FAST ALGORITHMS AND THEIR IMPLEMENTATION ON SPECIALIZED PARALLEL COMPUTERS

SPECIAL TOPICS IN SUPERCOMPUTING

Volume 5

Series Editors:

G. RODRIGUE
University of California at Davis
Lawrence Livermore National Laboratory
Livermore, CA, U.S.A.

S. FERNBACH
4 Holiday Drive
Alamo, CA, U.S.A.

G. MICHAEL
Lawrence Livermore National Laboratory
Livermore, CA, U.S.A.

VEDA
Publishing House
of the Slovak Academy of Sciences
Bratislava

NORTH-HOLLAND
Amsterdam • New York • Oxford • Tokyo

FAST ALGORITHMS AND THEIR IMPLEMENTATION ON SPECIALIZED PARALLEL COMPUTERS

J. MIKLOŠKO, M. VAJTERŠIC and I. VRŤO
Institute of Technical Cybernetics
Slovak Academy of Sciences
Bratislava, Czechoslovakia

R. KLETTE
Central Institute of Cybernetics and Information Processes
Academy of Sciences of GDR
Berlin, GDR

Edited by
J. MIKLOŠKO

VEDA
Publishing House
of the Slovak Academy of Sciences
Bratislava

1989

NORTH-HOLLAND
Amsterdam • New York • Oxford • Tokyo

Co-published by:

VEDA, Publishing House of the Slovak Academy of Sciences, Bratislava
and
Elsevier Science Publishers, B.V., Amsterdam

*Sole distributors for the East European socialist countries,
Democratic Republic of Vietnam, Mongolian People's Republic,
People's Democratic Republic of Korea, People's Republic of China,
Republic of Cuba*:

VEDA, Publishing House of the Slovak Academy of Sciences
Klemensova 19
814 30 Bratislava
Czechoslovakia

For the U.S.A. and Canada:

ELSEVIER SCIENCE PUBLISHING COMPANY, INC.
655 Avenue of the Americas
New York, N.Y. 10010
U.S.A.

For all other countries:

ELSEVIER SCIENCE PUBLISHERS B. V.
P.O. Box 103
1000 AC Amsterdam
The Netherlands

Copyright © 1989 by J. Mikloško, R. Klette, M. Vajteršic and I. Vrťo
Translation copyright © J. Hajnovičová

All rights reserved. No part of this publication may be reproduced, stored in a retrieval system or transmitted in any form or by any means, electronic, mechanical, photocopying, recording or otherwise, without the prior written permission of the publishers.

Special regulations for readers in the USA — This publication has been registered with the Copyright Clearance Center Inc. (CCC), Salem, Massachusetts. Information can be obtained from the CCC about conditions under which photocopies of parts of this publication may be made in the USA. All other copyright questions, including photocopying outside of the USA, should be referred to the copyright owners.

No responsibility is assumed by the Publishers for any injury and/or damage to persons or property as a matter of products liability, negligence or otherwise, or from any use or operation of any methods, products, instructions or ideas contained in the material herein.

ISBN 0-444-70141-9

Printed in Czechoslovakia

Introduction to the Series

Large scale computing is a growing field of research that plays a vital role in the advancement of science, engineering, and modern industrial technology. Computing is fast becoming the most frequently used technique to explore new questions. In just the last few years, the inclusion of computer modeling has produced results that were inconceivable a decade ago. They are an indispensable tool in many areas; from climate studies to chemical dynamics, from automated manufacturing to operating hospital intensive care units. Computer simulations of scientific processes provide, in many cases, substitutions for actual experiments. These simulations are less expensive and can address a wider range of problems. Computer simulations also provide an understanding of physical problems that cannot be obtained from experiments alone.

Research problems of many sorts are now becoming increasingly dependent on computer models, and numerical experiments are taking their place alongside the more traditional methods of research. Along with the theoretical and experimental, there is now a computational aspect of science as well.

Increasing sophistication in research has led to a need for bigger and faster computers — for Supercomputers. In this quest, supercomputers are themselves stimulating the redevelopment of the methods of computation. Results in one area are quickly adapted for another. The effect is making supercomputation a multi-disciplinary adventure. Research scientists in supercomputing come from a variety of interests and backgrounds and can be found in all universities, laboratories, and industries.

In supercomputing, a large overlap is found between the academic areas of engineering and physical sciences and the academic areas of mathematics, computer science, and computer engineering. The scientific jargons used in each of these areas are different and require translation or understanding before being able to make progress in the supercomputing sciences.

Although many advances have made the process easier in many cases, it has not kept pace with the dramatic increase in demands placed on the computer as well as the growing complexity of the computer hardware that has occurred over the past decade.

Special Topics in Supercomputing will take on two directions. First, in recognition of the fact that research in supercomputing is constantly embarking in new directions, a part of the series will be devoted to topics that have just begun to solidify as a well-defined research area. These volumes will contain manuscripts from researchers who are current leaders in the field.

Second, Special Topics in Supercomputing will include as part of its series a collection of monographs and contributed volumes on new- and well-established areas of supercomputing. As certain topics of supercomputing begin to solidify on a firm theoretical foundation, they will be coalesced into monograph or textbook form by author(s) who are experienced in the field. On the other hand, important areas of supercomputing are so new that few manuscripts can be collected to warrant a full-scale book. These topics will then be included in the contributed volumes of the series.

A hope of this enterprise will be to make supercomputing more widely understood, and more accessible in fields where it has not yet penetrated because of insufficient information.

G. Rodrigue

Contents

Introduction to the Series v
Introduction xi
Abbreviations xv

CHAPTER 1 — FAST PARALLEL ALGORITHMS
1.1 Introduction 1
1.2 Principles of construction of fast parallel algorithms 2
    1.2.1 Restructuring by suitable modification 2
    1.2.2 Aggregation of a serial algorithm 4
    1.2.3 Vector iteration 6
    1.2.4 Method "divide et impera" 8
    1.2.5 Parallel algorithms for systolic arrays 9
    1.2.6 Synchronous systolic algorithms 11
    1.2.7 Asynchronous systolic algorithms 17
    1.2.8 Vectorization of a scalar algorithm 20
    1.2.9 Parallel computation in bit slices 21
    1.2.10 Chaotic iteration 24
    1.2.11 Synchronous and asynchronous iterations 24
1.3 Matrix multiplication on parallel computers 28
1.4 Algorithms for solving the Poisson equation on parallel computers . . . 36
    1.4.1 Introduction 36
    1.4.2 Direct methods 37
    1.4.3 Iterative methods 47
References 52

CHAPTER 2 — FAST PARALLEL ALGORITHMS FOR ASSOCIATIVE COMPUTERS
2.1 Introduction 56
2.2 Associative memory and parallel associative processor 57
2.3 Logical algorithms for PAP 61
    2.3.1 Pattern matching 61
    2.3.2 Computation of the maximum element 61
    2.3.3 Selection of all the numbers which are equal, greater than or less than a pattern . . 62
2.4 Numerical algorithms for PAP 63

	2.4.1 Adding unity to a vector	63

2.4.1 Adding unity to a vector 63
2.4.2 Summation of two vectors 65
2.4.3 Summation of vector components 66
2.5 Sorting on an associative computer 67
2.6 Parallel implementation of Fast Fourier Transform 72
2.7 Parallel histogram algorithms for an associative parallel computer . . 77
    2.7.1 Introduction 77
    2.7.2 Image field-vector of gray level values algorithm 78
    2.7.3 Image field-comparand register histogram algorithm 79
    2.7.4 Non-redundant associative histogram algorithm 80
    2.7.5 Parallel histogram decoding algorithm 81
2.8 Linear algebra examples on a parallel associative SIMD-type computer 84
    2.8.1 Direct methods of solving the systems of linear equations . . . 86
    2.8.2 Iterative methods of solving the systems of linear equations . . 92
    2.8.3 Calculation of matrix inversion 98
    2.8.4 Calculation of eigenvalues of a symmetric matrix 100
References 109

CHAPTER 3 — SYSTOLIC ALGORITHMS AND THEIR IMPLEMENTATION ON SPECIALIZED PROCESSORS

3.1 Introduction 111
3.2 Characteristics of systolic arrays and algorithms 113
    3.2.1 Basic properties 113
    3.2.2 Classification of systolic algorithms 115
3.3 Numerical algorithms 117
    3.3.1 Matrix operations 117
    3.3.2 Recurrent relations 126
    3.3.3 Operations with polynomials 130
    3.3.4 Signal processing algorithms 133
3.4 Non-numerical algorithms 137
    3.4.1 Algorithms for data manipulation 137
    3.4.2 Algorithms on graphs 142
3.5 Complexity of systolic algorithms 144
    3.5.1 The model of a VLSI circuit 145
    3.5.2 Methods of lower bounds 147
3.6 Conclusion 154
References 155

CHAPTER 4 — ALGORITHMS FOR PIPELINE PROCESSORS, MATRIX PROCESSORS AND MULTIPROCESSORS

4.1 Introduction 160
4.2 Pipeline vector computers and their algorithms 161
4.3 Matrix processors and their algorithms 169
4.4 Multiprocessor computers and their algorithms 183
    4.4.1 Introduction 183
    4.4.2 Algorithms for multiprocessor computers 184
    4.4.3 Hierarchical EGPA multiprocessor 186

4.4.4 Algorithms for the EGPA multiprocessor	189
References	196

CHAPTER 5 — FAST ALGORITHM FOR SOLUTION OF A SYSTEM OF LINEAR ALGEBRAIC EQUATIONS ON SPECIALIZED VLSI COMPUTERS

5.1 Introduction	199
5.2 Single VLSI chip computer: SLEC1	203
5.2.1 Introduction	203
5.2.2 Structure of SLEC1	203
5.2.3 Instructions and program P1 for SLEC1	204
5.2.4 Complexity of program P1	206
5.3 VLSI chip with P-processors and cache memory: SLEC2	206
5.3.1 Introduction	206
5.3.2 Structure of SLEC2	207
5.3.3 Instructions and program P2 for SLEC2	208
5.3.4 Complexity of program P2	211
5.4 VLSI orthogonal pipeline vector processors: SLEC3r and SLEC3c	211
5.4.1 Introduction	211
5.4.2 Structures of SLEC3r and SLEC3c	212
5.4.3 Instructions and programs P3r and P3c for SLEC3r and SLEC3c . .	213
5.4.4 Complexity of P3r and P3c programs	216
5.5 VLSI systolic array: SLEC4	217
5.5.1 Introduction	217
5.5.2 Structure of SLEC4	218
5.5.3 Instructions and program P4 for SLEC4	219
5.5.4 Complexity of program P4	221
5.6 Conclusion	222
References	224

CHAPTER 6 — LOWER TIME BOUNDS FOR SIMD-TYPE ALGORITHMS

6.1 Introduction	225
6.2 The general SIMD model	225
6.3 OFF-NETs and ON-NETs	227
6.4 Local, global and total data transfer measures	237
6.5 Local, global and total data dependence measures	247
6.6 Data transfer lemma and applications	254
References	258

Subject index	259

Introduction

Over the whole 35-year history of modern computing technology, experts have been trying to solve problems that cannot be solved on modern computers: for example, large scientific-technological computations, direct real time control of complex objects, complex problems of artificial intelligence and robotics (pattern recognition, scene analysis, signal processing, image restoration, speech recognition, control and planning of activities of a robot, etc.). These problems very often bring about the necessity to process a large amount of information in real time. Satisfactory solutions of the above tasks can be achieved either by creating new fast algorithms or improving the parameters of present computers.

The limits of speed-up of algorithms are defined by results of their computational complexity and these imply that many of the yet existing serial algorithms cannot be accelerated any more. On the other hand, the limits of speed-up of computers are given by transmission rate of electrical signals, but the increase of the speed of logical elements has reached, practically, its limits. Further increase in the computational speed of solving different tasks can only be achieved by parallel algorithms implemented on parallel computers which cooperate mutually in solving a given task. The structure of their architecture is always influenced by the algorithms, so that all the parallel computers are more or less specialized. On the other hand, for a given parallel computer, specialized algorithms and programs should be constructed that are tightly bound to its architecture.

Also in the case of classical serial computers both the algorithm and the program had to be adapted to the architecture of a computer for the purpose of its optimal efficiency. If the efficiency ratio of a good program to a bad one was about 2—3 on a serial computer, on a parallel computer this ratio is often by one or even more orders higher, i.e. matching the algorithms and programs to the architecture of a parallel program is inevitable. Therefore, to create such algorithms and programs, precise knowledge of the computer they are to be implemented on, is required. High efficiency of computations can only be achieved by application of specialized parallel algorithms and programs on specialized computers.

Parallel computers offer the possibility to substantially speed up the computational processes. Their use, however, brings about new problems, especially those connected with creating parallel algorithms and programs. These problems cannot be solved by tools used in serial computations even though our approach is influenced by several centuries of serial mathematics, by 50 years of designing serial algorithms and by about 20 years of serial programming in FORTRAN.

In this monograph, we deal with problems of creating fast numerical and non-numerical algorithms, with analysis of their properties and possibilities of their efficient implementation on specialized parallel computers. The goal of this book is not to tackle these problems separately, but to deal with them in their complexity, taking into account their mutual relationships.

Attention is devoted to the following topics:
(1) methods of creating fast parallel algorithms;
(2) parallel algorithms for associative computers;
(3) systolic algorithms and their implementation on specialized processors;
(4) algorithms for pipeline and matrix processors and for multiprocessors;
(5) solution of a system of linear equations on specialized computers;
(6) lower time bounds for SIMD-type algorithms.

All the above topics, especially the topics 2, 3, 5, and 6 represent new, rapidly developing fields of research.

Each chapter is devoted to one topic. At the end of the chapter there is a list of quoted literature. All the papers listed in the literature are commented. In the text, especially those less known results which were found in journals and unpublished papers are given. By stressing the implementation view-point of algorithms described, the book is addressed to the broad circle of readers who use computers to solve their problems. We consider it useful for them to get a comprehensive overview of the ever growing number of new results which will enable them to become oriented in these new problems. The explanations throughout this monograph are subjected to this task and that is why there are no abstract theories and complex considerations involved in it.

The first chapter of this monograph is devoted to the problems of developing fast parallel algorithms. General principles of creating fast parallel algorithms and special examples of algorithms are demonstrated. Also, the development of parallel algorithms for fast computation of two important mathematical problems — matrix multiplication and solution of Dirichlet's problem for the Poisson equation on the square — are discussed.

In the second chapter we focus our attention on algorithms for parallel associative computers. Our goal is to demonstrate, using selected examples, the special features of associative information processing. For a parallel associative processor we shall describe some numerical and non-numerical algorithms. For a parallel associative computer of the SIMD-type we shall formulate several sorting algorithms, algorithms of Fast Fourier Transform and some basic tasks of linear algebra.

The third chapter deals with systolic algorithms which are suitable for implementation on specialized systolic arrays. We shall describe the properties of both systolic arrays and algorithms and discuss several systolic algorithms to solve various numerical and non-numerical problems. Attention will be paid to essential problems of complexity of systolic algorithms.

The fourth chapter is devoted to the study of algorithms for other types of parallel computers, such as pipeline processors, matrix processors and multi-processors. Along with the corresponding algorithms, the structures of architecture of a pipeline processor CRAY-1, of a matrix processor DAP and of a multiprocessor EGPA will be described.

In the fifth chapter of this monograph, four specialized VLSI computers to solve the systems of linear equations by modification of the Gauss—Jordan—Rutishauser algorithms are designed and analysed, such as: single chip computer, P-processors computer with cache memory on chip and off-chip active memory, orthogonal pipeline vector processor (row and column variants) and systolic array.

In the sixth chapter, a general theoretical approach to characterize the inherent complexity of computational problems in relation to different structures of SIMD-type computers is described. The given approach is important in the process of designing parallel hardware for a specific field of applications.

Throughout the monograph the following basic notations are used: $\lceil x \rceil$ denotes the minimum integer $\geq x$; $\lfloor x \rfloor$ denotes the maximum integer $\leq x$; $\log x$ means $\log_2 x$; $\ln x$ means $\log_e x$. The complexity of algorithms is characterized by the following asymptotic notations:

— $f(n) = O(g(n))$ means that there exists a positive constant c, for which $f(n) \leq cg(n)$, i.e. $f(n)$ grows no faster than $g(n)$;

— $f(n) = \Omega(g(n))$ means that there exists a positive constant c, for which $f(n) \geq cg(n)$, i.e. $f(n)$ is bounded from below by $g(n)$;

— $f(n) = \Theta(g(n))$ means that there exist positive constants c_1 and c_2, for which $c_1 g(n) \leq f(n) \leq c_2 g(n)$.

A parallel computer of the SIMD- type is understood to have a simple instruction stream with multiple data stream. Usually, it is represented by a set of processors which operate synchronously under single control. A computer of the MIMD-type is a multiprocessor computer with multiple instruction and data streams. A multiprocessor computer consists of at least two independent processors which are, in a certain way, interconnected. They can store data in a common memory, share peripheral equipment and execute programs of operating system.

This book is a result of cooperation between the Institute of Technical Cybernetics, Slovak Academy of Sciences in Bratislava (authors J. Mikloško, M. Vajteršic and I. Vrťo) and the Central Institute of Cybernetics and Information Processes, Academy of Sciences of GDR in Berlin (author R. Klette).

The authors' share in writing this monograph is as follows: RNDr. J. Mikloško, DrSc. (Chapter 1: Sections 1.1 through 1.3, Chapter 2: Sections 2.1 through 2.4, Chapter 4: Sections 4.1 through 4.3, Chapter 5); Dr. Reinhard Klette (Chapter 6); RNDr. M. Vajteršic, CSc. (Chapter 1: Section 1.4, Chapter 2: Sections 2.7 and 2.8, Chapter 4: Section 4.4); RNDr. I. Vrťo, CSc. (Chapter 3).

Because of the aim of the monograph and also because its authors are mathematicians, the problems of technical equipment of parallel computers have been tackled only at the level necessary to understand the design and implementation of the corresponding algorithms. Readers who are interested in equipment are recommended to consult papers or monographs listed below:

D. F. Barbe, *Very Large Scale Integration (VLSI). Fundamentals and Application*, Ed. D. F. Barbe (Springer-Verlag, Berlin, Heidelberg, New York, 1980).

D. J. Evans (Ed.), *Parallel Processing Systems* (Cambridge University Press, Cambridge, 1982).

C. C. Foster, *Content Addressable Parallel Processors* (Van Nostrand Reinhold Company, New York, 1976).

B. A. Golovkin, *Parallel Computational Systems* (in Russian) (Nauka, Moscow, 1980).

R. W. Hockney and C. R. Jesshope, *Parallel Computers* (Adam Hilger, Ltd., Bristol, 1981).

K. Hwang and F. A. Briggs, *Computer Architecture and Parallel Processing* (McGraw-Hill Book Company, New York, 1984).

C. Mead and L. Conway, *Introduction to VLSI Systems* (Addison-Wesley, Reading, 1980).

J. Mikloško and V. E. Kotov (Eds.), *Algorithms, Software and Hardware of Parallel Computers* (Springer-Verlag, Heidelberg — Veda, Bratislava, 1984).

I. Plander, Parallel and problem-oriented processors for artificial intelligence and robotics, *Počítače a umelá inteligencia* 1 (1982) 7—33.

J. D. Ullman, *Computational Aspects of VLSI* (Computer Science Press, Rockville, 1984).

In this way the authors would like to thank the Management of the Institute of Technical Cybernetics for good creative atmosphere at the Institute, to the scientific editor Prof. RNDr. A. Huťa, CSc. and the reviewers RNDr. A. Dávid, CSc. and Ing. RNDr. R. Zezula, CSc., for their constructive criticism of the manuscripts, RNDr. B. Otrubová and RNDr. M. Lucká for writing Sections 2.5 and 2.6.

J. Mikloško, Editor

Abbreviations

AGM	arithmetic-geometric mean
ALU	arithmetic-logic unit
AM	associative memory
AMM	associative memory modul
ASA	asynchronous systolic array
CCU	central control unit
CM	control memory
CP	control processor
CU	control unit
FIN-OFF-ON	
FIN-ON-IN	
FP	floating-point
GJR	Gauss–Jordan–Rutishauser elimination with partial pivoting
LR 21	
LRUD 21	
MP	matrix processor
OFF-IN	
OFF-NET	
OM	orthogonal memory
ON-IN	
ON-NET	
PAP	parallel associative processor
PE	processing element
PM 21	
PN	permutation network
PS	perfect shuffle
RAM	random access maching
SA	systolic array
SLEC	system of linear equation computer
WPM 21	

Chapter 1

Fast parallel algorithms

1.1 Introduction

The first chapter of this monograph is devoted to the methods of forming fast parallel algorithms. Various examples are used here to describe the general principles of developing fast parallel algorithms and to illustrate the application of actual algorithms for computation of the two significant mathematical problems: matrix multiplication and the solution of Dirichlet's problem for the Poisson equation on square. Recently, fast algorithms for serial computation of these tasks have noted remarkable development. Some examples of their parallel computation will also be described in this chapter.

Throughout the chapter attention will be paid to algorithms that are not naturally parallel. The parallel implementation of the serial version of such algorithms, gives rise to problems solvable by means of special methods described in this chapter.

In the 2nd section of this chapter, various principles of forming parallel algorithms are described (examples of algorithms applied are given in brackets). The simplest principles are restructuring of an algorithm by algebraic transformations (arithmetic expressions) or application of suitable relations to increase the parallelism of the algorithm (computation of high-powers). The next two methods of forming parallel algorithms described can be used to transform the strictly serial algorithms into parallel algorithms. It is the method of aggregation of the steps of a serial algorithm (computation of eigenvalues by Jacobi's method) and the method of vector iteration of the direct serial algorithm (elimination of a tridiagonal system of linear equations). Along with the "divide et impera" method (the general system of linear equations and computation of recurrence formulas) the algorithms derived are suitable especially for parallel computers of the SIMD-type.

The next part of this section is aimed at the principles of forming algorithms for special parallel computers — so-called systolic arrays. In this way synchronous systolic algorithms and arrays (repeated computation of arithmetic-geometric mean) as well as asynchronous systolic algorithms (iterative computation of a system of linear equations) are described. The procedure of vectorization of scalar algorithms (calculation of eigenvalues of symmetric tridiagonal matrix by Givens' method) and of parallel computation on the vectors in the bit slices (the CORDIC technique for computation of arithmetic operations and elementary functions) is important in forming parallel algorithms for associative computers. At the end of the second section some principles of constructing parallel algorithms for multiprocessor computers of the MIMD-type are given: chaotic implementation of an iterative method (a system of linear equations) and asynchronous implementation of an iterative algorithm.

An example of matrix multiplication is used in the third section to illustrate various forms of this algorithm. After a brief description of the most important ideas of speeding up serial algorithms of matrix multiplication, the parallel algorithms for computation of this task at various architecture structures will be discussed: computers of SIMD- and MIMD-types, pipeline processors of the STAR-100-type, matrix processors of the DAP-type, parallel computers with tree-communication networks and systolic hexagonal arrays.

In the fourth section, parallel computation of a more complex model problem has been chosen: Dirichlet's problem for the Poisson equation on square. Systematic descriptions of various direct, iterative and semi-iterative parallel algorithms are given together with their computational complexity from the view-point of their implementation on a matrix processor of the SIMD-type.

1.2 Principles of construction of fast parallel algorithms

1.2.1 Restructuring by suitable modification

Restructuring of a given algorithm to an algorithm that is numerically equivalent but of better parallelism can be accomplished using different algebraic procedures or applying suitable relationships that are more parallel compared with the original ones. The essential part of each numerical algorithm consists of arithmetic expressions. Their parallelism can be increased using associative, commutative and distributive laws. For instance, an expression $(((a + b) + c) + d)$ requires three computational steps [42]. However, with the help of the associative law, $(a + b) + (c + d)$ can be obtained in two parallel steps. The expression $a + bc + d$ requires three steps again, whereas when applying the commutative law, $a + d + bc$ is obtained again in two steps. Expression $a(bcd + e)$ is executed in four parallel steps whereby the situation cannot be improved by associative or commutative laws. Distributive law, however, yields $abcd + ae$ which, in turn, can be computed in three parallel steps.

In parallel computation an arithmetic expression can be represented by a binary tree, whose height defines the number of time steps of its implementation and whose nodes on the same level represent the number of active processors. For general arithmetic expressions algorithms have been constructed that are able to transform the corresponding trees into parallel equivalents by reducing their length. An optimum algorithm that uses associative and commutative laws was described by Baer and Bovet [3], an algorithm that makes use of the distributive law was described by Muraoka [53].

Let T_p be the time for implementation of the given arithmetic expression on a p-processor computer. It is known that with the help of associative, commutative and distributive laws every arithmetic expression with n operands and operations $+, -, \times :$ can be constructed in such a way that $T_p \leq 4 \lceil \log n \rceil$ for $p \leq 3n$ and $T_p \leq 2.88 \lceil \log n \rceil$ for $p > O(n)$ [13, 52]. The estimates with constants 2.46 and 2.08 hold for expressions without dividing.

Increase in parallelism of the computation by the use of suitable mathematical relationships will be demonstrated in the next example.

Have a polynomial of nth degree $f_n(x) = (x - w_1)(x - w_2)\ldots(x - w_n)$, where w_k, $k = 1, 2, \ldots, n$, represent its roots. Decompose $f_n^{-1}(x)$ into partial fractions

$$1/f_n(x) = \sum_{j=1}^{n} \frac{A_j}{x - w_j},$$

where

$$A_j = 1/f_n'(w_j) = 1 \bigg/ \prod_{\substack{k=1 \\ k \neq j}}^{n} (w_j - w_k).$$

Let $f_n(x) = x^n - 1$. Then w_j, $j = 1, 2, \ldots, n$, form a set of n unit roots, i.e. $w_j = \exp(2\pi i j/n)$, where $i = \sqrt{-1}$. It holds that $f_n'(w_j) = nw_j^{n-1} = n/w_j$, because $w_n = 1$. Then our decomposition assumes the form

$$x^n = 1 + n \bigg/ \sum_{j=1}^{n} \frac{w_j}{x - w_j}, \tag{1}$$

which was used by Kung [43] for parallel computation of x^n.

Let F be an array of complex numbers and $F(x)$ an array of rational expressions in x over F. Denote the times of addition, multiplication and division in $F(x)$ as A, M and D, respectively.

Kung's parallel algorithm of calculation x^n by means of (1) consists of computations of:

(1) Values w_j and $s_j = w_j/n$, $j = 1, 2, ..., n$;
(2) $a_j = x - w_j$, $j = 1, 2, ..., n$;
(3) $b_j = s_j/a_j$, $j = 1, 2, ..., n$;
(4) $c = \sum_{j=1}^{n} b_j$;
(5) $d = 1/c$;
(6) $y = d + 1$, whereby $y = x^n$.

Step (1) is independent of x and therefore it can be implemented in a preliminary computation. Steps (2) through (6) on n-processors can be executed in time A, D, $\lceil \log n \rceil$ A, D, A, and thus, the parallel computation of x^n using this interesting algorithm consumes time $T_n = \lceil \log n \rceil A + 2(A + D)$. At present, the best serial algorithm for computation of x^n requires time $M(\log n + O(\log n/\log \log n))$ [4]. If division is not used, the lower limit for the time of parallel computation of x^n (irrespective of the number of processors being used) is $M \lceil \log n \rceil$. It is reached when we use $\lfloor n/2 \rfloor$ processors and the algorithm of multiplication by pairs according to the diagram of its binary tree. From the above it follows that without division no parallel algorithm can be substantially faster than a serial algorithm for computation of this problem. Kung's algorithm shows that the situation is changed on using division.

If, for the given computer, it holds that $M > A$ and $\lceil \log n \rceil > 2(A + D)/(M - A)$, then Kung's algorithm is faster than the best up to now known parallel algorithm for computation of x^n in time $S_n = M \lceil \log n \rceil$. Since $\lim_{n \to \infty} S_n/T_n = M/A$, for large n this algorithm is (M/A) times faster. Kung [43] has also derived analogical algorithms for parallel computation of $\{x^2, x^3, ..., x^n\}$, $\prod_{i=1}^{n} (x + a_i)$ and $\sum_{i=0}^{n} a_i x^i$. If x is a multiple-precision number, or a square matrix in these expressions, then the multiplication time of such elements considerably exceeds the time of summation, and thus, the above algorithms are, in these cases, more efficient.

1.2.2 Aggregation of a serial algorithm

By the method of aggregation several successive steps of a seemingly serial algorithm are integrated into a single step, which can be implemented in parallel. For example, the classical serial algorithm of Jacobi's method computes all eigenvalues and eigenfunctions of real symmetric matrix $\mathbf{A}$ of n/n type in the following way:

If $\mathbf{A} = \mathbf{A}_1$, then the sequence $\mathbf{A}_{k+1} = (a_{ij}^{(k+1)})$, $k = 1, 2, ...$, is obtained by Jacobi's rotations $\mathbf{A}_{k+1} = \mathbf{R}_k \mathbf{A}_k \mathbf{R}_k^T$, whereby $\mathbf{A}$ is iteratively reduced to a diagonal matrix **D** with eigenvalues situated on diagonal lines. $\mathbf{R}_k = \mathbf{R}_k(p, q, \varphi)$ are matrices of planar rotations in the plane (p, q) with angle φ which is chosen so that the elements a_{pq} and a_{qp} are eliminated. $\mathbf{R}_k$ represents orthogonal matrices differing from unit matrix by elements $r_{pp} = r_{qq} = \cos\varphi$ and $r_{pq} = -r_{qp} = \sin\varphi$, only. In a serial algorithm all extradiagonal elements are successively eliminated, the succession being $(1, 2), (1, 3), ..., (1, n), (2, 3), (2, 4), ..., (2, n)...,$ etc. On ascending k, matrix **A** converges to the diagonal matrix $\mathbf{D} = \mathbf{RAR}^T$, where **R** is the product of all the rotation matrices, i.e. it contains the eigenvectors of the matrix **A**.

It is inefficient to apply this serial procedure to a parallel computer, since on every rotation only one matrix element is set to zero, while just two of its columns and rows are changed. In [62] it is shown how more than one extradiagonal element can be eliminated. Elimination is achieved by means of a matrix generated by multiplication of elementary rotation matrices with the property that all the planes (p_i, q_i) occurring in this product differ from each other.

If, for instance, matrix **A** is of order 4, then at the same time elements in position $(1, 4)$ and $(2, 3)$ along with their symmetric pairs can be set to zero using the general rotation

$$\mathbf{R}_1 = \begin{bmatrix} c_1 & 0 & 0 & s_1 \\ 0 & c_2 & s_2 & 0 \\ 0 & -s_2 & c_2 & 0 \\ -s_1 & 0 & 0 & c_1 \end{bmatrix},$$

where $\mathbf{R}_1$ is generated by multiplication of two rotations following each other, whereby all rows and columns of **A** [66] are changed. In this case, $c_i = \cos\varphi_i$, $s_i = \sin\varphi_i$, $i = 1, 2$, whereby φ_i are chosen so that they eliminate the elements in position $(1, 4)$ and $(2, 3)$. Chosing matrices $\mathbf{R}_2$ and $\mathbf{R}_3$ so that

$$\mathbf{R}_2 = \begin{bmatrix} c_3 & 0 & s_3 & 0 \\ 0 & c_4 & 0 & s_4 \\ -s_3 & 0 & c_3 & 0 \\ 0 & -s_4 & 0 & c_4 \end{bmatrix}, \quad \mathbf{R}_3 = \begin{bmatrix} c_5 & s_5 & 0 & 0 \\ -s_5 & c_5 & 0 & 0 \\ 0 & 0 & c_6 & s_6 \\ 0 & 0 & -s_6 & c_6 \end{bmatrix},$$

$\mathbf{R}_2$ eliminates the elements $(1, 3), (2, 4)$ and $\mathbf{R}_3$ the elements $(1, 2), (3, 4)$. When multiplying three generalized rotations following one after another, $\mathbf{Q}_1 = \mathbf{R}_3\mathbf{R}_2\mathbf{R}_1$ is obtained, i.e. the transformation changes all the extradiagonal elements **A**, whereby each of them is set to zero once. It is obvious that the computation of all angles φ is done in parallel, while with respect to the iteration principle of Jacobi's method every zero-setting of elements results in generating new non-zero elements in corresponding matrices. It holds that $\mathbf{D} = \mathbf{RAR}^T$, where $\mathbf{R} = ...\mathbf{Q}_{10}\mathbf{Q}_7\mathbf{Q}_4\mathbf{Q}_1$.

In general, every matrix $\mathbf{R}_k$ eliminates $\lfloor n/2 \rfloor$ extradiagonal elements and $\mathbf{Q}_k = \mathbf{R}_{2m+k-2} \cdots \mathbf{R}_{k+1}\mathbf{R}_k$, where $m = \lfloor (n+1)/2 \rfloor$, $k = 1, 2m, 4m-1, \ldots$ will change all the extradiagonal elements and eliminate each of them once.

Thus, a serial algorithm decomposed into individual steps was aggregated into larger steps which are implemented in parallel.

1.2.3 Vector iteration

Vector iteration of a serial algorithm can be demonstrated on the Gaussian elimination of tridiagonal systems of linear equations

$$\mathbf{A}\mathbf{x} = \mathbf{c}, \tag{2}$$

where, for the sake of simplicity

$$\mathbf{A} = \begin{bmatrix} 1 & b_1 & & & & 0 \\ a_2 & 1 & b_2 & & & \\ & \ddots & \ddots & \ddots & & \\ & & a_{n-1} & 1 & b_{n-1} \\ 0 & & & a_n & 1 \end{bmatrix}.$$

The classical Gaussian elimination consists of factorization $\mathbf{A} = (\mathbf{I} + \mathbf{K}) \cdot \mathbf{D}(\mathbf{I} + \mathbf{R})$ and of the solution of bidiagonal systems $(\mathbf{I} + \mathbf{K})\mathbf{f} = \mathbf{c}$ and $(\mathbf{I} + \mathbf{R})\mathbf{x} = \mathbf{D}^{-1}\mathbf{f}$, which in the recurrence form can be written as follows:

$d_1 = 1,$ $\quad d_j = 1 - a_j b_{j-1}/d_{j-1},$ $\quad\quad\quad\quad\quad\quad\quad\quad j = 2, 3, \ldots, n;$
$f_1 = c_1,$ $\quad k_j = a_j/d_{j-1},$ $\quad\quad f_j = c_j - k_j f_{j-1},$ $\quad j = 2, 3, \ldots, n;$
$r_j = b_j/d_j,$ $\quad\quad\quad\quad\quad\quad\quad\quad\quad\quad\quad\quad\quad\quad\quad\quad\quad j = 1, 2, \ldots, n-1;$
$g_j = f_j/d_j,$ $\quad\quad\quad\quad\quad\quad\quad\quad\quad\quad\quad\quad\quad\quad\quad\quad\quad j = 1, 2, \ldots, n;$
$x_n = g_n,$ $\quad x_j = g_j - r_j x_{j+1},$ $\quad\quad\quad\quad\quad\quad\quad\quad\quad\quad j = n-1, n-2, \ldots, 1.$

Serial recursions in the Gaussian elimination were in [34] replaced by successive vector iterations of the vectors $\mathbf{d}$, $\mathbf{f}$ and finally by $\mathbf{x}$. For example, the relationship for d_j can, for $j > 1$, be iterated as

$$d_j^{(i)} = 1 - a_j b_{j-1}/d_{j-1}^{(i-1)}, \qquad i = 1, 2, \ldots, \tag{3}$$

where the upper index denotes the iteration step number. In this way, having chosen the initial conditions in the appropriate way, all the vector elements of the vector $\mathbf{d}$ can be computed. Although such a parallel vector iteration requires many more operations compared with the original serial recursion, on parallel computers — pipeline processors, for example, — it can be implemented with great advantage. It can be derived from its matrix formulation as it will be done later on.

If matrix $\mathbf{A}$ has additive or multiplicative decomposition of the form $\mathbf{A} = \mathbf{A_K} + \mathbf{I} + \mathbf{A_R}$, or $\mathbf{A} = (\mathbf{I} + \mathbf{K})\mathbf{D}(\mathbf{I} + \mathbf{R})$, where $\mathbf{A_K}(\mathbf{A_R})$ is the matrix with non-zero diagonal below (over) the main diagonal, then

$$\mathbf{D} = \mathbf{I} - \mathbf{A_K}\mathbf{D}^{-1}\mathbf{A_R}, \tag{4}$$

and

$$\mathbf{K} = \mathbf{A_K}\mathbf{D}^{-1}, \quad \mathbf{R} = \mathbf{D}^{-1}\mathbf{A_R}.$$

Let $\mathbf{D} = \mathrm{diag}(d_1, d_2, \ldots, d_n)$, $\mathbf{K} = \mathrm{subdiag}(k_2, k_3, \ldots, k_n)$ and $\mathbf{R} = \mathrm{superdiag}(r_1, r_2, r_{n-1})$. Then, for the computation of d_j, k_j and r_j the above recurrence relationships hold.

From the relationship (4) there follows the iteration

$$\mathbf{D}^{(i)} = \mathbf{I} - \mathbf{A_K}(\mathbf{D}^{(i-1)})^{-1}\mathbf{A_R}, \qquad i = 1, 2, \ldots, \tag{5}$$

where $\mathbf{D}^{(0)}$ is supposed to be regular. From $\mathbf{D}^{(i)}\,\bar{\mathbf{K}} = \mathbf{A}_K(\mathbf{D}^{(i)})^{-1}$ and $\bar{\mathbf{R}} = (\mathbf{D}^{(i)})^{-1}\mathbf{A}_R$ can be calculated approximately. If $\mathbf{D}^{(i)} = \mathrm{diag}(d_1^{(i)}, d_2^{(i)}, \ldots, d_n^{(i)})$, then the iteration (5) coincides with (3).

The speed of convergence of iterations (3) can be increased, as $d_j^{(i)}$ depends not only upon $d_{j-1}^{(i-1)}$.

If, all the elements of $\boldsymbol{d}$ are first indexed as even and then as odd, using always the latest values that are at our disposal, then the results of odd-indexed elements will coincide with those obtained if the vector $\boldsymbol{d}$ is calculated twice.

From the bidiagonal systems in the Gaussian elimination it follows that $\boldsymbol{f} = \boldsymbol{c} - \mathbf{K}\boldsymbol{f}$ and $\boldsymbol{x} = \mathbf{D}^{-1}\boldsymbol{f} - \mathbf{R}\boldsymbol{x}$. Jacobi's iteration for these systems yields $\boldsymbol{f}^{(i)} = \boldsymbol{c} - \mathbf{K}\boldsymbol{f}^{(i-1)}$, or $\boldsymbol{x}^{(i)} = \boldsymbol{g} - \mathbf{R}\boldsymbol{x}^{(i-1)}$, which again, represent parallel vector iterations $f_j^{(i)} = c_j - k_j f_{j-1}^{(i-1)}$ or $x_j^{(i)} = g_j - r_j x_{j+1}^{(i-1)}$ which, similarly, can be accelerated.

On this principle, the speeded up parallel Gaussian elimination can be implemented by substituting vertical iterations as follows (let, for simplicity, n be an even number for horizontal recursion):

(a) Let $d^{(0)}$ be given and $d_1^{(i)} = 1$, for all i.
  For $i = 1, 2, \ldots, ID$ compute
  $d_j^{(i)} = 1 - a_j b_{j-1}/d_{j-1}^{(i-1)}$, j even,
  $d_j^{(i)} = 1 - a_j b_{j-1}/d_{j-1}^{(i)}$, j odd and >1.
(b) Define $\bar{k}_j = a_j/d_{j-1}^{(ID)}$ for all $j > 1$.
  Let $f^{(0)}$ be given and $f_1^{(i)} = c_1$ for all i.

For $i = 1, 2, \ldots, IF$ compute
$$f_j^{(i)} = c_j - \bar{k}_j f_{j-1}^{(i-1)}, j \text{ even},$$
$$f_j^{(i)} = c_j - \bar{k}_j f_{j-1}^{(i)}, j \text{ odd and } > 1.$$
(c) Define $\bar{g}_j = f_j^{(IF)}/d_j^{(ID)}$ for all j,
$$\bar{r}_j = b_j/d_j^{(ID)} \text{ for all } j < n.$$
Let $x^{(0)}$ be given and $x_n^{(i)} = \bar{g}_n$ for all i.
For $i = 1, 2, \ldots, IX$ calculate
$$x_j^{(i)} = \bar{g}_j - \bar{r}_j x_{j+1}^{(i-1)}, j \text{ odd},$$
$$x_j^{(i)} = \bar{g}_j - \bar{r}_j x_{j+1}^{(i)}, j \text{ even and } < n.$$

The approximate solution of system (2) is $\boldsymbol{x}^{(IX)}$. The values ID, IF and IX with the accuracy required can be determined a priori or by stabilization of iterations.

If matrix $\boldsymbol{A}$ in (2) is diagonally dominant, then the values ID, IF and IX do not depend on n, and thus the system (2) can be computed parallelly on $n/2$ processors in $O(1)$ steps.

1.2.4 Method "divide et impera"

The technique "divide et impera" will first be demonstrated using a method suggested by Pease [58] to solve the system of $n = 2^m$ linear equations with n unknowns, $\boldsymbol{Ax} = \boldsymbol{b}$ with the help of n-processors in $O(n^2 \log n)$ steps.

The system solved is transformed into

$$\begin{bmatrix} \boldsymbol{I} & \boldsymbol{F}_1 \\ \boldsymbol{F}_2 & \boldsymbol{I} \end{bmatrix} \begin{bmatrix} \boldsymbol{x}_1 \\ \boldsymbol{x}_2 \end{bmatrix} = \begin{bmatrix} \boldsymbol{g}_1 \\ \boldsymbol{g}_2 \end{bmatrix},$$

where $\boldsymbol{I}$ is the unit matrix of order 2^{m-1}. On multiplying by the matrix

$$\begin{bmatrix} \boldsymbol{I} & -\boldsymbol{F}_1 \\ -\boldsymbol{F}_2 & \boldsymbol{I} \end{bmatrix}$$

the original system will be split into two independent subsystems

$$(\boldsymbol{I} - \boldsymbol{F}_1 \boldsymbol{F}_2) \boldsymbol{x}_1 = \boldsymbol{g}_1 - \boldsymbol{F}_1 \boldsymbol{g}_2,$$
$$(\boldsymbol{I} - \boldsymbol{F}_2 \boldsymbol{F}_1) \boldsymbol{x}_2 = \boldsymbol{g}_2 - \boldsymbol{F}_2 \boldsymbol{g}_1,$$

in which the same procedure can be repeated by recursion. In this way, after $\log n$ steps, the required solution can be obtained.

A more complicated example of this method is the algorithm of recursive doubling of recurrent computations [41], suggesting that serial algorithm may contain much of hidden parallelism.

Direct computation of the recurrence relation $x_1 = b_1$, $x_i = a_i x_{i-1} + b_i$, $i = 2, 3, ..., n$, requires serially $n - 1$ multiplications.

By induction it can be proved that

$$x_{2i} = \prod_{r=i+1}^{2i} a_r q_{i1} + q_{2i, i+1}, \qquad (6)$$

where q_{mp} for $m \geq p$ is

$$q_{mp} = \sum_{j=p}^{m} \left(\prod_{r=j+1}^{m} a_r \right) b_j,$$

whereby $q_{i1} = x_i$.

By decomposition of the relationship (6) our problem was split into two independent partial problems of equal complexity, because the values q_{i1} and $q_{2i, i+1}$ are structurally identical and require the same number of multiplications and summations.

Their splitting can be continued further and so the parallel algorithm of recursion doubling can be obtained:
(1) $A_0(i) = a_i$, $i = 2, 3, ..., n$; $B_0(i) = b_i$, $i = 1, 2, ..., n$.
(2) For $k = 1, 2, ..., \lceil \log n \rceil$ parallel computation:
$B_k(i) = B_{k-1}(i) + A_{k-1}(i) B_{k-1}(i - 2^{k-1})$, $2^{k-1} < i \leq n$.
(3) $A_k(i) = A_{k-1}(i) A_{k-1}(i - 2^{k-1})$, $2^{k-1} + 1 < i \leq n$.

In steps 2 and 3 on $B_k(i)$ the values x_i, $i = 1, 2, ..., n$, are obtained successively. Thus on an n-processor computer, we compute x_i, $i = 1, 2, ..., n$, in the time of $\lceil \log n \rceil$ sums and $2 \lceil \log n \rceil$ products, i.e. in $O(\log n)$ steps.

1.2.5 Parallel algorithms for systolic arrays

Now we shall show how parallel algorithms for specialized parallel computers based on VLSI technology, the so-called systolic arrays, are generated. Let us mention several general principles of their construction as first.

Systolic systems are composed of input and output channels and of a great number of simple processors which are mutually interconnected by a communication network. The communication network is the key to making use of the parallelism in a systolic array. The structure of the processors is closely related to the algorithm implemented.

Designing a systolic system we try to project the selected algorithm with the help of a technical tool into the parallel computer structure. Since automatic design of such a structure is not possible at present, it must be implemented "manually", based on the detailed knowledge of the corresponding algorithm. Design of an algorithm for systolic implementation rests in the fact that from the set of algorithms to solve this problem such an algorithm is selected which, to the maximum possible extent, satisfies the following requirements [26, 44]:

(a) in computations pipelining and parallelism are used;
(b) each data item has multiple uses;
(c) data flow is simple and regular;
(d) it is composed of several types of simple operations;
(e) if possible, it is universal.

The systolic array is influenced by the above properties in such a way that:

(a) the data will flow through the processors in the network, while the right data will meet at the right moment in the right processor;

(b) input data will be distributed into all processors or they will travel through the processor arrays;

(c) processors will be interconnected by a regular, local, and as far as possible planar communication network;

(d) the array will only be implemented by means of various types of simple processors, whereby they can be extended modularly;

(e) on the basis of their input data it will be able to compute various problems.

The design of technical implementation of a systolic array must be preceded by design of [26]:

(a) suitable algorithm by which the whole structure of the chip will be determined;

(b) the types of these processors and of their location;

(c) the data flow and its control.

Success of this design of a "silicon-algorithm" depends on the cooperation of mathematicians, engineers and designers of integrated circuits.

In this section, principles of construction of synchronous and asynchronous systolic arrays which by technical tools implement the given algorithms in parallel will be discussed. As we are concerned here with new problems, this topic will be treated in more detail. Our explanation is especially of methodological importance; it indicates how these algorithms and rough sketches of systolic arrays can be designed.

Creation of synchronous systolic arrays will be illustrated using repeated computation of the Gaussian algorithm of the arithmetic-geometric mean [50]. Beside the diagrams of various modifications of the corresponding systolic arrays with their time analysis, these results are also interesting by the fact, that even though non-linear recurring relationships are concerned, on repeated computations on a systolic array the computation can be speeded up.

Asynchronous systolic arrays will be described in general as well as in their special form which represents an implementation of the Gauss—Seidel iteration method to solve a system of linear algebraic equations.

1.2.6 Synchronous systolic algorithms

The Gaussian algorithm of the arithmetic-geometric mean (AGM) is given by these relationships:

$$a_0 > b_0 > 0,$$
$$a_{i+1} = (a_i + b_i)/2, \quad b_{i+1} = \sqrt{a_i b_i}, \quad i = 0, 1, \ldots . \tag{7}$$

AGM represents a universal algorithm, since on choosing suitable a_0, b_0 it quadratically converges to various functions (e.g. to an elliptic integral, logarithmic function). It holds that $\lim_{i \to \infty} a_i = \lim_{i \to \infty} b_i = X$, where, for example, when $a_0 = 1$, $b_0 = \sqrt{1 - k^2}$, then according to [28]

$$\int_0^{\pi/2} \frac{d\varphi}{(1 - k^2 \sin^2 \varphi)^{1/2}} = \frac{\pi}{2X},$$

or, if $a_0 = 1$, $b_0 = 4/y$, then $\log y = \frac{\pi}{2X} [1 + O(y^{-2})]$ [11]. Further applications of this algorithm are described in [12].

Computation of the square root in (7), i.e. $\sqrt{C}$, is implemented by a convergent recurrence relationship

$$x_0 > 0, \quad x_{j+1} = (x_j + C/x_j)/2, \quad j = 0, 1, \ldots, \tag{8}$$

where $\lim_{j \to \infty} x_j = \sqrt{C}$.

In practical computations (7) and (8) these relationships are computed so long until it holds that

$$|(a_{i+1} - b_{i+1})/a_{i+1}| < \varepsilon, \quad \text{or} \quad |(x_{j+1} - x_j)/x_{j+1}| < \varepsilon,$$

where ε is the computation accuracy required. Termination of computation requires testing of these inequalities in each cycle. If there is a word size s in a computer with computer system basis β, then $\varepsilon = \beta^{-s}$. To avoid testing, let us suppose that in relationship (7) or (8) we know an a priori value of $i = I$, or

$j = J$, for which (7) or (8) is fixed to s places for all input values a_0, b_0 or x_0. Then, for the given I, J, a_0, b_0, x_0, the algorithm A calculates the value of X:

for $i = 1$ **to** $I - 1$ **do**
    begin $c := a_0 b_0$; $a_0 := (a_0 + b_0)/2$;
    for $j = 1$ **to** J **do** $x_0 := (x_0 + c/x_0)/2$;
    $b_0 := x_0$;
    end;
$X := (a_0 + b_0)/2$.

Let a, m, d, $d2$, p be actual times of computer implementation of operations of addition, multiplication, division and division by two, and assignment. Then, the actual time t_s of implementation of the algorithm A on a serial algorithm is

$$t_s = I[a + m + d2 + 3p + (J - 1)(a + d + d2 + p)]. \qquad (9)$$

Algorithms (7) and (8) are serial non-linear recurrence relations. Making them parallel is very difficult and it yields only a constant speed-up. Up to now algorithms of non-linear relationships made parallel just by finding a complex transform of variables [56] are of theoretical meaning only. Another technique of parallelization — so-called asynchronous iteration — is described in [45]. However, it cannot be applied to (7), because this relationship must be implemented as synchronous only, for $i = 0, 1, \ldots$. Asynchronous implementation of the branches for a_i and b_i need not converge at all, if it converges to erroneous results [74]. In paper [43] it is shown, that by making (8) parallel in any way using an arbitrary number of processors the computation can be speeded up at maximum three times.

Now, let us have the task to compute M results of the algorithm A for N various initial values a_0, b_0. The time of serial implementation of this task is $T_s = Mt_s$. Its M times speed-up can be accomplished by parallel implementation on M diverse processors. Further, we shall show that quite a good speed-up of computation can also be reached by implementation repeating the AGM of M times in a systolic array.

The first alternative $V1$ of the system will consist of processors of types AM and SQ. The structure and function of the AM processor is shown in Fig. 1.

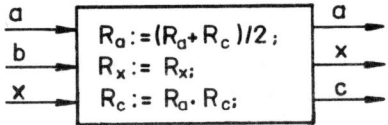

Fig. 1. AM processor.

It has three registers R_a, R_c and R_x. In each basic cycle of computation it delivers data a, b, x into R_a, R_c, R_x, respectively; it carries out the corresponding operation and the results are shifted to the output.

The SQ processor is shown in Fig. 2.

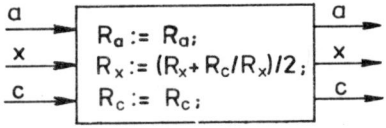

Fig. 2. SQ processor.

The unit SQRT by which the function of square root is implemented, comprises J processors of SQ which are connected sequentially.

Then, the alternative $V1$ will be formed by $I - 1$ repeated pairs AM, SQRT with the element AM, where in R_a is $a_i = X$ (Fig. 3).

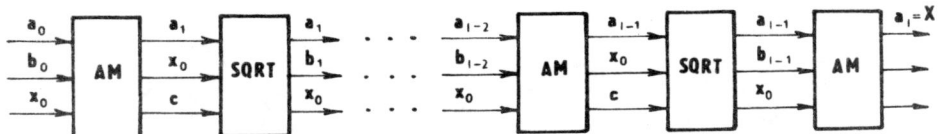

Fig. 3. Modification of $V1$ for AGM.

Thus, the algorithm AGM is split into $k = I(J + 1) - J$ steps. The time necessary to implement AM or SQ equals $a + m + d2 + 2p$ or $a + d + d2 + p$. If $d > m + p$, then the basic cycle of the computation $V1$ is $t = a + d + d2 + p$. The computation in each processor is done in such a way that all the processors carry out their computational functions and shift their input data to their outputs. When AGM is repeated M times, all the input constants are ready at the input $V1$. After starting the computation, this is propagated in $V1$ from left to right, whereby the first result is computed at the time $[I(J + 1) - J]t$ and all the M results are obtained at the time $T_p = (M + k - 1)t$.

On comparing the times consumed by a serial computation, T_s and T_p, we find that application $V1$ is only important for such M for which

$$T_s > T_p, \quad \text{i.e.} \quad MIJ + MI\frac{m + 2p - d}{t} > M + (J + 1)(I - 1),$$

which also implies that $T_p \approx T_s/IJ$, i.e. starting from a definite M it holds that the M-multiple serial computation of the AGM is IJ times longer than the computation on the array $V1$.

An alternative design to $V1$ is represented by the system $V1'$, in which each unit is modified according to Fig. 4 (Fig. 5).

Structures of processors SQ1 and SQ2 are shown in Fig. 6.

Fig. 4. Unit AM-SQRT-AM.

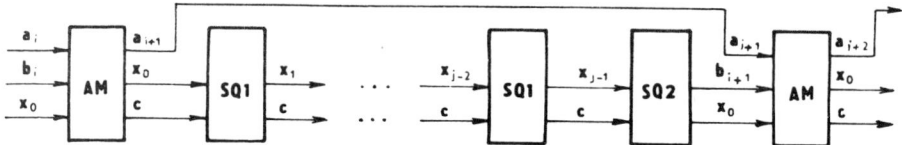

Fig. 5. Modification of $V1'$ for AGM.

$$\boxed{\begin{array}{l} R_x := (R_x + R_c / R_x) / 2; \\ R_c := R_c; \end{array}} \qquad \boxed{\begin{array}{l} R_x := (R_x + R_c / R_x) / 2; \\ R_c := R_x; \end{array}}$$

Fig. 6. Processors SQ1 and SQ2.

The advantage of this design is that that SQ1 and SQ2 have only 2 inputs and outputs and that each processor SQ2 will prepare by $R_c := R_x$ the initial value $x_0 = b_{i+1}$ for computation of b_{i+2}, which in the next cycle of the AGM will facilitate faster computation of the square root. With I increasing in AGM, the number of cycles per iteration for square root should decrease successively.

The main disadvantage of $V1'$ is represented by its inhomogeneity.

Another alternative, $V2$, will have the structure shown in Fig. 7.

The processor SQ2' is nearly coinciding with SQ2, SQ2' does not represent the implementation of $R_c := R_x$, because it has no output c. The element AM1 is similar to AM, its structure is shown in Fig. 8.

The input value of AM1 is represented by the latest value of arithmetic mean which with increasing i converges very quickly to its geometric mean.

Timing of computations $V1'$ and $V2$ is equal to that of $V1$. The alternatives treated up to now were not of regular structure because they were composed of several types of processors. The last alternative $V3$ will be "almost" regular as it will comprise, with few exceptions, just one type of processor MAD, which due to some excessive operations will be able to implement all the AGM operations.

The structure of the MAD processor is shown in Fig. 9.

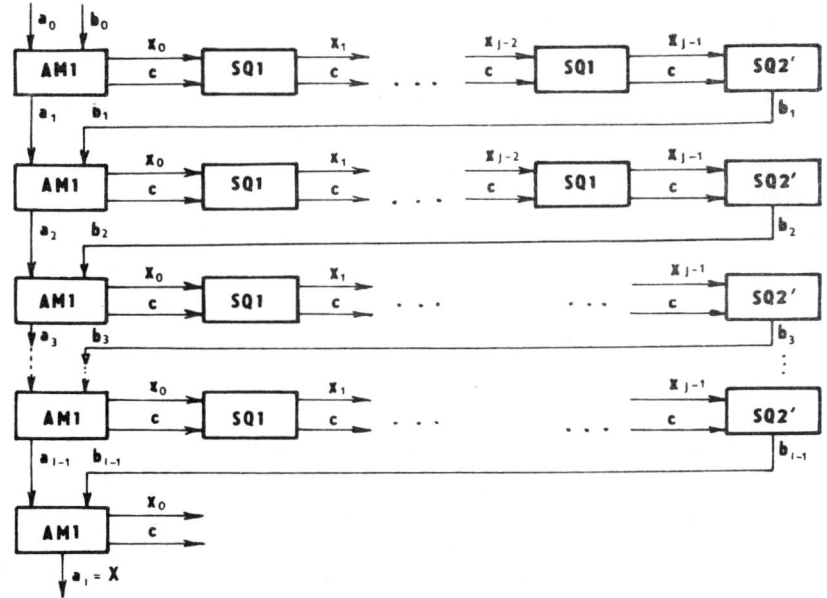

Fig. 7. Modification of $V2$ for AGM.

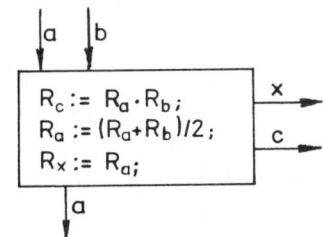

Fig. 8. AM1 processor.

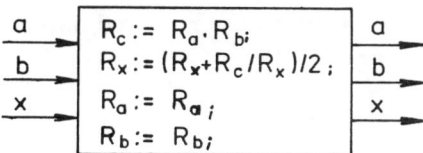

Fig. 9. MAD processor.

The structure of whole $V3$ is in Fig. 10.

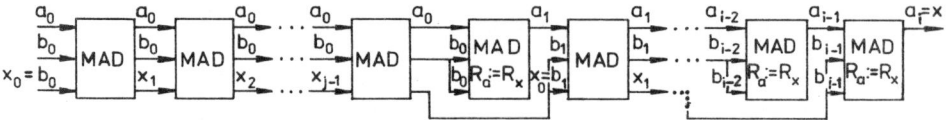

Fig. 10. Modification of $V3$ for AGM.

The basic cycle of implementation of MAD is $t + m + p$. Application of $V3$ is important for such M, for which

$$MI\left(J + \frac{m + 2p - d}{t}\right) > (m + p + 1)[M + (J + 1)(I - 1)],$$

and thus, in this case $T_p \approx T_s(m + p + 1)/IJ$.

The advantage of $V3$ is its being "almost" regular. It is composed of equal processors with the exception of one assignment $R_a := R_x$ in each terminal processor of the cycle and in the last processor. In the neighbourhood of these processors the communication network is changed, see Fig. 10.

Note. The complexity of the structure of processors may be influenced by the operation of division in (8). It can be avoided by computing the reciprocal value of $1/x_j$ from the quadratically converging iteration $y_{i+1} = y_i(2 - x_j y_i)$, $i = 0, 1, \ldots$, where y_0 is specified and $\lim_{i \to \infty} y_i = 1/x_j$. Another possibility is the computation of $\sqrt{C}$ from the quadratically converging iteration $x_{i+1} = x_i(3C - x_i^2)/2C$, $i = 0, 1, \ldots$, where x_0 is specified, $\lim_{i \to \infty} x_i = \sqrt{C}$, which in contrast to (8) does not cover the division with the changing variable [40].

Extending the division in (8) to a larger number of processors will promote a speed-up of M-multiple computations of AGM.

A systolic array (SA) can work synchronously or asynchronously. As we have seen in Section 1.2.6, a synchronous systolic array rhythmically processes, and with the help of central control cycles, moves the data through the system, where the computations are done in parallel and synchronously. On the other hand, in an asynchronous SA the control of data flow is distributed among processors, each processor is controlling its own data movement, whereby the computation is executed as soon as the required data is available. This can be obtained either as the input data or as results of other processors. Thus, asynchronous SA operates on the principle of data flow-controlled computation [20].

1.2.7 Asynchronous systolic algorithms

The third chapter is devoted to synchronous systolic arrays. In what follows we shall describe a general asynchronous systolic array (ASA) along with an illustrative example of ASA for the Gauss—Seidel iteration method to calculate a system of linear equations

$$\mathbf{A}\mathbf{x} = \mathbf{b}, \tag{10}$$

where $\mathbf{A} = (a_{ij})$ is a regular matrix of nth degree, $\mathbf{x} = (x_i)$, $\mathbf{b} = (b_i)$ [51]. Through input channels a general ASA is entered by input data, for which the ASA is specialized. An interprocessor communication network is built so as to make data transfers among separate processors as efficient as possible. If the processor p_{qr} uses in computations just the results of the processor p_{st}, then in ASA there is a channel of straight connection leading from p_{st} to p_{qr}.

Each processor p_{ij} in ASA has its input and output channels, input, constant and output registers, and starting and functional blocks that are implemented by technical means. The input (output) data of the task solved are flowing through the input (output) data channels into p_{ij} (from p_{ij}); the intermediate results computed by other processors (for other processors) are flowing through input (output) intermediate channels into p_{ij} (from p_{ij}). Obviously, each p_{ij} need not have all types of these channels.

Input registers of the processor are divided into data and intermediate registers. The input data for the whole task are stored in data registers, whereas intermediate registers serve the data that represent the results of other processors. Constant registers contain constants permanently stored in memory; these are necessary for the implementation of the functional block of the processor. After finishing the operation, results of each processor are stored in an input register from which they all are shifted immediately either into registers of other processors, or to the input of ASA.

The starting block of processor p_{ij} is composed of the starting word, semaphore and starting function. The starting word p_{ij} is a k-bit word $r_{ij} = \bigcup_{s=1}^{k} r_{ij}^{(s)}$, where k is the number of input registers, p_{ij}. Each of its bits $r_{ij}^{(s)}$ is connected to one input register, p_{ij}. If into an sth input register p_{ij} a data was stored, then $r_{ij}^{(s)} = 1$, whereas in the opposite case $r_{ij}^{(s)} = 0$. The semaphore of the processor p_{ij} is represented by the Boolean function $f(r_{ij}) = \bigcap_{s=1}^{k} r_{ij}^{(s)}$. If all $r_{ij}^{(s)} = 1$, then $f(r_{ij}) = 1$, i.e. all the input registers contain the data required so that the processor can start its operation. In the opposite case, $f(r_{ij}) = 0$, i.e. the processor waits for data. The starting function p_{ij} steadily implements the statement in the cycle

$$N_{ij}: \textbf{if } f(r_{ij}) = 0 \textbf{ then go to } N_{ij}.$$

This command is followed by a functional block p_{ij} which is implemented if $f(r_{ij}) \neq 0$. The functional block accomplishes the matching of input registers p_{ij} into output registers. It is ended by setting the bits in the starting word to zero, corresponding to intermediate registers; other bits r_{ij} stay unchanged. So, if needed, irrespective of the momentarily situation, the repeated operation of this processor in ASA is possible. Then, the whole operation of ASA is carried out in the following stages:

(1) Input registers and starting words r_{ij} of all processors p_{ij} are set to zero.

(2) Through input channels input data are successively read into the data registers of corresponding registers; after they have been recorded their starting words are changed and using the starting function the beginning of computation of functional blocks of the register is started to be tested.

(3) The calculated results flow out of the output channels; if all results are computed the computation is terminated, or the data of the next problem to be solved are read into.

Both the input and output of results to ASA and from ASA may, but need not, overlap with the computation of the functional blocks of individual processors.

Now we shall design a diagram of ASA for iterative solution of the system of linear equations (10) by the Gauss—Seidel algorithm. This algorithm is formed by a serial process in which the unknowns are iterated according to the relationship

$$x_i^{(k+1)} = c_i \left(b_i - \sum_{j=1}^{i-1} a_{ij} x_j^{(k+1)} - \sum_{j=i+1}^{n} a_{ij} x_j^{(k)} \right), \tag{11}$$

$$i = 1, 2, \ldots, n, \quad k = 0, 1, \ldots,$$

where $c_i = 1/a_{ii}$, $x_i^{(0)}$ are the given initial values, whereby the process of iterations is terminated, if for the given $\varepsilon > 0$ it holds $\max_i |x_i^{(k+1)} - x_i^{(k)}| < \varepsilon$. Provided that the iteration process is convergent (that occurs at each $x_i^{(0)}$, e.g., if **A** is a positive definite matrix), the corresponding ASA — for simplicity $n = 4$ — will have the structure shown in Fig. 11.

In each processor, its input data are stored in data registers in the left upper corner. The channels labelled by the symbol $\downarrow$ shift the intermediate results just into the next processor. The channels which pass data through all the corresponding processors are labelled by the symbol $\downarrow$. The function of each processor is recorded in it. We assume that the values c_i will be calculated from input data in preliminary computation, so that there is no operation included in the

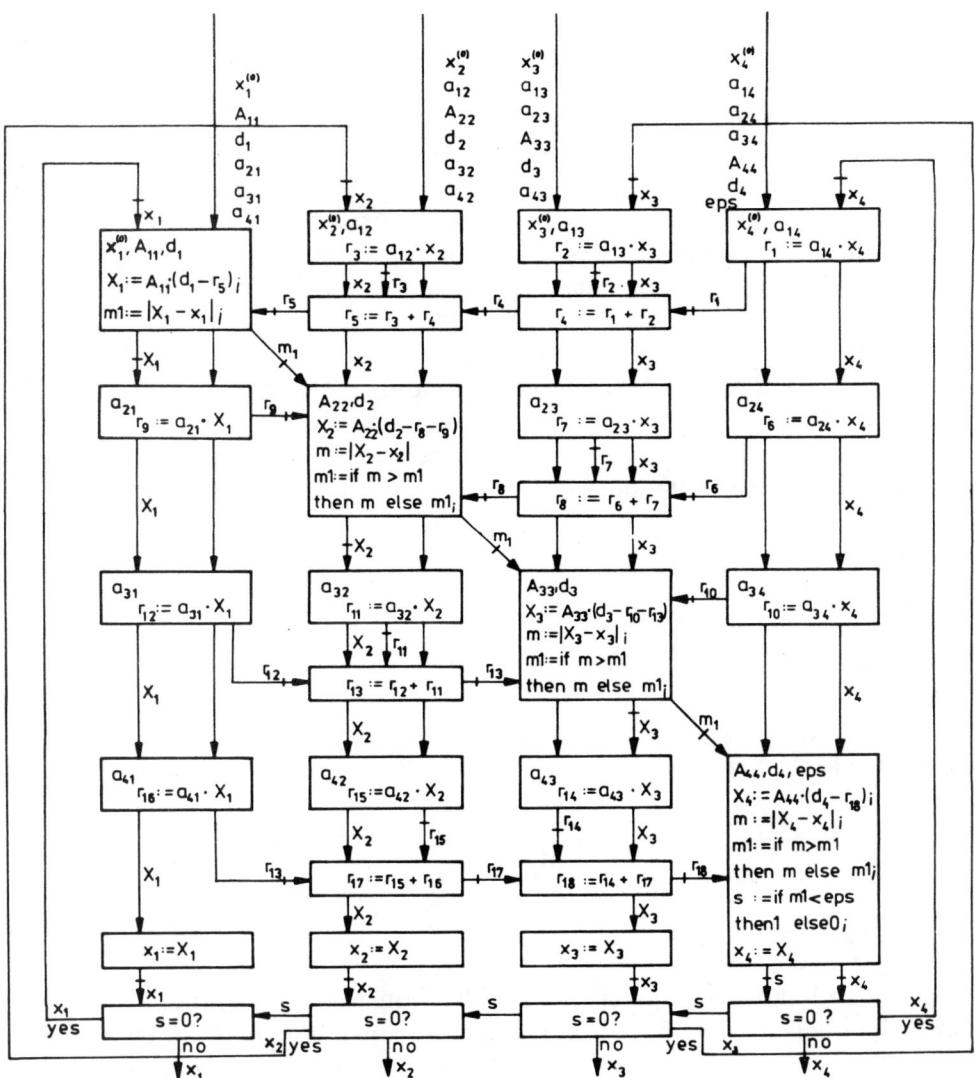

Fig. 11. ASP for the Gauss–Seidel algorithm.

diagram. This is advantageous from the view-point of its implementation. The diagram can be generalized for any n, or its modular use for iteration with block matrices is possible.

The designed ASA is computed as follows. After the data are inserted into the diagram in the given order, each processor which stores in its registers the data required, immediately implements its function and passes the obtained results further. So every unknown is asynchronously iterated by its speed, whereby the relationship (11) is obeyed. The computation of ASA is finished if all the results appear at output. In the above way, also the serial process (11) is parallelly asynchronously implemented on ASA.

ASA are suitable especially for less homogeneous algorithms. The synchronization is locally implemented by each processor, so that the system need not be controlled and synchronized as a whole. Asynchronous implementation also enables efficient utilization of hidden parallelism in the algorithm, because in this case each processor implements its function as soon as possible.

1.2.8 Vectorization of a scalar algorithm

Vectorization of a scalar algorithm can be demonstrated by the numerical computation of eigenvalues of symmetrical tridiagonal matrix **A** of degree n, i.e.

$$\mathbf{A} = \begin{bmatrix} a_1 & b_2 & & & 0 \\ b_2 & a_2 & b_3 & & \\ & \ddots & \ddots & \ddots & \\ 0 & & b_n & & a_n \end{bmatrix}$$

by the method of bisection. Let us suppose that all the eigenvalues of **A** lie in an interval $[a, b]$. Serial method of bisection is based on the following theorem [76]. For the fixed $\lambda \in [a, b]$ compute the recurrence relation

$$p_0(\lambda) = 1, \quad p_1(\lambda) = \lambda - a_1, \quad p_i(\lambda) = (\lambda - a_i)p_{i-1}(\lambda) - b_i^2 p_{i-2}(\lambda), \quad (12)$$
$$i = 2, 3, \ldots, n.$$

If $s(\lambda)$ is the number of sign changes in the sequence $\{p_0(\lambda), p_1(\lambda), \ldots, p_n(\lambda)\}$, then $s(\lambda)$ equals the number of eigenvalues **A** which are greater than λ.

Thus, for every subinterval $[\lambda_1, \lambda_2] \subset [a, b]$ the number of eigenvalues lying in $[\lambda_1, \lambda_2]$ is given by $s(\lambda_1) - s(\lambda_2)$.

The serial method of bisection rests in successive calculation of the relationship (12) until the interval containing just one eigenvalue is found. The eigenvalue can be computed using any method by which roots of non-linear equations are computed.

By vectorization of this algorithm the parallel algorithm is obtained, by which — on the assumption that we have $n + 1$ processors at our disposal — all the eigenvalues of **A** are computed at the same time.

Let us divide $[a, b]$ into n subintervals $[r_j, r_{j+1}], j = 0, 1, \ldots, n - 1$, using the points $r_j = a + j(b-a)/n$, $j = 0, 1, \ldots, n$. Let us denote the vector $r = (r_j)$, $j = 0, 1, \ldots, n$, and let us compute the vector relationship

$$P_0(r) = e_{n+1}, \quad P_1(r) = r - a_1 e_{n+1},$$
$$P_i(r) = (r - a_i e_{n+1}) P_{i-1}(r) - b_i^2 P_{i-2}(r), \quad i = 2, 3, \ldots, n, \quad (13)$$

in which $P_i(r) = (p_{ij})$ are the vectors of dimension $(n+1)$, e_{n+1} is the unit vector, whereby under the product of two vectors, multiplication of their corresponding components is understood.

When implementing this algorithm on a parallel computer, the jth processor ($j = 0, 1, \ldots, n$) implements the jth line of the relationship (13), namely the relationship (12) at the point r_j, where the number of sign changes of corresponding Sturm's sequence, i.e. $s(r_j)$, is calculated on the way.

Further on, the values $t_j = s(r_j) - s(r_{j+1})$, $j = 0, 1, \ldots, n-1$, yielding the number of eigenvalues lying in $[r_j, r_{j+1}]$ are calculated in parallel. The subintervals with $t_j = 0$ are excluded from further computations, the subintervals with $t_j = 1$ are stored in memory, or their eigenvalues are computed immediately. The sum of lengths of other subintervals is divided by n, what yields new vector elements of the vector r; the whole procedure is repeated until n subintervals with single eigenvalues are found. Another alternative is to obtain new r depending upon t_j, i.e. for larger t_j the subinterval is divided with greater density.

Parallel implementation of this procedure depends on the type of parallel computer. If a matrix processor of the SIMD-type is concerned, then the relationship (13) can be implemented on it with great advantage, provided each processor will hold $2n - 1$ elements of **A** in its memory. Searching for subintervals with single eigenvalues followed by their computation can also be accomplished asynchronously on a multiprocessor computer. Vector operations along with search for sign changes are operations applicable to an associative computer of the SIMD-type — description of vector bisection for this type of computer is in [49].

1.2.9 Parallel computation in bit slices

Computation of vectors in bit slices can be well implemented on parallel associative computers. It can be demonstrated using the so-called CORDIC algorithm, which is suitable for computation of some arithmetic operations and elementary functions. The CORDIC algorithm is an iterative computation of the type $t_i = F(t_{i-1})$, $i = 1, 2, \ldots, n$, where each iteration requires just the operations of summation and shifting. For example, division of two scalars

$z = x/y$, where x, y and z are numbers in binary code, is implemented as follows [5].

The values of y are expressed in the form

$$y = 1 \bigg/ \prod_{i=1}^{n} (1 + \xi_i 2^{-i}),$$

where ξ_i can be $+1$ or -1, and it holds $\xi_1 = \text{sign } y$ and

$$\xi_i = -\text{sign}\left[y \prod_{k=1}^{i-1} (1 + \xi_k 2^{-k}) - 1 \right], \qquad i = 2, 3, \ldots, n. \tag{14}$$

Then, for the result

$$z = x \prod_{i=1}^{n} (1 + \xi_i 2^{-i}). \tag{15}$$

The above implies that the algorithm contains just the sequence of operations $a(1 + \xi_i 2^{-i})$, i.e. the sum $a + \xi_i b$, where $b = a 2^{-i}$. If a is a number in binary code, then b is obtained by the shift of bits of the number a by i positions to the right. For $\xi_i = 1$ ($\xi_i = -1$) this means simple addition (subtraction) b with (from) a. Thus the whole operation of division is composed of computation of values ξ_i with the help of (14) and of implementation of (15), where both steps use just the operation of shift and addition, or subtraction.

The CORDIC algorithm can also be easily used for parallel division of two vectors by components. In this case the algorithm of division by bit slices can be well implemented on a parallel associative computer.

Let $\mathbf{X} = (x_i)$, $\mathbf{Y} = (y_i)$, $i = 1, 2, \ldots, m$, be two vectors. The vector $\mathbf{Z} = (z_k) = \mathbf{X}/\mathbf{Y} = (x_k/y_k)$, $k = 1, 2, \ldots, m$, can be computed with the accuracy of n bits on an m-processor computer by bit slices according to the following relationships: parallel computation for $k = 1, 2, \ldots, m$:

$$\xi_1^{(k)} = \text{sign } y_k;$$

$$z_k^{(1)} = x_k(1 + \xi_1^{(k)} 2^{-1}); \quad q_k^{(1)} = y_k(1 + \xi_1^{(k)} 2^{-1});$$

for $i = 2, 3, \ldots, n$ **do**
begin $\xi_i^{(k)} = -\text{sign}(q_k^{(i-1)} - 1);$
$\quad z_k^{(i)} = z_k^{(i-1)}(1 + \xi_i^{(k)} 2^{-i});$ **if** $i = n$ **then go to** A;
$\quad q_k^{(i)} = q_k^{(i-1)}(1 + \xi_i^{(k)} 2^{-i});$
end;

A: the results z_k are on $z_k^{(n)}$, $k = 1, 2, ..., m$.

Parallel implementation of this algorithm requires the memory reservation of six m-component arrays, Fs, $s = 1, 2, ..., 6$. On starting the computation the vectors **X** and **Y** are in $F1$ and $F2$ at the end the vector **Z** is in $F1$. During computation, the vector $\xi_i = (\xi_i^{(k)})$, $k = 1, 2, ..., m$, will be in $F3$; $F4$ and $F5$ remember the shifted intermediate results and $F6$ contains the unit vector. Parallel vector division by the CORDIC method will proceed in the following steps [49]:

(1) $j := 1$; $F1 := \mathbf{X}$; $F2 := \mathbf{Y}$; $F3 := \text{sign } F2$;
(2) $F4 := F1 \cdot 2^{-j}$; $F5 := F2 \cdot 2^{-j}$;
(3) $F1 := F1 + F3 \cdot F4$; $F2 := F2 + F3 \cdot F5$;
(4) $j := j + 1$; $F3 := -\text{sign}(F2 - F6)$;
(5) $F4 := F1 \cdot 2^{-j}$; $F5 := F2 \cdot 2^{-j}$;
(6) $F1 := F1 + F3 \cdot F4$; if $j = n$ **go to** (8);
(7) $F2 := F2 + F3 \cdot F5$; **go to** (4);
(8) Vector **Z** is on $F1$.

There also exists a variant of the CORDIC method described for scalar multiplication xy, planar vector rotations, as well as for the functions $\sqrt{x}$, $\exp(x)$, $\log x$, $\sin x$, $\text{arc tg } x$, etc., where x is a scalar [2, 5]. A function such as $z = \sqrt{x}$ is computed with accuracy of n bits from similar relationships [5]

$$\xi_1 = 1, \quad \xi_i = -\text{sign}\left[x \prod_{k=1}^{i-1}(1 + \xi_k 2^{-k})^2 - 1\right], \quad i = 2, 3, ..., n,$$

$$z = x \prod_{i=1}^{n}(1 + \xi_i 2^{-i}).$$

Vectorization of relationships occurring in computations in bit slices for an associative computer is analogous to the above-described algorithm of vector division. Thus, the CORDIC method can also be easily used for computation of $\sqrt{\mathbf{X}}$, $\exp(\mathbf{X})$, $\log \mathbf{X}$, $\sin \mathbf{X}$, $\text{arctg } \mathbf{X}$, etc., that is to compute these functions by individual components of vector argument **X**.

Because all the above functions represent basic algorithms of signal processing and matrix algebra, the general CORDIC algorithm was designed in [1] as a specialized chip based on VLSI technology. Its use for specialized parallel computer structures is described in [67]. In this paper a linear array of CORDIC processors is proposed for computation of the Fast Fourier Transform along with computation of eigenvalues of matrices by QR algorithm and a triangular array of CORDIC processors for Kholesky's decomposition of positive definite matrices and for Given's method for solving the systems of linear algebraic equations.

1.2.10 Chaotic iteration

Chaotic implementation of parallel algorithms was designed by Chazan and Miranker [16] for iterative computation of a system of linear equations $x = = Ax + b$, where A is a real matrix of degree n.

Here, individual components of the solution are iterated on various processors of a multiprocessor computer in random sequence, where they are stored as global variables in a memory shared by all processors. The iteration process is finished if certain conditions are fulfilled, which is checked by the processor reserved specially for this purpose. To secure the convergence of this diagram the sequence of iterations is limited, because there must exist a fixed positive integer s such that on implementing the ith iteration of any component the components of the jth iteration are used only if $j \geq i - s$ and, further it must be guaranteed that on steady operation of the algorithm each component of solution is iterated an arbitrary number of times. In [16] it is proved that this process will be convergent, if $\varrho(|A|) < 1$, where $\varrho(|A|)$ is the spectral radius of matrix $|A|$, i.e. a matrix each element of which is replaced by its absolute value. The larger s in this chaotic process — i.e. the older the iteration values can be used that exert some unfavourable influence upon its convergence — the less will the blocking of its operators be caused by waiting for suitable input data. Consequently, less administrative operations will occur, that is, the whole process will be implemented faster.

The problem of enlarging the chaotic principle to non-linear systems is solved in [60].

On using chaotic iteration, repeated checking of the state of individual iterations, hence also a certain form of synchronization cannot be avoided. Another disadvantage of this method is its very narrow specialized applicability in numerical mathematics, restricted to iterative method. Thus the so-called asynchronous implementation of algorithms which represents another method of construction of parallel algorithms for multiprocessor computer is more advantageous from the view-point of efficiency of its implementation and universal use.

1.2.11 Synchronous and asynchronous iterations

A parallel algorithm for a multiprocessor computer is a set of processes run in parallel, which, when solving the given problem, can operate simultaneously over common memory. Each process has so-called iteration points, at which it is capable of communication with other processors. By interaction points the whole process is divided into steps.

Usually for a multiprocessor computer, the time of a given step, hence of the whole process, is not constant. Variations in this time are unpredictable and are caused by the following reasons [45]:

(a) a multiprocessor can be composed of processors of various speeds, speed of the process depends on the processor it was assigned to;

(b) a process can be postponed by conflicts when access into common memory is claimed for by more processors;

(c) a processor which runs the given process can be interrupted and the computation replaced by another activity (i.e. a process of higher priority, input-output operation, etc.);

(d) in multiprogramming mode the speed of computation can be influenced by the number of other users of the system and their requirements;

(e) the work necessary for implementation of the given process can depend on its input data (e.g. the number of comparisons necessary for arranging n elements depends on their original arrangement, the computation time of a function depends on the position of the point in which it is computed, etc.).

From the above it follows that the execution time of an arbitrary process on a multiprocessor computer represents a random variable fulfilling certain distribution function. This fact can be made use of in designing algorithms for a multiprocessor computer [45].

Let us have a convergent method of iteration

$$x_{i+1} = \varphi(x_i), \qquad i = 0, 1, ..., \tag{16}$$

where x_0 is the given number. Parallel algorithm can be created from (16) either by parallel implementation of φ, or with the use of variations of the computation time of φ.

Parallel computation of φ can be accomplished synchronously or asynchronously. Let us suppose that (16) can be written in the form

$$x_{i+1} = F(g(x_i), h(x_i)), \qquad i = 0, 1, ... \tag{17}$$

On synchronous iteration, $g(x_i)$ and $h(x_i)$ are computed first; having finished these computations, one can compute x_{i+1}. Obviously, implementation times g and h can differ from each other and thus, the moment of computation of x_{i+1} is determined by the time of the function which is computed next.

In using asynchronous iteration the processes are not synchronized. Let, for example, computation time h be much longer than g. Then, an algorithm is constructed of two processes, P_1 and P_2, i.e.

P_1: $y_1 := g(y_3)$; $y_3 := F(y_1, y_2)$, until S does not hold,
P_2: $y_2 := h(y_3)$, until S does not hold.

The global variables y_1, y_2 and y_3 can be accessed by P_1 and P_2. S represents a global condition for termination of the process. At the beginning of computation $y_1 = g(x_0)$, $y_2 = h(x_0)$ and $y_3 = F(y_1, y_2)$. Whenever any of the processes finishes its computation, a new computation using the momentary values of global variables is started without delay. If the implementation time P_1 is less than P_2, then

$$x_{i+1} = F(g(x_i), h(x_j)), \qquad j \leq i, \tag{18}$$

i.e. an iteration different from (17) is concerned, and thus, new convergence conditions are to be derived. Synchronous and asynchronous iterations can be compromised by additional condition for (18), which has the form $i - j \leq k$, where k is an integer quaranteeing that the function $h(x)$ does not use too old values of x_j at iteration.

Thus, on synchronous iteration there exist some processes where some steps cannot start operating before the operation of the steps of other processes has been finished. Because the times of steps of the processes are random variables, synchronization can cause blocking of some processes at the given moment so that the total computation speed is decreased.

In asynchronous iteration there exists a set of global variables, which can be accessed by all necessary global variables. Then the latter are read into by the process and on the basis of their values and results obtained some global variables are modified, whereby the operations above them must be programmed as critical sections. The main advantage of asynchronous computation is that its processes never wait for data, but they always calculate with the global variables. Disadvantage, however, is that the processes can be blocked prior to the input to the critical sections.

Termination time of such process is given by the sum of times [45] of:

(1) processing, i.e. the sum of times necessary to run through all its steps;

(2) blocking, i.e. the sum of the times at which the process was blocked because of waiting for suitable data or for input to the critical section;

(3) synchronization, i.e. the sum of the times necessary to perform the synchronization or implementation of the critical sections.

Times of blocking and synchronization are substantially higher in synchronous than in asynchronous computations. It appears that there is a certain correlation among these times, i.e. if one of them is reduced, the others are increased and vice versa.

If the iteration (16) there is no parallelism in computation φ, then (16) is a strictly serial algorithm, which can be made parallel by only making use of the variation of the time of computation φ on a multiprocessor computer. In this case, under a parallel algorithm we understand a set of asynchronous processes communicating with each other via their global variables. Let us suppose that the iteration (16) is to be computed for $i = 0, 1, \ldots, n - 1$. Further, let there be a free processor always available for each implementable process. An algorithm which uses $k \geq 1$ asynchronous processes P_i, $i = 1, 2, \ldots, k$, to solve this task, consists of the following steps:

(1) If no process has finished any subtask, then the free process starts the execution of x_1;

(2) Else, if x_n has not finished by any process, the free process starts the execution of a subtask, which has not been finished yet and is ready for implementation.

For linear arrangement of the subtask, the 2nd step unambiguously defines the task to be realized.

Let us create three identical processes P_k, $k = 1, 2, 3$:

$$P_k: j := i + 1;\ x_j := \varphi(x_{j-1}); \tag{19}$$

if $i < j$, then $i := j$;

if S holds, then it is finished.

Variables i and x_i are global, and j is a local variable of every process, i is the index of a variable which was computed last. Statement (19) is programmed as a critical section. Processes P_1, P_2 and P_3 compute φ from input data that are available at the moment when their computation has just started. Let $t_1, t_2, \ldots, t_i < t_{i+1}$ be end moments of the processes. The diagram in Fig. 12 shows possible arrangement of our computation.

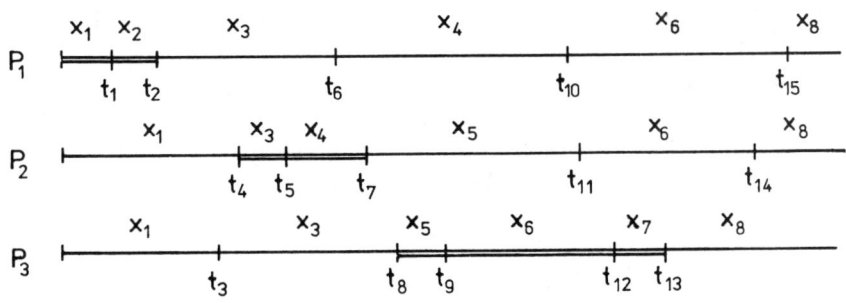

Fig. 12. Asynchronous implementation of a serial algorithm.

We can see that if P_3 finishes x_3 at the moment t_8, then P_2 is finished. Therefore, P_3 will omit x_4 and after x_3 it starts the realization of x_5. Similarly, P_1 omits x_5 and x_7, and P_2 omits x_2 and x_7. If each process implements 6 subtasks, then the algorithm implements $x_1, x_2, \ldots, x_8$, hence a speed-up was reached which does not follow from splitting of work to the processors but from the variation of implementation times of individual subtasks. From the diagram it can also be seen that at each time at least one process makes reasonable computations (double lines).

The speed of such computation can be further accelerated by interrupting the processes, computations of which are not useful anymore. Of course, under the assumption that the cost of this test and of the subsequent interruption is not too high.

The described algorithm makes the algorithms parallel by the use of asynchronous behaviour of a multiprocessor computer which never waits for input data, whereby advantage of fast processes is utilized. It facilitates essential speed-up, if the time variation of subtasks is relatively high.

1.3 Matrix multiplication on parallel computers

The problem of matrix multiplication is one of the most important numerical tasks, that frequently occurs when scientific and technological tasks are solved on a computer. From the view-point of complexity of algorithms it represents the key problem, as many numerical and non-numerical tasks can be transformed to matrix multiplication. Therefore any success in designing new fast matrix multiplication algorithms is met by a wide application area in this field.

In this section basic algorithms of serial matrix multiplication will be described. Then we shall focus our attention to various algorithms of parallel matrix multiplication algorithms implemented on different types of computer architectures. The computer architectures considered are described in more detail in other chapters of this monograph.

Let us have two square matrices of dimension n, $\mathbf{A} = (a_{ij})$ and $\mathbf{B} = (b_{ij})$. Their product

$$\mathbf{AB} = \mathbf{C} = (c_{ij}) \qquad (20)$$

is defined as

$$c_{ij} = \sum_{k=1}^{n} a_{ik} b_{kj}, \qquad i, j = 1, 2, \ldots, n. \qquad (21)$$

This classical procedure requires n^3 multiplications and $n^3 - n^2$ additions. In general, we can assume that $n = 2^m$.

Decomposition of the product (20) into square submatrices of dimension $n/2$ yields

$$\begin{bmatrix} \mathbf{A}_{11} & \mathbf{A}_{12} \\ \mathbf{A}_{21} & \mathbf{A}_{22} \end{bmatrix} \begin{bmatrix} \mathbf{B}_{11} & \mathbf{B}_{12} \\ \mathbf{B}_{21} & \mathbf{B}_{22} \end{bmatrix} = \begin{bmatrix} \mathbf{C}_{11} & \mathbf{C}_{12} \\ \mathbf{C}_{21} & \mathbf{C}_{22} \end{bmatrix}, \qquad (22)$$

then we have

$$\mathbf{C}_{ij} = \mathbf{A}_{i1}\mathbf{B}_{1j} + \mathbf{A}_{i2}\mathbf{B}_{2j}, \qquad i, j = 1, 2. \tag{23}$$

If the products obtained are subjected to the same recursive procedure, the number of operations $P(n)$ of this algorithm is given by the recursion $P(n) = 8P(n/2) + O(n^2)$ which implies that $P(n) = O(n^3)$. Very interesting decrease in the number of operations of matrix multiplication was reached by Strassen [69]. He has shown that four submatrices $\mathbf{C}_{ij}$ in (23) can be calculated employing just 7 multiplications and 18 additions using the following identities

$$\mathbf{C}_{11} = (\mathbf{A}_{11} + \mathbf{A}_{22})(\mathbf{B}_{11} + \mathbf{B}_{22}) + (\mathbf{A}_{12} - \mathbf{A}_{22})(\mathbf{B}_{21} + \mathbf{B}_{22}) + \mathbf{A}_{22}(\mathbf{B}_{21} - \mathbf{B}_{11}) - (\mathbf{A}_{11} + \mathbf{A}_{12})\mathbf{B}_{22},$$

$$\mathbf{C}_{12} = (\mathbf{A}_{11} + \mathbf{A}_{12})\mathbf{B}_{22} + \mathbf{A}_{11}(\mathbf{B}_{12} - \mathbf{B}_{22}),$$

$$\mathbf{C}_{21} = (\mathbf{A}_{21} + \mathbf{A}_{22})\mathbf{B}_{11} + \mathbf{A}_{22}(\mathbf{B}_{21} - \mathbf{B}_{11}),$$

$$\mathbf{C}_{22} = (\mathbf{A}_{11} + \mathbf{A}_{22})(\mathbf{B}_{11} + \mathbf{B}_{22}) + \mathbf{A}_{11}(\mathbf{B}_{12} - \mathbf{B}_{22}) - (\mathbf{A}_{21} + \mathbf{A}_{22})\mathbf{B}_{11} + (\mathbf{A}_{21} - \mathbf{A}_{11})(\mathbf{B}_{11} + \mathbf{B}_{12}).$$

The above algorithm does not use the commutativity of multiplication, so it can be recursively used for other submatrices. The number of multiplications $M(n)$, or of additions $A(n)$ of this method is given by recursion $M(n) = 7M(n/2)$, or $A(n) = 7A(n/2) + 18(n/2)^2$ which implies that $M(n) = 7^{\log n} = n^{\log 7} \approx n^{2.81}$ and also $A(n) = O(n^{2.81})$. Thus, instead of $O(n^3)$ operations of classical procedure (21) or (23) we have obtained an algorithm for matrix multiplication with $O(n^{2.81})$ operations, or more precisely an algorithm with less than $4.7n^{2.81}$ operations which from certain n represent less than $2n^3 - n^2$ operations of classical algorithm. Winograd [78] has shown that 7 is the minimum number of multiplications necessary for computation of problem (22) and Probert has proved that the optimum number of additions is 15 [59].

The algorithm for (22) with 7 multiplications and 15 additions can be expressed in graphical form as shown in Fig. 13 [57].

In Fig. 13, • (o) in the square $(\mathbf{A}_{ij}, \mathbf{B}_{kl})$ is represented by the term $+ (-)$ $\mathbf{A}_{ij}\mathbf{B}_{kl}$. The terms occurring in the products are represented by seven mutually interconnected groups of circles (e.g., the square generated by connecting 9 circles represents the term $(-\mathbf{A}_{11} + \mathbf{A}_{21} + \mathbf{A}_{22})(\mathbf{B}_{11} - \mathbf{B}_{12} + \mathbf{B}_{22})$). Blocks of the matrix $\mathbf{C}$ are, in turn, given by the following formulas

$$\mathbf{C}_{11} = a + b, \qquad \mathbf{C}_{12} = a + c + e + f,$$
$$\mathbf{C}_{21} = a + c + d + g, \qquad \mathbf{C}_{22} = a + c + d + e.$$

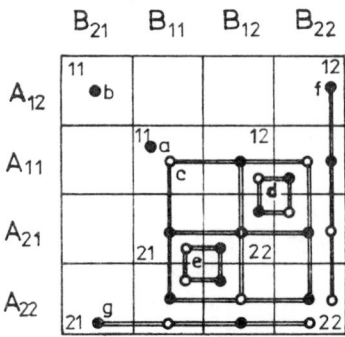

Fig. 13. Fast algorithm for multiplication of 2×2 matrices.

In spite of the optimality of this algorithm the number of its operations is again $O(n^{2.81})$. As the lower limit of the complexity of matrix multiplication is $O(n^2)$, many authors tried to decrease the upper limit of complexity. The first success in this field was achieved by Pan [54], who on the basis of new methods (so-called trilinear aggregating, uniting and cancelling) obtained and algorithm with the number of operations $O(n^{2.795})$, which was improved to $O(n^{2.780})$ in [55]. All the above algorithms belong to the class of accurate algorithms. Recently, the attention has also been paid to formulation of approximate algorithms which are used for computation of matrices with the accuracy ε.

Using the method of partial matrix multiplication of a triangular and full matrices, an approximate algorithm with $O(n^{2.779})$ operations was obtained in [8]. The efforts to reduce the complexity of approximate algorithms are continuing. The latest known result achieved by combining several methods is an algorithm of complexity $O(n^{2.495})$ described in [18].

With respect to practical applicability of these algorithms, Spiess [68] has shown that new accurate algorithms of matrix multiplication are of interest also for practical computations (for example, Strassen's algorithm using integer arithmetic is faster than the classical algorithm already from matrices of dimension 30). As all approximate algorithms reach the speed-up at large n only, they have had but theoretical meaning till now.

Very intensive research of serial algorithms for matrix multiplication has been carried on for 20 years. Many surprising and important results have been achieved in this period. Now, let us discuss some results that have been achieved in the field of parallel algorithms for matrix multiplications. Its study — along with designing new parallel computers — has started to develop in its full extent just recently.

Now, as an example of matrix multiplication (20) it will be shown how the formulas (21) can be modified in various ways in order to be efficiently implemented on various types of parallel architecture.

Formulas (21) represent n mutually independent scalar products, where each of them can be computed in parallel. Thus, an algorithm is obtained, which computes (20) in $\lceil \log n \rceil + 1$ steps with n^3 processors. Similarly, using the parallel implementation of Strassen's algorithm on $k \leq O(n^{\log 7})$ processors, the result is obtained in $3 \lceil \log n \rceil + 1$ steps [19]. However, these algorithms have rather theoretical meaning, because they require large number of processors and the price of communications is not being taken into account.

Formulas (21) can also be used directly on matrix processors, as well as on multiprocessor systems.

Consider a matrix processor with n processors which can operate over vectors with the rows of matrices. The program for computation of **C** for this computer will be as follows:

```
for i := 1(1)n do
   begin c_ik := 0 (k = 1(1)n);
   for j := 1(1)n do
       c_ik := c_ik + a_ij b_jk (k = 1(1)n);
end.
```

Notation $k = 1(1)n$ means that the operation in the given row is executed in parallel for all the given indices. The program computes all elements of the ith row simultaneously. Each element of the jth row **B** is in parallel multiplied by a_{ij}, so that this element is sent by the communication network to all processors at the same time.

The program of matrix multiplication on a multiprocessor system will be as follows:

```
for k := 1(1)n - 1 do
   Fork N;
   k := n;
N: for i := 1(1)n do
       begin c_ik := 0;
           for j := 1(1)n do
               c_ik := c_ik + a_ij b_jk;
       end;
Join n.
```

In this case the algorithm was divided into n processes, which are assigned to the free processors of the computer. Command **Fork** N means the start of the process, following the label N. Computation proceeds in parallel manner after **Fork** N. Command **Join** n will cause connection of n independent processes into a single flow of instructions. Program after **Join** n starts at that moment only, when n processes have executed **Join**. If there is no free processor for the newly established process, then the process queues up in a queue where it waits for its execution.

Another typical vector algorithm of computation (20) is represented by the set of relationships

$$c_j = \sum_{k=1}^{n} b_{kj} a_k, \qquad j = 1, 2, \ldots, n, \tag{24}$$

where c_j (a_k) is the jth (kth) column vector of **C** (**A**). Its execution is especially suitable for pipeline processors which require algorithms expressed in vector form. An example of pipeline processors is the STAR-100 computer. On this computer, the algorithm (24) requires time $1.5n^3 + 249n^2 - 187.5n + 94$, which is expressed in 40 ns units [47]. Another algorithm that can be easily vectorized for matrix multiplications on STAR-100 is that from [47], this algorithm requires matrices stored by diagonals, where one can compute matrix **C** by diagonals using the vectors of diagonals of **A** and **B**.

Let d_0 be the main diagonal **C** and d_k (d_{-k}), $k = 1, 2, \ldots, n - 1$, the first, second, …, $(n - 1)$st diagonal over (under) d_0. Then the algorithm for computation of d_k, $k = 0, 1, \ldots, n$, is informally as follows:

(1) Create a matrix A_k or B_k by omitting the lower k rows of **A** or of the upper k rows of B^T;

(2) Create a matrix $D_k := A_k \times B_k$, i.e. multiply mutually the equally positioned elements in matrices A_k and B_k of dimension $(n - k)/n$;

(3) Summation of the elements of the mth row, D_k, $m = 1, 2, \ldots, n - k$, yields the mth component of d_k.

Computation of d_k, $k < 0$ can be done in similar manner by omitting the upper k rows of **A** and the lower k columns of B^T at the first step. The time of this algorithm on STAR-100 is $1.5n^3 + 250(3n^2 - 3n + 1)$. While its starting time is about 3 times longer compared to the preceding algorithm, both algorithms for large n are equivalent. This algorithm has proved to be most advantageous for band matrices of small band width. If **A** and **B** are band matrices of band width $2p + 1$, then the band width of **C** is $4p + 1$ and time required for computation of **C** is $(2p + 1)^2(1.5n + 250)$. If, for example, **A** and **B** are tridiagonal matrices of dimension 1000, then the diagonal algorithm on STAR-100 compared to the preceding algorithm is more than 48 times faster [47].

Another advantage of this algorithm is that A^T can be obtained easily from the vectors of diagonals. If in algorithm (24) matrices are stored by columns and because STAR-100 assumes successive storing of vector elements one by another, A^T cannot be obtained easily.

The algorithm of matrix multiplication modified with respect to the architecture of matrix processor DAP is as follows [24]:
(1) $k := 0$; $\mathbf{C} := 0$;
(2) $k := k + 1$;
(3) Create a matrix $\mathbf{A}_k$ or $\mathbf{B}_k$, where in $\mathbf{A}_k$ ($\mathbf{B}_k$) all its columns (rows) are equal to the kth column of $\mathbf{A}$ (row of $\mathbf{B}$);
(4) $\mathbf{C} := \mathbf{C} + \mathbf{A}_k \times \mathbf{B}_k$;
(5) If $k < n$, go to 2.

The algorithm is based on the identity

$$\mathbf{C} = \sum_{k=1}^{n} \mathbf{A}_k \times \mathbf{B}_k,$$

where the operation $\times$ is again multiplication of equally positioned elements of corresponding matrices. Mechanism of constructing $\mathbf{A}_k$ and $\mathbf{B}_k$ is implemented by technical means, and that is why it occupies about 10% of the total computation time.

Another interesting algorithm of matrix multiplication, designed for a matrix processor specialized for computation of the Kálmán filter, is described in [70]. Let us suppose that the matrix processor consists of n^2 processors p_{ij}, $i, j = 1, 2, ..., n$, arranged in a square array in the following form (Fig. 14)

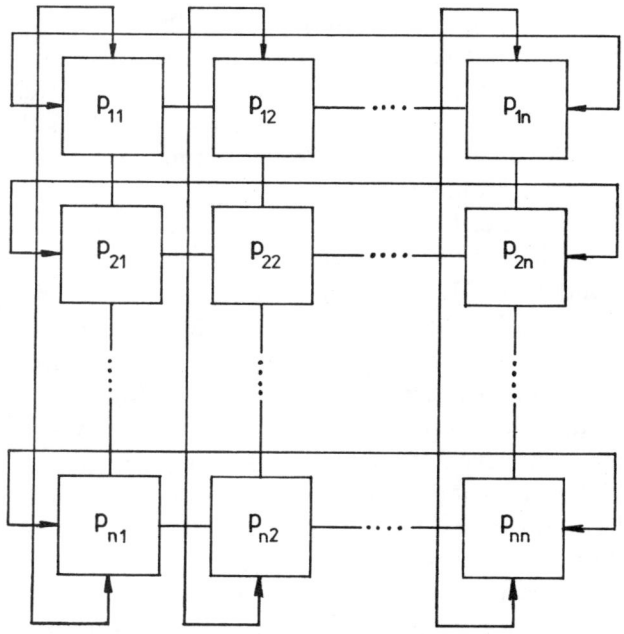

Fig. 14. Matrix processor for matrix product.

Each processor p_{ij} has four registers Ra^{ij}, Rb^{ij}, Rc^{ij} and Rt^{ij}. By a cyclic communication network it is connected with its four neighbours with which it can exchange its data. Matrix multiplication for such a system is given by the algorithm:

(1) $k := 0$; parallel input of **A**, **B** and zero setting of **C**;

$$Ra^{ij} = a_{ij}; \quad Rb^{ij} = b_{ij}; \quad Rc^{ij} = 0.$$

(2) For $i = 1, 2, \ldots, n$ do the cyclic shift of the ith row by $i - 1$ columns to the left.

(3) For $j = 1, 2, \ldots, n$ do the cyclic shift of the jth column of **B** by $j - 1$ rows upwards.

(4) $k := k + 1$; parallel multiplication in all processors: $Rt^{ij} = Ra^{ij} Rb^{ij}$.

(5) Parallel summation in all p_{ij}: $Rc^{ij} := Rc^{ij} + Rt^{ij}$.

(6) Do the cyclic shift of all contents of Ra^{ij} by one position to the right.

(7) Do the cyclic shift of all contents of Rb^{ij} by one position downwards.

(8) If $k < n$, then go to 4.

(9) The output of the elements c_{ij} of matrix **C** which are in registers Rc^{ij}.

The algorithm of matrix multiplication that is obtained by dividing the matrices into blocks, can be implemented with advantage on a parallel computer with tree-communication network [48]. For matrices **A**, **B**, **C** divided into blocks according to (22), the relationships (23) hold.

If the products of matrices of dimension $n/2$ are split again into smaller submatrices, then this decomposition can be continued until after $\log n$ steps we arrive at the product of matrices of dimension 1×1, i.e. to the products of individual elements **A** and **B**. By reverse combination of intermediate results the solution of the original problem is obtained.

A parallel tree-computer implementing this recursive decomposition has n^3 leaves in which products of two elements are implemented; the first product is from **A**, the second from **B**. The other processors in the tree compute the submatrices of the given level or they implement decomposition at forward run and aggregation of the corresponding submatrices at backward run. The tree-computer for matrix computation will then have $m = \log n$ levels of processors which will sum up the relevant matrices, and m levels which will split or integrate all submatrices into one level, in which parallel multiplication of two numbers will be executed. Thus, the total number of levels of the tree will be $2m + 1$. Each processor for decomposition and for aggregation has three successors, each processor for addition has two successors. The root-processor will store in its memory whole matrices and will split them into submatrices of half-dimension, these will be sent to a lower level of processors. After a successive splitting the level of multiplication will be executed, the levels of processors for addition will be alternated by those for aggregation. Thus, smaller and smaller matrices are to be sent and stored down the tree. That is why the communication requirements are maximum at the root of tree and minimum at the leaves. Because each element of the matrices has to travel through the whole tree in both directions, the number of steps of this algorithm is of order $O(n^2)$.

From the above algorithm it can be seen that mapping the recursion into a parallel recursive structure is quite a complex computation procedure. For this reason it cannot be expected that the implementation of the Strassen's recursive procedure by means of a tree-computer will bring any advantage with regard to the parallelism. Finally, we shall describe the systolic algorithm of multiplication of band matrices, which can be implemented with advantage on a specialized matrix array. Such a systolic array can be based on new technology of very large scale of integration (VLSI). This topic will be considered further in Chapter 3.

Let **A** and **B** in the product **AB** = **C** be band matrices with band widths w_1 and w_2. The hexagonal array with $w_1 w_2$ processors will compute **C** in $3n + \min(w_1, w_2)$ time steps. Then, the case $w_1 = w_2 = 4$ is given by

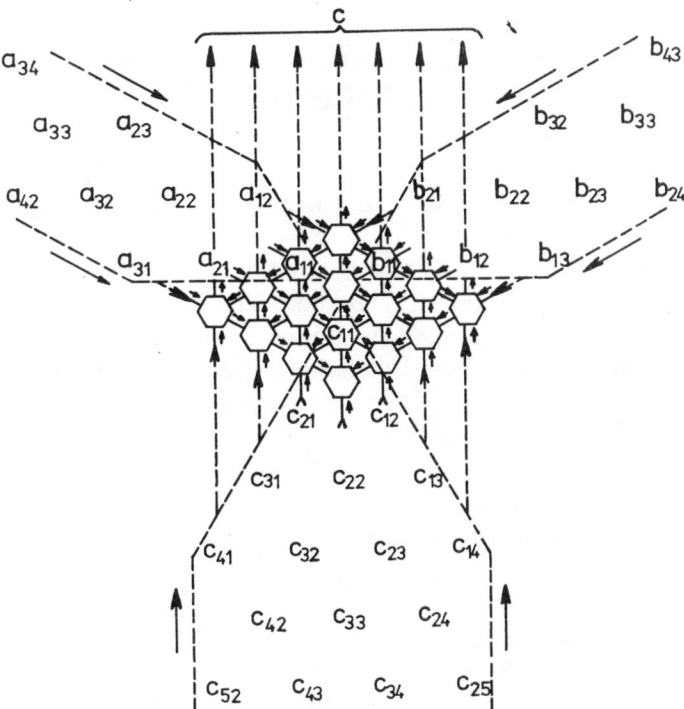

Fig. 15. Hexagonal systolic array for product of matrices.

$$\begin{bmatrix} a_{11} & a_{12} & & & & \\ a_{21} & a_{22} & a_{23} & & \text{\huge 0} & \\ a_{31} & a_{32} & a_{33} & a_{34} & & \\ & a_{42} & \ddots & \ddots & \ddots & \\ \text{\huge 0} & & \ddots & & & \ddots \end{bmatrix} \begin{bmatrix} b_{11} & b_{12} & b_{13} & & & \\ b_{21} & b_{22} & b_{23} & b_{24} & \text{\huge 0} & \\ & b_{32} & b_{33} & b_{34} & b_{35} & \\ & & b_{43} & \ddots & \ddots & \ddots \\ \text{\huge 0} & & & & \ddots & \end{bmatrix} = \begin{bmatrix} c_{11} & c_{12} & c_{13} & c_{14} & & 0 \\ c_{21} & c_{22} & c_{23} & c_{24} & \ddots & \\ c_{31} & c_{32} & c_{33} & c_{34} & \ddots & \\ c_{41} & c_{42} & \ddots & \ddots & \ddots & \\ 0 & & \ddots & & & \end{bmatrix}.$$

The corresponding systolic array is shown in Fig. 15 [44].

A systolic array consists of a network of processors which rhythmically compute and pass data through the communication network. The input data enters the array while the outputs are used for the results.

A network of hexagonal array consists of processors of scalar products. Each processor has three registers Ra, Rb and Rc. Each register has its input and output connections. Within each time interval, the data is synchronously carried by each processor into Ra, Rb and Rc and computes $Rc := Rc + RaRb$. The values from Ra and Rb, or the new value from Rc, are shifted to the output. Diagonals of the matrices **A**, **B** and **C** are synchronously shifted in three directions. At the beginning, zero c_{ij} enter the array from beneath, the final results leave the array through its upper boundary.

1.4 Algorithms for solving the Poisson equation on parallel computers

1.4.1 Introduction

The Poisson equation represents the fundamental problem in solving partial differential equations by numerical methods. In various branches of science (theoretical physics, meteorology, astronomy) it is necessary to solve this equation in two or more dimensions. It belongs among the problems solution of which is time-consuming. Especially in time-dependent applications, an urgent requirement emerges to reduce the number of operations to be executed to obtain the solution as well as to reduce the memory requirement. During the last 10 to 15 years, great attention has been paid to the design of fast algorithms for this equation. Because in the solution of this equation, a simple mathematical formula is applied to a great number of data, it belongs to the most frequent tasks run on parallel computers. Methods of its solution have also influenced the architecture design of the first parallel computers [15, 75].

In this section, some direct and iterative algorithms will be introduced for solving this task on parallel computers. To simplify the description of presented algorithms the Poisson equation

1.4 Algorithms for solving the Poisson equation

$$u_{xx} + u_{yy} = f$$

with given values of solution on the boundary

$$u = g$$

will be considered for the unit square.

Having created a square grid by discretizing the region in both directions by step $1/(N+1)$ (N is an appropriate natural number) and substituted the difference formulae [25] for partial derivatives, the problem is reduced to the solution of a linear block tridiagonal system

$$\mathbf{M}u = w, \qquad (25)$$

where $\mathbf{M} = (-\mathbf{I}, \mathbf{A}, -\mathbf{I})$, in which $\mathbf{A} = (-1, 4, -1)$ is a tridiagonal and $\mathbf{I}$ is a unit matrix of dimension N. The vectors u, w have N^2 components corresponding to interior points of the region located on N vertical lines of the grid.

The parallel computational complexity for the above algorithms will be given from the view-point of their implementation on a matrix computer of the SIMD-type. This computer is assumed to have a sufficient number of processors to execute in one time step one of four basic arithmetic operations and in it there occur no time penalties caused by the arrangement of data in memory [63].

1.4.2 Direct methods

In parallel algorithms based on direct methods, the properties of the block-tridiagonal matrix $\mathbf{M}$ are used. Its structure enables us to use efficient ways of elimination and decomposition leading to the design of fast algorithms.

In the following we shall describe algorithms using matrix decomposition and cyclic reduction, as well as special modifications to the method of shooting for the system (25), which indicate possible manner of their parallel implementation.

The fundamental idea upon which the method of matrix decomposition is based, further referred to as MD [14], is the existence of decomposition

$$\mathbf{A} = \mathbf{Q}\mathbf{D}\mathbf{Q}^T$$

of the diagonal block $\mathbf{A}$ of matrix $\mathbf{M}$, where

$$\mathbf{Q} = (Q_{ij}) = \sqrt{\frac{2}{N+1}} \sin \frac{ij\pi}{N+1}, \qquad i,j = 1, 2, \ldots, N, \qquad (26)$$

and the diagonal matrix

$$\mathbf{D} = (d_i) = 4 - 2\cos\frac{i\pi}{N+1}, \qquad i = 1, 2, \ldots, N.$$

Then, $\mathbf{QQ}^T = \mathbf{I}$, and after slight transformations the solution of system (25) can be obtained. From an algorithmical point of view, the computational procedure involves three stages:

(1) Calculation of $\mathbf{Q}^T \mathbf{w}_i = \mathbf{y}_i = (y_{1i}, \ldots, y_{Ni})^T$, $i = 1, 2, \ldots, N$;

(2) For $i = 1, 2, \ldots, N$ solution of the systems $\mathbf{D}_i \tilde{\mathbf{u}}_i = (y_{i1}, \ldots, y_{iN})^T$, where $\mathbf{D}_i = (-1, d_i, -1)$ and $\tilde{\mathbf{u}}_i = (\tilde{u}_{1i}, \ldots, \tilde{u}_{Ni})^T$;

(3) Computation of $\mathbf{u}_i = \mathbf{Q}(\tilde{u}_{i1}, \ldots, \tilde{u}_{iN})^T$, $i = 1, 2, \ldots, N$.

Because in the first part of the transformation with matrix $\mathbf{Q}$ the algorithm of Fast Fourier Transform (FFT) can be applied, and because the second part represents a solution to special tridiagonal systems, the entire algorithm can be implemented with considerable efficiency on a parallel computer. According to [63], the use of FFT algorithm for computation of one vector $\mathbf{y}_i$ requires $3\log N$ steps on N processors. The same holds for the computation of $\mathbf{u}_i$, so that both the first and the third part of the algorithm can be computed with N processors in $6\log N$ parallel arithmetic steps. Solution to each tridiagonal Toeplitz system in the second part can be obtained after $6\log N$ operations using N processors [63]. The computational complexity of solving a discretized Poisson equation on a square with N^2 interior points is thus $12\log N$ steps on N^2 processor elements.

In the algorithm of cyclic odd-even reduction [14] (in the following referred to as CR) the solution of the original system (25) of dimension N^2 (provided $N = 2^{m+1} - 1$, where m is a natural number) is reduced by successive reduction carried out in m phases to solve a system of dimension N.

In the first phase, in the triple of equations

$$-\mathbf{u}_{k-2} + \mathbf{A}\mathbf{u}_{k-1} - \mathbf{u}_k = \mathbf{w}_{k-1},$$
$$-\mathbf{u}_{k-1} + \mathbf{A}\mathbf{u}_k - \mathbf{u}_{k+1} = \mathbf{w}_k,$$
$$-\mathbf{u}_k + \mathbf{A}\mathbf{u}_{k+1} - \mathbf{u}_{k+2} = \mathbf{w}_{k+1},$$

the first and the third equation are multiplied by $-\mathbf{I}$, the second by $-\mathbf{A}$, and then all are summed up. The result splits the original system into two systems of half-dimension, namely

$$\begin{bmatrix} \mathbf{A} & & & & 0 \\ & \mathbf{A} & & & \\ & & \ddots & & \\ & & & & \\ 0 & & & & \mathbf{A} \end{bmatrix} \begin{bmatrix} \mathbf{u}_1 \\ \mathbf{u}_3 \\ \vdots \\ \vdots \\ \mathbf{u}_N \end{bmatrix} = \begin{bmatrix} \mathbf{w}_1 + \mathbf{u}_2 \\ \mathbf{w}_3 + \mathbf{u}_2 + \mathbf{u}_4 \\ \vdots \\ \vdots \\ \mathbf{w}_N + \mathbf{u}_{N-1} \end{bmatrix},$$

$$\begin{bmatrix} (2I - A^2) & I & & & 0 \\ I & (2I - A^2) & I & & \\ & \cdot & \cdot & \cdot & \\ & & \cdot & \cdot & \cdot \\ & & & & I \\ 0 & & & I & (2I - A^2) \end{bmatrix} \begin{bmatrix} u_2 \\ u_4 \\ \cdot \\ \cdot \\ \cdot \\ u_{N-1} \end{bmatrix} = \begin{bmatrix} -w_1 & -w_3 & -Aw_2 \\ -w_3 & -w_5 & -Aw_4 \\ \cdot & \cdot & \cdot \\ \cdot & \cdot & \cdot \\ \cdot & \cdot & \cdot \\ -w_N & -w_{N-2} & -Aw_{N-1} \end{bmatrix}.$$

Matrix of the system of unknown vectors with even indices has the same block structure as the original matrix M, such that it can be repetitively reduced using the above procedure. The result after m reductions is

$$M^{(m)} u_{2^m} = w_{2^m}^{(m)}.$$

Its dimensions are $N \times N$, and from it, the algorithm of matrix decomposition yields the vector of unknown values for the grid points lying on the central vertical line. Again, by m back substitutions the remaining unknown solutions on vectors are computed. Successively, for $r = 1, 2, \ldots, m$ the right-hand sides of reduced systems are formed according to the relationships

$$w_j^{(r)} = -w_{j-2^{r-1}}^{(r-1)} - w_{j+2^{r-1}}^{(r-1)} - A^{(r-1)} w_j^{(r-1)},$$
$$j = k 2^r, \quad k = 1, 2, \ldots, 2^{m+1-r} - 1,$$
(27)

starting from $w_j^{(0)} = w_j$ for $j = 1, 2, \ldots, N$. Matrices $A^{(r)}$, $r = 1, 2, \ldots, m$ satisfy the recurrent relationship

$$A^{(r)} = 2I - (A^{(r-1)})^2,$$
(28)

where $A^{(0)} = A$. For unknown u_j, $j = k 2^r$, $k = 1, 3, \ldots, 2^{m+1-r}$ computed in the rth phase of back substitution ($r = m, \ldots, 1, 0$) it holds

$$u_j = (A^{(r)})^{-1} (w_j^{(r)} + u_{j+2^r} + u_{j-2^r}),$$
(29)

where $u_0 = u_{2^{m+1}} = 0$.

The computation diagram for $m = 2$ is in Fig. 16, where $\bigcirc$ denotes the computation according to (27) and $\square$ stands for (29).

In each vertical level, the computation of reduction as well as that of substitution can be done in parallel [35]. Because each matrix $A^{(r)}$ from (28) can be expressed in the form of a product [7]

$$A^{(r)} = \prod_{i=1}^{r} (A - q_i^{(r)} I),$$

on the above array computer of the SIMD-type with N^2 processors, the computation of the relationship (27) for the given r requires $(3r^2 + 2)$ steps. The computational complexity of the reduction part of an algorithm is then $O(\log^3 N)$. Decomposition of $\mathbf{A}^{(r)}$ is also applied to the computation of (29) in which multiplication with $(\mathbf{A}^{(r)})^{-1}$ can be considered for recurrent solution of r tridiagonal systems [33]. Because systems with matrices are of the same form as those solved in the second part of algorithm MD, the computation for the given r can be executed in $(6r \log N + O(1))$ steps. For all r, the computational complexity for the substitution is $O(\log^3 N)$. This is also the computational complexity for such parallelly implemented cyclic odd-even reduction on N^2 processors.

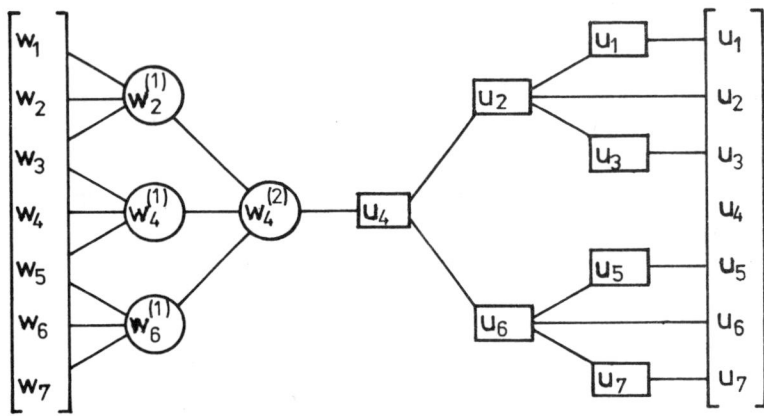

Fig. 16. Computational diagram of a cyclic odd-even reduction.

The computational complexity of the above procedure is higher than for the algorithm MD. Moreover, there also is a strict serial dependence in the horizontal direction and an inefficient use of processor elements caused by the tree-structure of the algorithm. This means that those parallel computers which do not have N^2 processors or in which the computation time is substantially influenced by communication among the processors, are unsuitable for this procedure. In an effort to reduce the parallel computational complexity, a modified procedure can be proposed.

Because for the matrices $\mathbf{A}^{(r)}$ it holds

$$\mathbf{A}^{(r)} = \mathbf{Q}\mathbf{D}^{(r)}\mathbf{Q}^T, \qquad r = 1, 2, ..., m,$$

where $\mathbf{Q}$ is a matrix given in (26) and $\mathbf{D}^{(r)}$ are diagonal matrices defined by the recurrent relationship

$$\mathbf{D}^{(0)} = \mathbf{D}, \quad \mathbf{D}^{(r)} = 2\mathbf{I} - (\mathbf{D}^{(r-1)})^2, \quad r = 1, 2, \ldots, m,$$

the values from (27) and (29) can be expressed in a transformed form. From the vectors $\mathbf{w}_i^{(0)} = \mathbf{Q}\mathbf{w}_i$, $i = 1, 2, \ldots, N$, the vectors of the right-hand side for individual phases of reduction can be computed in the form $\bar{\mathbf{w}}_j^{(r)} = \mathbf{Q}\mathbf{w}_j^{(r)}$, according to (27), as

$$\bar{\mathbf{w}}_j^{(r)} = -\bar{\mathbf{w}}_{j-2^{r-1}}^{(r-1)} - \bar{\mathbf{w}}_{j+2^{r-1}}^{(r-1)} - \mathbf{D}^{(r-1)}\bar{\mathbf{w}}_j^{(r-1)}, \tag{30}$$

because $\mathbf{Q}$ is an orthogonal matrix. Then, from these values the vectors $\bar{\mathbf{u}}_j = \mathbf{Q}\mathbf{u}_j$ can easily be obtained using the relationship

$$\bar{\mathbf{u}}_j = (\mathbf{D}^{(r)})^{-1}(\bar{\mathbf{w}}_j^{(r)} + \bar{\mathbf{u}}_{j+2^r} + \bar{\mathbf{u}}_{j-2^r}). \tag{31}$$

The actual result can be computed by inverse transformation of the vectors $\bar{\mathbf{u}}_j$.

Taking into account the computational complexity of this modification for N^2 processors, the computation of both transforms requires $6 \log N$ steps. In this case, the computational string has $2 \log N$ terms (number of reduction and substitution phases) and for computation of each of these terms, three steps are necessary. Thus, the computational complexity for SIMD-type computer with N^2 processors is reduced to $12 \log N$ steps. Synchronization of the computational process occurs automatically after the execution of each step.

It will be shown, that this procedure can also be applied advantageously to computers of the MIMD-type [22] which have at their disposal a smaller number of processors and in which the design of algorithm also considers the problems of synchronization. In Fig. 17 the computation for $N = 7$ on four

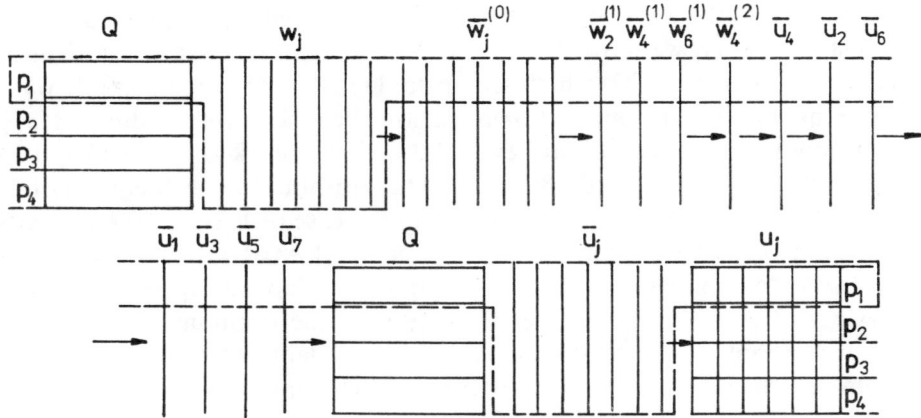

Fig. 17. Computational diagram of the MIMD-type computer.

processors p_1, p_2, p_3, p_4 is illustrated; the part of computation executed by selected processor p_1 is marked with dotted line.

The processor p_i holds only the ith horizontal block of matrix $\mathbf{Q}$ in its memory and computes the ith block of vectors $\bar{\mathbf{w}}_j^{(0)}$, $j = 1, 2, \ldots, N$, in the classical manner. The processor needs not wait for the other processors. The corresponding blocks of vectors $\bar{\mathbf{w}}_j^{(r)}$ can be computed serially, according to (30), along with the corresponding parts of $\bar{u}_j$ on the basis of (31). If the processor has the corresponding elements of matrices $\mathbf{D}^{(r)}$ in its memory, it can proceed with its computations irrespective of other processors, because $\mathbf{D}^{(r)}$ and $(\mathbf{D}^{(r)})^{-1}$ are diagonal matrices. Having computed the corresponding parts of vectors $\bar{u}_j$, synchronization and exchange of the computed values among the individual processors are necessary. If each processor stores in its memory the complete vectors $\bar{u}_j$, $j = 1, 2, \ldots, N$, the horizontal blocks of the resulting solution can again be computed on all the processors in parallel through matrix multiplication.

On the assumption that N is a multiple of p, the multiplication by $\mathbf{Q}$ at the starting and the final phase, when p-processors are used, requires $4(N/p)N^2$ steps. The number of vectors $\bar{\mathbf{w}}_j^{(r)}$ and $\bar{u}_j$, to be computed is of order $\log^2 N$ and N, respectively. Here, each processor executes $3(N/p)$ operations, and thus the computational complexity of (30) and (31) is $3(N/p)(N + \log^2 N - 1)/2)$. Because the time for multiplication is dominant, the result for the computational complexity is $(N/p)O(N^2)$. For $p = N$ processors this value is $4N^2 + 3N + 1.5\log^2 N$. However, using N processors, a vertical version can be proposed in which the computational complexity can be reduced to $O(N \log N)$. In this case at the beginning and at the end of computations, the vectors w_j and $\bar{u}_j$ are transformed using the FFT algorithm, where an additional synchronization step is required.

To demonstrate the ways of parallelizing odd-even reduction algorithms in a more illustrative way, we have chosen a variant of complete reduction defined by relationships (27) and (29) which are unstable [14]. One of the possible ways to achieve the stability of computation is the so-called incomplete reduction [37], in which only $s < m$ reductions are executed and the block tridiagonal system of order $2^{m+1-s} - 1$ is solved by the MD algorithm. In the literature, this algorithm is known as FACR(s) [38], which in the case of FACR(O) represents the algorithm of matrix decomposition, while for FACR(m) it is a notation corresponding to complete reduction. Its complexity depends upon s, as shown by Schwartztrauber in [65]. For serial computers the optimum value of this parameter is about $\log \log N$. Problems of the parallel implementation of this algorithm on a number of today available parallel computers are discussed by Hockney in [39], in which he has formulated two parallel versions of the algorithm. In algorithm SERIFACR, the parallel computation of s reduction

1.4 Algorithms for solving the Poisson equation

phases is followed by the solution of a block tridiagonal system, accomplished parallelly at vertical levels on vectors of length N. He has found that the optimum value of s for a grid $N \times N$ ($N < 500$) is 1 or 2 for CRAY-1, 0 or 1 for CYBER-205 and 0 for ICL DAP, where for a grid with $N < 100$ the lower from the above values is more convenient. In case of vector computers such as CYBER-205, it is more advantageous to work over longer vectors. In the PARAFACR algorithm the work has been made over vectors of length N^2, i.e. over the values of all grid points. Comparing both algorithms on the basis of implementation on the above parallel computers for a grid with a value $N > 64$, it can be concluded that for the CRAY-1 the SERIFACR is a more suitable alternative, whereas in case of grids of lower density PARAFACR is more suitable. On the contrary, for the CYBER-205 in most applications the PARAFACR is the most suitable alternative, with the exception of large grids ($300 < N < 1500$), when the SERIFACR is recommended.

The first algorithm for solving the system (25) with complexity $O(N^2)$ for serial computation was a special variant of the shooting method [6]. Here, instead of the original linear system a permuted system

$$\begin{bmatrix} -\mathbf{I} & \mathbf{A} & & & & \\ & \ddots & \ddots & & & \\ & & \ddots & \ddots & & \\ & & & \mathbf{A} & -\mathbf{I} & \\ \mathbf{0} & & & -\mathbf{I} & \mathbf{A} & \\ \mathbf{A} & -\mathbf{I} & & & & \mathbf{0} \end{bmatrix} \begin{bmatrix} \boldsymbol{u}_1 \\ \vdots \\ \vdots \\ \boldsymbol{u}_{N-1} \\ \boldsymbol{u}_N \end{bmatrix} = \begin{bmatrix} \boldsymbol{w}_2 \\ \vdots \\ \vdots \\ \boldsymbol{w}_N \\ \boldsymbol{w}_1 \end{bmatrix}$$

is solved in the following steps [7]

$$\boldsymbol{z}_{N-1} = -\boldsymbol{w}_N, \quad \boldsymbol{z}_{N-2} = \mathbf{A}\boldsymbol{z}_{N-1} - \boldsymbol{w}_{N-1}, \quad \boldsymbol{z}_{N-i} = \mathbf{A}\boldsymbol{z}_{N-i+2} - \boldsymbol{w}_{N-i+1},$$
$$i = 3, 4, \ldots, N, \tag{32a}$$

$$\mathbf{S}^{(N)} \boldsymbol{u}_N = -\boldsymbol{z}_0, \tag{32b}$$

$$\boldsymbol{u}_{N-1} = \mathbf{A}\boldsymbol{u}_N - \boldsymbol{w}_N, \quad \boldsymbol{u}_{N-i} = \mathbf{A}\boldsymbol{u}_{N-i+1} - \boldsymbol{u}_{N-i+2} - \boldsymbol{w}_{N-i+1},$$
$$i = 2, 3, \ldots, N-1, \tag{32c}$$

where $\mathbf{S}^{(N)}$ is the result of the recurrent computation

$$\mathbf{S}^{(0)} = \mathbf{I}, \quad \mathbf{S}^{(1)} = \mathbf{A}, \quad \mathbf{S}^{(i)} = \mathbf{A}\mathbf{S}^{(i-1)} - \mathbf{S}^{(i-2)}, \quad i = 2, 3, \ldots, N. \tag{33}$$

This version of algorithm is not parallel. To compute the recurrent relationships (32a) and (32c) a SIMD-type computer can be used, with N processors executing $O(N)$ steps. System (32b) can be solved again as a sequence of N diagonally dominant tridiagonal systems

$$(\mathbf{A} - q_i^{(N)}\mathbf{I})\mathbf{x}_i = \mathbf{x}_{i-1}, \qquad i = 1, 2, \ldots, N,$$

where

$$q_i^{(N)} = 2\cos\frac{i\pi}{N+1}$$

and $\mathbf{x}_0 = -\mathbf{z}_0$, $\mathbf{x}_N = \mathbf{u}_N$ [6]. To solve each of them, $O(\log N)$ steps on N processors must be executed. By the parallel computation on N processors, the computational complexity of $O(N \log N)$ is achieved.

This algorithm also can be parallelized. Its computational complexity is then $O(\log N)$ for a SIMD-type computer with N^2 processors. The orthogonal transform of the right-hand side of the system (25) is computed in $O(\log N)$ steps. Using a decomposition of $\mathbf{A}^{(r)}$ the relationships (32a) and (32c) will be computed with diagonal matrices $\mathbf{D}$. Then, to this computation the algorithm [17], which is adapted for vector arguments can be applied. In this case, the complexity remains $O(\log N)$. Here, the system (32b) is replaced by

$$\mathbf{D}^{(N)}\bar{\mathbf{u}}_N = \bar{\mathbf{w}}_N,$$

from which $\bar{\mathbf{u}}_N$ can be computed in $O(1)$ steps. Having computed the back recurrent relationships (32c), the resulting vector can be obtained by inverse transformation.

According to [6], algorithm (32a)—(32c) is only stable for $N \leq 8$. This fact is used in an algorithm in which solution of the original problem is decomposed into subregions, where it can be applied without any loss of accuracy. Thus, the problem of solving the system (25) is decomposed into partial problems leaving the form

$$\begin{bmatrix} \mathbf{A} & -\mathbf{I} & & & & \\ -\mathbf{I} & \mathbf{A} & -\mathbf{I} & & \mathbf{0} & \\ & \ddots & \ddots & \ddots & & \\ & & \ddots & \ddots & \ddots & \\ & \mathbf{0} & & -\mathbf{I} & \mathbf{A} & -\mathbf{I} \\ & & & & -\mathbf{I} & \mathbf{A} \end{bmatrix} \begin{bmatrix} \mathbf{u}_j \\ \mathbf{u}_{j+1} \\ \vdots \\ \\ \mathbf{u}_s \end{bmatrix} = \begin{bmatrix} \mathbf{u}_{j-1} \\ \mathbf{0} \\ \vdots \\ \mathbf{0} \\ \mathbf{u}_{s+1} \end{bmatrix},$$

where unknown solutions along the lines $(j-1)$ and $(s+1)$ are equal to $\mathbf{0}$. The solutions of these subsystems are integrated into larger blocks, from which the required residuals are computed. First, the solutions on boundary lines of regions and then insides of the regions are determined.

Computation for $N = k2^s - 1$, where k is the dimension of subregions, is carried out at the following steps [7]

(1) For $j = 1, 2, \ldots, 2^s - 1$ the systems

$$\mathbf{S}^{(k-1)}\mathbf{a}_j = \mathbf{S}^{(k-2)}(\mathbf{w}_{jk-1} + \mathbf{w}_{jk+1}) + \mathbf{S}^{(k-3)}(\mathbf{w}_{jk-2} + \mathbf{w}_{jk+2}) +$$
$$+ \ldots + \mathbf{S}^{(0)}(\mathbf{w}_{(j-1)k+1} + \mathbf{w}_{(j+1)k-1})$$

are solved, and the computation of $\mathbf{w}_j^{(0)} = \mathbf{w}_{jk} + \mathbf{a}_j$ is carried out;

(2) For $p = 0, 1, \ldots, s - 2$ and for $j = 2^{p+1}$ with step 2^{p+1} through $2^s - 1$ the systems

$$\mathbf{C}^{(2^p k)}\mathbf{e}_j^{(p)} = (\mathbf{w}_{j+2^p}^{(p)} + \mathbf{w}_{j-2^p}^{(p)})$$

are solved and computation $\mathbf{w}_j^{(p+1)} = \mathbf{w}_j^{(p)} + \mathbf{e}_j^{(p)}$, is carried out, where

$$\mathbf{C}^{(0)} = 2\mathbf{I}, \quad \mathbf{C}^{(1)} = \mathbf{A}, \quad \mathbf{C}^{(i)} = \mathbf{A}\mathbf{C}^{(i-1)} - \mathbf{C}^{(i-2)}, \qquad i = 2, 3, \ldots, N;$$

(3) For $p = s - 1, s - 2, \ldots, 0$ and for $j = 2^p$ with step 2^{p+1} through $2^s - 1$ the systems

$$\mathbf{S}^{(2^p k - 1)}\mathbf{d}_j = \mathbf{u}_{(j+2^p)k} + \mathbf{u}_{(j-2^p)k}, \quad (\mathbf{u}_0 = \mathbf{u}_{N+1} = \mathbf{0})$$
$$\mathbf{C}^{(2^p k)}\mathbf{u}_{jk} = \mathbf{S}^{(2^p k - 1)}(\mathbf{w}_j^{(p)} + \mathbf{d}_j);$$

(4) For $j = 1, 2, \ldots, 2^s$ computation of $\mathbf{u}_i$, $i = (j-1)k + 1, \ldots, jk - 2, jk - 1$ is done using the original algorithm according to (32).

The algorithm can be combined with both the MD algorithm and CR [7]. Algorithms generated in this way, can be very easily parallelized for a MIMD-type computer as was shown for the CR algorithm. In this case also, N^2 processors must be used, and using an orthogonal decomposition of matrices $\mathbf{S}^{(i)}$ and $\mathbf{C}^{(i)}$, the solution can be obtained in $O(\log N)$ steps.

Recently, solutions of the Poisson equation using multigrid methods [9, 32] have been applied with advantage. They are based on the idea that the task solved for a discretization step h is transformed into a task with a step $H > h$. Thus, the computation of the solution at the points of a dense grid is replaced by computation over a coarse grid and then, by interpolation it is spread to the original dense grid. This procedure is applied iteratively.

One iteration of the solution of equation (25) for the case $H = 2h$ can be expressed, according to [32], as follows (j denotes the iteration index, indexes h or H denote the discretization over grids with step h or H, respectively):

$$d_h^{(j)} = w_h - M_h u_h^{(j)} \quad \text{(computation of residuum of the } j\text{th iteration),}$$
$$d_H^{(j)} = E_h^H d_h^{(j)} \quad \text{(computation of residuum on a coarse grid),}$$
$$v_H^{(j)} = M_H^{-1} d_H^{(j)} \quad \text{(computation of accurate solution on a coarse grid),}$$
$$v_h^{(j)} = E_H^h v_H^{(j)} \quad \text{(spreading of solution onto a fine grid),}$$
$$u_h^{(j+1)} = u_h^j + v_h^j \quad \text{(computation of the } (j+1)\text{st iteration).}$$

Matrices M_h and M_H correspond to a five-point discretization relationship for the Laplace operator, E_h^H is a mapping of a discrete function $d_h^{(j)}$ from the grid with a step h onto a grid with a step $2h$, and operator E_H^h is the interpolation operator from the coarse grid onto the fine grid. Most frequently, a so-called weighing operator [32]

$$E_h^H = \frac{1}{16} \begin{bmatrix} 1 & 2 & 1 \\ 2 & 4 & 2 \\ 1 & 2 & 1 \end{bmatrix}_h^{2h}$$

and operator corresponding to the bilinear interpolation denoted, according to [32], as

$$E_H^h = \frac{1}{4} \begin{bmatrix} 1 & 2 & 1 \\ 2 & 4 & 2 \\ 1 & 2 & 1 \end{bmatrix}_{2h}^{h}$$

are used.

Since the above iterative process with the iteration matrix $(I_h - E_H^h M_H^{-1} E_h^H)$ converges slowly or it does not converge at all [32], it is combined with an iterative relaxation method. For this reason, prior to starting the computation of $d_h^{(j)}$ and after the computation of $(u_h^{(j)} + v_h^{(j)})$ a certain number of smoothing steps of some of the iteration methods is applied. The above algorithmic procedure is called a $(h, 2h)$ algorithm which forms the fundamental part of the so-called complete multigrid algorithm [32]. In this case, in one iteration cycle the computation is recursively transferred onto a grid with the minimum possible dimension.

In [31] the multigrid method was studied from the view-point of parallel implementation. It has been found that for a grid with $(2^r + 1) \times (2^r + 1)$ points, $9r^2$ products [10] are to be executed, i.e. the parallel arithmetic computational complexity of the algorithm is $O(\log^2 N)$. Another idea on how to parallelize this method is present in [71]. Extension of these works towards the analysis of the performance of multigrid algorithms on various parallel computer types is given in [27]. Together with the two existing variations of the multigrid technique, a new parallel algorithm has been developed which exploits a high level of computational concurrency.

The performance of these methods is analysed from the point of view of the parallel time complexity for parallel architectural models with various types of communication systems (e.g. mesh-connected arrays, mesh-shuffle connected systems, permutation networks and direct planar VLSI embeddings). The behaviour of these algorithms is also examined for some current architectures [10].

Among the latest results for the parallel solution of the Poisson equation, one should mention an adaptation of the multigrid principle to a supercomputer multiprocessor architecture [30]. The processors of the system perform the computational work over several grids simultaneously. The independent nature of the relaxation steps on different grids facilitates faster parallel execution of computation. The method has been run and tested numerically on the CRAY XMP-48 supercomputer. Though in most cases the values of the parallel arithmetic computational complexity for these methods are higher than for other parallel versions of fast direct methods, it is worth mentioning that the principle is applicable not only to this specific task but also to solving elliptic boundary problems over non-rectangular regions.

1.4.3 Iterative methods

There are a large number of papers dealing with iterative methods for solving Poisson equations. A detailed analysis of sequential methods is in [77].

On a parallel computer, the most naturally applicable algorithm is Jacobi's method. For the Poisson equation where each point is approximated by the five-point difference formula, Jacobi's method is given by the expression

$$u_{ij}^{(k+1)} = \frac{1}{4}(u_{i+1,j}^{(k)} + u_{i-1,j}^{(k)} + u_{i,j+1}^{(k)} + u_{i,j-1}^{(k)}) + w_{ij}.$$

This continues until, for a chosen accuracy $\varepsilon > 0$, we obtain

$$|u_{ij}^{(k+1)} - u_{ij}^{(k)}| < \varepsilon. \qquad (34)$$

In a SIMD-type computer each point of the grid can be assigned one processor. Then, computation of one iteration will be done in five steps, but the number of iterations required to achieve precision of N^{-2} on unit square using this method is $(2/7)N^2 \log N$ [21, 73].

When solving this task on a SOLOMON-II parallel computer [15], points of the network were divided into 4-tuples. All 4-tuples associated with a point M are its neighbours denoted by N, S, W, E from the top, bottom, right and left, respectively. The computation was executed in parallel on $N^2/4$ processors whereby individual 4-tuples were evaluated simultaneously. Each newly computed value was immediately used for computation in next points according to formulas

$$u_1^{(k+1)}(M) = \frac{1}{4}(u_2^{(k)}(W) + u_3^{(k)}(N) + u_3^{(k)}(M) + u_2^{(k)}(M)) + w_1(M),$$

$$u_2^{(k+1)}(M) = \frac{1}{4}(u_1^{(k+1)}(M) + u_1^{(k+1)}(E) + u_4^{(k)}(N) + u_4^{(k)}(M)) + w_2(M),$$

$$u_3^{(k+1)}(M) = \frac{1}{4}(u_1^{(k+1)}(M) + u_1^{(k+1)}(S) + u_4^{(k)}(W) + u_4^{(k)}(M)) + w_3(M),$$

$$u_4^{(k+1)}(M) = \frac{1}{4}(u_2^{(k+1)}(M) + u_2^{(k+1)}(S) + u_3^{(k+1)}(M) + u_3^{(k+1)}(E)) + w_4(M).$$

This is the Gauss—Seidel iteration for which the number of iterations necessary to achieve precision of N^{-2} is about $(1/7)N^2 \log N$ [21]. One iteration computed on $N^2/4$ processors is 4 times as demanding as the computation using Jacobi's method. Two successive iteration values are compared immediately after evaluation of the corresponding set of equally denoted grid points. Iterative computation is terminated when the convergence criterion is fulfilled for all the four point groups at the same time.

An iterative procedure on $N^2/2$ processors is explained in [72]. Grid points are arranged by diagonals as shown in Fig. 18.

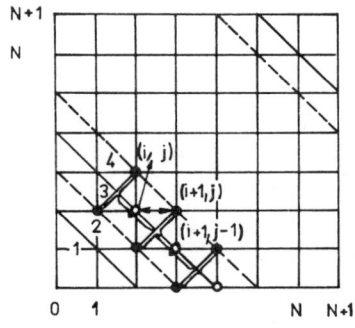

Fig. 18. Enumeration of network points along diagonal lines.

The values on the even diagonals are computed first and, after shifting the processors by one step to the right, computation on odd diagonals is performed. Because the values on odd diagonals depend only on the even ones, and vice versa, the computation can be accomplished by altering the diagonals. Because some intermediate results can be used twice, computation of one iteration on an SIMD computer will be carried out in four sums, two products and two tests (34). Also, since the computation is always based on newly computed values, a modification of Gauss—Seidel method is achieved.

If we compare the previous procedures to this iterative method on a SIMD computer, it can be shown that computation by diagonals is not only twice as fast but also the communication among individual processors is simpler [72]. However, because the use of diagonal notation doubles the number of processors, it can be said that from an efficiency a view-point both procedures are equivalent.

Similarly, the successive over-relaxation (SOR) can be adapted inspite of its internal serial character for implementation on parallel computer [63]. Based on properties of the matrix **M**, there exists a permutation matrix **W**, such that the system (25) can be solved in the form

$$\mathbf{WMW}^T \bar{u} = \begin{bmatrix} 4\mathbf{I} & \mathbf{R}^T \\ \mathbf{R} & 4\mathbf{I} \end{bmatrix} \bar{u} = \bar{w},$$

where $\bar{u} = \mathbf{W}u$, $\bar{w} = \mathbf{W}w$ and **R** is a banded matrix of dimension $N^2/2$ which has not more than four non-zero elements in the same row. Then, the iteration process for $k = 0, 1, 2, \ldots$ is

$$(\mathbf{I} - \omega \mathbf{L}) \bar{u}^{(k+1)} = ((1 - \omega)\mathbf{I} + \omega \mathbf{L}^T) \bar{u}^{(k)} + \frac{\omega}{4} \bar{w},$$

where

$$\mathbf{L} = \frac{-\omega}{4} \begin{bmatrix} 0 & 0 \\ \mathbf{R} & 0 \end{bmatrix}.$$

For the optimum convergence parameter ω, the number of arithmetic steps for computation of solution with accuracy N^{-2} is $(15/7) N \log N$ for N^2 processors [63]. Let us note that the algorithm for implementation of this method for chess-like arrangement of points on associative computer is explained in another chapter of this book.

Considering the number of steps to compute the solution in parallel, there is the more efficient implicit method of alternating direction (ADI) [63], in which one iteration is computed in two stages

$$(\mathbf{S} + r_{k+1}\mathbf{I}) \tilde{u}_{k+1} = (r_{k+1}\mathbf{I} - \mathbf{T}) u_k + w,$$

$$(\mathbf{T} + r_{k+1}\mathbf{I}) u_{k+1} = (r_{k+1}\mathbf{I} - \mathbf{S}) \tilde{u}_{k+1} + w,$$

where r_{k+1} is the parameter of iteration, **S** and **T** are matrices of a sum decomposition of matrix **M** [73]. If the computation of one iteration on N processors can be done in $24 + 12\log N$ steps, then the whole computation can be done with $(1/5)\log^2 N$ iteration, with an accuracy of N^{-2}. Totally, the iterative method comparable with the accuracy for direct method requires $(12/5)\log^3 N$ steps.

The next class of methods which can be adapted to parallel computation of (25) represent the so-called semi-iterative methods given by the expression

$$\mathbf{M}_1 u^{(k+1)} = \mathbf{M}_2 u^{(k)},$$

where $\mathbf{M} = \mathbf{M}_1 - \mathbf{M}_2$. Here, $\mathbf{M}_1$ is chosen such that the corresponding system is easily solved by a suitable direct method.

One of the possible ways is to denote the network points according to a multi-row arrangement such that they would correspond to the division of the original array into narrow and long rectangles. An example of a two-row arrangement for part of an array of 24 internal points is shown in Fig. 19.

1	3	5	7	9	11
2	4	6	8	10	12
13	15	17	19	21	23
14	16	18	20	22	24

Fig. 19. Two-row arrangement of network points.

In this case **M** assumes the form

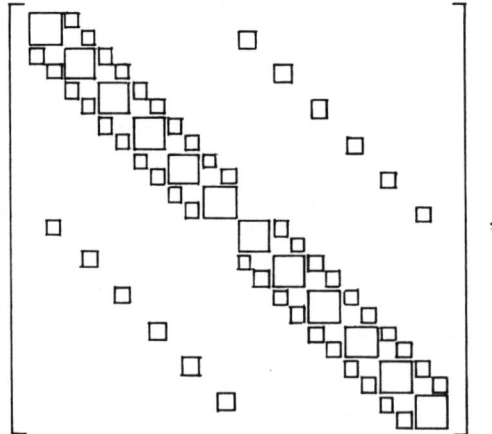

Scheme 1

where $\boxed{}$ denotes the matrix $\begin{bmatrix} 4 & -1 \\ -1 & 4 \end{bmatrix}$ and $\square$ the values of -1. **M** is its block diagonal part composed of three pentadiagonal symmetric matrices of half-dimension. In this way the new iteration can be computed either as a solution to two independent symmetric pentadiagonal systems or, after $\mathbf{M}_1$ is complemented by zeros, as a solution of one large pentadiagonal system where a suitable parallel algorithm is used to solve the banded linear systems [23, 36].

In the case of the two-row ordering, the convergence of the SOR method is twice as fast as that of a naturally ordered grid [70]. This problem of multi-row ordering along with the description of the structure of matrices **M** and $\mathbf{M}_1$ can be found in [35].

Another suitable type of arrangement is the spiral arrangement [35]. An example for a grid 4×4 is shown in Fig. 20.

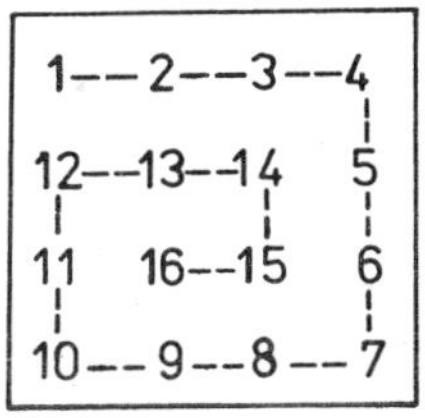

```
1----2----3----4
                |
12---13---14    5
 |              |
11    16---15   6
 |              |
10---- 9---- 8----7
```

Fig. 20. Spiral arrangement of network points.

In this arrangement, $\mathbf{M}_1$ is a symmetric tridiagonal matrix with values of 4 on its main diagonal and with values of -1 on subdiagonals. For such system parallel algorithms described in [29] can be used.

For a linearly connected set of processors, three iterative algorithms for the numerical solution of self-adjoint elliptic boundary value problems have been proposed in [61]. Here, the cyclic Chebyshev semi-iterative scheme, a preconditioned conjugate gradient method and a block generalization of Stiefel iterations are considered for a computational model where the time consumption for a transmission of one floating-point number from one processor to either of its two neighbours are greater than those for one time step.

Note. In most cases the above methods work fast when implemented on serial computers. For example, the complexity of the iterative method ADI is $O(N^2 \log^2 N)$, the complexity of direct FACR algorithm is $O(N^2 \log N)$ and for the Lorenz modification of shooting method [46] as well as for multigrid methods [32] the lower bound $O(N^2)$ is achieved.

Because the actual speed of execution of algorithms on a given computer depends on the technique of implementation, a competition in 1977 in Kernforschungszentrum, Karlsruhe, was organized for the fastest serial procedure to solve a given problem. Specifically, on an IBM 360/168 computer the Poisson equation was to be solved on a grid composed of 128 × 32 points.

The fastest was the FACR(3) method, by which the required precision was achieved. The computation time for fastest direct method was of the order of tens of seconds. By comparison it was found that the iterative ADI method and the row version of SOR were about ten times slower compared to direct methods [64].

References

[1] H. M. Ahmed, J. M. Delosme and M. Morf, "Highly concurrent computing structures for matrix arithmetic and signal processing", *Computer* **1** (1982) 65–82.

[2] M. Andrews and D. A. Eggerding, "A pipelined computer architecture for unified elementary function evaluation", *Computer Electr. Engng.* **5** (1978) 189–202.

[3] J. L. Baer and D. P. Dovet, "Compilation of arithmetic expressions for parallel computations", *Proc. IFIP Congress* (Edinburgh, 1968) pp. 340–346.

[4] A. Bauer, "An addition chain", *Bull. Amer. Math. Soc.* **45** (1939) 736–739.

[5] V. D. Baikov and V. B. Smolov, *Hardware Implementation of Elementary Function in Digital Computers* (in Russian) (Izd. Leningradskogo universiteta, Leningrad, 1975).

[6] R. E. Bank and D. J. Rose, "An $O(n^2)$ method for solving constant coefficient boundary value problems in two dimensions", *SIAM J. Number. Anal.* **12** (1975) 529–540.

[7] R. E. Bank and D. J. Rose, "Marching algorithms for elliptic boundary value problems, I, The constant coefficient case", Techn. Rep. 14 (Aiken Comp. Lab., Harward University, 1975).

[8] D. Bibi, M. Capovani, G. Lotti and F. Romani, "$O(n^{2.7799})$ complexity for matrix multiplication", *Inform. Proc. Lett.* **8** (1979) 234–235.

[9] A. Brandt, "Multilevel adaptive technique (MLAT) for fast numerical solution to boundary value problems", Lecture Notes in Physics 18 (Springer-Verlag, Berlin, 1973) pp. 82–89.

[10] A. Brandt, "Multigrid solvers on parallel computers", in *Elliptic Problem Solvers*, Ed. M. H. Schulz (Academic Press, New York, 1981) pp. 39–84.

[11] R. P. Brent, "Multiple precision zero-finding methods and the complexity of elementary function evaluation", Techn. Rep. (Comp. Sci. Dep., Carnegie-Mellon University, Pittsburgh, 1975).

[12] R. P. Brent, "Fast multiple-precision evaluation of elementary function", *J. ACM* **23** (1976) 242–251.

[13] R. P. Brent, "The parallel evaluation of general arithmetic expressions", *J. ACM* **21** (1974) 201–206.

[14] B. L. Buzbee, G. H. Golub and C. W. Neilson, "On direct methods for solving Poisson's equation", *SIAM J. Numer. Anal.* **7** (1970) 627–656.

[15] A. B. Carroll and R. T. Wetherald, "Application of parallel processing to numerical weather prediction", *J. ACM* **14** (1967) 591–614.

[16] D. Chazan and W. Miranker, "Chaotic relaxation", *Linear Algebra and its Application* **2** (1969) 199–222.

[17] S. C. Chen and D. J. Kuck, "Time and parallel processor bounds for linear recurrence systems", *IEEE Trans. Comp.* **C-24** (1975) 701–717.

[18] D. Coppersmith and S. Winograd, "On the asymptotic complexity of matrix multiplication",

Proc. 22nd Annual Symp. on Foundations of Computer Science (IEEE, Nashville, 1981) pp. 82—90.
[19] L. Csanky, "On the parallel complexity of some computational problems", Dissertation (University of California, Berkeley, 1974).
[20] J. B. Dennis, "Data flow supercomputers", Computer **11** (1980) 48—56.
[21] F. W. Dorr, "The direct solution of the discrete Poisson equation on a rectangle", SIAM Rev. **12** (1970) 248—263.
[22] P. H. Enslow, Jr., "Multiprocessor organization — A survey", Comp. Surv. **9** (1977) 103—112.
[23] D. J. Evans, A. Hadjidimos and D. Noutsos, "The parallel solution of banded linear equations of the new quadrant interlocking factorization (Q.I.F.) method", Int. J. Comp. Math. **9** (1981) 151—161.
[24] P. M. Flanders et al., "Efficient high speed computing with the distributed array processor", in *High Speed Computer and Algorithm Organization*, Eds. D. J. Kuck, D. H. Lawrie and A. H. Sameh (Academic Press, New York, 1977) pp. 113—128.
[25] G. E. Forsythe and W. R. Wasow, *Finite Difference Methods for Partial Differential Equations* (J. Wiley, New York, 1960).
[26] M. J. Foster and H. T. Kung, "Design of special-purpose VLSI chips: Example and opinions", Techn. Rep. (Comp. Sci. Dep., Carnegie-Mellon University, 1979).
[27] D. Gamnon and J. V. Rosendale, "Highly parallel multigrid solvers for elliptic PDE's: An experimental analysis", Techn. Rep. (ICASE, NASA Langley Res. Center, 1982).
[28] W. Gautschi, "Computational methods in special functions — A survey", in *Theory and Application of Special Functions* (Academic Press, New York, 1975) pp. 1—98.
[29] J. Grcar and A. Sameh, "On certain parallel Toeplitz linear system solvers", SIAM J. Sci. Stat. Comp. **2** (1981) 238—256.
[30] A. Greenbaum, "A multigrid method for multiprocessors", Techn. Rep. UCRL-92211 (Lawrence Livermore National Laboratory, Livermore, 1985).
[31] C. E. Grosch, "Performance analysis of Poisson solvers on array computers", in *Infotechnical State of the Art Report: Supercomputers*, Vol. 2, Eds. C. R. Jesshope and R. W. Hockney (Infotech Int. Ltd, Maidenhead, 1979).
[32] W. Hackbusch and U. Trottenberg, "Multigrid methods", Lecture Notes in Mathematics 960 (Springer-Verlag, Berlin, 1982).
[33] D. E. Heller, "Some aspects of the cyclic reduction algorithm for block tridiagonal linear systems", Techn. Rep. (Comp. Sci. Dep., Carnegie-Mellon University, Pittsburgh, 1977).
[34] D. E. Heller, D. K. Stevenson and J. P. Traub, "Accelerated iterative methods for the solution of tridiagonal system on parallel computers", J. ACM **23** (1976) 636—654.
[35] D. E. Heller, "Direct and iterative methods for block tridiagonal linear systems", Techn. Rep. (Comp. Sci. Dep., Carnegie-Mellon University, Pittsburgh, 1977).
[36] D. E. Heller, "A survey of parallel algorithms in numerical linear algebra", SIAM Rev. **2** (1978) 740—777.
[37] R. W. Hockney, "Rapid elliptic solvers", in *Numerical Methods in Applied Fluid Dynamics* (Academic Press, New York, 1980) pp. 1—48.
[38] R. W. Hockney and C. P. Jesshope, *Parallel Computers — Architecture, Programming and Algorithms* (Adam Hilger, Bristol, 1981).
[39] R. W. Hockney, "Optimizing the FACR(l) Poisson-solver on parallel computers", Proc. Int. Conf. on Parallel Processing (Bellaire, 1982) pp. 62—71.
[40] W. H. Hwang, "A recurrence relation for the square root", J. Approx. Theor. **9** (1973) 299—306.
[41] O. Kogge, "Parallel solution of recurrence problems", IBM J. Res. Develop. **18** (1974) 138—148.

[42] D. J. Kuck, "Parallel processing of ordinary programs", *Advances in Computers*, Vol. 15 (Academic Press, New York, 1977) pp. 119—179.
[43] H. T. Kung, "New algorithms and lower bounds for the parallel evaluation of certain rational expressions", Techn. Rep. (Comp. Sci. Dep., Carnegie-Mellon University, Pittsburgh, 1974).
[44] H. T. Kung and Ch. E. Leiserson, "Systolic arrays (for VLSI), Techn. Rep. (Comp. Sci. Dep., Carnegie-Mellon University, Pittsburgh, 1978).
[45] H. T. Kung, "Synchronized and asynchronous parallel algorithms for multiprocessors", in *Algorithm and Complexity*, Ed. J. F. Traub (Academic Press, New York, 1976) pp. 153—200.
[46] E. N. Lorenz, "A rapid procedure for inverting del-square with certain computers", *Montly Weather Rev.* **104** (1976) 961—966.
[47] N. K. Madsen et al., "Matrix multiplication by diagnosis on a vector parallel processor", *Inform. Proc. Lett.* **5** (1976) 41—45.
[48] C. Mead and L. Conway, *Introduction to VLSI Systems* (Addison-Wesley, Reading, Mass., 1980).
[49] J. Mikloško and M. Lucká, "Fast parallel algorithms for associative computer", *Proc. 2nd Int. Conf. on Artificial Intelligence and Inform. Control Systems of Robots* (Smolenice, 1982) pp. 162—166.
[50] J. Mikloško and O. Sýkora, "Special-purpose systolic arrays", *Computers and Artif. Intelligence* **2** (1983) 127—145.
[51] J. Mikloško, "Systolic systems for the linear equations systems and matrix inversion", *Computers and Artif. Intelligence* **2** (1983) 361—372.
[52] D. E. Muller and F. P. Preparata, "Restructuring of arithmetic expressions for parallel evaluation", *J. ACM* **23** (1976) 534—542.
[53] Y. Muraoka, "Parallelism exposure and exploitation in programs", Techn. Rep. 71-424 (Comp. Sci. Dep., University of Illinois, Urbana, 1971).
[54] V. Ya. Pan, "Strassen's algorithm is not optimal", *Proc. 19th Annual Symp. on Foundations of Computer Science* (Ann Arbor, Mich., 1978) pp. 166—176.
[55] V. Ya. Pan, "New fast algorithms for matrix operations", *SIAM J. Comput.* **9** (1980) 321—342.
[56] D. S. Parker, "Nonlinear recurrence and parallel computation", in *High Speed Computer and Algorithm Organization* (Academic Press, New York, 1977) pp. 317—321.
[57] M. S. Paterson, "Complexity of product and closure algorithms for matrices", *Proc. Int. Congress on Mathematics* (Vancouver, 1974) pp. 483—489.
[58] M. C. Pease, "The C(2, m) algorithm for matrix inversion", Techn. Rep. (Stanford Research Institute, Menlo Park, Cal., 1974).
[59] L. R. Probert, "On the additive complexity of matrix multiplication", *SIAM J. Comput.* **5** (1976) 187—203.
[60] F. Robert, M. Charnay and F. Musy, "Iterations chaotique serie pour des equations non lineares de point fixe", *Appl. Math.* **1** (1975) 1—38.
[61] Y. Saad and A. H. Sameh, "Iterative methods for the solution of elliptic difference equations on multiprocessors", in *CONPAR '81*, Ed. W. Händler (Springer-Verlag, Berlin, 1981) pp. 395—411.
[62] A. Sameh, "On Jacobi and Jacobi-like algorithm for a parallel computer", *Math. Comp.* **25** (1971) 115—123.
[63] A. H. Sameh, S. C. Chen and D. J. Kuck, "Parallel Poisson and biharmonic solvers", *Computing* **17** (1976) 219—230.
[64] U. Schumann, "On fast direct methods for the solution of discretized elliptic equations", *Proc. GAMM-Workshop on Fast Solution Methods for the Discretized Poisson Equation*, Ed. U. Schumann (Advance Publications, London, 1977) pp. 1—27.
[65] P. N. Schwarztrauber, "The methods of cyclic reduction, Fourier analysis and the FACR

algorithm for the discrete solution of Poisson's equation on a rectangle", *SIAM Rev.* **19** (1977) 490—501.
[66] D. L. Slotnick and A. Sameh, "Numerical calculation and computer design", *Comp. Methods with Applications* **3** (1978) 201—210.
[67] L. Snyder, "Introduction to the configurable, highly parallel computer", *Computer* **1** (1982) 47—56.
[68] J. Spiess, "Untersuchungen des Zeitgewinns durch neue Algorithmen zur Matrix-Multiplikation", *Computing* **17** (1976) 23—36.
[69] V. Strassen, "Gaussian elimination is not optimal", *Numer. Math.* **13** (1969) 354—356.
[70] K. J. Thurber, *Large Scale Computer Architecture, Parallel and Associative Processors* (Hayden Book Comp., Rochelle Park, N.J., 1976).
[71] U. Trottenberg, "Schnelle Lösung partieller Differenzialgleichungen — Idee und Bedeutung des Mehrgitterprinzips", Jahresbericht 1980/1981 der Gesellschaft für Mathematik und Datenverarbeitung (Bonn, 1981) pp. 85—95.
[72] M. Vajteršic, "Parallel algorithm for fast computation of numerical solution of Laplace equation", *Proc. 3rd Symp. on Algorithms in Computing Technology* (High Tatras, 1975) pp. 151—161.
[73] R. Varga, *Matrix Iterative Analysis* (Prentice-Hall, Englewood Cliffs, 1962).
[74] I. Vrťo, Personal communication, 1982.
[75] R. Wilhelmson, "Solving partial differential equations using ILLIAC IV", *Proc. Symp. on Constructive and Comp. Methods for Differential and Integral Equations*, Lecture Notes in Mathematics 430 (Springer-Verlag, Berlin, 1974) pp. 543—576.
[76] J. H. Wilkinson, *The Algebraic Eigenvalue Problem* (Clarendon Press, Oxford, 1965).
[77] D. M. Young, *Iterative Solution of Large Linear Systems* (Academic Press, New York, 1971).
[78] S. Winograd, "On multiplication of 2×2 matrices", *Linear Algebra and its Application* **4** (1971) 318—388.

Chapter 2

Fast parallel algorithms for associative computers

2.1 Introduction

This chapter is focused on parallel data processing algorithms on parallel associative computers. Its aim is to demonstrate the particularities of associative information processing. This is illustrated by diverse algorithms on several examples.

In the second section the concept of an associative memory is formulated as well as that of an associative processor. Also some of its basic instructions are defined. A rough diagram of an associative computer of the SIMD-type is described where, in contrast to the previous concepts, it is possible to better characterize the structure of an associative computer. In the next sections various parallel algorithms for associative processing by such fictitious means of computation are described.

In the third and fourth sections a detailed explanation of three logical and arithmetic algorithms will be given. These are illustrated on several models of programs for a parallel associative processor. Algorithm of exact matching (MATCH), computation of maximum (MAX) and retrieval of all the numbers equal, less and greater than the given number (GEL) will be explained in the third section. Algorithm of adding the unity to a vector (ADD1), of the sum of two vectors (ADDV) and the summation of elements of the vector (SUMV) will be described in the fourth section. The algorithms will be expressed by means of instructions of a parallel associative processor in a language similar to ALGOL, where comments to the corresponding commands will be written in brackets.

For better illustration, the formation of separate masks may be given in some algorithms only. The algorithms are presented in the form where the maximum associative memory word size is used. Naturally, in practical applications the size of words is chosen according to the need.

All the algorithms in the third and fourth sections were taken from [7] and modified for the set of given instructions. The description of these algorithms is aimed to focus the reader's attention to the problems of associative data processing in bit slices. Actual algorithms of associative processing have to take into account the architecture of real associative computers. For this reason, the 5th, 6th, 7th, and 8th sections of this chapter are devoted to the complexity and non-traditional aspects of these problems. This will be demonstrated on three various non-trivial examples of algorithms for a parallel associative computer of the SIMD-type.

For this purpose the following algorithms were chosen: sorting, Discrete Fourier Transform and numerical solution of a system of linear algebraic equations.

In the fifth section Batcher's sorting algorithm will be introduced, where, based on the principle of bitonic sorting, a sequence of N elements can be arranged within $O(\log^2 N)$ steps. Parallel algorithm for Fast Fourier Transform is described along with a procedure for its implementation on an associative computer in the sixth section. Associative algorithms for the parallel computation of a histogram for multilevel digitalized image are described in the seventh section.

In the concluding eighth section, algorithms for solving problems of linear algebra on an associative computer are introduced. Here, various parallel modifications of the algorithms for computation of systems of linear algebraic equations are given as well as those of matrix inversion and of eigenvalues of real symmetric matrix. Attention is also paid to solving systems of linear equations originating from elliptic partial differential equations.

2.2 Associative memory and parallel associative processor

A classical model of a serial computer of the von Neuman type has an arithmetic-logic and a control unit, input and output units and memory with individually addressed cells. Each cell can store one item, where it can be used either as a number or an instruction. When communicating with memory, the central processor reads by giving to the memory the address of the cell. The contents are then read in by the memory and, after a certain delay, the memory delivers the contents of this cell.

One of the obstacles preventing the speed acceleration in classical computers is that its computation and memory capacities are separated from each other, that is, computation requires transfers between the processing units and memories. These transfers are executed by buses slowing down the computation rate. By inserting the computer capacity into memory this disadvantage is removed. In this respect, an associative memory (AM), i.e. memory addressed by its contents, proved to be the best choice. An AM is a facility capable of storing information, comparing it with other information and discovering agreement or disagreement [7]. It can quickly answer questions, such as: "Does there exist a position in AM that contains an item x?" or "What is the maximum value of the components of a given vector?" In each cell of AM, there are logicals that determine in parallel whether a given cell does or does not contain data, having given properties. Later, a type of AM will be studied that works in parallel over its words and serially over its bits, i.e. computations are executed serially in bit slices. A diagram of an associative memory is shown in Fig. 21 [7].

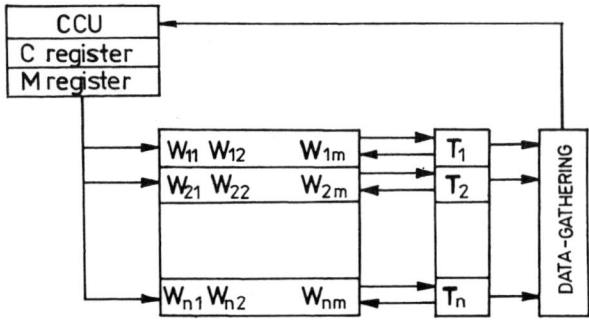

Fig. 21. Diagram of associative memory.

An AM has n cells W_i, $i = 1, 2, ..., n$, where each cells has m bits $W_i = W_{i1} W_{i2} ... W_{im}$. Each cell W_i is connected a tag bit T_i. A response register T is formed by the bits T_i, $i = 1, 2, ..., n$, and is connected by a data-gathering device with the central control unit (CCU). From the CCU, instructions go in parallel to each cell W_i. The CCU contains a comparand register $C = C_1 C_2 ... C_m$ and a mask register $M = M_1 M_2 ... M_m$. C contains the word that is to be compared in parallel with all or with selected words in the AM. Bits that are to be compared in these words in the AM. Bits that are to be compared in these words are determined by register M. If the jth place in M is 1 and the other $M_i = 0, i = 1, 2, ..., m, i \neq j$, then the jth bit of each word will be compared with C_j, namely the jth bit slice. In the cells where, on comparing C_j with W_{ij}, $i = 1, 2, ..., n$, equality occurs, $T_i = 1$ is set and in other cells T_i is set to zero. The pattern is stored in the register C, where, on the basis of some condition, it is compared serially bit by bit, but in parallel with all or with selected cell contents W_i, $i = 1, 2, ..., n$. The result of this operation is a subset of the original array containing all of the elements that satisfy the given retrieval condition. Such a condition can be exact match, less than, greater than, nearest less than, nearest greater than, etc. Among these operations there also belongs searching for minima and maxima and searching for all of the elements lying or not lying in a given interval.

Also, the concept of parallel associative processor (PAP) can be defined. Basically, it is an associative memory capable of a parallel recording of information into all the words that report agreement [7]. The main advantage of such an organization of computation is the speed acceleration. On a classical computer the execution of n identical operations over m-bit words lasts n times as long as the execution of one operation. Computation on a PAP does not depend on n because it can be executed in parallel; it depends on m where usually $n \gg m$. For example, searching for the maximum from n elements, where each element has m bits, takes n steps on classical computers, whereas on a PAP requires just m steps. Serial comparison of elements with each other requires n^2 steps, whereas on a PAP it are nm steps, etc.

A serial computer has a fixed word size. Computations on a serial computer are run either with single precision or by multiple word size (which, in turn, causes substantial prolongation of the computation time). A PAP enables flexible selection of precision of arithmetic operations. The word size as well as the way of rounding off can be selected arbitrarily. Depending on the problem solved, this helps to spare memory and computation time. Arithmetic operations on PAP are of vector type, where the individual operation, such as addition, multiplication, square root, exponential, sinus, arctg, etc. is executed in parallel over all vector components.

Now, let us define some basic instructions of a PAP [7], that enable searching for cells and executing of given operations in an AM. On the basis of these instructions, selected parallel algorithms will be described.

Instruction **SET** causes all the bits of a register T to be set to 1, i.e. $T_i = 1$, $i = 1, 2, ..., n$. Instruction **COMPARE** will cause a parallel comparison of one bit C_j in register C with the bit slice W_{ij}, $i = 1, 2, ..., n$. Comparison will be accomplished only in the case where $M_j = 1$ in the register M. It is executed for those words only, where $T_i = 1$. If we write explicitly, e.g. **COMPARE** $C_j = 0$, then, irrespective of the momentary state of registers C and M, a comparison $C_j = 0$ is done in the jth bit slice of the AM over all the cells with $T_i = 1$. Instruction **WRITE** $A = B$ will execute the recording of a bit slice B into a bit slice A in an AM where recording will only be accomplished in those cells of an AM where $T_i = 1$. Also, the register T can play the role of B. However, a change in the register T can only be achieved by **SET** or as a result of **COMPARE**. Instruction **WRITE** will record one bit of C into a bit slice of an AM, according to M and T. The result of the next three instructions **REPORT**, **FIRST** and **COUNT** is reported to the CCU. Instruction **REPORT** announces whether at least one bit in the register T is unit. If so, then **REPORT** = 1, else = 0. Instruction **FIRST** reports the index k, for which $T_k = 1$, where all $T_i = 0$, for

$i < k$. At the same time, it sets all the bits of register T except T_k to zero. If **COUNT** $= k$, then k units occur in register T. Instruction **INPUT** (**W**) causes the input of an array **W** into the AM. The symbol **DEF** $X = Y$ defines the position of the bit slice Y in an AM and is called X.

To be able to implement algorithms of higher complexity a parallel associative computer of the SIMD-type consists of the fundamental parts listed below (Fig. 22) [21]:
— associative memory module (AMM),
— arithmetic-logic unit (ALU),
— permutation network (PN),
— control memory (CM),
— control unit (CU).

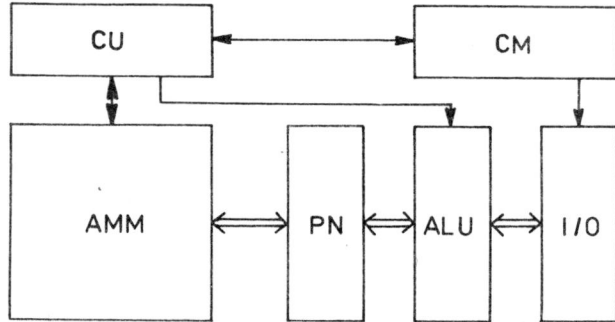

Fig. 22. Parallel associative computer of the SIMD-type.

In an AMM the data is stored over which the associative computer operates. Parallel arithmetic-logic operations over the words of an AMM are executed by an ALU. Part of the ALU is a selector that with various combination of zeros and ones forms masks. By means of ones (zeros) in a mask, the words in an AMM are determined, where the result of an arithmetic or logic operation is (is not) recorded. PN enables the rearrangement of data. In a CM, the program for an associative computer is stored as well as the required or generated data that are not contained in the AMM. The associative computer is controlled by the CU.

According to [7], the algorithms for a PAP are divided into logical and arithmetic algorithms. Logical algorithms search for a class of operands for certain properties while arithmetic algorithms execute arithmetic operations over this class of operands. The logical and arithmetic operations for associative processing will be described in the following sections.

2.3 Logical algorithms for PAP

2.3.1 Pattern matching

Let us have an m-bit word $c = c_1 c_2 \ldots c_m$ and a binary vector $\mathbf{w} = (w_i) = (w_{i1} w_{i2} \ldots w_{im})$, $i = 1, 2, \ldots, n$. We want to know where there are binary words in the vector $\mathbf{w}$, that are identical with c.
Algorithm of a task for PAP is as follows.

Algorithm MATCH:
   begin INPUT ($\mathbf{w}$); (input of the vector $\mathbf{w}$ into the AM)
        $C := c$; (the word under comparison is recorded into register C)
        $j := 0$;
        SET;
  A: $j := j + 1$;
        $M := 2^{m-j}$; (the equation $M_j = 1$ is recorded into register M)
        COMPARE; (comparison of C_j with the bit slice w_{ij}, $i = 1, 2, \ldots, n$)
        if $j < m$ **then go to** A; (the cycle is repeated m times)
  end.

SET sets all $T_i = 1$, $i = 1, 2, \ldots, n$. In register M, M_j is successively changed (from left to right) from 0 to 1, such that during the operation **COMPARE** C_j is compared in bit slices with w_{ij}, $i = 1, 2, \ldots, n$. In the cells where $C_j = w_{ij}$, T_i remains unchanged, if $C_j \neq w_{ij}$, then $T_i = 0$ is set. In the following cycle, comparison is only performed with those words where $T_i = 1$.
At completing the algorithm, there is an absolute equality of C with w_i in those cells where $T_i = 1$.

2.3.2 Computation of the maximum element

Let us have a vector $\mathbf{w} = (w_i) = (w_{i1} w_{i2} \ldots w_{i, m-1})$, $i = 1, 2, \ldots, n$, in which all the elements w_i are positive numbers. Let us find the maximum of them and also its position in W.
The algorithm by which this problem can be solved is as follows.

Algorithm MAX:
   begin INPUT ($\mathbf{w}$); (input of $\mathbf{w}$ into AM)
        DEF $X = (w_{im})$, $i = 1, 2, \ldots, n$; (definition of the position of the bit
            slice X)
        $C := 11 \ldots 1$; (the maximum possible element is written into C)

```
          j := 0;
          SET;
A:        j := j + 1;
          if j > m - 1 then go to B; (jump to end after m - 1 cycles)
          M := 2^{m-j}; (writing of M_j = 1 into register M)
          WRITE X = T; (storing of the state of register T into the bit slice X)
          COMPARE; (comparison of C_j with the bit slice w_{ij}, i = 1, 2, ..., n)
          if REPORT = 0 then (if all w_{ij} = 0, i = 1, 2, ..., n, then set C_j to zero;
                             since in this case all T_j are zero, we store the contents
                             of register T into X)
          begin C_j := 0; WRITE T = X end;
          go to A;
B:        end.
```

The algorithm compares the bit slices w_{ij}, $i = 1, 2, ..., n$, in succession, with ones in C. The cells in which agreement occurs when executing **COMPARE**, are recorded into T, those in which inequality occurs are excluded from further computations. In case that equality does not occur over the whole bit slice, we change the corresponding bit in C to 0. In the next cycle, we work over the same cells as have been used in the preceding step and the state of register T is stored into X. At the end of the computation, the value of maximum element is in the cells, where $T_i = 1$ and also in register C. If there are several maximum elements in w, the first occurrence will be determined by instruction **FIRST**.

2.3.3 Selection of all the numbers which are equal, greater than or less than a pattern

Have a $(m - 2)$-bit word $c = c_1 c_2 ... c_{m-2}$ and a binary vector $\mathbf{w} = (w_i) = w_{i1} w_{i2} ... w_{i, m-2}$, $i = 1, 2, ..., n$, the elements of c and w are positive numbers. Determine in **w** all the elements that are equal, greater than or less than c.

Reserve in AM, after each element w_i, two bits $XY = (w_{i, m-1} w_{im})$. If after ending the program $XY = 10, 01, 00$, it holds that $w_i = c$, $w_i > c$, $w_i < c$, respectively.

The algorithm for this computation of AM is as follows.

Algorithm GEL:
  begin INPUT (w);
        DEF $X = (w_{i, m-1})$, $Y = (w_{i, m})$, $i = 1, 2, ..., m$; (we define bit slice X
            and Y after w)

        $C := c$;
        SET;
        WRITE $X := 1$; **WRITE** $Y := 0$; (10 is recorded into XY of each cell)
        $j := 0$;
        SET;
A: $j := j + 1$;
        COMPARE $X = 1$; (set $T_i = 1$ for all the cells which are not decided)
        if $c_j = 1$ **then** (make decision on less and greater elements in the jth
                bit slice)
        begin COMPARE $c_j = 0$; **WRITE** $X = 0$ **end**
        else begin COMPARE $c_j = 1$; **WRITE** $X = 0$;
                WRITE $Y = 1$ **end**;
        if $j < m - 2$ **then go to** A;
end.

At the beginning, 10 is inserted into all the bits XY, as if all the elements of **w** were equal to c. Computation proceeds from the highest bits in $m - 2$ cycles. Among the words which are not yet decided, if the bit c_j is 1 or 0, we search for such words that have 0 or 1 at the jth position. $XY = 00$ ($XY = 01$) are recorded into words that are less (greater) than c. At the end of the algorithm the words that have maintained the value 10 in XY are equal to c.

2.4 Numerical algorithms for PAP

2.4.1 Adding unity to a vector

Let us have an integer positive vector $\boldsymbol{w} = (w_i)$, $i = 1, 2, \ldots, n$, in which each element w_i has $m - 1$ bits, i.e. $w_i = (w_{i,m-1} w_{i,m-2} \ldots w_{i1})$ (further the bits of the numerical elements will be numbered from right to left).

Let us add unity to each element of **w**.

AM will be reserved for **w**. In each word of the AM, the bit w_{im} will be reserved for storing transfers. At the beginning of computation the bits w_{im}, $i = 1, 2, \ldots, n$, are set to unity, which will be added to all the elements of **w**.

The algorithm for computation of the task on PAP is as follows.

Algorithm ADD1:
  begin INPUT (**w**);
        $M := 2^{m-1}$; (put $M_1 = 1$)
        $C := 2^{m-1}$; (put $C_1 = 1$)
        SET;

        WRITE; (write unity into the bit slice w_{im}, $i = 1, 2, ..., n$)
        $j := 0$;
A: $j := j + 1$;
        $M := 2^{m-1}$;
        $C := 2^{m-1}$;
        SET;
        COMPARE; (select the words with transfer bit = 1)
        $M := 2^{j-1}$; (put $M_{m-j+1} = 1$)
        COMPARE; (of the selected words find those, which have the jth
                    bit = 0)
        $C := 2^{j-1}$;
        WRITE; (put the jth bit = 1 in words with $T_i = 1$)
        $M := 2^{m-1}$;
        WRITE; (set the transfer bits to zero in words with $T_i = 1$)
        $C := 2^{m-1}$;
        SET;
        COMPARE; (selection of the words with the transfer bit = 1)
        $M := 2^{j-1}$;
        $C := 2^{j-1}$;
        COMPARE; (of the selected words find those, which have the jth
                    bit = 1)
        $C := 2^{m-1}$;
        WRITE; (set the jth bits to zero in words with $T_i = 1$)
        $M := 2^{m-1}$;
        WRITE; (set the transfer bits = 1 in words with $T_i = 1$)
        if $j < m - 1$ **then go to** A;
end.

For better illustration, the forming of individual masks in the algorithm is described in more detail. During computation two possibilities can emerge: the transfer bit of the cell is 1 and, at the same time, its jth bit is 0, or the transfer bit and the jth bit are equal to 1. In cells with the transfer bit set to zero, adding of unity was executed, so they are no longer taken into account. Because $1 + 0 = 1$, in the first case it is necessary to store 0 into transfer bit and 1 into the jth bit. In the latter case, because $1 + 1 = 10$, the transfer bit is set to 1 and the jth bit is set to 0.

After $m - 1$ cycles, the result is in array **W**, the maximum bit of every result being the transfer bit, because transfer occurred at the maximum bit of numbers w_i.

2.4.2 Summation of two vectors

We have integer positive vectors $\boldsymbol{x} = (x_i)$ and $\boldsymbol{y} = (y_i)$, $i = 1, 2, \ldots, n$, where the elements $x_i = (x_{i,k} x_{i,k-1} \ldots x_{i1})$ and $y_i = (y_{ik} y_{i,k-1} \ldots y_{i1})$ are k-bit integers. Let us compute the vector $\boldsymbol{z} = x + y = (z_i) = (z_{i,k+1} z_{ik} \ldots z_{i1})$.

Vectors $\boldsymbol{x}$, $\boldsymbol{y}$ and $\boldsymbol{z}$ are stored into AM such that in each cell the bits 1, 2, $\ldots$, k are reserved for the elements $\boldsymbol{x}$, bits $k + 1, k + 2, \ldots, 2k$ for $\boldsymbol{y}$, bits $2k + 1$, $2k + 2, \ldots, 3k + 1$ for the result $\boldsymbol{z}$ and bit $3k + 2$ will be the flag bit. The bit reserved for $z_{i,k+1}$ will play the role of carry bit at the sum $x_i + y_i$; at the conclusion of the algorithm this bit will represent the maximum bit of the result. Now denote the bit slice of the flag bits of cells by $F = (F_1 F_2 \ldots F_n)$. If on summation of the jth bits $F_i = 0$, then this indicates that summation of the jth bits in the ith cell has been accomplished. On the contrary, $F_i = 1$ means that summation has not been accomplished yet. Therefore, in these cells comparison of their bits still needs to be executed. With respect to the memory size, the inequality $3k + 2 \leq m$ is to be fulfilled.

Preceding states (prior to summation) and new states (after summation) of the jth bits and the transfer bit are listed in Table 1.

Table 1

Case	Preceding state			New state	
	x_{ij}	y_{ij}	$z_{i,k+1}$	$z_{i,k+1}$	z_{ij}
1	0	0	0	0	0
2	1	0	0	0	$\underline{1}$
3	0	1	0	0	$\underline{1}$
4	0	0	1	$\underline{0}$	$\underline{1}$
5	1	1	0	$\underline{1}$	0
6	1	0	1	1	0
7	0	1	1	1	0
8	1	1	1	1	$\underline{1}$

If the bits of the jth slice have already been set to zero, then the changes which need to be made in the individual cases, are underlined in Table 1. Thus, the cases 1, 6 and 7 need not be taken into account.

The algorithm for summation of two vectors on PAP is as follows.

Algorithm ADDV:
    begin INPUT $(\boldsymbol{x}, \boldsymbol{y})$;
        DEF $P = (w_{i,2k+1})$, $F = (w_{i,3k+2})$,

$i = 1, 2, \ldots, n$; (definition of the bit slices P and F)
$j := 0$;
SET; WRITE $P = 0$; (zero setting of transfer bits)
A: $p := k - 1$; $q := 2k - j$; $r := 3k + 1 - j$;
SET; WRITE $F = 1$; (denoting the candidates of summation of the
$(j + 1)$st bits)
WRITE $C_r = 0$; (zero setting of the $(j + 1)$st bit slice of the
vector **z**)
COMPARE $C_p = 1$; COMPARE $C_q = 0$ (test case 2)
WRITE $C_r = 1$; WRITE $F = 0$; (record the change, set the flag bits of
these cells to zero)
SET; COMPARE $F = 1$; (put $T_i = 1$ for the cells where summation
has still not been executed)
COMPARE $C_p = 0$; COMPARE $C_q = 1$; (test case 3)
WRITE $C_r = 1$; WRITE $F = 0$;
SET; COMPARE $F = 1$;
COMPARE $C_p = 0$; COMPARE $C_q = 0$; (case 4)
COMPARE $P = 1$;
WRITE $P = 0$; WRITE $C_r = 1$; WRITE $F = 0$;
SET; COMPARE $F = 1$;
COMPARE $C_p = 1$; COMPARE $C_q = 1$; (case 5)
COMPARE $P = 0$;
WRITE $P = 1$; WRITE $F = 0$;
SET; COMPARE $F = 1$;
COMPARE $C_p = 1$; COMPARE $C_q = 1$; (case 8)
COMPARE $P = 1$; WRITE $C_r = 1$;
$j := j + 1$;
if $j < k$ then go to A;
end.

In the algorithm, cases 2, 3, 4, 5 and 8 in the summation table are tested step by step and inevitable changes in bit slices are recorded. The cells in which summation has been executed are excluded from further testing. After k cycles, the array **z** contains the resulting sum **x** + **y**.

2.4.3 Summation of vector components

Let us have an integer positive vector $\boldsymbol{x} = (x_i) = (x_{i1} x_{i2} \ldots x_{im})$, $i = 1, 2, \ldots, n$. Let us compute

$$S = \sum_{i=1}^{n} x_i.$$

If the number of units in the jth bit slice x_{ij}, $i = 1, 2, ..., n$, is denoted by a symbol a_j, then the computation of S is equivalent to the computation of a polynomial with coefficients $a_1, a_2, ..., a_m$ at the point 2, i.e. [7]

$$S = \sum_{i=1}^{m} a_i x^{m-i}$$

for $x = 2$. S can be computed using Horner's method, i.e. the algorithm

$$S = a_1, \quad S = Sx + a_i, \quad i = 2, 3, ..., m.$$

The algorithm for PAP will be as follows.

Algorithm SUMV:
   begin INPUT (x);
      $S := 0$;
      $j := 1$;
A: **SET**;
      $C := 2^{m-j}$; (put $C_j = 1$)
      $M := 2^{m-j}$; (put $M_j = 1$)
      COMPARE;
      $N := $ **COUNT**; (sum the number of ones in the jth slice)
      $S := 2S + N$;
      $j := j + 1$;
      if $j \leq m$ **then go to** A;
   end.

After m cycles of this algorithm in S we get the sum of the components of vector **x**.

2.5 Sorting on an associative computer

In this section the Batcher sorting algorithm will be presented. The Batcher sorting algorithm belongs to the most efficient parallel algorithms for solving this task. In case that the given parallel computer is able to simultaneously execute $N/2$ operations of comparison and exchange, its complexity is $O(\log^2 N)$.

In Batcher algorithm of bitonic sorting, generalized perfect reordering, so-called perfect shuffle, is used to a large extent.

Definition [19]. Have the sequence $a_0, a_1, \ldots, a_{N-1}$, where $N = 2^m$ and $N \geq 4$ and at the same time $N = kn, k, n \geq 2$. We say, that the sequence $b_0, b_1, \ldots, b_{N-1}$ has originated from the original sequence by generalized perfect shuffle $PS(k, n)$, if:

$$b_i = \begin{cases} a_{ki}, & \text{if } 0 \leq i \leq n-1, \\ a_{ki+1-N}, & \text{if } n \leq i \leq 2n-1, \\ \vdots \\ a_{ki+j(1-N)}, & \text{if } jn \leq i \leq (j+1)n-1, \\ \vdots \\ a_{ki+(k-1)(1-N)}, & \text{if } (k-1)n \leq i \leq kn-1. \end{cases}$$

By means of the permutation network of an associative computer, $PS(k, n)$ can be implemented efficiently.

The algorithm of bitonic sorting is based on the following definition and theorem [18].

Definition. Sequence of real numbers $a_0, a_1, \ldots, a_{N-1}$ is bitonic if

(a) there exists an index i, $0 \leq i \leq N-1$ such that $a_0, a_1, \ldots, a_i$ is a monotonic increasing sequence and $a_i, \ldots, a_{N-1}$ is a monotonic decreasing sequence, or

(b) the sequence can be cyclically shifted such that the condition (a) is satisfied.

Theorem. Let $a_0, a_1, \ldots, a_{N-1}$ be a bitonic sequence. If $b_i = \min(a_i, a_{i+N/2})$, $c_i = \max(a_i, a_{i+N/2})$ for $0 \leq i \leq N/2 - 1$, then the sequences $b_0, b_1, \ldots, b_{N/2-1}$ and $c_0, c_1, \ldots, c_{N/2-1}$ are also bitonic and $b_i \leq c_j$ holds for all indices i and j, $0 \leq i, j \leq N/2 - 1$.

Sorting of a bitonic sequence composed of N elements is shown in Fig. 23.

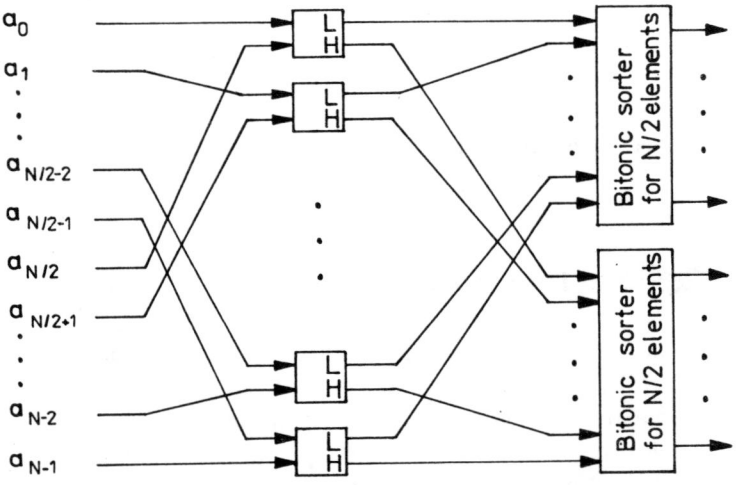

Fig. 23. Bitonic sorter for N elements.

At the output L (H) of the module $\begin{array}{c}\rightarrow\boxed{\begin{array}{c}L\\H\end{array}}\rightarrow\\\rightarrow\end{array}$ there is the minimum (maximum) element of the input elements. From the above theorem it follows that the sequences entering the upper or the lower sorter for $N/2$ elements are bitonic, and it holds that all elements of the upper sequence are less than or equal to the elements of the upper sequence. After $\log N$ steps of comparison and exchange, a sorted sequence is obtained.

For the module $\rightarrow\boxed{\begin{array}{c}L\\H\end{array}}\rightarrow$ notation $\boxed{L}$ will be used. In the Batcher sorting algorithm also module $\rightarrow\boxed{\begin{array}{c}H\\L\end{array}}\rightarrow$ is used, which orders the elements in a non-increasing order. For this module notation $\boxed{H}$ will be used.

The following symbols will be used in the description of the Batcher algorithm for a parallel associative computer:

A — input sequence of a length N which is to be sorted,

B — resulting ordered sequence,

M — mask of a length N that determines which of the modules, $\boxed{L}$ or $\boxed{H}$, will be used in the comparison and exchange of elements,

F — array of an associative memory of a length N,

R — auxiliary vector of a length N forming the mask,

$\oplus$ — logical operation XOR defined in Table 2.

Table 2

v	w	v ⊕ w
0	0	0
0	1	1
1	0	1
1	1	0

$PS(k, n)(X)$ means that $PS(k, n)$ was applied to X. **COMEX**(F, M) means that in an array F comparison and exchange of neighbouring elements are executed depending on the present state of the mask M. Let $M = (m_0, m_1, ..., m_{N-1})$. Let $i = 0, 1, ..., N/2 - 1$. When m_{2i} and m_{2i+1} are zeros (ones), then for comparison of the elements F_{2i} with F_{2i+1} the module $\boxed{L}$ ($\boxed{H}$) is used.

In general, we can assume that $N = 2^m$.

Comments in the algorithm are enclosed in asterisks.

The Batcher sorting algorithm [18] consists of the following steps

(1) $F \leftarrow A$;

(2) $R \leftarrow (0, 1, 0, 1, ..., 0, 1)$;

(3) * Initiation of the mask *

Repeat m times: $[M \leftarrow M \oplus \boldsymbol{R}; M \leftarrow \text{PS}(2, N/2)(M)]$;
(4) $F \leftarrow \textbf{COMEX}(F, M)$;
(5) **If** $m = 1$, **go to** (7);
(6) ∗ Successive generating of still greater bitonic sequences in an array F, until a single bitonic sequence is generated, which will be merged into ordered sequence.
$i := m - 1$;
(6.0) **If** $i = 0$, **go to** (7);
$\boldsymbol{R} \leftarrow \text{PS}(2, N/2)(\boldsymbol{R}); M \leftarrow M \oplus \boldsymbol{R};$ ∗ Modification of the mask ∗
$j := i$;
go to (6.j);
(6.j) $F \rightarrow \text{PS}(2, N/2^j)(F)$;
$F \leftarrow \textbf{COMEX}(F, M)$;
$F \leftarrow \text{PS}(N/2^j, 2)(F)$;
If $j = m - 1$, **then** $[F \leftarrow \textbf{COMEX}(F, M); i := i - 1;$ **go to** (6.0)], **else** $[j := j + 1;$ **go to** (6.j)];
(7) $B \leftarrow F$.

The Batcher algorithm works correctly even when some elements of the input sequence are identical.

For better understanding, the algorithm is illustrated using an example with 16 elements.

First, we explain how the mask was changing. Having accomplished step 3, the initial mask was obtained

$$M = M_0 = (0, 0, 1, 1, 1, 1, 0, 0, 1, 1, 0, 0, 0, 0, 1, 1).$$

The algorithm went through step (6.0) three times, because $m = 4$. After the first transition, the mask

$$M = M_1 = (0, 0, 0, 0, 1, 1, 1, 1, 1, 1, 1, 1, 0, 0, 0, 0),$$

was obtained, after the second transition

$$M = M_2 = (0, 0, 0, 0, 0, 0, 0, 0, 1, 1, 1, 1, 1, 1, 1, 1)$$

and after the third transition

$$M = M_3 = (0, 0, 0, 0, 0, 0, 0, 0, 0, 0, 0, 0, 0, 0, 0, 0).$$

Let the input sequence be

$$A = (8, 7, 10, 12, 1, 14, 5, 13, 16, 9, 2, 3, 6, 4, 11, 15).$$

2.5 Sorting on an associative computer

The diagram illustrating sorting is shown in Fig. 24. The arrow situated above the figure indicates when the algorithm went through step (6.0), at which the

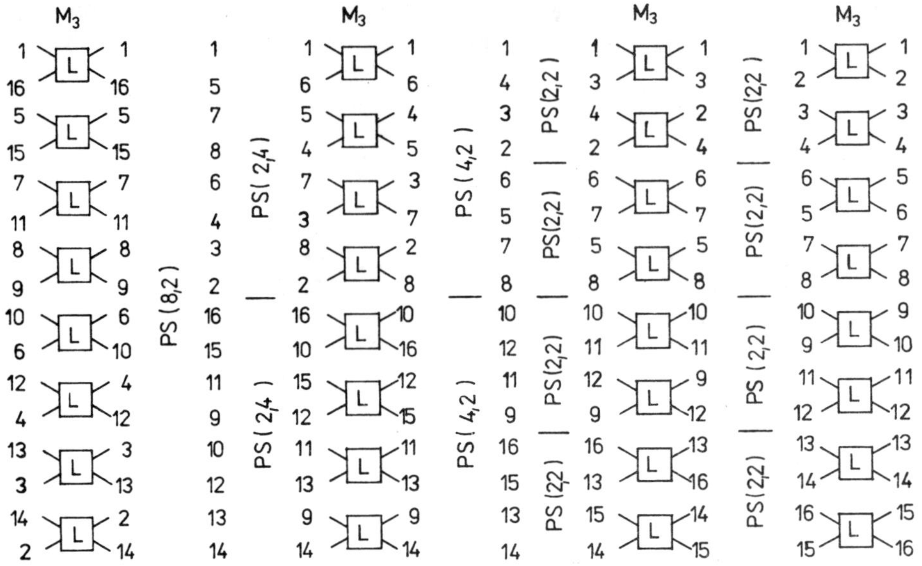

Fig. 24. Sorting of 16 elements with the use of the Batcher sorting algorithm.

mask was changed. Above the steps of comparison and exchange there is a mask that was used in these steps.

The complexity of balanced sorting [5] is of the same order as that of Batcher's sorting, namely $O(\log^2 N)$. However, when compared with the latter it has the advantage that it is not necessary to generate and change the mask, because all elements of the sequence in each step of the algorithm are ordered in non-decreasing order.

2.6 Parallel implementation of Fast Fourier Transform

Discrete Fourier Transform (DFT) of a set of N data has the form

$$F(n) = \sum_{k=0}^{N-1} f(k) w^{nk}, \quad n = 0, 1, ..., N-1, \qquad (35)$$

where $w = \exp(-i2\pi/N)$ and i is an imaginary unit. Computation of the vector $F = (F(n))$ from the vector $f = (f(n))$, $n = 0, 1, ..., N-1$, by means of (35) requires approximately N^2 arithmetic operations. An efficient method to computate the DFT is Fast Fourier Transform (FFT) decreasing the number of operations to $O(N \log N)$. In what follows, we shall briefly describe the principles of this method and then the design of its implementation on an associative computer.

We shall assume that $N = 2^m$, where m is a positive integer. Relationship (35) is shown in Fig. 25.

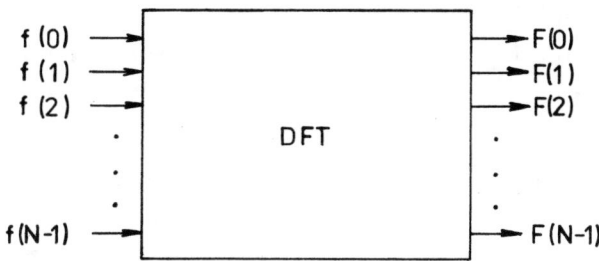

Fig. 25. Discrete Fourier Transform.

If relationship (35) is rearranged in such a way that the even and odd terms are grouped together, we get

$$F(n) = B_n + w^n C_n,$$

where

$$B_n = \sum_{k=0}^{N/2-1} f(2k) w^{2nk},$$

$$C_n = \sum_{k=0}^{N/2-1} f(2k+1) w^{2nk}.$$

It holds that $B_n = B_{n+N/2}$ and $C_n = C_{n+N/2}$, $n = 0, 1, ..., N/2 - 1$, and thus, a DFT of dimension N can be decomposed into two DFTs of dimension $N/2$. Using the relationship

$$w^{n+N/2} = -w^n$$

is a decomposition for $N = 8$ shown in Fig. 26.

The computation of vectors B_n and C_n for $n = 0, 1, ..., N/2 - 1$ is a DFT of dimension $N/2$; each of them can be decomposed again into two transformations of dimension $N/4$. Thus, by splitting, the FFT algorithm is obtained. From the above it follows that the input vector f is not ordered in sequential order. The required ordering of the vector f at input can be obtained so that the element $f(i)$ is interchanged with the element $f(j)$ if the bits of the bit representation of the number i are arranged in reverse order than are the bits of the number

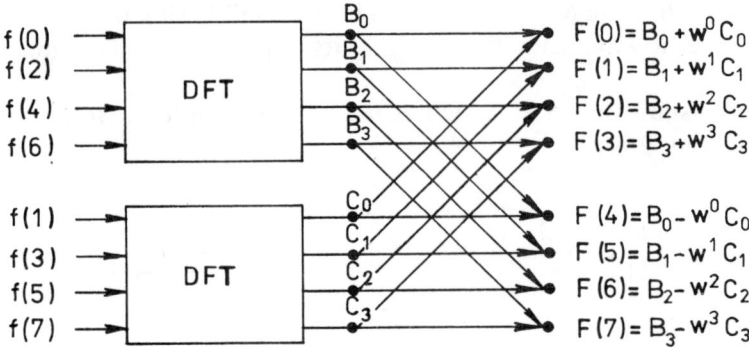

Fig. 26. First step of the DFT decomposition.

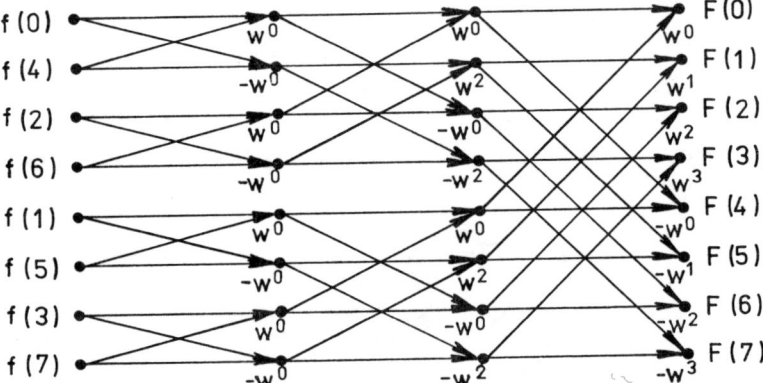

Fig. 27. FFT for $N = 8$ (input in bit-reversed order).

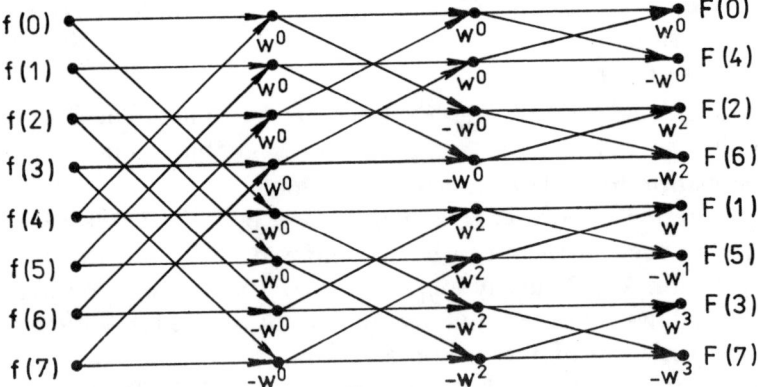

Fig. 28. FFT for $N = 8$ (input in sequential order).

j, e.g. $i = 1 = 001 \Rightarrow j = 100 = 4$, i.e. $f(1)$ is changed with $f(4)$. This ordering of elements of the input vector is called bit-reverse ordering. The corresponding FFT algorithm for $N = 8$ is shown in Fig. 27.

In some of the applications of signal and image processing it is necessary that the input signal be in sequential order. A computing diagram of the FFT for the vector $\boldsymbol{f}$ of dimension $N = 8$, where the input is in sequential order and the output in bit-reverse order, is shown in Fig. 28.

Let us denote the components of the input vector $\boldsymbol{f}$ in sequential order by $\boldsymbol{f}_0(k)$, $k = 0, 1, \ldots, N - 1$, and the results of the rth computational step by $\boldsymbol{f}_r(k)$, $r = 0, 1, \ldots, m - 1$. Then, the FFT algorithm can be expressed as follows

for $r = 1, 2, \ldots, m$,
   begin
     $\boldsymbol{f}_r(k) = f_{r-1}(k) + w^p f_{r-1}(k + N/2^r)$;
     $\boldsymbol{f}_r(k + N/2^r) = f_{r-1}(k) - w^p f_{r-1}(k + N/2^r)$;
   end;
$\boldsymbol{F}(n) = \boldsymbol{f}_m(n)$, $n = 0, 1, \ldots, N - 1$.

Exponent p in the algorithm will be determined as follows [3]:
(1) Index k will be written in binary form with m bits;
(2) This number will be shifted $m - r$ bits to the right, whereby the bits on the left will be filled by zeros;
(3) The obtained number will be written in bit-reverse order — it will be equal to p.

As can be seen from Fig. 28 and from the above relationships for the computation of the rth computation step, the operations of multiplication, summation, or subtraction can be executed in parallel over the whole vector $\boldsymbol{f}_r(k)$, $r = 0, 1, \ldots, m - 1$ (provided that there is a suitable inter-processor communication network). Such network is, for example, the inter-processor communication network for the associative computer STARAN where the FFT can be implemented very efficiently [2].

Now we shall describe a parallel FFT algorithm for an associative computer of the SIMD-type. In this algorithm, the vector $\boldsymbol{F}$ is in bit-reverse order, whereas vector $\boldsymbol{f}$ is in sequential order.

As seen from Fig. 28, flopping of the vectors in computation of the FFT is executed depending on the computation step. This flopping in the rth step will be denoted by FL_r.

Later, we say that the vector $\boldsymbol{g}'(k)$ was generated from the vector $\boldsymbol{g}(k)$ by flopping FL_r, if

$$\boldsymbol{g}'(k) = \boldsymbol{g}((k + N/2^r) \bmod (N/2^{r-1})), \qquad r = 1, 2, \ldots, m, \quad k = 0, 1, \ldots, N - 1.$$

Because all vectors in the FFT are complex in general, special arrays $F1 - F5$ are reserved for their components in associative memory. Arrays $F1 - F4$ have equal word length while the array $F5$ has a double word length. Width of arrays can be determined arbitrarily depending on the required precision and the width of associative memory.

In the real (imaginary) components of the vector f_0 are put into array $F1$ ($F2$), the FFT computation is carried out in the following $O(\log N)$ steps:

(1) $r := 1$;
(2) Input of proper values of functions $\cos x$ and $\sin x$ into arrays $F3$ and $F4\,(M_r)$;
(3) Exchange of elements of arrays $F1$ and $F2$ by means of $FL_r(M_r)$;
(4) $F3 := FL_r(F3)$;
(5) $F4 := FL_r(F4)$; $F4 := F4(-1)\,(M_r)$;
(6) $F5 := F2F4$;
(7) $F5 := FL_r(F5)$;
(8) $F5 := F5 + F2F3$;
(9) $F2 := F1 - F5$; $F1 := F1 + F5$;
(10) Exchange of elements of arrays $F1$ add $F2$ by means of $FL_r(M_r)$;
(11) $r := r + 1$; **if** $r \leq m$, **then go to** (2).

Notation (M_r) in the third, fifth and tenth steps means that in recording the results into associative memory, the mask M_r of the following form was used

$$M_r = (\mathbf{0, I, 0, I, ..., I}),$$

where $\mathbf{0}$ or $\mathbf{I}$ are the vectors containing $N/2^r$ zeros or ones, respectively.

The complex product of components of the vectors f_r with w^p can be computed using the relationship

$$(a + ib)(c + id) = ((a + b)(c - d) + ad - bc) + i(ad + bc),$$

$F1$	$F2$	$F3$	$F4$	$F5$	Step
$R1$	$I1$	0	0	0	2, 3
$R2$	$I2$	C	S	0	
$R1$	$R2$	C	S	0	4, 5
$I1$	$I2$	C	$-S$	0	
$R1$	$R2$	C	S	$-I2\cdot S$	6, 7
$I1$	$I2$	C	$-S$	$R2\cdot S$	
$R1$	$R2$	C	S	$R2\cdot C - I2\cdot S$	8
$I1$	$I2$	C	$-S$	$I2\cdot C + R2\cdot S$	
$R1 + R2\cdot C - I2\cdot S$	$I1 + I2*C + R2\cdot S$	C	S	$R2\cdot C - I2\cdot S$	9, 10
$R1 - R2\cdot C + I2\cdot S$	$I1 - I2*C - R2\cdot S$	C	$-S$	$I2\cdot C + R2\cdot S$	

Scheme 2

where four multiplications and two additions are replaced by three multiplications and five additions. In an associative computer, these can by reduced to two multiplications, two additions and two floppings (using suitable flopping of the vectors). The steps of the algorithm are shown in Scheme 2. Only one computation block of dimension $N/2^{r-1}$ is shown in each step (computation, however, is executed simultaneously over the whole array, i.e. over 2^{r-1} blocks).

2.7 Parallel histogram algorithms for an associative parallel computer

2.7.1 Introduction

The histogram procedure represents a basic routine for image processing systems. For an image with m possible gray levels $0, 1, \ldots, m-1$, the histogram is represented by numbers $H[0], H[1], \ldots, H[m-1]$, where $H[j]$ gives the number of jth level pixels.

On a sequential computer, the complexity of evaluation of m-level histogram for an image with n^2 pixels is proportional to $O(n^2 m)$. Since pixels can be processed by histogram evaluations independently, parallel processing can reduce this complexity estimate. Some results have already been achieved in parallel histogram algorithms [12, 16]. However, the problem of histogram evaluation is also of a more general importance because it occurs in many other areas (i.e. traffic sumulations, plasma physics, pattern recognition [12]).

This section presents four parallel variants for histogram evaluation on a specialized associative computer system with an APM memory block that operates under a SIMD-type parallel mode working in the "vector parallel — bit serial" manner [13].

An m-level image G of size $n \times n$ will be assumed. Its location in the APM will be in $s = n^2/p$ fields Gi, $i = 1, 2, \ldots, s$, of length p and width $\log m$, where p will be the number of processors in the ALU (n and p are powers of 2). The following notation for algorithm explanation will be used:

$F_j, j = 1, 2, \ldots, r$ — jth 1-bit slice of an r-bit field F;

$(F)_j, j = 1, 2, \ldots, q$ — jth component of a q-length field F;

$F[i], i = 1, 2, \ldots, r$ — ith block of a q-length field F where the length of Fi, $i = 1, 2, \ldots, r$, is q/r;

$FR \leftarrow F01$ **op** $F02$ — parallel execution of an operation "**op**" on operand fields $F01$, $F02$ with a result in FR;

$FR \leftarrow F01$ **op** $F02\,(M)$ — masked parallel execution of "**op**" where 1's and 0's in M respectively indicate those words in FR where the result should or should not be written in;

$F \leftarrow$ **SHIFT** $F^{+(-)}$ — cyclic shift of $F1$ one position up (down);

$F \leftarrow F_{2^k, 2^{k+1}}$, $k = 0, 1, \ldots, l-1$ — permutation of a q-length field F ($q = 2^l, l \geq 1$), with a permutation factor 2^k, within 2^{k+1}-length blocks $F[i]$ of F, defined as $(F[i])_j \leftarrow (F[i])_r$ for $i = 1, 2, \ldots, q/2^{k+1}, j = 1, 2, \ldots, 2^{k+1}$, where $k = 0, 1, \ldots, l-1$ and $r = (j + 2^k) \bmod 2^{k+1}$;

$Y \leftarrow$ **COMPARE** F, C — register Y contains 1's on those positions where components of F are equal to the content of comparand register C;

$Y \leftarrow$ **EQF** $F01, F02$ — 1's are in register Y where corresponding components of operand fields coincide;

COUNT Y — gives the number of 1's in register Y;

FIND Y — gives the address of the first 1 from the top in Y;

$\emptyset, I$ — 1-bit fields with the respective 0 and 1 in all components;

TG — log m-bit field where $(TG)_j = j - 1, j = 1, 2, \ldots, m$;

MTG — mask with 1's in first m positions (from the top).

2.7.2 Image field-vector of gray level values algorithm

This algorithm can be considered as a straightforward parallel comparison strategy where each from s image fields $G1, G2, \ldots, Gs$ in APM is compared with the field TG containing gray level values $0, 1, \ldots, m-1$. Supposing $p \geq m$, the

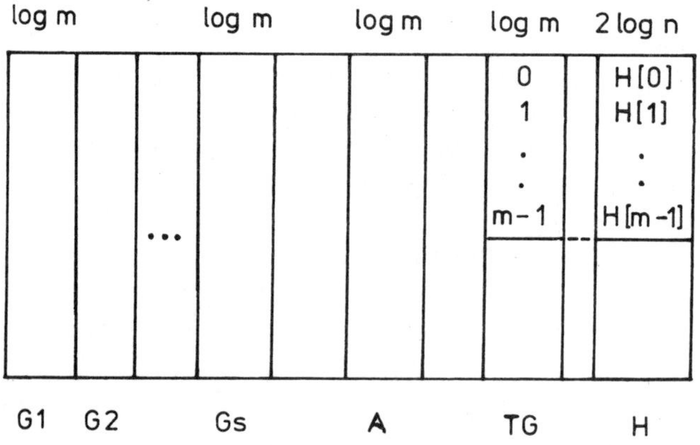

Fig. 29. Comparing histogram algorithm.

mask *MTG* (with 1's in the first *m* positions) can be constructed. The image fields are subsequently located in an auxiliary field *A* and then processed by comparing with the field *TG* in *p* comparison steps. These comparisons are executed using the mask *MTG*. In each step, the field *A* is shifted one position upwards and a content of register *Y* is added to $2\log n$-bit histogram field *H*. Having processed all image fields, $(H)_j$, $j = 1, 2, ..., m$, contains a number of image pixels possessing a gray level $j - 1$. The location of fields considered in an AMM is illustrated in Fig. 29.

This algorithm can be written in terms of the above notation's rules as follows

INPUTS Gi, $i = 1, 2, ..., s$, TG, MTG
    for $i = 1, 2, ..., s$
        $A \leftarrow Gi$
        for $j = 1, 2, ..., p$
            $A \leftarrow$ **SHIFT** A^+
            $Y \leftarrow$ **EQF** TG, $A(MTG)$
            $H \leftarrow H + Y$

Counting the costs of all used instructions [17], the total complexity C_1 of this algorithm is

$$C_1 \approx 2n^2 \log m/p + 7n^2 \log m + 6n^2 \log n = O(n^2 \log k),$$

$$k = \max(m, n).$$

2.7.3 Image field-comparand register histogram algorithm

In one comparison pass of this algorithm, image fields Gi, $i = 1, 2, ..., s$, are compared to one from the gray level values $0, 1, ..., m - 1$ in a straightforward manner. The comparison passes for $j = 0, 1, ..., m - 1$ are performed starting from 0 to $m - 1$. In one comparison pass, each image field Gi, $i = 1, 2, ..., s$, is compared with a given value of j stored in the comparand register. The number of pixels in Gi possessing a jth gray level is given by the number of 1's in register Y. For this reason, 1-bit intermediate fields Ei, $i = 1, 2, ..., s$, will serve to store contents of register Y as the results of comparisons of Gi's with C. The summation of Ei, $i = 1, 2, ..., s$, follows in a tree-sum manner [10]. In each ith step, $i = 1, 2, ..., \log s$, $s/2^i$ vector pairs are added. The width of the respective operand vectors and a result are i and $i + 1$ bits. The final result will be located in the field $E1$ of the width $\log s + 1$. The number of 1's in all Ei, $i = 1, 2, ..., s$, is then obtained as a sum of components of $E1$. It can be done in $O(m) + O(\log m \log p)$ steps.

INPUTS Gi, $i = 1, 2, ..., s$
  $M = (0, 0, ..., 1)$
  for $j = 0, 1, ..., m - 1$
    $C \leftarrow j$
    $M \leftarrow M^-$
    for $i = 1, 2, ..., s$
      $Y \leftarrow \textbf{COMPARE } Gi, C$
      $Ei \leftarrow Y$
    for $i = 1, 2, ..., \log s$
      for $k = 1, 2, ..., s/2^i$
        $l = 1 + (k - 1) 2^i$
        $l1 = l + 2^{i-1}$
        $El \leftarrow El + El1$
    for $i = 1, 2, ..., \log p$
      $E11 \leftarrow E1_{2^{i-1}, 2^i}$
      $E1 \leftarrow E1 + E11$
    $H \leftarrow H + E1(M)$

The complexity is

$$C_2 \approx 22ms + ms \log m + 6m \log s \log p = O(mn^2 \log m/p).$$

2.7.4 Non-redundant associative histogram algorithm

In this algorithm each column is only compared with those gray level values that it contains. Thus the redundancy of the preceding algorithm (where Gi's were compared with all m gray level values) will be avoided. A 1-bit field Bi is used to control the number of processed pixels in Gi, $i = 1, 2, ..., s$ (Fig. 30). A

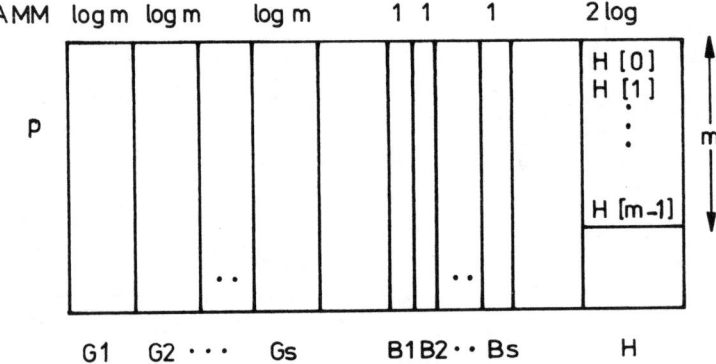

Fig. 30. Non-redundant histogram algorithm.

given Gi is processed from top to bottom whereby the first unclassified pixel is found by **FIND**. The gray level of this pixel is moved into C. Gi is compared with the content of C and the number of 1's is added to H with a corresponding mask. The next column is processed after Gi has been examined.

INPUTS Gi, $i = 1, 2, ..., s$, TG
   for $i = 1, 2, ..., s$
     $Bi \leftarrow \emptyset$
L1: $Y \leftarrow$ **COMPARE** Bi, $\emptyset$
     $M \leftarrow$ **FIND** Y
     $C \leftarrow Gi(M)$
     $Y \leftarrow$ **COMPARE** TG, C
     $M \leftarrow Y$
     $Y \leftarrow$ **COMPARE** Gi, C
     $Bi \leftarrow Bi + Y$
     $H \leftarrow H +$ **COUNT** $Y(M)$
     $Y \leftarrow$ **COMPARE** Bi, I
     if **COUNT** $Y \neq p$ **go to** L1

Using the estimation pm/n for the mean number of gray levels in one image field, then

$$C_3 \approx 2mn \log m + 10mn \log n + 4n^2 = O(mn \log k),$$

$$k = \max(m, n).$$

2.7.5 Parallel histogram decoding algorithm

Another approach to histogram evaluation is based on a decoding technique which can be named a "histogram filter". The decoding represents a jth level

Gi \ j	0	1	2	3	4	5	6	7
2	0	0	1	0	0	0	0	0
1	0	1	0	0	0	0	0	0
0	1	0	0	0	0	0	0	0
3	0	0	0	1	0	0	0	0
5	0	0	0	0	0	1	0	0
7	0	0	0	0	0	0	0	1
1	0	1	0	0	0	0	0	0
6	0	0	0	0	0	0	1	0

Fig. 31. Decoded image field.

pixel by a 1 exactly in the histogram position corresponding to $H[j]$. The number of pixels of a given gray level is given by the number of 1's in the corresponding column of the decoding block. For $m = 8$, $p = 8$ an example of decoded image field Gi is shown in Fig. 31.

The decoding technique is very simple. To decode pixels represented by $\log m$ bits, $\log m + 1$ intermediate fields Di, $i = 0, 1, ..., \log m$ (each of a width 2^i bits) will be constructed (Fig. 32). If an image field Gi is composed of $\log m$ bit slices Gi_l, $l = 1, 2, ..., \log m$, it can be decoded in $\log m$ steps.

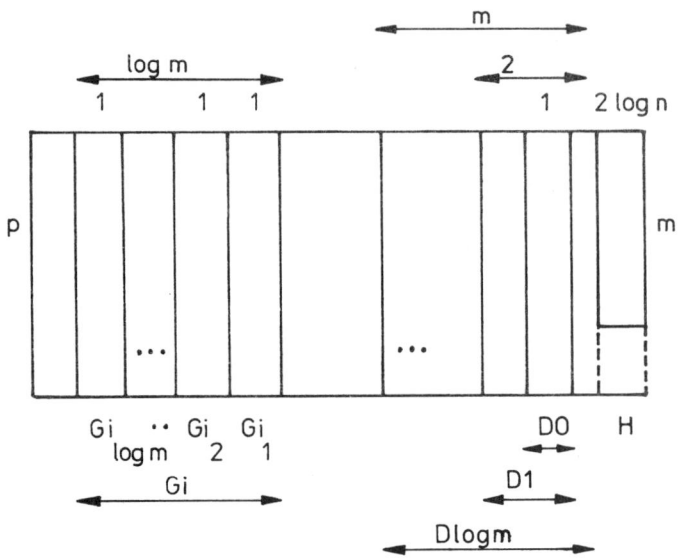

Fig. 32. Decoding approach.

At the beginning of decoding, $D0 = I$. Then in each lth step, $l = 1, 2, ..., \log m$, the field Dl is constructed either by shifting components of $Dl - 1$ 2^{l-1} bits to the left and setting 2^{l-1} bits from the right zero, or by keeping $Dl - 1$ without any change and setting 2^{l-1} bits from the left zero. We note that by constructing a new field, the old one can be overwritten. Hence, in AMM memory only m-bit field has to be reserved for result $D \log m$ of decoding. For a more transparent explanation, the operation of the lth decoding step, $l = = 1, 2, ..., \log m$, can be expressed as a masked multiplication of $Dl - 1$ by $2^{2^{l-1}}$ where the mask is represented by Gi_l. Figure 33 shows decoding steps for the above example (see Fig. 31). After decoding each image field, $D \log m$ can be seen as a $p \times m$ Boolean matrix. In order to obtain the number of 1's for each gray level, its rows $D \log m_j$, $j = 1, 2, ..., p$, have to be added. The resulting vector of this addition is added to vector H.

D_3	D_2	D_1	$D0$	$Gi_1 Gi_2 Gi_3$	Gi
0 0 0 0 0 1 0 0	0 1 0 0	0 1	1	0 1 0	2
0 0 0 0 0 0 1 0	0 0 1 0	1 0	1	0 0 1	1
0 0 0 0 0 0 0 1	0 0 0 1	0 1	1	0 0 0	0
0 0 0 0 1 0 0 0	1 0 0 0	1 0	1	0 1 1	3
0 0 1 0 0 0 0 0	0 0 1 0	1 0	1	1 0 1	5
1 0 0 0 0 0 0 0	1 0 0 0	1 0	1	1 1 1	7
0 0 0 0 0 0 1 0	0 1 0 0	0 1	1	0 0 1	1
0 1 0 0 0 0 0 0	0 1 0 0	0 1	1	1 1 0	6

Fig. 33. Position matrix.

Construction of this algorithm for the associative parallel computer is as follows

INPUTS Gi, $i = 1, 2, ..., s$
  $H \leftarrow \emptyset$
  for $i = 1, 2, ..., s$
  $D0 \leftarrow I$
  for $l = 1, 2, ..., \log m$
    $M \leftarrow Gi_l$
    $Dl \leftarrow (Dl - 1) 2^{2^{i-1}}(M)$
  for $i = 1, 2, ..., p$
    $Ei \leftarrow D \log m_i$
  for $i = 1, 2, ..., \log p$
    for $k = 1, 2, ..., p/2^i$
      $(l = 1 + (k-1)2^i, l1 = l + 2^{i-1})$
      $El \leftarrow El + El1$
  $H \leftarrow E1 + H$

Counting the complexities of macroinstructions in the algorithm, we get a total number of operation steps [8]

$$C_4 \approx 6n^2 \log m/p + 8n^2 \log n/p - 4n^2 \log p/p + 18n^2 + 3n^2 m/p = O(mn^2/p).$$

Finally, let us analyse complexity estimations of the algorithms developed. Four cases will be assumed

  (a) $n = m = p$,
  (b) $n = p \gg m$,
  (c) $n \gg m = p$,
  (d) $n = 2p = 4m$.

Comparing the corresponding complexities, the following relationships hold

(a) $C_4 < C_2 < C_3 < C_1$,
(b) $C_2 < C_3 < C_4 < C_1$,
(c) $C_3 < C_2 < C_4 < C_1$,
(d) $C_2 < C_4 < C_3 < C_1$.

As seen, the most effective algorithms are those which make use of the tree-sum technique [10], where the asymptotically optimal value has been achieved for the algorithm with the decoding technique.

The algorithms have been formulated for one associative computer module under restriction that $m \leq p$, i.e. the number of gray level values must not exceed the number of processors. An open question is how to design the algorithms organization if $p < m$ and more than one associative module is available.

2.8 Linear algebra examples on a parallel associative SIMD-type computer

In this section we cover the efficient use of associative computers for solving some tasks in linear algebra. It is necessary to formulate suitable algorithms for implementing these problems on associative computers.

First, we show how Gauss and Gauss—Jordan elimination methods can be adapted to solve a system of dimension N on the associative parallel computer described in the introduction to Chapter 2. Both order N and order N^2 space complexity algorithms are considered. For the Gaussian method the algorithm includes solving the resulting triangular system. From the class of iterative methods, single step methods with a constant iteration matrix will be described. Since systems of linear equations frequently emerge in connection with the numerical solutions of differential equations, a procedure to solve some elliptic equations will be designed for an associative computer.

Matrix inversion will be illustrated with the Gauss—Jordan method with pivoting. This chapter ends with the computation of the eigenvalues of a symmetric matrix using Jacobi's method.

All the numbers will be n-bits long. In the description of algorithms, as in Section 2.7, commands are of the form $F3 \leftarrow F1$ **op** $F2(M)$, where the Fi are operand fields **op** is the arithmetic operation and M is the mask. On dividing or multiplying two fields, only the first n-bits of each element in the resulting will be considered for the result. The number of components of the mask M corresponds to the number of words in the operand fields. These components are 1 (0) for the corresponding words where the result is (is not) to be stored. When the mask M is missing, the results are stored into all of the field elements.

$F1 \leftarrow F2$ indicates that the components from the field $F2$ will be transferred into the field $F1$. An acyclic shift of the field F by one word up (down), where 0 will be inserted into the empty location, will be written as $F \leftarrow F^+$ (F^-).

We now define some useful masks.

In the algorithms for directly solving linear systems, the masks

$$m_i = (\underbrace{0, ..., 0}_{i-1}, 1, 0, ..., 0)$$

will be used to select elements from the matrix diagram and the masks

$$m_i^* = (\underbrace{0, ..., 0}_{i}, 1, ..., 1)$$

will be used to select all elements below the diagonal element. These masks are of dimension N. The masks

$$M_i = (\underbrace{\boldsymbol{0}, ..., \boldsymbol{0}}_{i-1}, \boldsymbol{I}, \boldsymbol{0}, ..., \boldsymbol{0}), \quad \bar{M}_i = (\underbrace{\boldsymbol{I}, ..., \boldsymbol{I}}_{i-1}, \boldsymbol{0}, \boldsymbol{I}, ..., \boldsymbol{I})$$

are of dimension $N(N+1)$, where $\boldsymbol{I}$ is a vector of all 1's, $\boldsymbol{0}$ is a vector of all 0's and both have N elements. For the iterative method the mask $\tilde{M} = (m_1, m_2, ..., m_N)$ of dimension N^2 is used.

In algorithms for $N(N+1)$ memory words, each array, F, will be considered as a vector composed of N memory blocks F_j. Then the ith component of each memory block will be denoted as $(F_j)_i$. In the N-word implementation, the ith component of the array F will be denoted by $(F)_i$.

$\boldsymbol{I}$ or $\boldsymbol{0}$ will be the compatible arrays with all entries 1 or 0, respectively. Cyclic permutation of a 2^k component vector F with code 2^p for blocks of length 2^q, where $0 \leq p < q \leq 2k$, will be denoted as $F(2^p, 2^q)$. For example, if $\mathbf{F}$ is a 4×4 matrix containing indices of elements in row order, then $F(2^2, 2^3)$ will represent the permutation that takes

$$F = (11\ 12\ 13\ 14\ 21\ 22\ 23\ 24\ 31\ 32\ 33\ 34\ 41\ 42\ 43\ 44) \text{ to}$$

$$F(2^2, 2^3) = (21\ 22\ 23\ 24\ 11\ 12\ 13\ 14\ 41\ 42\ 43\ 44\ 31\ 32\ 33\ 34).$$

C will be a reserved variable indicating a comparand register. C will compare the elements of the matrix $\mathbf{F}$ with the contents of register C by writing compare

$F[C]$. Spreading of the contents of register C into field F with the mask M will be written as $F \leftarrow$ spread $C(M)$.

2.8.1 Direct methods of solving the systems of linear equations

A system of linear algebraic equations can be written as

$$\mathbf{A}\mathbf{x} = \mathbf{a}_{N+1}, \tag{36}$$

where $\mathbf{A} = (a_{ij}^{(0)})$ is an $N \times N$ square matrix, and $\mathbf{x} = (x_i)$ and $\mathbf{a}_{N+1} = (a_{i,N+1}^{(0)})$ are N vectors. The Gaussian elimination of the augmented matrix $[\mathbf{A}: \mathbf{a}_{N+1}]$ is described in the following algorithm [6]:

> **for** $i = 1, 2, \ldots, N$ (for each row)
>   **for** $j = i, \ldots, N+1$ (for all remaing columns plus RHS)
>   **begin** $a_{ij}^{(i)} = a_{ij}^{(i-1)}/a_{ii}^{(i-1)}$;
>   **for** $k = i+1, \ldots, N$
> $a_{kj}^{(i)} = a_{kj}^{(i-1)} - a_{ki}^{(i-1)} a_{ij}^{(i)}$;
> **end**.

The original system is reduced to an upper triangular system of equations denoted

$$\mathbf{A}^{(N)} \mathbf{x} = \mathbf{a}_{N+1}^{(N)}. \tag{37}$$

The right-hand side of this system of equations is

$$\mathbf{a}_{N+1}^{(N)} = (a_{i,N+1}^{(i)}), \quad i = 1, 2, \ldots, N.$$

This system is solved by back substitution to obtain $\mathbf{x}$.
We can calculate the back substitution by computing

$$d_i^{(j)} = a_{i,N+1}^{(i)} - \sum_{k=N-j+1}^{N} a_{ik} x_k, \quad i = 1, 2, \ldots, N \text{ and } j = 1, 2, \ldots, N-i.$$

For ease of reading the notation

$$\mathbf{a}_i = (a_{i1}^{(0)}, a_{i2}^{(0)}, \ldots, a_{i,N+1}^{(0)}), \quad i = 1, 2, \ldots, N,$$

will denote the ith augmented row and

2.8 Linear algebra examples on SIMD-type computer

$$\bar{a}_i = (a_{1i}^{(0)}, a_{2i}^{(0)}, ..., a_{Ni}^{(0)}) \quad \text{for} \quad i = 1, 2, ..., N + 1$$

the ith column.

Let's begin with the Gaussian method using N memory words. Here, not all of the coefficients of the system can be placed into memory at one time. We need bidirectional communication of intermediate results between the associative memory module and the external memory which we denote P. The elimination procedure for $i = 1$ is in Table 3.

Table 3

m_1	m_1^*	$F1$	$F2$	
1	0	$a_{11}^{(0)}$	$a_{11}^{(0)}$	· $a_{1,N+1}^{(0)}$
0	1	$a_{21}^{(0)}$	$a_{21}^{(0)}$	· $a_{2,N+1}^{(0)}$
0	1	$a_{31}^{(0)}$	$a_{31}^{(0)}$	· $a_{3,N+1}^{(0)}$
⋮	⋮	⋮	⋮	⋮
0	1	$a_{N-1,1}^{(0)}$	$a_{N-1,1}^{(0)}$	· $a_{N-1,N+1}^{(0)}$
0	1	$a_{N1}^{(0)}$	$a_{N1}^{(0)}$	· $a_{N,N+1}^{(0)}$

$F3$		$F2$		$F4$			$F2$	
1 · · $a_{1,N+1}^{(1)}$	1 · · $a_{1,N+1}^{(1)}$					1 · $a_{1,N+1}^{(1)}$		
1 · · $a_{1,N+1}^{(1)}$	$a_{21}^{(0)}$ · · $a_{2,N+1}^{(0)}$	$a_{21}^{(0)}$	·	$a_{21}^{(0)} a_{1,N+1}^{(1)}$	0	· $a_{2,N+1}^{(1)}$		
1 · · $a_{1,N+1}^{(1)}$	$a_{31}^{(0)}$ · · $a_{3,N+1}^{(0)}$	$a_{31}^{(0)}$	·	$a_{31}^{(0)} a_{1,N+1}^{(1)}$	0	· $a_{3,N+1}^{(1)}$		
⋮	⋮	⋮	⋮	⋮	⋮	⋮		
1 · · $a_{1,N+1}^{(1)}$	$a_{N1}^{(0)}$ · · $a_{N,N+1}^{(0)}$	$a_{N1}^{(0)}$	·	$a_{N1}^{(0)} a_{1,N+1}^{(1)}$	0	· $a_{N,N+1}^{(1)}$		

Reserve space in associative memory for fields $F1$ and $F2$ both of dimension N with word width n, and for fields $F3$ and $F4$ also of dimension N but with word of width $2n$. Begin by loading the 1st column vector $\bar{a}_1$ into field $F1$. Into field $F2$ each unfinished column of the evolving matrix $\mathbf{A}^i$ will be loaded successively. In $F3$, using the mask m_1, the coefficient $a_{1,N+1}^{(1)}$ is computed and then copied into all elements of $F3$. Then, using the mask m_1^*, the components of fields $F1$ and $F3$ are multiplied in parallel and then this product is subtracted from $F2$ also in parallel. In field $F2$, the columns of the final triangular system are denoted $\bar{z}_j$, $j = 1, 2, ..., N + 1$, and computed in increasing order. The computation of other elements is done in the same way. This is caused by the masks m_i and m_i^* selecting the next column for each i. Upon completion the elimination process the components of the column vectors $\bar{z}_i$, $i = 1, 2, ..., N + 1$, will be stored in external memory. These correspond to columns of the system (37). The algorithm for the associative computer is as follows

    for $i = 1, 2, ..., N$
        begin SET m_i, m_i^* ;

$F1 \leftarrow \bar{z}_i$; (read in from P)
for $j = i, \ldots, N+1$
  begin $F2 \leftarrow \bar{z}_j$;
    $F3 \leftarrow F2/F1\,(m_i)$; (computation of $a_{ij}^{(i)}$)
    $F2 \leftarrow F3\,(m_i)$;
    $F3 \leftarrow ((F3)_i, (F3)_i, \ldots, (F3)_i)$; (copy $a_{ij}^{(i)}$ into all $F3$)
    $F4 \leftarrow F1 \cdot F3\,(m_i^*)$;
    $F2 \leftarrow F2 - F4$; (calculation of $\bar{z}_j$)
    $P \leftarrow F2$; (store new column $\bar{z}_j$ into P)
  end
end.

At the ith step, the eliminations over $N - i + 2$ vectors are performed, hence the computational complexity for this procedure is $O(N^2 n^2)$.

Table 4 shows the computation for two first steps of the back substitution.

Table 4

$F1$	m_i	$F2$	$F3$	$F4$
$a_{1,N+1}^{(1)}$	0	x_N	$a_{1N}^{(1)}$	$a_{1N}^{(1)} x_N$
$a_{2,N+1}^{(2)}$	0	x_N	$a_{2N}^{(2)}$	$a_{2N}^{(2)} x_N$
$\vdots$	$\vdots$	$\vdots$	$\vdots$	$\vdots$
$a_{N-1,N+1}^{(N-1)}$	0	x_N	$a_{N-1,N}^{(N-1)}$	$a_{N-1,N}^{(N-1)} x_N$
$a_{N,N+1}^{(N)}$	1	x_N	1	x_N
$d_1^{(1)}$	0	x_{N-1}	$a_{1,N-1}^{(1)}$	$a_{1,N-1}^{(1)} x_{N-1}$
$d_2^{(1)}$	0	x_{N-1}	$a_{2,N-1}^{(2)}$	$a_{2,N-1}^{(2)} x_{N-1}$
$\vdots$	$\vdots$	$\vdots$		
			$a_{N-2,N-1}^{(N-2)}$	$a_{N-2,N-1}^{(N-2)} x_{N-1}$
$d_{N-1}^{(1)}$	1	x_{N-1}	1	x_{N-1}
0	0	x_N	0	0

From the vector $\bar{z}_{N+1} = (a_{i,N+1}^{(N)})$, $i = 1, 2, \ldots, N$, into the array $F2$ using the mask m_N, the value $a_{N,N+1}^{(N)} = x_N$ is selected. The x_N is then copied into all words of $F2$. Into $F3$, $\bar{z}_N$ is read in, and in $F4$ the product of $F1$ with $F3$ is stored. This product is then subtracted from $F1$ yielding the values $d_i^{(1)}$, $i = 1, 2, \ldots, N-1$. Here, $d_{N-1}^{(1)} = x_{N-1} x_{N-1}$ is moved with mask m_{N-1} into the $(N-1)$st word of $F2$. Computation of the second step is performed with x_{N-1} stored in all words of $F2$ except the last one. This procedure for back solving the triangular system (37) can be formulated into the following algorithm

$F1 \leftarrow \bar{z}_{N+1}$;
for $i = N, N-1, ..., 2$
begin SET m_i;
$\quad F2 \leftarrow F1(m_i)$; (move x_i from $F1$ into $F2$)
$\quad$ **for** $j = i-1, ..., 1$
$\quad (F2)_j \leftarrow (F2)_i$; (locating of x)
$\quad F3 \leftarrow \bar{z}_i$; (read the ith column)
$\quad F4 \leftarrow F2 \cdot F3$;
$\quad F1 \leftarrow F1 - F4$; (calculation of $d_j^{(j)}, j = N-i, ..., 1$)
end.
$F2 \leftarrow F1(m_1)$.

The computational complexity of the above algorithm is $O(Nn^2)$, since there are N steps, and in each of these steps, there are $O(n^2)$ multiplications of n-bit vectors [11].

In the Jordan method, contrasted with the Gaussian procedure, the ith step coefficients of the ith column are also eliminated. This is like combining the back substitution algorithm with the Gaussian method. In the ith step, the Gaussian algorithm given previously is changed for the loop with index k because all rows, except the ith one, are calculated. The results are represented directly by the values $x_i = a_{i, N+1}^{(N)}$, $i = 1, 2, ..., N$. The advantage of this method is that no separate back substitution algorithm is needed.

For the Jordan method an algorithm will be formulated which requires at least $N(N+1)$ memory words. The results of the computation of the first two reduction steps are given in the left or right parts of arrays $F1$ and $F2$ (n-bit), and $F3$ and $F4$ ($2n$-bit), in Table 5.

The program begins by reading the coefficients of the linear system into array $F1$. By copying each coefficient $a_{i1}^{(0)}$ ($N+1$) times into the corresponding block of $F2$, the $F2$ array is set up. With mask M_1, the ratio $F1/F2$ will be generated and stored in $F3_1$. This calculates the values $(1, a_{12}^{(1)}, ..., a_{1N}^{(1)})$ of the first reduced matrix $\mathbf{A}^{(1)}$. Further on, the values of block $F3_1$ are copied into all other blocks of $F3$. According to the mask M_1, the product $F2F3$ is calculated and stored into $F1$, the difference $F1 - F4$ is stored into $F3$. Since both these operations were made with mask M_1 in array $F3$, the first block vector has not been changed. In the other blocks the coefficients $a_{ij}^{(1)}$, $i = j = 2, 3, ..., N$, were calculated. Thus, the coefficients of the off-diagonal elements of the first column were reduced to zero.

By moving the field $F3$ into $F1$, the computation of the second iteration with masks M_2 and $\bar{M}_2$ can proceed as above.

Table 5

	F1	M_i	F2	F3	$\bar{M}_i$	F4	F3
$a_{11}^{(0)}$	1	1	$a_{11}^{(0)}$	1	0	0	0
$a_{12}^{(0)}$	$a_{12}^{(1)}$	1	$a_{11}^{(0)}$	$a_{12}^{(1)}$	0	$a_{12}^{(1)}$	0
...	...	...	...	...	...	...	$a_{13}^{(2)}$
$a_{1,N+1}^{(0)}$	$a_{1,N+1}^{(1)}$	1	$a_{11}^{(0)}$	$a_{1,N+1}^{(1)}$	0	$a_{12}^{(1)} a_{23}^{(2)}$	$a_{1,N+1}^{(2)}$
$a_{21}^{(0)}$	0	0	$a_{21}^{(0)}$	1	1	$a_{21}^{(0)}$	
$a_{22}^{(0)}$	$a_{22}^{(1)}$	0	$a_{21}^{(0)}$	1	1	$a_{21}^{(0)} a_{12}^{(1)}$	0
...	...	...	...	$a_{23}^{(2)}$	...	...	$a_{22}^{(1)}$
$a_{2,N+1}^{(0)}$	$a_{2,N+1}^{(1)}$	0	$a_{21}^{(0)}$	$a_{2,N+1}^{(2)}$	1	$a_{21}^{(0)} a_{1,N+1}^{(1)}$	$a_{2,N+1}^{(1)}$
$a_{31}^{(0)}$	0	0	$a_{31}^{(0)}$	1	1	$a_{31}^{(0)}$	0
$a_{32}^{(0)}$	$a_{32}^{(1)}$	0	$a_{31}^{(0)}$	1	1	$a_{31}^{(0)} a_{12}^{(1)}$	0
...	...	...	...	$a_{23}^{(2)}$	...	$a_{32}^{(1)} a_{23}^{(2)}$	$a_{33}^{(2)}$
$a_{3,N+1}^{(0)}$	$a_{32}^{(1)}$	0	$a_{31}^{(0)}$	$a_{2,N+1}^{(2)}$	1	$a_{31}^{(0)} a_{1,N+1}^{(1)}$	$a_{3,N+1}^{(2)}$
...	...	...	...	...	...	...	...
$a_{N-1,1}^{(0)}$	0	0	$a_{N-1,1}^{(0)}$	1	1	$a_{N-1,1}^{(0)}$	0
$a_{N-1,2}^{(0)}$	$a_{N-1,2}^{(1)}$	0	$a_{N-1,1}^{(0)}$	1	1	$a_{N-1,1}^{(0)} a_{12}^{(1)}$	0
...	...	...	...	$a_{23}^{(2)}$	...	$a_{N-1,2}^{(1)} a_{23}^{(2)}$	$a_{N,3}^{(2)}$
$a_{N-1,N+1}^{(0)}$	$a_{N-1,N+1}^{(1)}$	0	$a_{N-1,1}^{(0)}$	$a_{2,N+1}^{(2)}$	1	$a_{N-1,1}^{(0)} a_{1,N+1}^{(1)}$	$a_{N-1,N+1}^{(2)}$
$a_{N1}^{(0)}$	0	0	$a_{N1}^{(0)}$	1	1	$a_{N1}^{(0)}$	0
$a_{N2}^{(0)}$	$a_{N2}^{(1)}$	0	$a_{N1}^{(0)}$	1	1	$a_{N1}^{(0)} a_{12}^{(1)}$	0
...	...	...	...	$a_{23}^{(2)}$	...	$a_{N2}^{(1)} a_{23}^{(2)}$	$a_{N3}^{(2)}$
$a_{N,N+1}^{(0)}$	$a_{N,N+1}^{(1)}$	0	$a_{N1}^{(0)}$	$a_{2,N+1}^{(2)}$	1	$a_{N1}^{(0)} a_{1,N+1}^{(1)}$	$a_{N,N+1}^{(2)}$

The computation procedure is described by the following algorithm

for $j = 1, 2, ..., N$;
    $F1_j \leftarrow a_j$; (read the matrix **A** by rows)
for $i = 1, 2, ..., N$;
begin SET $M_i, \bar{M}_i$;
    for $j = 1, ..., i-1, i+1, ..., N$;
        $F2_j \leftarrow ((F1_j)_i, ..., (F1_j)_i)^T$;
    $F3 \leftarrow F1/F2\,(M_i)$; (computation $a_{ij}^{(i)}, j = 1, 2, ..., N$)
    for $j = 1, ..., i-1, i+1, ..., N$;
        $F3_j \leftarrow F3_i$; (loading of the ith equation)
    $F4 \leftarrow F2 \cdot F3\,(\bar{M}_i)$;
    $F3 \leftarrow F1 - F4\,(\bar{M}_i)$; (computation of $a_{kj}^{(i)}, j, k = 1, 2, ..., N, k \neq i$)
    $F1 \leftarrow F3$;
end.

The output $x_i, i = 1, 2, ..., N$, is in the $(N+1)$st words of array $F1$. Since in each step elimination of all rows is performed in parallel, complexity of this algorithm is $O(Nn^2)$.

If any of the diagonal elements $a_{ii}^{(j)}, i = 1, 2, ..., N$, are zero (or close to zero), the solution cannot be computed by either the Gauss or the Jordan algorithm, or the computation will be unstable. In this case either complete or partial pivoting may stabilize the algorithm. Pivoting means choosing the maximum element (in absolute value) from the whole array or from the ith row or column. The order of the unknowns stays unchanged in the following implementation.

For the Jordan method on the associative computer, we shall show partial pivoting by selecting the pivot element from the columns. This way of pivoting is suitable for the associative computer, since searching for the component vector for the maximum absolute value represents a typical associative operation. For each i, this selection will be made between the ith components of all blocks of an array $F1$. For the given i, this component is stored in block F_j and thus computation of the ith step is done according to the original algorithm with masks M_j and $\bar{M}_j$ instead with M_i and $\bar{M}_i$. Not to change the order of unknowns during the computation, it is necessary to exchange the coefficients of the ith and jth equations stored in blocks $F1_i$ and $F1_j$. Moving words within an associative memory is complicated since only if the two addresses are powers of 2 can the permutation network be used efficiently. Therefore, we avoid moving the blocks of memory, but instead store the changing order of the unknowns into an auxiliary array $F1$ of $\log N$ bits width. In the ith step of the computation with the leading element in the ith row, the value j is recorded into the $(N+1)$st word of block $F1_j$. After terminating the ith computational step, the $(N + 1)$st word of array $F1$ will have the components of the solution vector with indices in the $(N + 1)$st word of array $F1$.

Another possible organization of the computation is to store the system components by columns. But note that, in this way, the computation on the associative computer cannot be simplified, since the ith and jth components must be exchanged in all $N + 1$ blocks of the array $F1$ in order to evidence the change in the order of the unknowns gathered in its $(N + 1)$st block.

Detailed analysis and formulation of the algorithms for the implementation of the Gauss—Jordan method on this computer is presented in [20]. From the above analysis it follows that, for the number of memory moves as well as for the computational speed, the Jordan algorithm is the best choice not only for $N(N + 1)$-word algorithms, but also for the N-word implementations when the coefficients of the system are stored by columns.

2.8.2 Iterative methods of solving the systems of linear equations

For the problems where large sparse systems of linear equations are solved, direct methods are not suitable, since they cannot make use of the advantage following from a large number of zeros occurring in the matrix of the system. In these cases iterative methods are applied, which can be implemented on parallel computers effectively.

First, we shall describe and formulate an algorithm for a solution of the linear systems by stationary iterative methods. Since the iterative methods are frequently used in solving partial differential equations, we shall describe the implementation of approximation formulas for basic elliptic equations. According to the latter, in computation, the same sequence of arithmetic operations over a large number of discretization grid points must be implemented. Therefore, this problem can also be solved by a parallel associative computer. In all these cases, we shall assume that the number of words in associative memory is large enough to store all N^2 input data into one array.

Provided that the initial vector $\boldsymbol{x}$ is given, the stationary one-step methods can be expressed in the form:

$$\boldsymbol{x}^{(k+1)} = \boldsymbol{T}\boldsymbol{x}^{(k)} + \boldsymbol{w}, \qquad k = 0, 1, 2, \ldots, \tag{38}$$

where $\boldsymbol{T} = (t_{ij})$ is a matrix of degree N. Computation of (38) is terminated when for a given norm $\|\cdot\|$ the criterion

$$\|\boldsymbol{x}^{(k+1)} - \boldsymbol{x}^{(k)}\| < \varepsilon \tag{39}$$

is satisfied. On execution of computation of (34) a multiplication of a matrix with a vector has to be executed in each iteration, as well as the sum of two vectors and a comparison (39).

In the proposed procedure the computation of odd iterations will differ from that of even ones. Computation of odd or even iterations will be demonstrated on computation of vectors $\mathbf{x}^{(1)}$ and $\mathbf{x}^{(2)}$, respectively.

On starting the computation, the coefficients of matrix $\mathbf{T}$ are loaded into fields $F1$ and $F2$ of the associative memory (Table 6), and, similarly, values of

Table 6

$F1$	$F2$	$F3$	$F4$	$F5$		$F6$		$F7$	
t_{11}	t_{11}	w_1	w_1	$x_1^{(0)}$	$x_1^{(1)}$	$t_{11}x_1^{(0)}$	$t_{11}x_1^{(1)}$	$x_1^{(1)}$	$x_1^{(2)}$
t_{21}	t_{12}	w_2	w_1	$x_1^{(0)}$	$x_2^{(1)}$	$t_{21}x_1^{(0)}$	$t_{12}x_2^{(1)}$	$x_2^{(1)}$	$x_1^{(2)}$
$\vdots$	$\vdots$	$\vdots$	$\vdots$	$\vdots$	$\vdots$	$\vdots$	$\vdots$	$\vdots$	$\vdots$
t_{N1}	t_{1N}	w_N	w_1	$x_1^{(0)}$	$x_N^{(1)}$	$t_{N1}x_1^{(0)}$	$t_{1N}x_N^{(1)}$	$x_N^{(1)}$	$x_1^{(2)}$
t_{12}	t_{21}	w_1	w_2	$x_2^{(0)}$	$x_1^{(1)}$	$t_{12}x_2^{(0)}$	$t_{21}x_1^{(1)}$	$x_1^{(1)}$	$x_2^{(2)}$
t_{22}	t_{22}	w_2	w_2	$x_2^{(0)}$	$x_2^{(1)}$	$t_{22}x_2^{(0)}$	$t_{22}x_2^{(1)}$	$x_2^{(1)}$	$x_2^{(2)}$
$\vdots$	$\vdots$	$\vdots$	$\vdots$	$\vdots$	$\vdots$	$\vdots$	$\vdots$	$\vdots$	$\vdots$
t_{N2}	t_{2N}	w_N	w_2	$x_2^{(0)}$	$x_N^{(1)}$	$t_{N2}x_2^{(0)}$	$t_{2N}x_N^{(1)}$	$x_N^{(1)}$	$x_2^{(2)}$
$\vdots$	$\vdots$	$\vdots$	$\vdots$	$\vdots$	$\vdots$	$\vdots$	$\vdots$	$\vdots$	$\vdots$
t_{1N}	t_{N1}	w_1	w_N	$x_N^{(0)}$	$x_1^{(1)}$	$t_{1N}x_N^{(0)}$	$t_{N1}x_1^{(1)}$	$x_1^{(1)}$	$x_N^{(2)}$
t_{2N}	t_{N2}	w_2	w_N	$x_N^{(0)}$	$x_2^{(1)}$	$t_{2N}x_N^{(0)}$	$t_{N2}x_2^{(1)}$	$x_2^{(1)}$	$x_N^{(2)}$
$\vdots$	$\vdots$	$\vdots$	$\vdots$	$\vdots$	$\vdots$	$\vdots$	$\vdots$	$\vdots$	$\vdots$
t_{NN}	t_{NN}	w_N	w_N	$x_N^{(0)}$	$x_N^{(1)}$	$t_{NN}x_N^{(0)}$	$t_{NN}x_N^{(1)}$	$x_N^{(1)}$	$x_N^{(2)}$

the vector $\mathbf{w}$ are loaded into fields $F3$ and $F4$. Prior to starting the iterative process, the components $x_j^{(0)}$, $j = 1, 2, ..., N$, are loaded into each word of the jth block of field $F5$. The product of fields $F1$ and $F5$ will be stored in $F6$. Its components are summed in such a way that in the ith word ($i = 1, 2, ..., N$) of each block of this field, the result of the summation over all the ith components is stored. This can be done in $\log N$ steps by means of successive flipping of the components of the field $F6$. The summation of the first two components of a four-block field is illustrated in Fig. 34, where $a = \sum_{i=1}^{4} a_i$, $b = \sum_{i=1}^{4} b_i$. Upon adding the field $F3$ to the result, the vector of the first iteration is obtained in each block of the field $F7$. By testing (39), it is necessary to compare the values of the first iteration with initial values. Since the location of the components of vectors $\mathbf{x}^{(0)}$ and $\mathbf{x}^{(1)}$ in fields $F5$ and $F7$ is different, this comparison is done according to the mask $\tilde{M}$ which has 1 in the positions of the corresponding values of both iterations. The second iteration starts with the computation of the product of fields $F5$ and $F2$, resulting in $F6$. Summation of its components is done only within separate blocks — that means, in each word of the given block the sum of its components is generated. In each block, this summation is executed in parallel, so that all the corresponding values are obtained in $\log N$ steps. $F4$ is added to the resulting sum in field $F7$ and thus, the values of the second iteration are obtained and distributed in such a way that in the jth block each word is occupied by $x_j^{(2)}$. According to the mask $\tilde{M}$, the relationship (39) is tested again, and in the case that it is not satisfied, $F3$ is moved into $F5$, so the third iteration may follow.

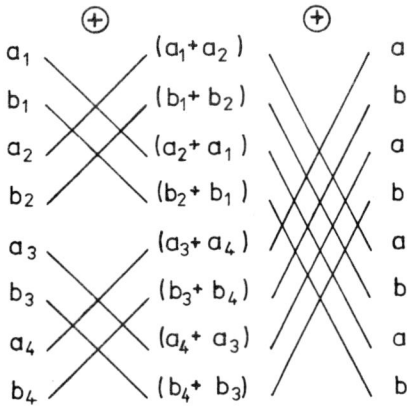

Fig. 34. Parallel addition of four two-component arrays.

This method can be expressed in the form of an algorithm as follows

for $j = 1, 2, \ldots, N$
begin
    $F1_j \leftarrow (t_{1j}, t_{2j}, \ldots, t_{Nj})^T$; (loading **T** into $F1$ by columns)
    $F2_j \leftarrow (t_{j1}, t_{j2}, \ldots, t_{jN})^T$; (loading **T** into $F2$ by rows)
    $F3_j \leftarrow (w_1, w_2, \ldots, w_N)^T$; (loading **w** into blocks of $F3$)
    $F4_j \leftarrow (w_j, w_j, \ldots, w_j)^T$; (loading the components of **w**)
    $F5_j \leftarrow (x_j^{(0)}, x_j^{(0)}, \ldots, x_j^{(0)})^T$; (loading the components of $\boldsymbol{x}^{(0)}$ into blocks of $F5$)
end;
I: $F6 \leftarrow F5 \cdot F1$;
    $j = 1, 2, \ldots, N$;
    for $r = 1, 2, \ldots, N$
        $(F7_j)_r \leftarrow \sum_{r=1}^{N} (F6_r)_j$; (addition for odd iterations)

$F7 \leftarrow F7 + F3$;
if $\|F7 - F5\|(\tilde{M}) < \varepsilon$, **go to** K;
$F5 \leftarrow F7$;
$F6 \leftarrow F5 \cdot F2$;
    for $j = 1, 2, ..., N$
        for $r = 1, 2, ..., N$
            $(F7_j)_r \leftarrow \sum_{r=1}^{N} (F6_j)_r$; (addition for even iterations)
$F7 \leftarrow F7 + F4$;
    if $\|F7 - F5\|(\tilde{M}) > \varepsilon$, **go to** I;
K: **end**.

The difference between the procedure given in [9] and the algorithm proposed rests in the execution of the summation phases. In the first case, the addition in each iteration is done within individual blocks with the use of a log sum algorithm and the result is stored in the first word of the corresponding block. In order to locate the new iteration values in each block of the corresponding memory array, they have to be concentrated from the first words of the individual blocks into the first block and then this has to be spread over all the other blocks of the given array. Such data operations require $2 \log N$ transfer steps. In the proposed algorithms, any additional operations have been avoided successfully by introducing two more memory fields ($F1$, $F3$).

On numerical solution of partial differential equations, the computation of an iteration value in one grid point, according to the approximation relationship, requires only constant number of arithmetic steps. Since the prescribed operations are executed simultaneously for a large number of points, they are suitable for parallel processing.

The implementation of a five-point difference relationship

$$u_{ij} = (u_{i-1,j} + u_{i+1,j} + u_{i,j+1} + u_{i,j-1})/4$$

for the solution of the Laplace equation on a square for an associative computer is described in [9].

The computational diagram is based on a chessboard, i.e. black-and-white arrangement of points in the region. Since the points in white points (W_i) depend only on the black points (B_i) and vice versa, the computation of all the points of the same colour can be executed in parallel. In an associative memory, the values of the points of the same colour will be located in a separate array and the values of two neighbouring points will be stored in the same word. The location of the points W_i and B_i in the ith memory word depends on the numbering of the grid points. In the case of N interior points, this can be done as shown in Fig. 35, where k is the number of pairs of the points in one grid row. The computation of W_i depends on B_i, B_{i+1}, B_{i-k}, B_{i+k+1}, and that of B_i, on W_i, W_{i-1}, W_{i-k-1} and W_{i+k}, i.e. the computation of the values in the ith memory word depends on the values in the words $i - k - 1, i - k, i + 1, i + k, i + k + 1$, that can be moved to the position in place of the ith word.

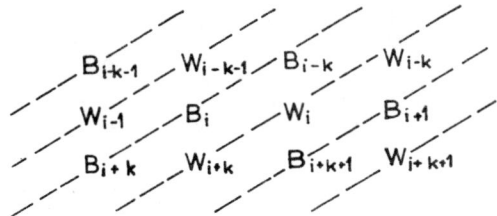

Fig. 35. Chessmate arrangement of network points.

The above procedure cannot be used for the solution of equations with mixed derivatives, or, in the case when they are approximated by higher-order differences. In these cases, so-called multicolour methods are used. For example, a diagram of parallel implementation of the difference relationship

$$u_{ij} = (u_{i+1,j} + u_{i-1,j} + u_{i,j+1} + u_{i,j-1} + (a/4)(u_{i+1,j+1} - u_{i-1,j+1} + u_{i-1,j-1} + u_{i+1,j-1}))/4 \qquad (40)$$

for the differential equation

$$u_{xx} + au_{xy} + u_{yy} = 0$$

on the unit square is proposed in [1]. The computation of one point depends on the values of the eight nearest neighbours. For this equation, the distribution of grid points in four colours (white, black, green, rose) can be proposed in the following way (Fig. 36).

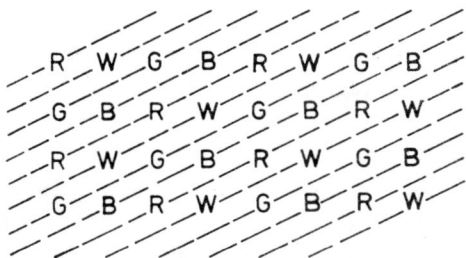

Fig. 36. Arrangement of network points into a diagram according to four colours.

The points of one colour can be calculated simultaneously according to (40) since they only depend on the points of the rest of colours. So, N^2 interior grid points can be divided into four disjoint sets and their corresponding iterative values can be stored in four arrays of an associative memory. Numbering of individual quadruples (W, B, G, R) is as follows

$$\begin{array}{ccc} (i-k-1) & & (i-k) \\ (i-1) & (i) & (i+1). \\ (i+k) & & (i+k+1) \end{array}$$

The number of quadruples of the points in the same row is k. The notation of the corresponding quadruple is given by the number of this word in the associative memory where its values are stored. For individual points of the ith quadruple, the following dependence on the points of the neighbouring quadruples can be determined

$$R_i: (W_i, W_{i+k}, W_{i-k-1}, G_{i-k-1}, G_{i+k}, G_{i-1}, B_{i-k-1}, B_{i+k}),$$
$$W_i: (R_{i+k+1}, R_{i-k}, R_i, B_i, B_{i+k}, B_{i-k-1}, G_{i+k}, G_{i-k-1}),$$
$$G_i: (W_{i+1}, W_{i+k+1}, R_{i-k}, R_{i+k+1}, B_{i-k}, B_i, B_{i+k+1}),$$
$$B_i; (W_i, W_{i-k}, W_{i+k+1}, G_{i-k}, G_{i+k+1}, G_i, R_{i+1}, R_{i-k}).$$

Using the above relationships, in the vector computation of all points of a given colour, the corresponding values of the arrays with points of neighbouring colours have to be moved accordingly. The number of these shifts is larger than that for a two-colour scheme, but it can be implemented on an associative computer.

As mentioned in [1], the majority of problems that lead to systems with 10^4 unknowns can be solved by the help of six colours. Using m colours, the number of necessary words in an associative memory, where the values are stored in m arrays according to individual colours, decreases m times approximately. Since, for every set of points, the computation is done using Jacobi's method, the computational complexity of one iteration is proportional to the complexity valid for Jacobi's method.

Consequently, we may say that the associative computer is a device that is suitable for iterative solving of a system of linear equations. From the viewpoint of its computational complexity, the computation of one iteration, according to the method (38) with a full matrix, requires $O(N^2)$ operations on a serial computer, while when implemented over N memory words, this complexity is $O(\log N)$. For sparse systems with N^2 unknowns the complexity of serial computation of one iteration is $O(N^2)$. For N^2-word implementation on an associative computer, it yields only $O(1)$.

2.8.3 Computation of matrix inversion

For an associative computer, the Gauss—Jordan method with storing the matrix by rows, has been chosen. Using this procedure, the organization of an AMM as well as the properties of PN can be assumed.

Since, $\mathbf{A}^{-1}\mathbf{A} = \mathbf{I}$, the unit matrix can be transformed into $\mathbf{A}^{-1}$ by using the same elementary operations as those for transforming $\mathbf{A}$ into $\mathbf{I}$. The computation of $\mathbf{A}^{-1}$ is executed in N steps of the Gauss—Jordan elimination. If the ith step of this elimination corresponds to multiplying $\mathbf{A}$ by the transformation matrix $\mathbf{B}_i$, $i = 1, 2, ..., N$, from the left, then from the original matrix $[\mathbf{A}, \mathbf{I}]$ of dimension $N \times 2N$ the matrices $[\mathbf{B}_1\mathbf{A}, \mathbf{B}_1\mathbf{I}]$, $[\mathbf{B}_2\mathbf{B}_1\mathbf{A}, \mathbf{B}_2\mathbf{B}_1\mathbf{I}]$, ..., $[\mathbf{B}_N\mathbf{B}_{N-1}, ..., \mathbf{B}_1\mathbf{A}, \mathbf{B}_N\mathbf{B}_{N-1}, ..., \mathbf{B}_1\mathbf{I}]$ are obtained successively. Thus, since $\mathbf{B}_N\mathbf{B}_{N-1}, ..., \mathbf{B}_1\mathbf{A} = \mathbf{I}$ and $\mathbf{B}_N\mathbf{B}_{N-1}, ..., \mathbf{B}_1\mathbf{I} = \mathbf{A}^{-1}$ the sought inverse matrix is obtained.

In the algorithm, the pivot element $a_{pq}^{(i-1)}$, its replacing by one and replacing of other values of the leading column by zeros is performed for each $i = 1, 2, ..., N$.

Next, the values $a_{pr}^{(i)} = a_{pr}^{(i-1)}/a_{pq}^{(i-1)}$ of the pivot row will be computed and elimination of other values of the matrix, according to $a_{kr}^{(i)} = a_{kr}^{(i-1)} - a_{kq}^{(i-1)}a_{pr}^{(i)}$, $k = 1, 2, ..., N$, $k \neq p$, will be done. If in computation $p \neq q$, then the order of rows and columns is changed, i.e. the pth row of the resulting matrix is occupied by the qth row of $\mathbf{A}^{-1}$, and its qth column, by its pth column. That is why it is necessary to secure remembering of the changed order of the elements of the inverse matrix and denote the elements among which further selection need not be done. The matrix $\mathbf{A}$ will be stored by rows in array $F1$.

To make better use of the properties of PN, we suppose that each row is completed by zeros up to the nearest power of $2^{\tilde{n}}$, i.e. $2^{\tilde{n}-1} < N \leq 2^{\tilde{n}}$. Also, the number of blocks will be filled into $2^{\tilde{n}}$ by zero blocks. The coordinates of elements of the systems will be stored in arrays R (rows) and S (columns), starting with 0 through $2^{\tilde{n}} - 1$. In the array PI, those elements will be denoted by 1, over which the selection of the pivot element is to be done. For the pivot, at position (p, q), the mask M will have 1 in all the words of the pth block. In the mask $\bar{M}$, qth positions of all blocks will be occupied by 1.

The algorithm can be formulated as follows

for $i = 1, 2, ..., 2^{\tilde{n}}$
    $(S)_i \leftarrow (0, 1, ..., 2^{\tilde{n}} - 1)$;
    $(R)_i \leftarrow \underbrace{(i - 1, i - 1, ..., i - 1)}_{2^{\tilde{n}}}$,

$PI \leftarrow 0$; $F1 \leftarrow 0$;
for $i = 1, 2, ..., N$

2.8 Linear algebra examples on SIMD-type computer

$$(F1)_i \leftarrow (a_{i1}^{(0)}, \ldots, a_{iN}^{(0)}, \underbrace{0, \ldots, 0}_{2^{\tilde{n}} - N});$$

(load A)

$$(PI)_i \leftarrow (1, \underbrace{1, \ldots, 1}_{N}, 0, \underbrace{0, \ldots, 0}_{2^{\tilde{n}} - N});$$

for $i = 1, 2, \ldots, N$
begin $Y \leftarrow \max |F1|(PI);$
 $M \leftarrow 0; \bar{M} \leftarrow 0$ (selection of the leading element)
 $C1 \leftarrow R(Y);$
 $C2 \leftarrow S(Y);$
 $M \leftarrow$ compare $R[C1];$ (generating M)
 $\bar{M} \leftarrow$ compare $S[C2];$ (generating $\bar{M}$)
 $R \leftarrow$ spread $C2(M);$
 $S \leftarrow$ spread $C1(\bar{M});$ (spreading of the row and column index)
 $F2 \leftarrow 0;$
 $F2 \leftarrow F1(\bar{M});$
 for $j = 0, 1, \ldots, \tilde{n} - 1$
  $F2 \leftarrow F2 + F2\,(2^j, 2^{j+1});$
 $F1 \leftarrow 0;$
 $F3 \leftarrow F1/F2(M)$ (computation of the leading element)
 for $j = 0, 1, \ldots, \tilde{n} - 1$
  $F3 \leftarrow F3 + F3\,(2^{\tilde{n}+j}, 2^{\tilde{n}+j+1})$
 $F4 \leftarrow F2 \cdot F3;$
 $F1 \leftarrow F1 - F4;$
 $F1 \leftarrow F3(M);$ (elimination phase)
 $PI \leftarrow PI - (M \vee \bar{M});$
end.

Masks M and $\bar{M}$ are generated by comparing the arrays R or S with the content of the segments $C1$ or $C2$ of the register C. (In $C1$ or $C2$ the value of the row or column index of the pivot element is stored.) By successive spreading of $C1$ (according to $\bar{M}$) and $C2$ (according to M) over S, or R, the new permuted order of row and column indices is defined. Then, into each block $F2$ there get the values stored in the corresponding blocks of the array $F1$ in the qth position. In place of the pivot element 1 is stored and in the remaining blocks 0 is stored in place of qth words. The pivot row (with inverse value of the pivot element) is spread over all the blocks of array $F3$. On computation of the ith elimination step, also the back transfer of the pivot row is performed. The relevant elements for the $(i + 1)$st step are denoted by 1 in PI.

Parallel arithmetic computational complexity of the algorithm is $O(N)$. The number of transfers in each execution phase is $2n$, and thus the transport complexity of the algorithm is $O(N \log N)$.

2.8.4 Calculation of eigenvalues of a symmetric matrix

Eigenvalue problems can be implemented using the Jacobi-like algorithms. The Jacobi method for a real symmetric matrix $\mathbf{A}$ of order N generates a sequence of rotation matrices $\mathbf{Q}^{(p)}$, $p = 1, 2, \ldots$ with non-zero elements $q_{ii}^{(p)} = q_{jj}^{(p)} = c_{ij}$, $q_{ij}^{(p)} = s_{ij}$, $q_{ji}^{(p)} = -s_{ij}$ which annihilate the off-diagonal elements $a_{ij}^{(p)}$, $a_{ji}^{(p)}$ ($i < j$) of a matrix $\mathbf{A}^{(p)}$ by constructing

$$\mathbf{A}^{(p+1)} = [\mathbf{Q}^{(p)}]^T \mathbf{A}^{(p)} \mathbf{Q}^{(p)} \tag{41}$$

with $\mathbf{A}^{(1)} = \mathbf{A}$. The rotation coefficients c_{ij} and s_{ij} are computed for given i, j as proposed in [14]:

$$x_{ij} = \frac{(a_{jj}^{(p)} - a_{ii}^{(p)})}{2 a_{ij}^{(p)}}, \tag{42}$$

$$y_{ij} = \frac{\text{sign}(x_{ij})}{(|x_{ij}| + \sqrt{1 + x_{ij}^2})}, \tag{43}$$

$$c_{ij} = \frac{1}{\sqrt{1 + y_{ij}^2}}, \tag{44}$$

$$s_{ij} = y_{ij} c_{ij}. \tag{45}$$

Comparing the matrices $\mathbf{A}^{(p+1)}$ and $\mathbf{A}^{(p)}$, the new values are only in rows and columns i and j. The formulas for the modified values are

$$a_{ii}^{(p+1)} = a_{ii}^{(p)} - y_{ij} a_{ij}^{(p)}, \quad a_{jj}^{(p+1)} = a_{jj}^{(p)} + y_{ij} a_{ij}^{(p)}, \tag{46}$$

$$a_{ij}^{(p+1)} = a_{ji}^{(p+1)} = 0, \tag{47}$$

$$\begin{aligned} a_{iq}^{(p+1)} &= c_{ij} a_{iq}^{(p)} - s_{ij} a_{jq}^{(p)}, \\ a_{jq}^{(p+1)} &= c_{ij} a_{jq}^{(p)} + s_{ij} a_{iq}^{(p)}, \quad q \neq i, j, \end{aligned} \tag{48}$$

$$\begin{aligned} a_{qi}^{(p+1)} &= c_{ij} a_{qi}^{(p)} - s_{ij} a_{qj}^{(p)}, \\ a_{qj}^{(p)} &= c_{ij} a_{qj}^{(p)} + s_{ij} a_{qi}^{(p)}, \quad q \neq i, j. \end{aligned} \tag{49}$$

The efficiency of the algorithm depends critically on the ordering that the elements are annihilated. One of the schemes for sequential computation (scheme PERSEQ) is defined by

$$(i, j) = \{(1, 2), (1, 3), ..., (1, N), (2, 3), ...,$$
$$(2, N), (3, 4), ..., (N - 1, N). \tag{50}$$

The number of iterations (41) in one annihilation cycle is $N(N - 1)/2$ for PERSEQ.

It was found that more than one orthogonalization can be performed in one iteration. Three parallel schemes will be formulated in terms of the operations of the permutation network. For an arbitrary $N = 2^r$, rules for estimating corresponding permutation parameters are given.

To demonstrate how to use these schemes in parallel algorithms for solving real symmetric eigenvalue problem, we have used an example of one iteration for Sameh's scheme. Special features of the algorithms for the two other schemes are also described. In each algorithm, $O(N)$ matrix transpose operations are saved in one orthogonalization cycle because of the efficient performance of rotations (48, 49). Assuming N^2 processors, the number of arithmetic steps is $O(1)$ for each iteration. The total parallel arithmetical complexity for the algorithms developed is $O(N)$. The number of data transports is $O(\log N)$ per iteration.

The results obtained by a simulation of the algorithms developed and their comparison to a sequential process, based on the scheme (50), will also be given.

Now, we shall present three ordering strategies for parallel execution of the orthogonalization process from the point of view of its effective realization on a parallel machine with the capability to perform the following data transfer functions in one instruction:

SHUP $2^k R$, (SHDOWN $2^k R$) — the cyclic shift of the blocks of a field R by 2^k blocks up (down),

shup $2^k P$, (shdown $2^k P$) — the cyclic shift of the elements in each block by 2^k positions up (down),

$P2^k R$, $P2^k R$ — cyclic permutation of the blocks of a field R (of elements within each block of R) where the lth block (lth element in each block) is stored in place of the mth block (element), where $m = (l + 2^k) \bmod N$.

The goal is to achieve exactly one rotation of each row and column in one iteration. The first scheme was developed by Sameh in [15]. The illustration for

Table 7

k	0	1	2	3	4	5	6	7	0
1	1	1 2	1 4	1 6	1 8	1 3	1 7	1 5	1
2	2	2 1	4 1	6 1	8 1	2 4	2 8	2 6	2
3	3	3 4	3 6	3 8	3 2	3 1	7 1	3 7	3
4	4	4 3	6 3	8 3	2 3	4 2	8 2	4 8	4
5	5	5 6	5 8	5 2	5 4	5 7	5 3	5 1	5
6	6	6 5	8 5	2 5	4 5	6 8	6 4	6 2	6
7	7	7 8	7 2	7 4	7 6	7 5	3 5	7 3	7
8	8	8 7	2 7	4 7	6 7	8 6	4 6	8 4	8
		$P2^0$	$P2^0$	$P2^0$	$P2^0$	$P2^1$	$P2^1$	$P2^2$	
		$SHUP2^0$	$SHUP2^0$	$SHUP2^0$	$SHUP2^0$	$SHUP2^1$	$SHUP2^1$	$SHUP2^2$	

$N = 8$ is given in Table 7. The respective row index i and column index j of elements $a_{ij}^{(k)}$, $a_{ji}^{(k)}$ annihilated in the kth iteration, $k = 1, 2, ..., N - 1$, are represented for a corresponding k by the left and the right column of permuted integers. (Further, instead of $a_{ij}^{(k)}$ only the index pair ij will be used.) According to the permutation functions given below in Table 7, the scheme PERSAM can be defined for an arbitrary $N = 2^r$ by $N - 1$ steps PERSAM$_k$, $k = 1, 2, ..., N - 1$, as follows

$$\text{PERSAM}_k \begin{cases} P2^0 \quad SHUP2^0 & k = 1, 2, ..., N/2, \\ P2^1 \quad SHUP2^1 & k = N/2 + 1, ..., N - N/4, \\ \vdots & \vdots \\ P2^{r-1} SHUP2^{r-1} & k = N - 1. \end{cases} \quad (51)$$

One of the schemes where one annihilation cycle is divided into N iterations was developed by Modi and Pryce. Its form is shown in Table 8.

The numbers in brackets correspond to the elements ij not annihilated in odd

Table 8

k	0	1	2	3	4	5	6	7	8	0
1		2 3	1 3	1 5	3 5	3 7	5 7	5 8	7 8	8
2		3 2	3 1	5 1	5 3	7 3	7 5	8 5	8 7	7
3		4 5	2 5	2 7	1 7	1 8	3 8	3 6	5 6	6
4		5 4	5 2	7 2	7 1	8 1	8 3	6 3	6 5	5
5		6 7	4 7	4 8	2 8	2 6	1 6	1 4	3 4	4
6		7 6	7 4	8 4	8 2	6 2	6 1	4 1	4 3	3
7		[8] 8	6 8	[6] 6	4 6	[4] 4	2 4	[2] 2	1 2	2
8		[1] 1	8 6	[3] 3	6 4	[5] 5	4 2	[7] 7	2 1	1
		TO	TE	TO	TE	TO	TE	TO	TE	

iterations. TO and TE denote transformation strings for odd and even iterations, respectively. The scheme PERMOPRY can be formulated using definitions of TO and TE as follows

$$\text{PREMOPRY}_k \begin{cases} \text{SHUP2}^0 \ P2^0 \ (\text{masked 2 last terms}) \ \text{SHDOWN2}^0 \ (=\text{TO}) \\ \qquad\qquad\qquad\qquad\qquad\qquad\qquad k = 1, 3, \ldots, N-1, \\ \text{SHUP2}^0 \ P2^0 \ \text{SHDOWN2}^0 \quad k = 2, 4, \ldots, N. \end{cases}$$

(52)

Note that after the Nth permutation, the even cycles start with reversed ordering of elements. However, this does not cause any difficulty because the permutations in even cycles can remain as defined.

We have developed a parallel scheme in which only "power of 2 permutations" $P2^r$ and $p2^r$ occur.

The diagram for $N = 8$ is shown in Table 9. The formulation for $N = 2^r$ is

$$\text{PERORD}_k \begin{cases} P2^0 & k = 1, 3, 5, \ldots, N-1, \\ P2^1 & k = 2, 6, \ldots, N-2, \\ \vdots & \\ P2^r & k = N/2. \end{cases}$$

(53)

As seen, the column index j of annihilated elements is permuted whereby the row index i remains without any change.

Table 9

k	0	1	2	3	4	5	6	7	0
1	1 2	1 4	1 3	1 7	1 8	1 6	1 5	1	
2	2 1	2 3	2 4	2 8	2 7	2 5	2 6	2	
3	3 4	3 2	3 1	3 5	3 6	3 8	3 7	3	
4	4 3	4 1	4 2	4 6	4 5	4 7	4 8	4	
5	5 6	5 8	5 7	5 3	5 4	5 2	5 1	5	
6	6 5	6 7	6 8	6 4	6 3	6 1	6 2	6	
7	7 8	7 6	7 5	7 1	7 2	7 4	7 3	7	
8	8 7	8 5	8 6	8 2	8 1	8 3	8 4	8	
	$P2^0$	$P2^1$	$P2^0$	$P2^2$	$P2^0$	$P2^1$	$P2^0$	$P2^2$	

The aim of the parallel associative algorithms based on the above three schemes is to perform all arithmetic operations required by the process (42)—(49) on vectors in parallel. Therefore, the matrix **A** that is to be orthogonalized will be located by rows in the associative memory. Also the data transfers needed in one iteration will be minimized.

The programming structures of these algorithms are essentially similar. Each iteration consists of the following parts which can be computed in parallel:
— permutation of elements for a given iteration according to corresponding step of a given permutation scheme,
— evaluation of c_{ij} and $\pm s_{ij}$ values for given pairs ij,
— orthogonal transformation on rows,
— orthogonal transformation on columns.

For simplicity of explanation, the evaluation of one iteration will be shown on the second iteration for the scheme PERSAM. Then, assuming $N = 4$, elements ij, ji for $i = 1, 3$ and $j = 2, 4$ are annihilated. As a result of the previous iteration, the matrix elements are ordered in field A of the memory (see Table 10) according to the first step of PERSAM.

As given by PERSAM$_2$, elements of the field A are shifted: $A \leftarrow \text{shup}2^0 A$, $A \leftarrow \text{SHUP}2^0 A$ (Table 10). Elements ii, $i = 1, 2, \ldots, 4$, are obtained in field D by $D \leftarrow A(M)$ where M is a mask with 1's in positions ii. The blocks of A and M are then permuted with the factor 2^0, which corresponds to the second step of PERSAM. The results $B \leftarrow P2^0 A$, $MB \leftarrow P2^0 M$ are shown in Table 10. From B, one can obtain in fields E and F elements ij and jj ($i = 1, 3, j = 2, 4$) by $E \leftarrow B(M)$ and $F \leftarrow B(MB)$, respectively. In order to get the non-zero elements of F in positions that correspond to the non-zero elements of fields D and E (Table 10), the field F has to be permuted within blocks by the factor 2^0 assigned to the step PERSAM$_2$, i.e. $F \leftarrow p2^0 F$. The operation $X \leftarrow (F - D)/2 * E$ on fields D, E, F gives respective values x_{ij} and $-x_{ij}$ in those positions in X, where elements jj and ii are stored in A. Hence, according to (43), the values of $\pm y_{ij}$ are obtained in the same positions in a field Y. Performing functions prescribed by (44) on vectors, we get the values c_{ij} in a field C in positions of $\pm y_{ij}$. The values s_{ij} and $-s_{ij}$ are obtained in a field S in positions of y_{ij} and $-y_{ij}$, respectively (Table 10).

The transformation (46) of diagonal elements (marked by $\bigcirc$) is computed by $A \leftarrow D - Y * E(M)$. The annihilations (47) in A are done with mask MB as $A \leftarrow O(MB)$, where O is a zero vector. In order to parallelly transform the rows of A by (48), i.e. to compute the matrix product

$$\begin{bmatrix} c_{14} & 0 & 0 & -s_{14} \\ 0 & c_{23} & -s_{23} & 0 \\ 0 & s_{23} & c_{23} & 0 \\ s_{14} & 0 & 0 & c_{14} \end{bmatrix} \begin{bmatrix} \text{⑪} & 12 & 13 & 0 \\ 21 & \text{㉒} & 0 & 24 \\ 31 & 0 & \text{㉝} & 34 \\ 0 & 42 & 43 & \text{㊹} \end{bmatrix} = \begin{bmatrix} \text{⑪} & 12' & 13' & 0 \\ 21' & \text{㉒} & 0 & 24' \\ 31' & 0 & \text{㉝} & 34' \\ 0 & 42' & 43' & \text{㊹} \end{bmatrix} =$$

$$= \begin{bmatrix} \text{⑪} & c_{14}12 - s_{14}42 & c_{14}13 - s_{14}43 & 0 \\ c_{23}21 - s_{23}31 & \text{㉒} & 0 & c_{23}24 - s_{23}34 \\ c_{23}31 + s_{23}21 & 0 & \text{㉝} & c_{23}34 + s_{23}24 \\ 0 & c_{14}42 + s_{14}12 & c_{14}43 + s_{14}13 & \text{㊹} \end{bmatrix}, \quad (54)$$

Table 10

1st iter.									2nd iteration													3rd iter.
A	A	M	D	B	MB	E	F	F	X	Y	C	S	A	CR	SR	MC	A	B	A	CC	SC	A	A
22	11	1	11	41			41	44	x_{14}	y_{14}	c_{14}	s_{14}	11	c_{14}	s_{14}	0	11	0	44	c_{14}	s_{14}	44	11
21	14			44	1		44						0	c_{14}	s_{14}	0	0	44	0	c_{14}	$-s_{14}$	0	12
24	13			43									13	c_{14}	s_{14}	1	13	43'	42'	c_{23}	$-s_{23}$	42	13
23	12			42									12	c_{14}	s_{14}	1	12	42'	43'	c_{23}	s_{23}	43	14
12	41		44	11	1			11	$-x_{14}$	$-y_{14}$	c_{14}	$-s_{14}$	0	c_{14}	$-s_{14}$	0	0	11	0	c_{14}	s_{14}	0	21
11	44	1		14		14							44	c_{14}	$-s_{14}$	0	44	0	11	c_{14}	$-s_{14}$	11	22
14	43			13									43	c_{14}	$-s_{14}$	1	43	13'	12'	c_{23}	$-s_{23}$	12	23
13	42			12									42	c_{14}	$-s_{14}$	1	42	12'	13'	c_{23}	s_{23}	13	24
42	31			21				22	$-x_{23}$	$-y_{23}$	c_{23}	$-s_{23}$	31	c_{23}	$-s_{23}$	1	31	21'	24'	c_{14}	s_{14}	24	31
41	34			24		23							34	c_{23}	$-s_{23}$	1	34	24'	21'	c_{14}	$-s_{14}$	21	32
44	33	1	33	23			22						33	c_{23}	$-s_{23}$	0	33	0	22	c_{23}	$-s_{23}$	22	33
43	32			22	1								0	c_{23}	$-s_{23}$	0	0	22	0	c_{23}	s_{23}	0	34
32	21			31			33		x_{13}	y_{23}	c_{23}	s_{23}	21	c_{23}	s_{23}	1	21	31'	34'	c_{14}	s_{14}	34	41
31	24			34	1	32							24	c_{23}	s_{23}	1	24	34'	31'	c_{14}	$-s_{14}$	31	42
34	23		22	33				33					0	c_{23}	s_{23}	0	0	33	0	c_{23}	$-s_{23}$	0	43
33	22	1		32									22	c_{23}	s_{23}	0	22	0	33	c_{23}	s_{23}	33	44

it is necessary to spread the non-zero values of fields C and S within their blocks. It is done in $\log N$ steps where for $k = 0, 1, \ldots, \log N - 1$, operations

$$CR \leftarrow CR + p2^k CR, \qquad SR \leftarrow SR + p2^k SR \tag{55}$$

are realized from starting vectors $CR = C$, $SR = S$ (Table 10). Then, the transformation (54) can be obtained as

$$A \leftarrow [CR * A - SR * B](MC),$$

where $MC = \overline{M + MB}$.

The orthogonalization (49) of columns can be expressed as

$$\begin{bmatrix} \text{\textcircled{11}} & 12' & 13' & 0 \\ 21' & \text{\textcircled{22}} & 0 & 24' \\ 31' & 0 & \text{\textcircled{33}} & 34' \\ 0 & 42' & 43' & \text{\textcircled{44}} \end{bmatrix} \begin{bmatrix} c_{14} & 0 & 0 & s_{14} \\ 0 & c_{23} & s_{23} & 0 \\ 0 & -s_{23} & c_{23} & 0 \\ -s_{14} & 0 & 0 & c_{14} \end{bmatrix} = \begin{bmatrix} \text{\textcircled{11}} & 12 & 13 & 0 \\ 21 & \text{\textcircled{22}} & 0 & 24 \\ 31 & 0 & \text{\textcircled{33}} & 34 \\ 0 & 42 & 43 & \text{\textcircled{44}} \end{bmatrix}.$$

$$\cdot \begin{bmatrix} \text{\textcircled{11}} & c_{23}12' - s_{23}13' & c_{23}13' + s_{23}12' & 0 \\ c_{14}21' - s_{14}24' & \text{\textcircled{22}} & 0 & c_{14}24' + s_{14}21' \\ c_{14}31' - s_{14}34' & 0 & \text{\textcircled{33}} & c_{14}34' + s_{14}31' \\ 0 & c_{23}42' - s_{23}43' & c_{23}43' + s_{23}42' & \text{\textcircled{44}} \end{bmatrix}. \tag{56}$$

In a straightforward implementation of (49) a transpose of the field A is needed. However, it can be done without this operation which can be rather complicated and expensive on this type of parallel computer. For this reason, the field A is permuted by the given permutation factor in blocks as well as within the blocks, i.e. $B \leftarrow P2^0 A$, $A \leftarrow p2^0 B$ (Table 10). The components of the fields C and S are spread by blocks in fields CC and SC. These fields can be constructed by

$$\begin{aligned} CC &\leftarrow CC + P2^k CC \\ SC &\leftarrow SC + P2^k SC, \qquad k = 0, 1, \ldots, \log N - 1, \end{aligned} \tag{57}$$

where the process starts with $CC = C$, $SC = S$. Then the transformation (56) follows from

$$A \leftarrow [CC * A + SC * B](MC).$$

The next iteration begins with shift operations on A, according to the factor prescribed by the third step of the permutation scheme PERSAM. All further steps are performed in the same manner as described above. However, the new value of the permutation factor is 2^1 instead of 2^0.

As seen, the number of vector operations is constant in the evaluation of one iteration ("additions" in (45) and (47) are not arithmetic but data manipulation operations which do not contribute to the arithmetic count). Because of the $\log N$ steps in (55) and (57), the parallel data transfer complexity is $O(N)$ and $O(N \log N)$.

The algorithm which realizes the scheme **PERMOPRY** is structured analogously to the above algorithm whereby the permutations required are prescribed by (52). The only difference is the evaluation of odd-numbered iterations. It is caused by the irregularity of these iterations where always one pair of elements is not annihilated. In order to keep the corresponding pair of rows and columns without any change, the vector operations are masked. Two constant masks are constructed where elements of the two last blocks and the two last elements in all blocks, respectively, are 0.

The arithmetic complexity remains the same as in the preceding algorithm, whereas the data transfer complexity is increased only by the cost of one additional shift operation.

The advantage of the parallel associative algorithm applied in the last scheme **PERORD** is that no shift operations are needed. However, to avoid transposition of the matrix, the algorithm requires the orthogonalizations from both sides on four vectors instead of one as it was the case in the two preceding algorithms.

It is caused by the fact that in evaluating the values (42) and hence, the coefficients (44), (45), a permuted vector in the original ordering $1, 2, ..., N$ is also needed.

The orthogonalization computations of the kth iteration, $k = 1, 2, ..., N-1$, will be performed on elements of the $(k-1)$st iteration, which are located in the four fields AO, AR, AC, ARC that are ordered as follows:

AO — original ordering in blocks and within the blocks,
AR — permutation of blocks corresponding to PERSAM_{k-1}, original ordering within the blocks,
AC — permutation within the blocks, according to PERSAM_{k-1}, original ordering in blocks, \hfill (58)
ARC — permutation in blocks and also within the blocks, according to PERSAM_{k-1}.

Then orthogonalization coefficients (44), (45) can be obtained in fields C and S analogously to the logarithm formulated above. Their arrangement in fields CR, SR and CC, SC, respectively, is the same as in (55) and (57) where a given permutation factor is used. The transformation of vectors (58) from the left is easy performed in a vector-like manner by

$$AO' \leftarrow CR*AO - SR*AR,$$
$$AR' \leftarrow CR*AR + SR*AO,$$
$$AC' \leftarrow CR*AC - SR*ARC,$$
$$ARC' \leftarrow CR*ARC + SR*AC.$$

Similarly, the column transformation does not require additional data transport operations because it can be done by

$$AO \leftarrow CC*AO' - SC*AC',$$
$$AR \leftarrow CC*AR' - SC*ARC',$$
$$AC \leftarrow CC*AC' + SC*AO',$$
$$ARC \leftarrow CC*ARC' + SC*AR'.$$

The number of parallel arithmetic operations reaches the constant value only, i.e. it remains $O(1)$ for one iteration. As mentioned above, the number of data manipulation is reduced and its value is $O(\log N)$.

Finally, it is worth noting that all the three strategies can be applied to solving the singular value problem (SVD) on the associative machine.

The parallel algorithms based on the three different ordering schemes have been simulated on a PDP 11/40 computer. The eigenvalue problem was solved for real symmetric matrices of order N for $N = 4, 8, 16$. Using a random number generator the matrix elements were uniformly and independently distributed in [0, 1]. The orthogonalization process was terminated after the initial sum of squares of off-diagonal elements had been reduced to 10^{-12}. Table 11 summarizes the results for the schemes PERSAM, PERMOPRY and PERORD, for $t = 100, 10, 5$, where t gives the number of trials. As an illustrative comparison, the results for the classical scheme PERSEQ are given. The values in the table are mean numbers of k iteration cycles that are necessary to satisfy the termination criterion. (The maximum and minimum numbers of cycles for each experiment was $\lceil a \rceil + 1$ and $\lceil a \rceil$, respectively, where $\lceil \ \rceil$ denotes an integer part of a given value.)

Table 11

n	t	PERSAM	PERMOPRY	PERORD	PERSEQ
4	100	3.11	3.40	3.11	3.20
8	10	4.10	4.30	4.50	3.90
16	5	5.00	5.20	5.20	4.40

The PERORD and PERSAM schemes yield the best results for $N = 4$. It follows, however, that all parallel schemes considered yield approximately the same results for the given values of N. As far as the numbers of parallel arithmetic and transfer steps are concerned, it is the algorithm based on the PERSAM scheme that is most efficient for this type of parallel computers. Since the analysis of the convergence of different parallel orderings for Jacobi's method is difficult, the simulation results concerning the convergence of our algorithms are promising.

References

[1] L. Adams and J. Ortega, "A multi-color SOR method for parallel computation", *Proc. Int. Conf. on Parallel Processing* (Bellaire, 1982) pp. 53—56.

[2] *Application of STARAN to Fast Fourier Transform*, GER-16109 (Goodyear Aerospace Corporation, Akron, 1974).

[3] R. P. Brent, F. T. Luk and Ch. van Loan, "Computation of the singular value decomposition using mesh-connected processors", Techn. Rep. 82-528 (Department of Computer Science, Cornell University, Ithaca, 1983).

[4] E. O. Brigham, *The Fast Fourier Transform* (Prentice-Hall, Englewood Cliffs, 1974).

[5] M. Dowd, Y. Perl, M. Saks and L. Rudolph, "The balanced sorting network", Techn. Rep. DCS-TR-127 (Department of Computer Science, Rutgers University, New Brunswick, 1983) pp. 1—25.

[6] D. K. Faddeyev and V. N. Faddeyeva, *Computational Methods of Linear Algebra* (in Russian) (Fizmatgiz, Moscow, 1963).

[7] C. C. Foster, *Content Addressable Parallel Processors* (Van Nostrand Reinhold, New York, 1976).

[8] Giang Vu Thang and M. Vajteršic, "Histogram parallel algorithms for the associative parallel computer of the SIMD type", *Proc. 1st Int. Conf. on Automatic Image Processing* (Berlin, 1985) pp. C4/1—C4/4.

[9] P. A. Gilmore, "Matrix computations on an associative processor", *Proc. Sagamore Computer Conf.*, Lecture Notes in Computer Science 24 (Springer-Verlag, Berlin 1975) pp. 272—290.

[10] A. Hübler, "Some image processing algorithms for an associative parallel computer", Report (Basic Laboratory of Artificial Intelligence, Institute of Technical Cybernetics, Slovak Academy of Sciences, Bratislava, 1985).

[11] *Macro-Apple Programming Manual*, Techn. Rep. GER-15648 (Goodyear Aerospace Corporation, Akron, 1973).

[12] K. Preston, Jr. and L. Uhr (Eds.), *Multicomputers and Image Processing — Algorithms and Programs* (Academic Press, New York, 1982).

[13] K. Richter, "Parallel Computer System SIMD", *Proc. Conf. on Artificial Intelligence and Inf. Control Syst. of Robots* (North-Holland, Amsterdam, 1984) pp. 309—313.

[14] H. Rutishauser, "The Jacobi method for real symmetric matrices", in *Handbook for Automatic Computation* (Springer-Verlag, Berlin, 1971).

[15] A. H. Sameh, "On Jacobi and Jacobi-like algorithms for a parallel computer", *Math. Comput.* **25** (1971) 579—590.

[16] L. J. Siegel, H. J. Siegel and P. H. Swain, "Parallel algorithm-performance measures", in *Multicomputers and Image Processing — Algorithms and Programs* (Academic Press, New York, 1982) pp. 241—252.

[17] J. Skákala, "Standard macroinstructions of ASPL language", Techn. Rep. (in Slovak) (Institute of Technical Cybernetics, Slovak Academy of Sciences, Bratislava, 1981).
[18] H. S. Stone, "Parallel processing with the perfect shuffle", *IEEE Trans. Comp.* **C-20** (1971) 153—161.
[19] O. Sýkora, "The generalization of the perfect shuffle principle and its application", in *Vorträge zu Problemen der Parallelverarbeitung*, Heft 39 (Technische Universität, Dresden, 1979) pp. 92—100.
[20] M. Vajteršic, "Solution of systems of linear algebraic equations on the parallel computer of associative type", Techn. Rep. III-8-1/10 (in Slovak) (Institute of Technical Cybernetics, Slovak Academy of Sciences, Bratislava, 1982) pp. 118—143.
[21] S. S. Yan and H. S. Fung, "Associative processor architecture — Survey", *Comp. Surv.* **9** (1977) 1—27.

Chapter 3

Systolic algorithms and their implementation on specialized processors

3.1 Introduction

On the basis of the production technology of integrated circuits with the density of the order of 10^4 transistors (LSI — Large Scale Integration) it is possible to build up various computer subsystems on chip. The progress in the production technology of integrated circuits makes it possible to place more than 10^5 transistors per chip using VLSI technology, and this density is still increasing each year [88]. This new technology allows a single chip to contain not only general-purpose microprocessors but also specialized parallel computer structures — so-called systolic arrays (SAR). The result is a transition from integrated circuits to integrated systems [22].

The problem of systolic algorithms (SAL), i.e. algorithms that can be implemented on systolic arrays, is tackled in this chapter. SARs are composed of a large number of simple processors (p) which are interconnected with a communication network. These processors perform synchronous data processing and transfer data among themselves. In parallel with the computations performed on the processors, data from memory are read-in by inputs, the results are sent back to the memory via the outputs. The essential principles of a systolic architecture are illustrated in Fig. 37 [45]. The adjective "systolic" originated as an analogy between the function of memory and the activity of the human heart. The memory periodically sends data (blood) to a systolic array, which are then propagating from one processor to another. The systolic arrays allow the connection of an SAR to a bus of a standard computer in a role of peripheral

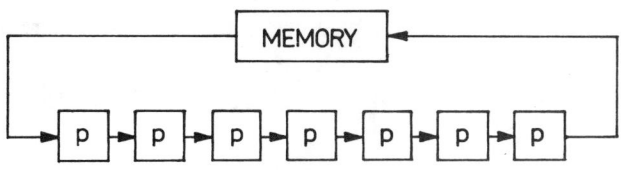

Fig. 37. Systolic architecture.

device for speeding up the computation of various functions, or to be used as parts of problem-oriented computers.

The first papers on SAR and algorithms date back to the beginnings of the VLSI technology at the end of the seventies. It is worth noting that the above problems appeared in previous research papers on iterative arrays and cellular automata [35, 68, 92]. While the processors — cells of iterative arrays and cellular automata represented only simple logical systems and were interconnected either by a linear or square orthogonal network, the processors in systolic arrays, as it will be shown later, can perform much more complicated operations and are interconnected with various networks.

The complete design of an SAR for implementing the problem introduced involves the following steps [29, 85]:

(1) Algorithmic level

The design of the SAR starts with the choice of an algorithm. Usually, a number of algorithms are available to solve a given problem. The task is to choose or to propose one that would be the most convenient alternative for the SAR architecture. The algorithm must involve the description of processors and the communication system as well as the input-output operations and the control design.

(2) Logical level

The logical level represents synthesis of logical circuits of functional units (processors, memories, control, data channels, etc.) that were designed at the first step. The logical design depends on the technology of integrated circuits.

(3) Transistor level — electric design

The electric design represents the transformation of logical circuits to the corresponding wiring diagram.

(4) Geometric level — design of chip morphology

This step transforms the electrical wiring circuits to the set of polygons corresponding to various technological levels (masks) that define both the vertical and the horizontal structure of a chip.

From the above it follows that a successful design of SAR depends on the cooperation of mathematicians and designers of integrated circuits.

This chapter is only confined to the problems of algorithmic level. In its first section the problems of systolic arrays and algorithms are described and algorithms classified with respect to communication networks.

Several SARs for implementing numerical and non-numerical problems are presented in the second and third sections.

The basic principles of the theory of complexity of systolic algorithms are explained in the fourth section.

3.2 Characteristics of systolic arrays and algorithms

3.2.1 Basic properties

Originally, SAR was designed by Kung and Leiserson [50] as an architecture for implementation of the algorithm of matrix multiplication on a hexagonal processor network. This algorithm has been mentioned in another connection in the first chapter. Our interpretation of the properties of SAR and SAL starts with an illustrative example of multiplication of a matrix by a vector [46].

Let us consider a problem **Ax** = **y**, i.e. multiplication of a band matrix **A** = (a_{ij}) of the type $n \times n$ with band width w by a vector **x** = (x_i). The vector **y** = (y_i), $i = 1, 2, ..., n$, is calculated from the relations

$$y_i^{(1)} = 0,$$
$$y_i^{(k+1)} = y_i^{(k)} + a_{ik}x_k,$$
$$y_i = y_i^{(n+1)}, \quad i = 1, 2, ..., n.$$

For example, for $w = 4$, we get

$$\begin{bmatrix} a_{11} & a_{12} & & & & & \\ a_{21} & a_{22} & a_{23} & & \text{\huge 0} & & \\ a_{31} & a_{32} & a_{33} & a_{34} & & & \\ & a_{42} & a_{43} & a_{44} & a_{45} & & \\ & & a_{53} & \cdot & \cdot & & \\ \text{\huge 0} & & & \cdot & \cdot & & \\ & & & \cdot & \cdot & & \end{bmatrix} \begin{bmatrix} x_1 \\ x_2 \\ x_3 \\ x_4 \\ \cdot \\ \cdot \\ \cdot \end{bmatrix} = \begin{bmatrix} y_1 \\ y_2 \\ y_3 \\ y_4 \\ \cdot \\ \cdot \\ \cdot \end{bmatrix}.$$

The above recurrent relations can be executed on an SAR consisting of a linear array of w processors with bidirectional data flow, according to Fig. 38.

Label the processors in SAR from left to right as $p_1, p_2, ..., p_w$. The $y_i^{(l)}$ enters the array from the right with value 0 and elements $y_i^{(k)}$ are shifted to the left. Values of x_i enter SAR from the left and they are shifted to the right. The elements a_{ij} enter the array from above, according to Fig. 38. To let the algorithm work properly, the input data must be organized in such a way as to enable the elements x_i, $y_i^{(k)}$, a_{ij} to get to the right place at the right moment. The operation of processors is synchronized by steps. Vector elements of the vectors **x**, **y** and of the diagonals of the matrix **A** enter the array delayed by 2 steps. Consequently, even and odd processors are active in alternating steps.

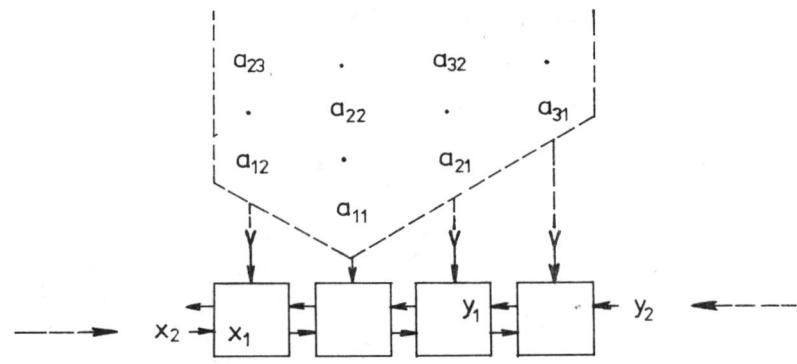

Fig. 38. Systolic array for multiplication of a band matrix by vector.

For precise description of SAL the following lebelling will be used. Let R_u^i, R_c^i be the registers p_i and let c be a constant. Then $R_u^i \leftarrow R_c^j$ means shifting of the contents of a register R_c^j into R_u^i; $R_u^i \leftarrow c$ means reading in of a constant into register R_u^i; R_u^i **op** R_c^j denotes an operation on the register contents.

Processor p_m has three registers R_x^m, R_y^m and R_a^m which are set to zero before starting operation. Each processor has three input lines for x, y, a and two output lines for x and y (Fig. 39).

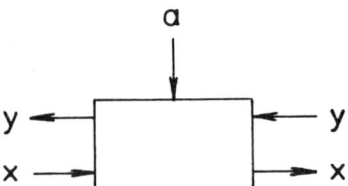

Fig. 39. Processor for scalar product.

Active processor p_m performs in one step an operation that involves shifting and computation

$$R_a^m \leftarrow a_{ij},$$
$$R_x^m \leftarrow R_x^{m-1} \quad \text{for } m \neq 1, \quad (R_x^m \leftarrow x_k \quad \text{for } m = 1),$$
$$R_y^m \leftarrow R_y^{m+1} \quad \text{for } m \neq w, \quad (R_y^m \leftarrow 0 \quad \text{for } m = w),$$
$$R_y^m \leftarrow R_y^m + R_x^m R_a^m.$$

Consider the computation of the element y_2 according to the situation shown in Fig. 38. In the next step, x_1 is shifted to the processor p_2 and $y_2^{(1)} = 0$ enters

p_4. In the following step, x_1, $y_2^{(1)}$, a_{21} are met in p_3 and $y_2^{(2)} = a_{21}x_1$ is computed. In an other step, x_2, $y_2^{(2)}$, a_{22} are gathered in p_2 and $y_2^{(3)} = a_{21}x_1 + a_{22}x_2$ is computed. At the end, the result of $y_2 = a_{21}x_1 + a_{22}x_2 + a_{23}x_3$ is computed in p_1. Using the above procedure the vector **y** is obtained in $2n + w$ steps. For comparison — the serial computation would take $O(wn)$ steps. The proposed SAR is characterized by the following properties:

(1) Function of the processor; each processor executes one step of the scalar product.

(2) Interprocessor communication network; a linear processor array is concerned.

(3) Data flow is bidirectional.

(4) Multiple use of input data; x is used in each processor.

The definition of SAR can be formulated using a more detailed specification of these properties.

Definition. A systolic array represents a processor network of the following properties

(a) processors perform simple operations with minimum memory, and control requirements. A small number of different types of processors occur in the array,

(b) all processors are interconnected via regular communication network,

(c) data flow is simple and synchronous,

(d) at computation pipelining and parallelism are used,

(e) input data are shared by several processors.

These five properties enable straightforward implementation of SAR based on the VLSI technology. The area of the chip and the computation time are influenced by the function of the processors and by the communication network. Modularity of the system is increased by a regular network. Properties (d) and (e) facilitate a fast computation although the number of input-output lines is limited for technological reasons.

Thus, systolic algorithms have the following properties:

(a) they consist of a small number of different types of simple operations,

(b) data flow in them is simple and regular,

(c) properties of parallelism and pipelining are used in the computation,

(d) each data item is used several times,

(e) their application enables implementation of a wider scope of problems.

3.2.2 Classification of systolic algorithms

Classification of SAL using linear, orthogonal and hexagonal array as well as tree and perfect shuffle communication networks is proposed in [47]. On the basis of the latest results, several more arrays can be added to this classification, such as a mesh of trees [67] and a cube connected cycles [74] (Fig. 40).

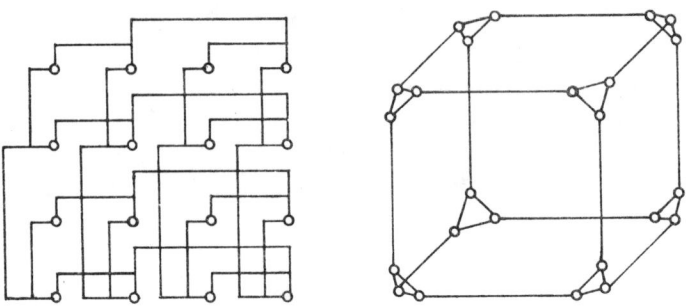

Fig. 40. Mesh of trees and cube connected cycles.

In the following paragraph there is a short survey of SALs proposed for the above communication networks. Today there exist hundreds of SALs and for almost every important parallel computation problem a systolic implementation has been designed. For this reason a finer classification of SAL with respect to the problems solved could be made, for instance, SAL for matrix multiplication, sorting, convolution, etc. The algorithms to be treated in this chapter are written in italics.

Linear array: *multiplication of matrix by a vector* [46], filtration [46], *multiplication and division of polynomials* [45], *Fourier Transform* [46], *recurrent relations* [50], *implementation of a triangular system of linear equations* [50], *odd-even sorting* [87, 98], *computation of elementary functions* [7], priority queue [55], *connected components* [76], matrix multiplication [43], convolution [45], maximum element [95], greatest common division [14], word recognition [8].

Orthogonal array: *matrix multiplication* [71], dynamic programming [34], Fourier Transform [89], sorting [87, 52], graph algorithms [34], database operations [48], *system of linear equations* [22], *matrix inversion* [64], *two-dimensional convolution* [49], matrix triangulation [33], eigenvalues [33, 17], *transitive closure* [34], implementation of the Toeplitz system of linear equations [16], speech recognition [31], matrix inversion [41].

Hexagonal array: matrix multiplication [50], *LU-decomposition* [50], QR factorization [33], the longest common substring [6].

Trees: searching [11], addition [15], matrix multiplication [50], satisfiability of a set of clauses [84], minimum spanning tree [11], database operations [69].

Perfect shuffle: *Fourier Transform* [88], sorting [88], matrix transposition [82].

Mesh of trees: matrix multiplication [67], *sorting* [87], minimum spanning tree [67], computational geometry [83].

3.3 Numerical algorithms

In this section several SALs to implement numerical problems are described. The section is divided into parts, according to algorithms for matrix operations, recurrent relations, operations of polynomials, etc.

3.3.1 Matrix operations

In this part algorithms for matrix multiplication are described as well as the **LU**-decomposition, solution of a triangular or general system of linear equations and algorithms for matrix inversion.

Matrix multiplications

In [20] an algorithm was proposed for matrix multiplication on a parallel computer with orthogonal processor network. Because the algorithm had typical properties of a SAL, in [71] it was adapted to SAR.

Let the square matrices $\mathbf{A} = (a_{ij})$, $\mathbf{B} = (b_{ij})$ be of dimension n. The elements of matrix $\mathbf{C} = (c_{ij})$, $\mathbf{C} = \mathbf{AB}$ can be obtained from recurrent relations $c_{ij}^{(1)} = 0$, $c_{ij}^{(k+1)} = c_{ij}^{(k)} + a_{ik}b_{kj}$, $c_{ij} = c_{ij}^{(n+1)}$, where $i, j, k = 1, 2, ..., n$. The above relations can be computed on an orthogonal array of processors. This array, for $n = 4$, is shown in Fig. 41.

Let the processor in the ith row and the jth column be p_{ij}, where $i, j = 1, 2, ..., n$. The elements of matrix $\mathbf{A}$ ($\mathbf{B}$) enter the array from the left (from above) and proceed in the specified directions by one processor further per step. The processor p_{ij} has registers R_a^{ij}, R_b^{ij}, R_c^{ij} and two input (output) lines for input (output) of the element of $\mathbf{A}$ ($\mathbf{B}$). Figure 41 illustrates the situation at the 0th step. In the kth step the processor p_{ij} performs

(1) Shift

$$\forall_i, R_a^{i1} \leftarrow a_{i, k-i-j+2}, \quad R_a^{ij} \leftarrow R_a^{i, j-1} \quad \text{for } j = 2, 3, ..., n,$$

$$\forall_j, R_b^{1j} \leftarrow b_{k-i-j+2, j}, \quad R_b^{ij} \leftarrow R_b^{i-1, j} \quad \text{for } i = 2, 3, ..., n.$$

(2) Computation

$$R_c^{ij} \leftarrow R_c^{ij} + R_a^{ij} R_b^{ij}.$$

$c_{ij}^{(2)}$ is computed in $i+j-1$ steps in the processor p_{ij}. In the next step, $c_{ij}^{(3)}$ is determined in p_{ij}, etc., until after $i+j+n-2$ steps the result c_{ij} is stored in the register R_c^{ij}. Using this procedure the matrix **C** is obtained in register R_c^{ij} in $3n-2$ steps; the output of this matrix requires n more steps. From the above it follows that during computations just one third of processors are working all the time. Efficient use of all processors can be achieved by solving the problem through pipelined computation of multiple matrix products of dimension n: $\mathbf{C}_i = \mathbf{A}_i \mathbf{B}_i$, $i = 1, 2, 3, \ldots$. Overlapping of computations of the matrix $\mathbf{C}_i$ with the output of data $\mathbf{C}_i$ in [38] is proposed as follows: one more register R_d^{ij} will be added to each processor p_{ij}, where the neighbouring registers will be interconnected with horizontal line. The inputs of matrices **A** and **B** will be delayed by two steps. Once the computation is finished c_{ij} is sent from R_c^{ij} into R_d^{ij}, from where (in following steps) it leaves the array through the registers R_d^{ik}, $k = j-1, j-2, \ldots, 1$.

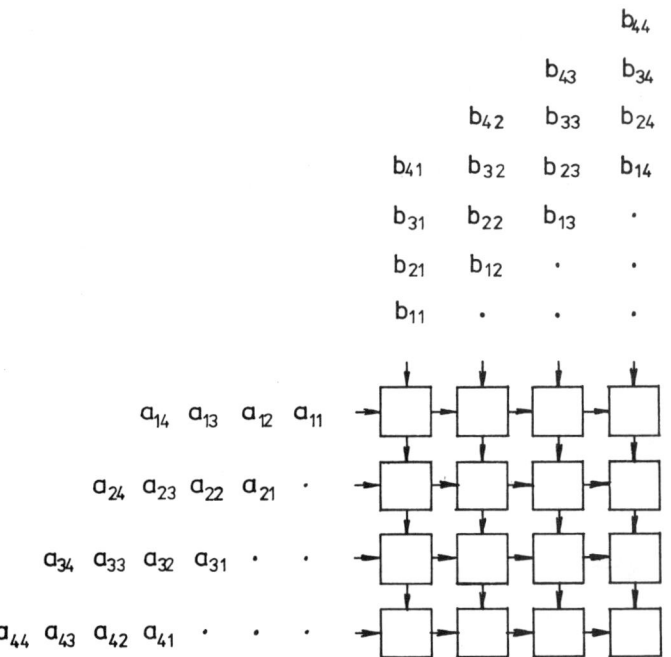

Fig. 41. Multiplication of matrices on a rectangular processor array.

This algorithm is area optimal: $A = O(n^2 k)$, where k is the number of bits of elements $k \geqslant \log n$ [37]. Definition of the area complexity can be found in conclusion to this chapter. Matrix multiplication is effectively computed also on linear SAR of n processors, $O(n)$ in area each [43].

LU-*decomposition*

LU-decomposition is a decomposition of a square matrix **A** of order n, into product of a lower and upper triangular matrices **L**, **U**, i.e. **A** = **LU** [75]. On the assumption that the matrix **A** can be decomposed using Gaussian elimination without pivoting [75], the matrices **L** = (s_{ij}) and **U** = (u_{ij}) can be determined from recurrent relations for $i, j, k = 1, 2, ..., n$

$$a_{ij}^{(1)} = a_{ij}, \quad a_{ij}^{(k+1)} = a_{ij}^{(k)} + s_{ik}(-u_{kj}),$$

$$s_{ik} = \begin{cases} 0 & \text{for } i < k, \\ 1 & i = k, \\ a_{ik}^{(k)} u_{kk}^{-1} & i > k, \end{cases}$$

$$u_{kj} = \begin{cases} 0 & k > j, \\ a_{ik}^{(k)} & k \leqslant j. \end{cases}$$

Now we demonstrate the computation of these relationships on a hexagonal array of processors [50]. Figure 42 demonstrates a band matrix of bandwidth $w = 7$. The matrix **A** enters at the bottom and the elements of the matrix **L** (**U**) leave at the left (right) upper boundary.

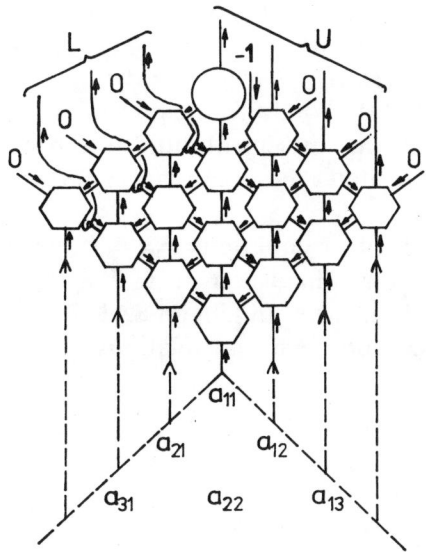

Fig. 42. Computation of **LU**-decomposition on a hexagonal processor array.

The processor labelled by a circle has a register R. Following operations are executed in an active step:

(1) The value $a_{kk}^{(k)}$ stored in the register R_a of the lower neighbouring processor is shifted to R_s and at the same time it is assigned to the output variable u_{22}.

(2) $R_s \leftarrow 1/R_s$ is computed.

The other processors which perform one step of scalar product will be as follows

(a) The processors in the left upper row have registers R_0, R_a and R_s. An active processor reads in within one step the contents R_s (R_a) of the right upper (lower) processor into register R_s (R_a). It performs $R_0 \leftarrow 0$, $R_s \leftarrow R_0 + R_a R_s$. The contents of R_s is assigned to the corresponding output variable s_{ik}.

(b) The processors in the right upper row have registers R_0, R_1 and R_u. The contents R_1 of the left upper neighbouring processor is shifted into R_1 in one step, whereby the number -1 is stored into the top R_1. R_0 is set to zero. The contents R_a of the lower neighbouring processor is shifted into the register R_u. The contents R_u is assigned to the corresponding output variable u_{kj}. Then, $R_u \leftarrow R_0 + R_1 R_u$ is computed.

(c) The remaining processors have the registers R_a, R_s and R_u. In a single step the contents R_a of the lower neighbouring processor is shifted by an active processor into R_a, the contents R_s (R_u) of the left (right) upper processor is read in into R_s (R_u). Then $R_a \leftarrow R_a + R_s R_u$ is executed.

In this way, the homogeneity of the above SAR is achieved by excessive computational operations of the processors of (a) and (b) types.

Solution of a triangular system of linear equations

This section will be tightly bound to the preceding one, because the **LU**-decomposition followed by the implementation of a system of linear equations with triangular matrix facilitates the computation of the general system of linear equations.

We have a system of linear equations $\mathbf{A}\mathbf{x} = \mathbf{b}$, where $\mathbf{A} = (a_{ij})$ is a lower triangular regular matrix of dimension $n \times n$, $\mathbf{b} = (b_i)$ and the vector of unknowns is $\mathbf{x} = (x_i)$, $i = 1, 2, \ldots, n$. In [50] an SAR is designed which computes the elements of vector $\mathbf{x}$ from recurrent relations

$$y_i^{(1)} = 0, \quad y_i^{(k+1)} = y_i^{(k)} + a_{ik}x_k, \quad i, k = 1, 2, \ldots, n,$$
$$x_i = (b_i - y_i^{(i)})/a_{ii}, \quad i = 1, 2, \ldots, n.$$

The computation procedure for band matrix $\mathbf{A}$ of bandwidth $w = 4$ is shown in Fig. 43.

Values y_i and elements of the vector $\mathbf{b}$ and of diagonal lines of the matrix $\mathbf{A}$ enter the array delayed by two steps, hence odd and even processors work in alternating steps. The processor p_1 has four registers R_a^1, R_b^1, R_x^1, R_y^1 and in its active step it performs

$$R_y^1 \leftarrow R_y^2, \quad R_a^1 \leftarrow a_{ii}, \quad R_b^1 \leftarrow b_i,$$
$$R_x^1 \leftarrow (R_b^1 - R_y^1)/R_a^1.$$

The processor p_m, $m \neq 1$ has three registers R_a^m, R_x^m, R_y^m and in its active step it performs

$$R_x^m \leftarrow R_x^{m-1}, \quad R_a^m \leftarrow a_{ij},$$
$$R_y^m \leftarrow R_y^{m+1}, \quad \text{for } m = w \quad R_y^m \leftarrow 0,$$
$$R_y^m \leftarrow R_y^m + R_a^m R_x^m.$$

The value x_i is obtained from the register R_x^w of processor R_w in $2w + 2i - 2$ steps. The whole computation takes $2w + 2n - 2$ steps.

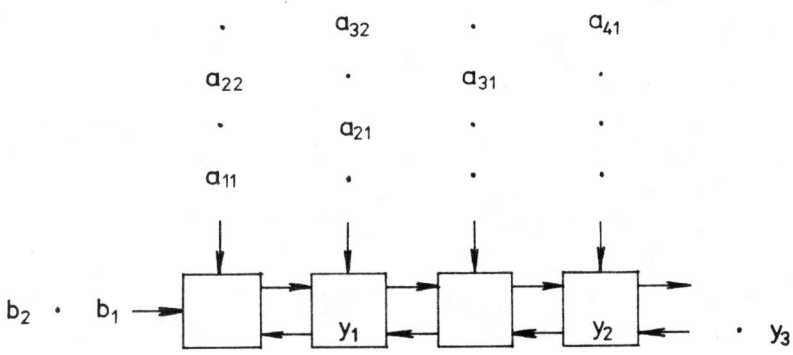

Fig. 43. Systolic array for solving a triangular system of linear equations.

Systolic array for a system of linear equations

The first systolic array for computation of a system of linear algebraic equations

$$\mathbf{A}\mathbf{x} = \mathbf{a}, \tag{59}$$

where $\mathbf{A} = (a_{ij})$ is a regular matrix of dimension n, $\mathbf{x} = (x_i)$, $\mathbf{a} = (a_{i,n+1})$, $i, j = 1, 2, \ldots, n$, was described by Kung and Leiserson in [50]. The system implements the **LU**-decomposition of matrix **A**. For computation of triangular systems, $\mathbf{L}\mathbf{y} = \mathbf{a}$ and $\mathbf{U}\mathbf{x} = \mathbf{y}$, a systolic system with a linearly ordered array of processors was proposed [50]. In [80] these systems are integrated into a single unit, so-called CHIP-processor. Design of a systolic system with local communication network for computation of (59) using Given's method is described in

[22]. Given's algorithm is based on application of a sequence of elementary orthogonal transformations of rows of matrix **A**; the result of this procedure is a triangular matrix. Its advantage is that no pivoting is needed in **A**; disadvantage, however, is that it uses a sequence of planar rotations that claim also the computation of functions $\sin x$, $\cos x$, $\sqrt{x}$ and arctg x. In [2] these functions are implemented using the CORDIC-algorithm on a special processor on which they are computed iteratively using only the operations of addition and shift. Consequently, the planar rotation does not take more time than the serial bitwise multiplication. Thus, from the view-point of algorithmic complexity — according to [2] — Given's method is as good as the Gaussian elimination without pivoting.

In this section, planar synchronous SAR will be proposed for system (59), in order to efficiently implement the Jordan elimination algorithm [75]. This algorithm is parallel and homogeneous enough to be implemented in form of SAR. In Jordan's algorithm the matrix **A** is processed in parallel by rows in system (59) into a unit matrix such that the solution x is obtained in place of the vector at the right hand-side of **a**.

The corresponding SP is generated by a matrix of processors with n rows and $n + 1$ columns, which are interconnected with a square communication network. Each processor, p_{ij}, $i = 1, 2, ..., n$, $j = 1, 2, ..., n + 1$, has registers R_a^{ij}, R_x^{ij} or R_y^{ii}. Its operation is implemented over the contents of these registers. The elimination algorithm is implemented on SAR synchronously in parallel steps. The steps will be labelled as follows

$$\forall_i: \quad i = 1, 2, ..., n,$$
$$\forall_j: \quad j = 1, 2, ..., n + 1,$$
$$\forall_{i(k)}: \quad i = 1, 2, ..., k - 1, k + 1, ..., n;$$

input $\downarrow a_{ij} \Rightarrow R_a^{ij}$; (input of the element a_{ij} from the top down to register R_a^{ij}),
transfer $\rightarrow R_a^{i1} \Rightarrow R_x^{ij} \forall_j$; (transfer of the contents of register R_a^{i1} into registers R_x^{ij}, $\forall_j$),
transfer $\downarrow R_a^{ij} \Rightarrow R_y^{ij} \forall_i$; (transfer of the contents of R_a^{1j} to the bottom of $R_y^{ij} \forall_j$),
$\forall_i \forall_j$ **cyclic shift** $\uparrow R_a^{ij} \Rightarrow R_a^{i-1,j}$; (cyclic shift of the above registers from the bottom $R_a^{0j} = R_a^{nj}$),
$\forall_i \forall_j$ **cyclic shift** $\leftarrow R_a^{ij} \Rightarrow R_a^{i,j-1}$; (cyclic shift of the above registers to the left, where $R_a^{i0} = R_a^{in}$),
do $R_a^{ij} \Leftarrow R_a^{ij}$ **op**$_1$ R_x^{ij} **op**$_2$ R_y^{ij}; (execution of **op**$_1$ and **op**$_2$ over the corresponding registers and storing of the result into R_a^{ij}),
$R_a^{ij} \Leftarrow c$; (storing of c into R_a^{ij}),
output $\rightarrow R_a^{ij}$; (output of the contents of R_a^{ij} to the right).

Using the above symbols the algorithm of Jordan's elimination of system (59) is executed by the corresponding SAR in the following steps

(0) $k := 0$;
(1) $\forall_i \forall_j$ **input** $\downarrow a_{ij} \Rightarrow R_a^{ij}$;
(2) $k := k + 1$;
 $\forall_i$ (**transfer** $\rightarrow R_a^{i1} \Rightarrow R_x^{ij} \forall_{j(1)}$);
(3) $R_a^{11} \Leftarrow 1$; $\forall_{j(1)}$ **do** R_a^{1j}/R_x^{1j};
(4) $\forall_{j(1)}$ **transfer** $\downarrow R_a^{1j} \Rightarrow R_y^{ij} \forall_{i(1)}$);
(5) $\forall_{i(1)} R_a^{i1} \Leftarrow 0$; $\forall_{i(1)}\forall_{j(1)}$ **do** $R_a^{ij} \Leftarrow R_a^{ij} - R_x^{ij} R_y^{ij}$;
(6) $\forall_i \forall_j$ **cyclic shift** $\uparrow R_a^{ij} \Rightarrow R_a^{i-1,j}$;
(7) $\forall_i \forall_{j(n+1)}$ **cyclic shift** $\leftarrow R_a^{ij} \Rightarrow R_a^{i,j-1}$;
(8) **if** $k < n$ **then go to** (2);
(9) $\forall_i$ **output** $\rightarrow R_a^{i,n+1}$.

Step (5) is executed by elimination of the corresponding submatrix. Steps (6) and (7) secure that the next leading element of elimination gets into processor p_{11}. The algorithm is executed without pivoting, i.e. we suppose that no division by zero may occur, what is guaranteed, for instance, when **A** is a positive definite or diagonally dominant matrix. The solution x_i is in $R_a^{i,n+1}$.

Let the actual execution time of operations of addition, multiplication, division, transfer, cyclic shift, assignment in arithmetic expression, input and

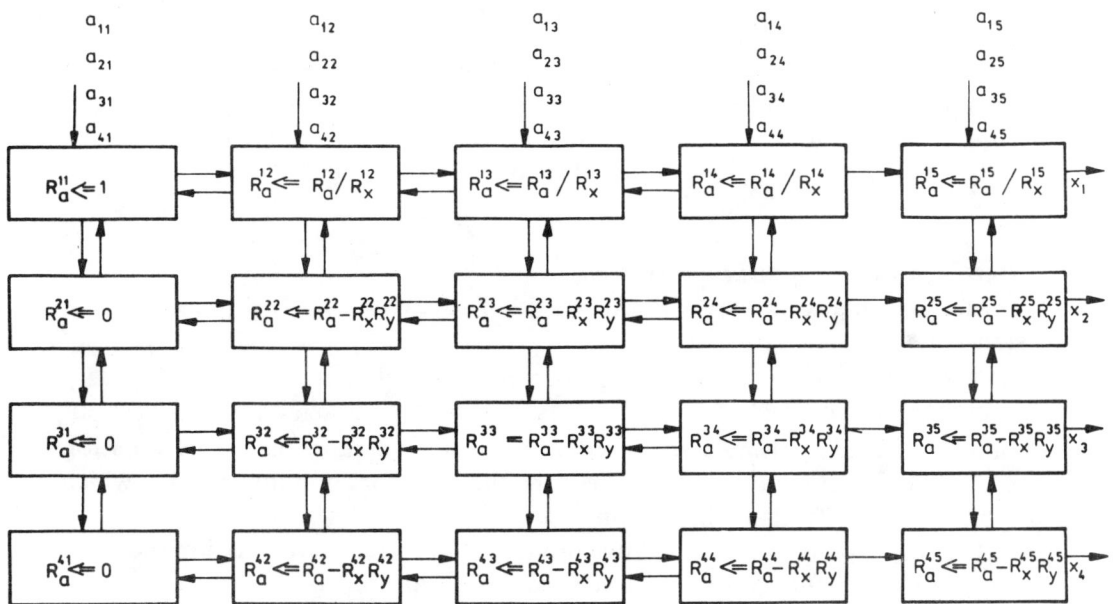

Fig. 44. Orthogonal systolic array for solving a system of linear equations.

output of n elements be a, m, d, t, s, p, i, o, respectively. Then the total execution time of SAR to implement the system (59) is

$$T_n^s = n[a + m + d + i + 2(t + s + p)] + o.$$

The structure of SAR for $n = 4$ is shown in Fig. 44.

In the general diagram of this SAR there are three types of processors: n processors p_{i1}, $\forall_i$ implement a simple assignment, n processors p_{1j}, $\forall_{j(1)}$ perform the operation of division in floating point, and $n^2 - n$ processors p_{ij}, $\forall_{i(1)}$, $\forall_{j(1)}$ execute the operations of multiplication and subtraction in floating point. The result of division by leading element in p_{11} is 1, elimination step in p_{i1}, $\forall_{i(1)}$ yields 0. With respect to homogeneity of the diagram, the elimination step can also be implemented in the first column of SAR. The resulting rounding-off errors may cause the problem that after elimination the matrix **A** will not be reduced to the unit matrix. Still, the accuracy of results is not affected by this disadvantage. Another alternative of SAR of lower complexity is obtained, if division by the leading element is only executed in p_{11}, while the remaining processors in the first row perform multiplication only.

Note. If any of the leading elements of the eliminated matrix in SAR is ≈ 0, then the above algorithm does not work well. This phenomenon can be avoided either by cyclic shifts of rows up, or of columns to the left, until the first non-zero element is found, or by partial pivoting, i.e. by selecting the maximum element in the corresponding column and by shifting it to the processor p_{11}. In our SAR, these operations are not taken into account. On selecting the maximum element this operation should by built into the processors p_{i1}, $\forall_i$, what would make the diagram more complicated. The above algorithm differs from the preceding one in that in one step it requires one value to be broad-casted to all processors in a row or a column. Algorithms of this property are called semisystolic [45].

Systolic array for matrix inversion

The computation of inversion of a regular square matrix $\mathbf{A} = (a_{ij})$ of dimension n, i.e.

$$\mathbf{B} = \mathbf{A}^{-1} = (b_{ij}) \tag{60}$$

on a systolic array using a sequence of elementary orthogonal transformation was tackled in [66]. Now, we shall describe the SAR for computation [42], which is based on the Jordan elimination.

The matrix **A** is transformed by eliminations to unit matrix. Using the same operations also $\mathbf{A}^{-1}$ can be obtained from the unit matrix.

The corresponding SAR is generated by a matrix of processors with n rows and n columns which, again, are interconnected with a square communication network. The processors in the first row of the SAR, with registers R_a^{1j}, R_x^{1j}, perform the operation of division. The other processors have the registers R_a^{1j}, R_x^{1j}, R_a^{ij}, R_x^{ij} and R_y^{ij}. They perform the operations of multiplication and subtraction. The algorithm for computation of **A**$^{-1}$ is executed SAR synchronously in the following steps (in this case, $\forall_j$ means $j = 1, 2, ..., n$)

(0) $k := 0$;
(1) $\forall_i \forall_j$ **input** $\downarrow a_{ij} \Rightarrow R_a^{ij}$;
(2) $k := k + 1$;
    $\forall_i$ (**transfer** $\to R_a^{i1} \Rightarrow R_x^{ij} \forall_j$);
(3) $R_a^{11} \Leftarrow 1$; $\forall_{i(1)} R_a^{i1} \Leftarrow 0$;
(4) $\forall_j$ **do** $R_a^{1j} \Leftarrow R_a^{1j}/R_x^{1j}$;
(5) $\forall_j$ (**transfer** $\downarrow R_a^{1j} \Rightarrow R_y^{ij} \forall_{i(1)}$);
(6) $\forall_{i(1)} \forall_j$ **do** $R_a^{ij} \Leftarrow R_a^{ij} - R_x^{ij} \cdot R_y^{ij}$;
(7) $\forall_i \forall_j$ **cyclic shift** $\uparrow R_a^{ij} \Rightarrow R_a^{i-1,j}$;
(8) $\forall_i \forall_j$ **cyclic shift** $\leftarrow R_a^{ij} \Rightarrow R_a^{i,j-1}$;
(9) if $k < n$ then go to (2);
(10) $\forall_i \forall_j$ **output** $\downarrow R_a^{ij}$.

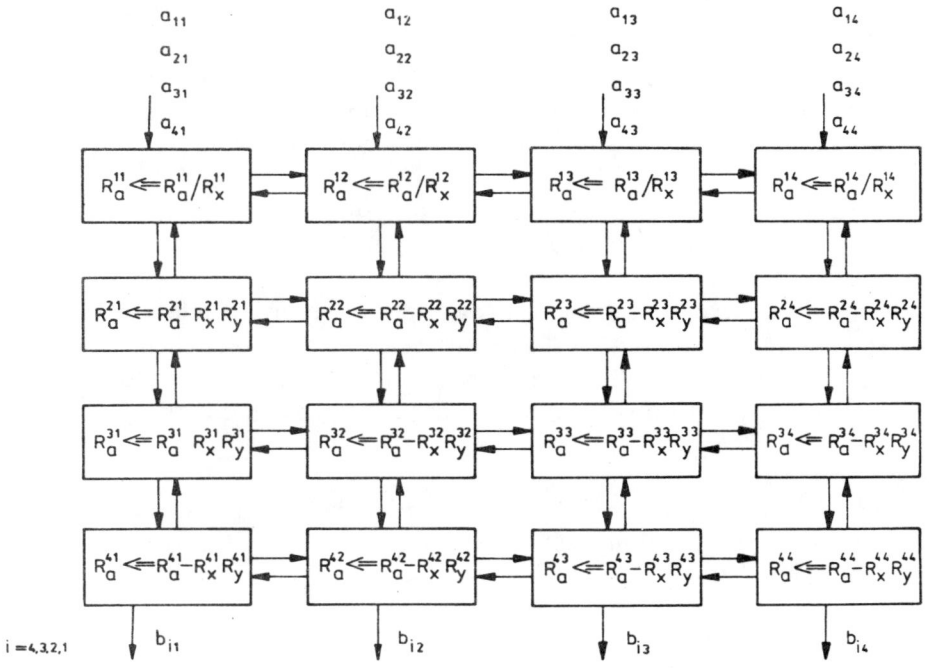

Fig. 45. Systolic array for matrix inversion.

By step (5) elimination on matrix **A** as well as on the unit matrix is performed in such a way that $n - k$ columns of matrix **A** and k columns of matrix $\mathbf{A}^{-1}$ are processed in the kth cycle of the algorithm. Steps (7) and (8) are analogous to steps (6) and (7) mentioned previously. Again, we suppose that in the algorithm no division by zero occurs in matrix **A**. The elements $\mathbf{A}^{-1} = b_{ij}$ are in R_a^{ij}, step (10) performs their transfer from the top to the bottom.

The total execution time of the SAR to compute $\mathbf{A}^{-1}$ is

$$T_n^{(i)} = n(a + m + d + i + o + 2t + 2s + 3p).$$

The time to compute inversion and a system of linear equations by elimination is $2:1$ compared to that on a serial computer. Not considering the times of data input and data output, this ratio is $1:1$ on SAR. The structure of a SAR for computation of $\mathbf{A}^{-1}$, $n = 4$, is shown in Fig. 45.

There are two types of processors in the general diagram: n processors p_{1j}, $\forall_j$ execute division and the operations of multiplication and subtraction are performed by $n^2 - n$ processors p_{ij}, $\forall_{i(1)}$, $\forall_j$. The input of data, similar to the preceding case, does not overlap with computation; the data on new problem may enter the SAR only after the preceding computation was finished.

Also this algorithm is semisystolic — because it uses global broadcasting of data. In [41] a SAL is designed on an orthogonal array of processors, which computes $\mathbf{A}^{-1}$ in time $\theta(nk)$ on an area of $\theta(n^2k)$, where k is the number of bits of elements, and it uses just local data transfer among processors. Also note, the last two algorithms that are optimal with respect to the area of $\mathbf{A} = \theta(n^2k)$ [37].

3.3.2 Recurrent relations

In this section we shall deal with two types of recurrent relations. First, we describe a SAL for computing the linear recurrent relation. Then, we propose a method to implement the recurrent relation with small order and apply it to computation of elementary functions using continued fractions.

Linear recurrent relation

In the linear recurrent relation of kth order the initial values of x_0, x_1, ..., x_{k-1} are specified along with coefficients $\{a_{ji}\}$, $j = 1, 2, ..., k + 1$, $i = k$, $k + 1$, ..., and

$$x_i = a_{1i}x_{i-1} + a_{2i}x_{i-2} + ... + a_{ki}x_{i-k} + a_{k+1,i}$$

is to be computed.

Solution to this problem for linear SAR is in [50]. Solution to the third order relations with constant coefficients $a_{ji} = a_j$, $j = 1, 2, ..., k + 1$, is illustrated in Fig. 46.

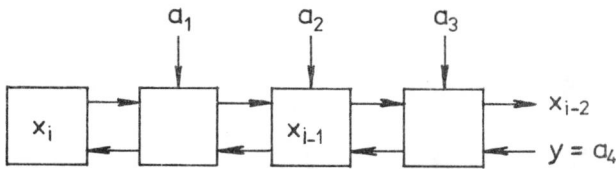

Fig. 46. Systolic array for computation of a linear recurrent relation.

The array consists of $k + 1$ processors $p_1, p_2, ..., p_{k+1}$. The auxiliary variable $y = a_{k+1}$ enters p_{k+1} in every other step. In p_1, x_i are generated in every other step, which in the next steps proceed to the right. Thus, the even and odd processors work in alternating steps. Processor p_j, $j = 2, 3, ..., k + 1$, has the registers R_a^j, R_x^j and R_y^j. In alternating steps, p_j executes

$$R_x^j \leftarrow R_x^{j-1}, \quad R_a^j \leftarrow a_{j-1},$$
$$R_y^j \leftarrow R_y^{j+1}, \quad (R_y^{k+1} \leftarrow a_{k+1}),$$
$$R_y^j \leftarrow R_y^j + R_a^j R_x^j.$$

Processor p_1 has the register R_x^1 and in its active step it executes $R_x^1 \leftarrow R_y^2$. The first $2k$ steps of computation require a special operating mode. During them, the initial values of $x_0, x_1, ..., x_{k-1}$ are read into R_x^1 with a time delay of two steps. The actual computation starts as soon as x_0 gets into p_{k+1} and meets a_k and a_{k+1}. The resulting values x_i leave p_{k+1} within $2k + 2$ steps.

The methods based on the theory of iterative arrays [35] are most suitable for computation of the recurrent relations of low order. Let $x_i = f(a_i, x_{i-1})$, $i = 1, 2, ..., n$, be a recurrent relation of first order with initial value x, where f is an arbitrary function of two variables and only x_n is to be computed. Computation of x_i, $i = 1, 2, ..., n$, is executed on n pipeline processors, as shown in Fig. 47, where the 0th step of computation is illustrated.

The processors from left to right are labelled by $p_1, p_2, ..., p_n$. The processor p_i, $i = 1, 2, ..., n$, has the registers R_x^i and R_a^i. In the ith step, p_i performs

$$R_a^i \leftarrow a_i,$$
$$R_x^i \leftarrow R_x^{i-1}, \quad (R_x^1 \leftarrow x_0),$$
$$R_x^i \leftarrow f(R_a^i, R_x^i).$$

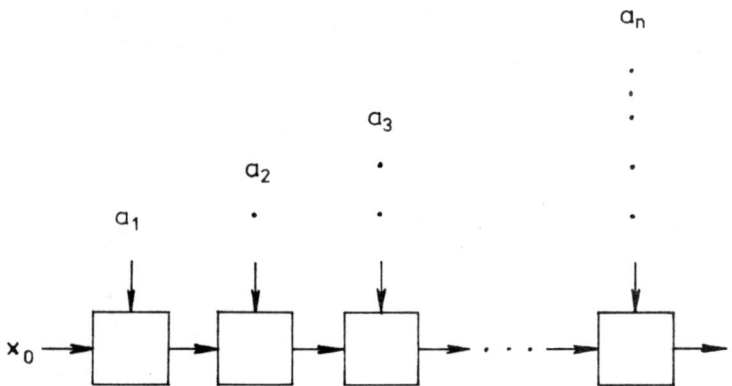

Fig. 47. Pipeline computation of a recurrent relationship of first order.

Using the above diagram we may implement as many as n problems with different initial conditions.

Now, we shall develop the application of this diagram to the computation of elementary functions.

A more general view of the iterative SAR is presented in [36], where several types of iterative SARs are characterized and their computational power, properties and limitations studied.

Computation of elementary functions

In this section a universal SAL for computation of elementary functions is proposed, based on the method of continued fractions.

The functions tg x, tgh x, arctg x and arctgh x are the base functions, because using arithmetic operations and square root all other elementary functions can be computed from them [7]. Our explanation is based on continued fractions [97]

$$\operatorname{tg} x = \frac{x}{1-} \frac{x^2}{1.3-} \frac{x^2}{3.5-} \cdots \frac{x^2}{-(2n-1)(2n+1)-} \cdots,$$

$$\operatorname{tgh} x = \frac{x}{1+} \frac{x^2}{1.3+} \frac{x^2}{3.5+} \cdots \frac{x^2}{+(2n-1)(2n+1)+} \cdots,$$

$$\operatorname{arctg} x = \frac{x}{1+} \frac{x^2}{1.3+} \frac{4x^2}{3.5+} \cdots \frac{n^2 x^2}{+(2n-1)(2n+1)+} \cdots,$$

$$\operatorname{arctgh} x = \frac{x}{1-} \frac{x^2}{1.3-} \frac{4x^2}{3.5-} \cdots \frac{n^2 x^2}{-(2n-1)(2n+1)-} \cdots.$$

(61)

We assume that for functions (61) the argument x lies in the interval of fast convergence of continued fractions, to achieve the required precision, it suffices to calculate the nth approximant of the continued fraction.

Denote

$$f(x) = \frac{x}{1+} \frac{b_2}{1+} \cdots \frac{b_n}{+1},$$

$$c_j = \frac{1}{(2j-3)(2j-1)}, \quad d_j = \frac{(j-1)^2}{(2j-3)(2j-1)}, \quad j = 2, 3, \ldots, n.$$

Then the equations can be formulated as follows

$$f(x) = \begin{cases} \text{tg } x, & b_j = c_j t, & t = -x^2, \\ \text{tgh } x, & b_j = c_j t, & t = x^2, \\ \text{arctg } x, & b_j = d_j t, & t = x^2, \\ \text{arctgh } x, & b_j = d_j t, & t = -x^2. \end{cases} \quad (62)$$

Values of $f(x)$ are determined through the computation of continued fractions [63]. According to it, $f(x)$ is computed from the relations

$$y_1 = y_2 = 1,$$
$$y_k = y_{k-1} + b_{n+3-k} y_{k-2}, \quad k = 3, 4, \ldots, n+1, \quad (63)$$

$$f(x) = \frac{x y_n}{y_{n+1}}. \quad (64)$$

An SAR for computation of relations (63) and (64) consists of two interconnected linear processor arrays (Fig. 48).

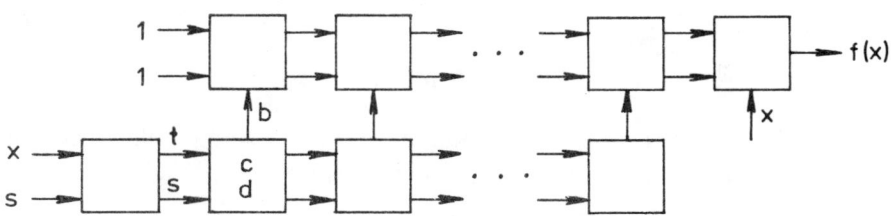

Fig. 48. Systolic array for computation of elementary functions.

Coefficients b_i, $i = 2, 3, \ldots$, are generated in the lower row, relationships (63) and (64) are computed in the upper row. Label the processors in the upper (lower) row from left to right by p_i (q_i), $i = 1, 2, \ldots, n$, respectively. Now introduce the variable s; its values will determine, which of the functions (61) is to be computed. Processor q_1 has the registers R_t^1, R_s^1 and in each step it executes

$$R_t^1 \leftarrow x,$$
$$R_s^1 \leftarrow s,$$
$$R_t^1 \leftarrow \pm (R_t^1)^2,$$

where the sign is chosen such as to correspond to s and equations (62). Processor q_i, $i = 2, 3, \ldots, n$, has the registers R_c^i and R_d^i in which, c_{n+1-i} and d_{n+1-i} are stored. Furthermore, q_i has the registers R_t^i, R_s^i and R_b^i. In one step it performs

$$R_s^i \leftarrow R_s^{i-1}, \quad R_t^i \leftarrow R_t^{i-1},$$
$$R_b^i \leftarrow \begin{cases} R_c^i R_t^i, & \text{for tg } x, \text{tgh } x, \\ R_d^i R_t^i, & \text{for arctg } x, \text{arctgh } x. \end{cases}$$

Processor p_i, $i = 1, 2, \ldots, n$, has the registers R_a^i, R_y^i and R_z^i. In every step, the processors p_i, $i < n$, execute

$$R_a^i \leftarrow R_b^{i+1}, \quad R_y^i \leftarrow R_z^{i-1}, \quad (R_y^1 \leftarrow 1),$$
$$R_z^i \leftarrow R_y^{i-1}, \quad (R_z^1 \leftarrow 1),$$
$$R_z^i \leftarrow R_y^i + R_a^i R_z^i.$$

In every step, the processor p_n computes relation (64)

$$R_a^n \leftarrow x,$$
$$R_y^n \leftarrow R_y^{n-1},$$
$$R_z^n \leftarrow R_z^{n-1},$$
$$R_z^n \leftarrow R_a^n R_y^n / R_z^n.$$

The value of function $f(x)$ is stored in the register R_z^n. Using pipelined computation, the proposed SAR yields in every step a new value of function $f(x)$.

3.3.3 Operations with polynomials

In this section we shall describe SAL for multiplication and division of polynomials, according to [42].

Multiplication of polynomials

Consider the polynomials

$$A_m(t) = \sum_{i=0}^{m} a_i t^i,$$

$$B_n(t) = \sum_{i=0}^{n} b_i t^i.$$

The coefficients of their product

$$C_{m+n}(t) = \sum_{i=0}^{m+n} c_i t^i$$

are defined in the following way

$$c_i = \sum_{k=0}^{i} a_k b_{i-k}, \quad i = 0, 1, \ldots, m+n,$$

where

$$a_i = 0 \quad \text{for } i > m,$$
$$b_i = 0 \quad \text{for } i > n.$$

Computation of c_i is executed using recurrent relations

$$c_i^{(-1)} = 0,$$
$$c_i^{(k)} = c_i^{(k-1)} + a_k b_{i-k},$$
$$c_i = c_i^{(i)} \quad \text{for } k = 0, 1, \ldots, i$$

on an SAR that consists of $m + 1$ processors. The computation for $m = 2$ is shown in Fig. 49.

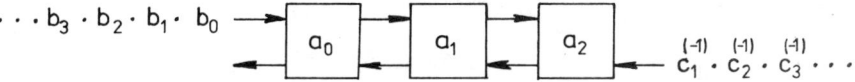

Fig. 49. Multiplication of polynomials.

The processors from left to right are labelled by $p_0, p_1, \ldots, p_m$. Because the values b_i (c_i^{-1}) enter the array from the left (right) delayed by two steps, the even and odd processors are working in alternating steps. Processor p_j has the registers R_a^j, R_b^j and R_c^j. Prior to starting the multiplication the value a_j is stored into R_a^j. In its active step the processor executes

$$R_b^j \leftarrow R_b^{j-1}, \quad (R_b^0 \leftarrow b_j),$$
$$R_c^j \leftarrow R_c^{j+1}, \quad (R_c^m \leftarrow c_i^{(-1)}),$$
$$R_c^j \leftarrow R_c^j + R_a^j R_b^j.$$

The resulting value c_i is obtained from processor p_0. The whole computation takes $O(m+n)$ steps.

The above algorithm is an optimal solution with respect to the area **A** = $= \theta(nk)$ [95, 96], where k is the number of bits of the coefficients, provided the computation is performed over the ring of residual numbers [96, 97]. In [78], a recursive algorithm is proposed for multiplication of polynomials, which is optimal with respect to the measure AP^2. Paper [45] is devoted to one-dimensional convolution, which in fact, represents a sort of multiplication of polynomials. Here there are 6 systolic and semisystolic algorithms described for this problem.

Division of polynomials

Now we have the polynomials $C_{m+n}(t)$, $A_m(t)$ and we search for the polynomials $B_n(t)$ and $R_k(t)$

$$R_k(t) = \sum_{i=0}^{k} r_i t^i,$$

such that it holds

$$C_{m+n}(t) = A_m(t) B_n(t) + R_k(t),$$

where $k < n$ and the polynomials A, B, C have been specified in the preceding section. Division of polynomials is an inverse operation to multiplication. Consequently, for its computation the SAR from the preceding section can be used, in which the data flow of b, c is changed to the opposite flow and the function of processor p_m is adapted. The whole procedure for $m = n = 2$ is shown in Fig. 50.

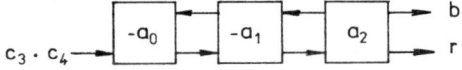

Fig. 50. Division of polynomials.

In an active step, the processor p_j, $j = 0, 1, ..., m-1$, executes

$$R_b^j \leftarrow R_b^{j+1},$$

$$R_c^j \leftarrow R_c^{j-1}, \quad (R_c^0 \leftarrow c_j),$$
$$R_c^j \leftarrow R_c^j + R_a^j R_b^j.$$

The value of $-a_j$ is stored in R_a^j. Processor p_m has the registers R_a^m, R_b^m and R_c^m; a_m is stored in R_a^m. In an active step the processor p_m executes

$$R_c^m \leftarrow R_c^{m-1},$$
$$R_b^m \leftarrow R_c^m / R_a^m,$$

and the contents of R_b^m gives the corresponding b_i. As soon as the computation b_0 has been finished, the operation $R_b^m \leftarrow 0$ is executed in p_m, and the coefficients of the remainder $R_k(t)$ start to be generated in the processor p_{m-1}. They are obtained from the register R_c^m. The time complexity of division of polynomials on the above SAR is $O(n)$.

3.3.4 Signal processing algorithms

According to [42], the SARs are most advantageously applied in implementing the problems that arise in signal processing. To the most common signal processing methods there belong various types of filtrations, convolutions and transformations. The following sections are devoted to algorithms of two-dimensional convolution and Fourier Transform.

The reader interested in this subject is referred to monograph [32] which is devoted to VLSI algorithms to solve the problems of image processing and pattern recognition.

Two-dimensional convolution

We have matrices $\mathbf{X} = (x_{ij})$ of dimension $n \times n$ and $\mathbf{W} = (w_{ij})$ of dimension

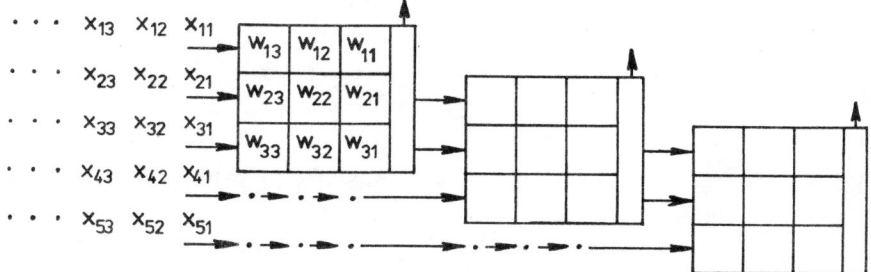

Fig. 51. Systolic array for two-dimensional convolution.

$k \times k$. Without loss of generality we can suppose that $k = 3$. A two-dimensional convolution is defined as follows.

For each $r, s, 2 \leq r, s \leq n - 1$ compute

$$y_{rs} = \sum_{i=1}^{3} \sum_{j=1}^{3} w_{ij} x_{r+i-2, s+j-2}.$$

The SAR for a two-dimensional convolution is described in [49]; for $n = 5$ it is shown in Fig. 51.

A systolic array is composed of $n - 2$ identical processors, each of them containing 10 modules. The matrix elements of **W** are permanently stored in nine square modules. In the ith row ($i = 1, 2, 3$) of the modules, the temporary results are computed in parallel

$$y_{rs}^i = \sum_{j=1}^{3} w_{ij} x_{r+i-2, s+j-2}$$

while in the rectangular module the terms are summed up

$$y_{rs} = \sum_{i=1}^{3} y_{rs}^i.$$

The operation of the modules is synchronized. The arrangement and timing of input matrix elements of **X** can be seen in Fig. 51. Now, we can describe the procedure by which the computation of y_{rs}^i is implemented. Label the modules in the ith row from left to right by q_1, q_2 and q_3, respectively. The module q_k, $k = 1, 2, 3$, has the registers R_x^k, R_y^k, R_z^k and R_w^k. The weighing coefficient $w_{i, 4-k}$ is stored in R_w^k. The processor q_k executes in each step the following operations

$$R_y^k \leftarrow R_y^{k-1}, \quad (R_y^1 \leftarrow 0),$$
$$R_z^k \leftarrow R_x^k, \quad R_x^k \leftarrow R_z^{k-1}, \quad (R_x^1 \leftarrow x_{ij}),$$
$$R_y^k \leftarrow R_y^k + R_w^k R_x^k.$$

The resulting value y_{rs}^i is obtained from the register R_y^3 in three steps.

Fourier Transform

Fourier Transform (FT) is one of the most frequently used mathematical techniques in signal processing. Much effort was devoted especially to its implementation on serial and parallel computers in its discrete form (DFT). In the present section two SALs for computation of the DFT on an SAR will be described, according to [89]. Formally, the DFT is defined as

3.3 Numerical algorithms

$$y = Ax, \quad x = (x_i), \quad y = (y_i), \quad i = 0, 1, 2, \ldots, n-1,$$

where A is a matrix of dimension $n \times n$ with the i, jth element $w^{(i-1)(j-1)}$, whereby w is the nth primitive root of unity [3].

Algorithm 1

To compute the DFT, an SAR for multiplication of a matrix by a vector from Section 3.2 will be used. Because the elements of matrix A have a special form, they will be generated in the SAR. In general, we may suppose that n is even. The case of $n = 4$ is demonstrated in Fig. 52.

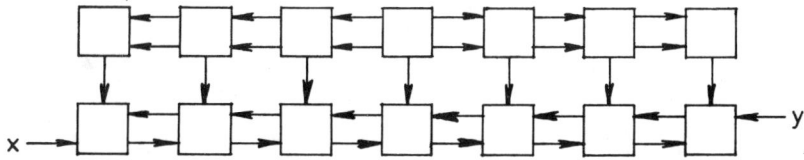

Fig. 52. Systolic array for computation of DFT.

The SAR consists of $4n - 2$ processors. The lower row of processors is functionally identical with the SAR from the algorithm for multiplication of a matrix by a vector. The elements of matrix A are computed in the upper row. Label the processors in the lower (upper) row from left by p_i (q_i), $i = 1, 2, \ldots, 2n - 1$. The processor q_n has the registers Q_a^n, Q_t^n and Q_w^n. At the beginning, 1's are stored in Q_a^n and Q_t^n and the value of w is in R_w^n. In an even step, q_n executes

$$Q_a^n \leftarrow Q_a^n (Q_t^n)^2 Q_w^n,$$
$$Q_t^n \leftarrow Q_t^n Q_w^n.$$

The processor q_i, $i < n$, for even (odd) i, has the registers R_a^i, R_t^j. In an even (odd) step, it executes

$$Q_a^i \leftarrow Q_a^{i+1},$$
$$Q_t^i \leftarrow Q_t^{i+1},$$
$$Q_a^i \leftarrow Q_a^i Q_t^i.$$

The processors q_i, for $i > n$, operates similarly, with the exception that the data transfer among the processors proceeds from left to right. The processor p_i, for even (odd) i, in an odd (even) step performs the transfer

$$R_a^i \leftarrow Q_a^i,$$

whereas all other operations are the same as in the algorithm for multiplication of a matrix by a vector. The computation of the DFT starts with the first step, when x_0 enters p_n and 1 from Q_a^n gets into R_a^n.

As follows from results of [26], this algorithm represents an optimal solution with respect to the area $A = \theta(nk)$, where k is the number of bits of the elements.

Algorithm 2

Another algorithm is the algorithm of Fast Fourier Transform, which was adapted by Thompson to computation on an SAR [89]. We shall assume that $n = 2^k$, k being a natural number. The general scheme of computation for $n = 16$ is shown in Fig. 53.

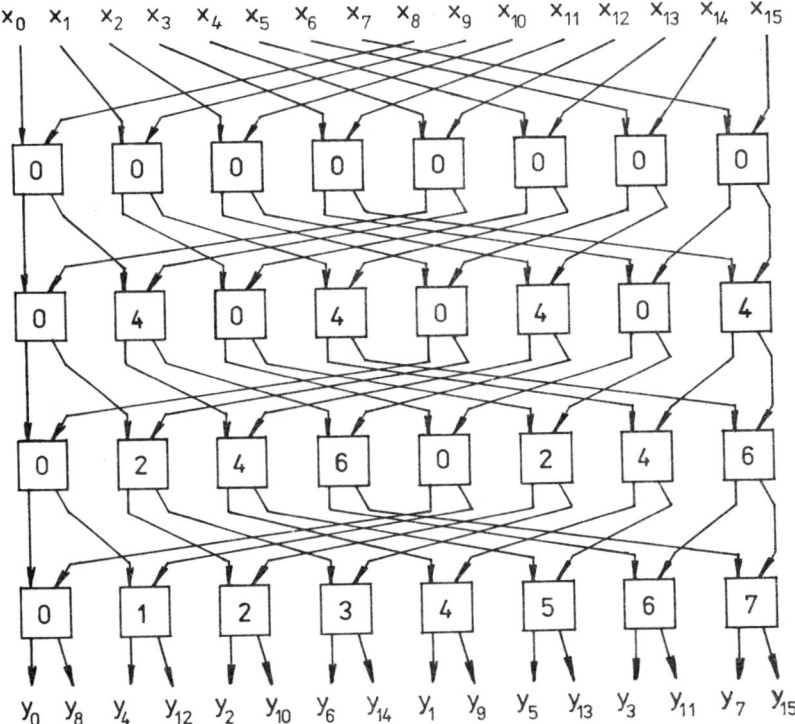

Fig. 53. Systolic array for computation of FFT.

The vector elements of **x** input from the top, while the elements of **y** output from the bottom. The SAR is composed of k-rows, each of them having $n/2$ processors; and they are interconnected with the perfect shuffle network. Label the processors of the ith row and the jth column by p_{ij}, $i = 1, 2, ..., k, j = 0, 1, ..., n/2 - 1$. The processor p_{ij} has the registers R_w^{ij}, R_{2j}^i and R_{2j+1}^i. The constant $w^{a_{ij}}$ is stored in R_w^{ij}, where $a_{ij} = 2^{k-1} j \pmod{n/2}$.

Let $s = 2j, 2j + 1$. The processor p_j executes in one step $R_s^i \leftarrow R_m^{i-1}$ for $m = (ns/2 + \lfloor s/2 \rfloor) \bmod n$, $i = 2, 3, ..., k$, $R_s^1 \leftarrow X_{\bar{s}}$, where $\bar{s}$ is s, expressed in bit-reversal code

$$R_{2j}^i \leftarrow R_{2j}^i + R_w^{ij} R_{2j+1}^i,$$
$$R_{2j+1}^i \leftarrow R_{2j}^i - R_w^{ij} R_{2j+1}^i.$$

The resulting vector is obtained from registers R_s^k in k steps, the element $y_{\bar{s}}$ is stored in R_s^k.

3.4 Non-numerical algorithms

In this section several algorithms for solving the non-numerical problems are presented. Special attention is paid to the algorithms for data manipulation as well as to algorithms of graphs.

3.4.1 Algorithms for data manipulation

Here special emphasis is put on the algorithms for pattern matching, sorting and selection of the maximum element.

Pattern matching

Assume to have an infinite sequence of characters $s_1, s_2, ..., s_k, ...$ and a definite k-character pattern $p_1, p_2, ..., p_k$, where

$$s_i = s_i^n s_i^{n-1} ... s_i^1, \qquad i = 1, 2, ...,$$
$$p_j = p_j^n p_j^{n-1} ... p_j^1, \qquad j = 1, 2, ..., k,$$

are bit-representations of characters. The task is to detect each coincidence of the pattern with a k-tuple of successive characters of the sequence. Let $r_1, r_2, r_3, ...$ be the sequence of comparison results, the step of pattern matching, for $i = 1, 2, ...,$ can then be formulated as follows

$$R_i = \begin{cases} 1, & \text{if for every } j, j = 1, 2, ..., k, s_{i-k+j} = p_j, \\ 0, & \text{in other cases.} \end{cases}$$

To solve the above problem Kung and Foster have suggested an orthogonal SAR [29] which, for $n = 4, k = 4$, is shown in Fig. 54. The SAR is composed of

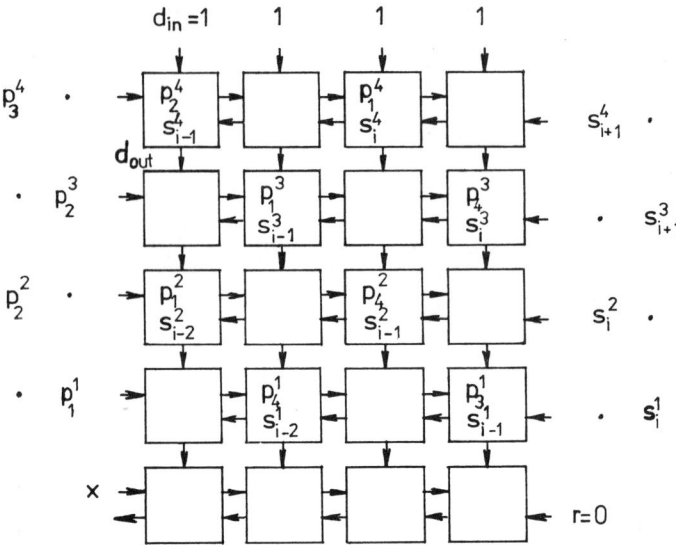

Fig. 54. Orthogonal systolic array for pattern matching.

two types of $(n+1)k$ processors which are labelled by p_{ij}, $i = 1, 2, \ldots, n+1$, $j = 1, 2, \ldots, k$, in the usual matrix form. The corresponding bits of characters of the pattern are compared with those of the sequence in rows $1, 2, \ldots, n$ and the result of comparison with the pattern is generated in the $(n+1)$st row. The arrangement and timing of input bits can be seen in Fig. 54. The processors p_{ij} operate for $i+j$ even or odd in alternating steps. The processor p_{ij} has the input (output) variables p_{in}, s_{in}, d_{in} (p_{out}, s_{out}, d_{out}) for input (output) of bits of pattern, sequence and the result of comparison of these bits. In an active step it executes

$$p_{\text{out}} \leftarrow p_{\text{in}},$$
$$s_{\text{out}} \leftarrow s_{\text{in}},$$
$$d_{\text{out}} \leftarrow d_{\text{in}} \wedge (p_{\text{in}} = s_{\text{in}}),$$

whereas in processors $p_{1j}, j = 1, 2, \ldots, k$, d_{in} is of value 1. The processor $p_{n+1,j}$, $j = 1, 2, \ldots, k$, has the input (output) variables x_{in}, d_{in}, r_{in} (x_{out}, r_{out}), and the register t. The variable x denotes the end of the pattern, while d_{in} yields the results of comparison of one pattern character to one sequence character; r is the result of comparison of the whole pattern. The temporary result of comparison of the first m, $m < k$ character is stored in the register t. In active step the processor $p_{n+1,j}$ performs

$$x_{\text{out}} \leftarrow x_{\text{in}},$$

whereas for $p_{n+1,1}$ it holds

$$x_{\text{in}} = \begin{cases} 1, & \text{if the last bit of pattern } p_k^1 \text{ was} \\ & \text{read into SAR in the preceding step,} \\ 0, & \text{in other cases,} \end{cases}$$

$$r_{\text{out}} \leftarrow t \wedge d_{\text{in}}, \quad t \leftarrow 1, \qquad \text{if } x_{\text{in}} = 1,$$

$$r_{\text{out}} \leftarrow r_{\text{in}}, \qquad t \leftarrow t \wedge d_{\text{in}}, \quad \text{if } x_{\text{in}} = 0,$$

while for $p_{n+1,k}$, $r_{\text{in}} = 0$.

The results of pattern matching are obtained in every other step from processor $p_{n+1,1}$.

Sorting

Sorting is one of the tasks most frequently solved on computers. In paper [87], thirteen algorithms are proposed for sorting on SAR. In this section, just the odd-even sorting algorithm and rank sorting are treated.

Odd-even sorting

Have n numbers $a_1, a_2, \ldots, a_n$ that are to be ordered according to their magnitude. Consider the linear SAR consisting of the processors $p_1, p_2, \ldots, p_n$ and suppose n to be even. The processor p_i, $i = 1, 2, \ldots, n$, has registers R^i, a^i. Prior to starting the sorting, the number a_i is in R^i. In odd steps, the processors p_{2j-1}, $j = 1, 2, \ldots, n/2$, execute

$$Q^{2j-1} \leftarrow R^{2j},$$
$$R^{2j} \leftarrow \max(Q^{2j-1}, R^{2j-1}),$$
$$R^{2j-1} \leftarrow \min(Q^{2j-1}, R^{2j-1}).$$

In even steps, the processors p_{2j}, $j = 1, 2, \ldots, n/2$, operate as follows

$$Q^{2j} \leftarrow R^{2j+1},$$
$$R^{2j+1} \leftarrow \max(Q^{2j}, R^{2j}),$$
$$R^{2j} \leftarrow \min(Q^{2j}, R^{2j}).$$

After n steps, the numbers a_i, $i = 1, 2, \ldots, n$, will be stored in an order according to their values in registers R^i, the smallest number being in R^1.

Practical implementation of this algorithm on a single chip for $n = 6$ of 8-bit numbers is dealt with in paper [18]. For $k = c \log n$, $c > 1$, the above algorithm is an optimal solution with respect to the area [2, 7, 79]. See Section 3.5.2.

Rank sorting

Again, we have the numbers $a_1, a_2, \ldots, a_n$ and search for the n-tuple of $v_1, v_2, \ldots, v_n$, such that v_i, $i = 1, 2, \ldots, n$, denotes the rank of the number a_i in an arrangement of the numbers $a_1, a_2, \ldots, a_n$ into sorted sequence. The mesh of trees is obtained from an orthogonal network of processors p_{ij}, $i, j = 1, 2, \ldots, n$, such that each of the n processors in a row (column) is connected to a binary tree processor network. A mesh of trees for $n = 4$, is shown in Fig. 55.

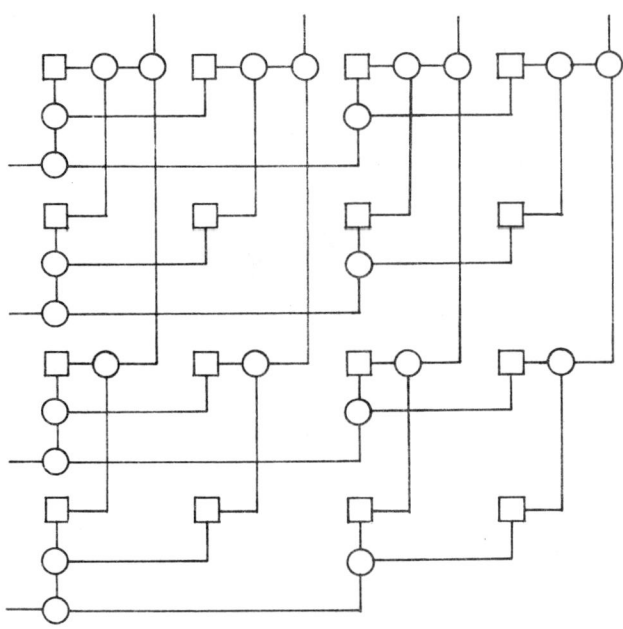

Fig. 55. Mesh of trees for $n = 4$.

Label the binary tree by $T_i(S_i)$, the tree's leaves are the processors in the ith row (column), $i = 1, 2, \ldots, n$. The processors in the vertices of $T_i(S_i)$ (leaves being an exception) perform in a single step the following functions.

(a) they create two copies of input data received from the father and send them to the sons;

(b) they sum up the input data received from the sons and send the result to the father.

The processors p_{ij} have the registers R_T^{ij}, R_S^{ij} and R^{ij}. Rank sorting is accomplished in four steps.

(1) Place the number a_i into the root processor T_i (S_i) and send it in $\log n$ steps to the leaf processors such that

$$R_S^{ij} \to a_i,$$
$$R_S^{ij} \leftarrow a_i, \quad j = 1, 2, \ldots, n.$$

(2) Processors p_{ij}, $i, j = 1, 2, \ldots, n$, execute in one step

$$R^{ij} \leftarrow \begin{cases} 1, & \text{if } R_T^{ij} > R_S^{ij} \text{ or } (R_T^{ij} = R_S^{ij} \text{ and } i < j), \\ 0, & \text{in other cases.} \end{cases}$$

(3) The tree of processors T_i, $i = 1, 2, \ldots, n$, sums up in parallel the contents of registers R^{ij}, $j = 1, 2, \ldots, n$, and in $\log n$ steps the values of v_i will be stored in the root processors T_i.

(4) The values v_i are sent to the processors p_{ij} through the trees T_i where the operations are executed. If $v_i = j$, the content of R_T^{ij} is sent to the root processor of the tree S_j. Thus, on the root processors of trees S_i, the required sorted sequence appears. The time complexity of rank sorting is $O(\log n)$ steps.

Maximum element

From n non-negative integers $a_1, a_2, \ldots, a_n$ we shall select the maximum one.
Let $a_i = a_i^{k-1} a_i^{k-2} a_i^{k-3} \ldots a_i^0$, $i = 1, 2, \ldots, n$, be the binary expression for a_i. Denote $m = \max(a_1, a_2, \ldots, a_n)$. The maximum number m will be selected on a SAR composed of $(n-2)k^2 + k(k+1)/2$ processors of two types. The SAR $n = 5$, $k = 4$ is shown in Fig. 56.

From the left and from the downside values a_i^j, $i = 1, 2, \ldots, n$, $j = 0, 1, \ldots, k - 1$, enter the SAR. The arrangement and timing can be seen in Fig. 56. The operation $\max(\max(a_1, a_2, \ldots, a_i), a_{i+1})$, $i = 1, 2, \ldots, n - 1$, is executed in the ith slanting row of square processors. The comparison of two numbers starts from the highest bits, the jth bits of maximum element, $j = 0, 1, 2, \ldots, k - 1$, are generated in the jth horizontal row. Each processor labelled by a circle performs identity functions; in one step it assigns the horizontal (vertical) input to horizontal (vertical) output. The direction of data flow can be seen from Fig. 56. The processor labelled by a square compares in one step the input bits p_{in}, q_{in} on the basis of the state of $x_{in} y_{in}$ (which stores the results of the comparison of higher bits). Further, it produces the result p_{out} and the new state of $x_{out} y_{out}$. Let $x_{in} y_{in} = 10$ (01) if the number entering from the left of the slanting row of the processor is larger (less) than the numbers entering from the bottom, let $x_{in} y_{in} =$ $= 00$ if these numbers coincide in the bits compared up to now. The square processor executes the following Boolean functions.

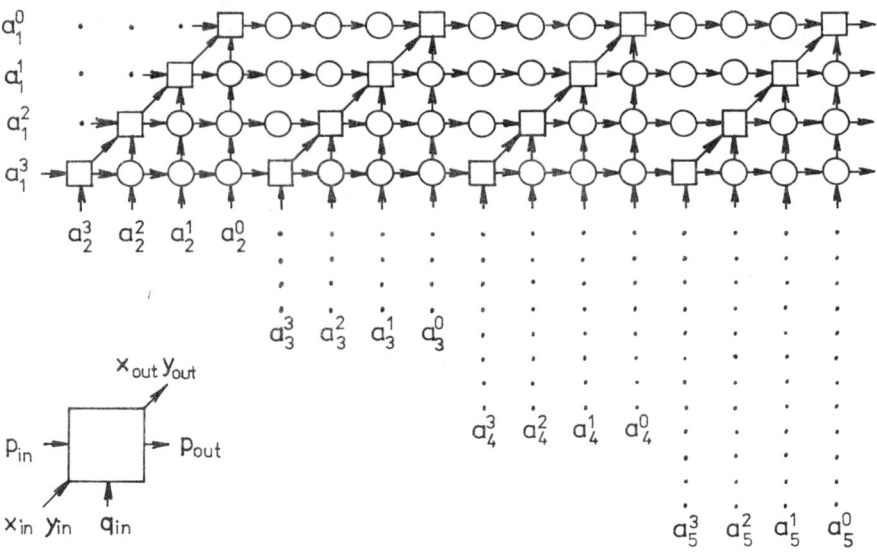

Fig. 56. Orthogonal systolic array for searching the maximum element.

$$p_{out} \leftarrow p_{in}\bar{y}_{in} + q_{in}\bar{x}_{in},$$
$$x_{out} \leftarrow x_{in}\bar{y}_{in} + p_{in}\bar{x}_{in}\bar{y}_{in}\bar{q}_{in},$$
$$y_{out} \leftarrow \bar{x}_{in}y_{in} + \bar{p}_{in}\bar{x}_{in}\bar{y}_{in}\bar{q}_{in}.$$

The advantage of the above scheme is that it makes it possible to simultaneously implement as much as nk problems and that in each step one computation is completed. In [95] there are several optimal SALs suggested for the maximum element with respect to measures A, AT, AT^2 in a linear model. For linear model of a VLSI circuit see Section 3.5.1.

3.4.2 Algorithms on graphs

Let us consider a graph $G = (V, H)$, where $V = \{1, 2, ..., n\}$ and $H \subset \binom{V}{2}$. Under the notion "a connected component" we understand a maximum connected subgraph of the graph G. One of the possibilities how to describe all the connected components of the graph G is to construct a function $f: V \leftarrow \{1, 2, ..., n\}$ such that if one component consists of vertices $v_1, v_2, ..., v_i$, than $f(v_k) = \min(v_1, v_2, ..., v_i)$, $k = 1, 2, ..., i$. A linear SAR composed of $n + 1$ processors $p_1, p_2, ..., p_{n+1}$, which constructs the function f is suggested in [77].

Input data of the SAR are represented by graph edges (u, v) which in every other step enter p_1. The processor p_i, $i = 1, 2, \ldots, n$, has the registers R_u^i, R_v^i, R_x^i, R_y^i, $R_{u'}^i$, $R_{v'}^i$, R_{max}^i, R_{min}^i, R_f^i and R^i. Prior to starting the computation, the number i is stored in R_f^i, R^i, while the other registers are set to zero. In an active step, p_i performs

$$R_u^i \leftarrow R_u^{i-1}, \quad R_v^i \leftarrow R_v^{i-1}, \quad (R_u^1 \leftarrow u, \quad R_v^1 \leftarrow v),$$

$$R_x^i \leftarrow R_x^{i-1}, \quad R_y^i \leftarrow R_y^{i-1}, \quad (R_x^1 \leftarrow 0, \quad R_y^1 \leftarrow 0),$$

$$R_{u'}^i \leftarrow R_{u'}^{i+1}, \quad R_{v'}^i \leftarrow R_{v'}^{i+1}, \quad R_{max}^i \leftarrow R_{max}^{i+1}, \quad R_{min}^i \leftarrow R_{min}^{i+1}.$$

If $R_f^i = R_{max}^i$, then $R_f^i \leftarrow R_{min}^i$.
If $R_u^i = R^i$, $(R_v^i = R^i)$, then $R_x^i \leftarrow R_f^i$, $(R_y^i \leftarrow R_f^i)$.
If $R_u^i = R_{max}^i$, $(R_v^i = R_{max}^i)$, then $R_x^i \leftarrow R_{min}^i$, $(R_y^i \leftarrow R_{min}^i)$.

At the beginning, the registers R_x^{n+1}, R_y^{n+1}, $R_{u'}^{n+1}$, $R_{v'}^{n+1}$, R_{max}^{n+1} and R_{min}^{n+1} of the processor p_{n+1} are set to 0. In an active step, p_{n+1} performs

$$R_{u'}^{n+1} \leftarrow R_u^n, \quad R_{v'}^{n+1} \leftarrow R_v^n,$$

$$R_x^{n+1} \leftarrow R_x^n, \quad R_y^{n+1} \leftarrow R_y^n,$$

$$R_{max}^{n+1} \leftarrow \max(R_x^{n+1}, R_y^{n+1}),$$

$$R_{min}^{n+1} \leftarrow \min(R_x^{n+1}, R_y^{n+1}).$$

If the graph G has m edges, $2m + 2n$ steps are needed to compute values $f(i)$ into R_f^i.

Another algorithm for connected components based on the computation of transitive closure is given in [91].

Transitive closure

Let G be an oriented graph with vertices $1, 2, \ldots, n$ and **A** be a Boolean matrix of type $n \times n$ with elements $a_{ij} = 1$, $i, j = 1, 2, \ldots, n$, iff in G there exists an oriented edge from i to j. A transitive closure of matrix **A** is a Boolean matrix **A***, whose i, jth element is equal to 1, iff in G there exists an oriented path leading from i to j. In [34] it has been shown that to solve the above problem a rectangular SAR for matrix multiplication can be used (see Section 3.3), with the following modifications.

(1) Matrix **B** is replaced by matrix **A** and register R_a^{in} (R_b^{ni}) is connected with R_a^{i1} (R_b^{1i}), $i = 1, 2, \ldots, n$.

(2) Function of the processors does not change, the only exception being the arithmetic operations of addition and multiplication that are replaced by opera-

tions of logical addition and multiplication. In the case a_{ij} is moved to R_a^{ij} (R_b^{ij}), the following operation is executed

$$R_a^{ij} \leftarrow R_c^{ij}, \quad (R_b^{ij} \leftarrow R_c^{ij}).$$

The elements of matrix **A**, which have reached the processors p_{in} (p_{ni}), $i = 1, 2, \ldots, n$, are moved in one step to p_{i1} (p_{1i}). After three repeated transitions of matrices through the SAR, the matrix **A*** will be stored in register R_c^{ij}. The proof of correctness of the above algorithm and its detailed analysis can be found in [91].

3.5 Complexity of systolic algorithms

Invention of SAL has given rise to the theory of complexity of systolic algorithms. The traditional complexity measures for parallel algorithms are not satisfactory any more. These measures were only aimed at following the number of arithmetic or logic operations, the number of processors and memory space. The input-output operations and interprocessor communication were neglected. Because the SAL is usually implemented on a single chip, a new general measure of complexity, i.e. the area of a VLSI circuit, has been introduced. This measure involves the area of processors, memory, input-output ports and interprocessor connections. Another important complexity measure is the computation time of an algorithm, which covers the input-output operations, shifts (transfers) and computations on processors. Exact definitions will be given in the next section.

The complexity problem of SAL involves

(1) lower bounds, i.e. determination of a limit with respect to a certain measure necessary for computation of a definite class of algorithms to solve the problem under consideration,

(2) upper bounds, i.e., construction of an algorithm for the given problem, whose complexity measure is minimum.

If the lower and the upper bounds are equal, we say that the algorithm is optimal. In an effort to achieve an optimal algorithm and to design the upper bounds, the conditions imposed on SAL are often weakened. That is why in the present section, under SAL an arbitrary algorithm implemented on a single chip will be understood. Description of a model of a VLSI circuit, definition of complexity measures and the most important methods used in determining the lower bounds are presented in the next two sections.

3.5.1 The model of a VLSI circuit

Today there exist several models of VLSI circuits different in their degree of abstraction as well as in their special properties. In this section, the most common models are introduced and discussed along with their special properties. These properties enable extension and modification of the models, if necessary. We shall start with the first model of VLSI, according to [88].

A VLSI circuit is a computational device by which a set of m Boolean functions $(y_1, y_2, ..., y_m) = F(x_1, x_2, ..., x_n)$ is realized. Let the function f be defined on a domain $D \subset E^n$. Let X (Y) denote the set of input (output) variables.

Input (output) variables are assigned to input (output) nodes of the circuits. Computation in the circuit is performed by combinatioíinal and sequential circuits.

A model of a VLSI circuit is also called a communication graph (CG). The CG originates, when each simple logic system in the circuit is assigned a vertex CG, each wire is assigned an oriented edge of the graph, and the following conditions are satisfied:

(1) Geometrical conditions

The CG is laid out into a square mesh of distance λ (length unit) and it holds that

(a) each edge is represented by path directed along horizontal and vertical lines of the grid,

(b) at one point at maximum, p edges can have intersection. It is assumed that the edges are led in p different levels. Usually, $p \leq 3$,

(c) the CG occupies convex domain,

(d) it is assumed, that the degree of a vertex is limited by a constant b and the vertex is represented by a square of side d, if d is the number of edges entering this square,

(e) no pairs of vertices coincide with each other.

(2) Time conditions

(a) time unit τ is given, whose integer multiples specify discrete time, in which CG computes,

(b) the delay of each vertex is τ (see 3(a)),

(c) unit bandwith of edges.

(3) Conditions for the function of vertices

(a) each vertex represents a finite automaton. It has a vector of input (output) variable $\boldsymbol{x} = (x_1, x_2, ..., x_i)$ ($\boldsymbol{y} = (y_1, y_2, ..., y_j)$), respectively, where $i + j < b$, b is a constant and a vector of state variables $\boldsymbol{s} = (s_1, s_2, ..., s_k)$, where k is limited by a constant c. Behaviour of the vertex at time t is described by the transition function

$$[s(t + \tau), y(t + \tau)] = F[s(t), x(t)],$$

(b) in the CG there exist special vertices, i.e. input-output ports, through which the variables are input (output).

(4) Conditions for input-output operations
(a) each input variable enters the CG just once,
(b) each I/O variable is time and place determinate (is available at prespecified time and port, for all instances of problem),
(c) input-output ports lie on the boundary of the convex hull of the CG.

An important consequence of conditions (3) is that the area of the input-output port and the area necessary to store one bit of information occupy a constant number of area units (at least λ^2).

The existing models of VLSI circuits can be classified into three groups according to the time $T(h)$ necessary to transfer one bit of information along an edge of length h:
(1) Constant model [15]: $T(h) = \tau$;
(2) Logarithmic model [88]: $T(h) = O(\log h)$;
(3) Linear model [19]: $T(h) = O(h)$.

The above basic models can be further modified or weakened as follows:
— each input variable is read in several times [39, 78],
— condition 4(b) is weakened in such a way that only the order of variables in which they enter the input port is known before [40],
— condition 4(c) is usually omitted, especially for the reason of reaching the optimal upper bounds,
— one additional condition is imposed, the aspect ratio of the CG is constant [91].

The main complexity measures can be defined on the basis of this model of a VLSI circuit.

Area A. Under the area of a CG the area of the minimum rectangle covering of the CG is understood.

Time T. Computation time is the time which elapses between the input of the first bit and the output of the last bit of result.

Period P. Let us suppose that more problems with different inputs are computed by CG in pipelined way. Consequently, it is advantageous to define the time interval P (period) that passes between the input of two identical variables of two successive instances.

Area-time tradeoff. The cost of a circuit is reflected in the area occupied by the circuit. When optimizing the cost of a circuit, the time decreases and vice versa [61]. Thus, it is useful to compromise the cost and time aspects, which is expressed by the measures of area-time tradeoffs AP, AT, AP^2, AT^2, APT, or — in general $A^\alpha T^\beta P^\gamma$.

3.5.2 Methods of lower bounds

Let us consider the function $(y_1, y_2, ..., y_m) = f(x_1, x_2, ..., x_n)$ computed by a VLSI circuit. In this section we shall deal with methods of estimating the complexity measure of the function f with respect to measures T, A, AT^α, $1 \leqslant \alpha \leqslant 2$. All the results will be related to the models described in the preceding section, though some of them can also be applied to other models. Cases where it is necessary to impose some additional conditions to the model will be specified separately.

Lower bounds for time

Let $y_j = f_j(x_1, x_2, ..., x_n)$ be a partial function of the function f. Assume that f_j satisfies the property V_0: $\forall_i$, $i = 1, 2, ..., n$, there exist constants $a_1, a_2, ..., a_{i-1}$, $a_{i+1}, ..., a_n$ such that $f_j(a_1, a_2, ..., a_{i-1}, 0, a_{i+1}, ..., a_n) \neq f_j(a_1, a_2, ..., a_{i-1}, 1, a_{i+1}, ..., a_n)$, i.e. y_j depends on each variable x_i.

Theorem 1. Let f_j satisfy condition V_0. Then, for computation of f the time

$$T = \Omega(\log n) \text{ in constant model [96],}$$

$$T = \Omega(\log n \log \log n) \text{ in logarithmic model [1],}$$

$$T = \Omega(\sqrt{n}) \text{ in linear model [19]}$$

is necessary.

Proof. We shall prove only the third lower bound.

Let the CG have p input ports $1 \leqslant p \leqslant n$. The time of computation is at least $T = \Omega(n/p)$, since all n input values have to be read in. Another consequence of the property V_0 is that there exists an oriented path from each input port to an output port for y_j. Since the input-output ports lie at the boundary of a convex domain, there exists at least one oriented path of length $\Omega(p)$ [19]. Thus, in a linear model, the time is, at least $T = \Omega(p)$. These estimates yield the theorem.

The bound is optimal for addition using a carry look-ahead adder [13]. In the same paper optimal upper bounds for cyclic shift and multiplication of numbers are proved.

In a constant model the $\Omega(\log n)$ bound is tight for operations, such as addition of numbers. The fact that the highest bit of the sum depends on all input bits is easy to prove.

The estimate is optimal and can be achieved by a carry look-ahead adder [15].

Lower bounds for area

In this section we shall describe two fundamental methods for finding lower bounds on area. We shall compare their computational power; a number of important results obtained by their use will be introduced. Let the sequence $t_0, t_1, \ldots$ denote the discrete time. Let n_i be the number of input bits which were read in at time t_i. Define $N_0 = 0$, $N_i = N_{i-1} + n_i$, $i = 1, 2, \ldots$, where N_i is the number of bits which were read in before t_i. Let s_i be the number of information bits stored in CG at time t_i. Let Y_i denote the set of output variables which were still not computed at time t_i. Let S_i be the number of all the possible sets of results which can be output by variables in Y_i.

Method I [9, 15]

Theorem 2 [9]. The area of a circuit computing the function f is

$$A \geq n_i + s_i,$$

where

$$s_i \geq \log S_i - (N - N_i).$$

Proof. In the circuit $n_i + s_i$ bits information are stored while $N - N_{i+1}$ is not yet read in. From these bits, $2^{N - N_{i+1}} 2^{m_i + s_i}$ different states can be generated, this number being not less than S_i.

Moreover, if f is subjective and f_j, $j = 1, 2, \ldots, n$, has the property V_0, a very important consequence follows from Theorem 2 [15].

Consequence 1. $A = \Omega(\log |f[D]|)$, where $|f[D]|$ denotes the cardinality of the image of the function f.

Proof. Let t_i be the time at which the last bits are read in. Obviously,

$$N_i + n_i = N_{i+1} = n \quad \text{and} \quad S_0 = |f[D]|.$$

Since each output depends on each input, output variables could not yet have been computed. Hence it holds that $S_i = S_0$. Substituting these equations into lower bounds for area, we obtain the consequence.

On estimating lower bounds by the above method, only Consequence 1 is usually used in practice. It was applied, for instance, in developing lower bounds, such as:

— multiplication of two n-bit numbers requires the area $A = \Omega(n)$ [15],

— Discrete Fourier and Walsh–Hadamard Transforms of n k-bit elements require the area

$$A = \Omega(nk) \quad [26],$$

— sorting of n k-bit numbers requires the area [12, 27, 79]

$$A = \begin{cases} \Omega(n \log n) & \text{if } k \geq 2 \log n, \\ \Omega(n(k - \log n)) & \text{if } 2 \log n > k > \log n, \\ \Omega(n) & \text{if } k = \log n, \\ \Omega(2^k (\log n - k)) & \text{if } k < \log n. \end{cases}$$

The above method has one serious disadvantage — it is not applicable in the case of small m. For instance, for $m = 1$ it only yields a trivial lower bound. Now we shall introduce another method, which can yield non-trivial estimates even for single-output functions:

Method II [77, 91, 96]

Again, consider the same situation as in Method I, at time t_i.

Theorem 3. If there exist Q_i distinct subfunctions of the function f, originating by assigning all the possible values to the variables read in at time t_i and by omitting the output variables from $Y - Y_i$, then

$$A = \Omega(\max(n_i, \log Q_i)).$$

Proof. Sketch. On the one hand, the circuit at time t_i reads in n_i bits and that is why $A = \Omega(n_i)$. On the other, the circuit has to provide at least $\log Q_i$ memory bits at time t_i to be able to distinguish among Q_i possible branches of computation.

This method, for $m = 1$ and $N_i = n/2$, was derived by Yao [99]. Yet, there arises a question, which of the methods is stronger? The answer is in the following theorem.

Theorem 4. The lower bound obtained by Method II is not less than the lower bound obtained by Method I.

Proof. It follows from a simple fact that $Q_i \geq S_i/2^{n-N_i}$. Thereby, several single-output functions exist, for which, using Method II, linear lower bounds [60] can be derived. Another application of Method II can be found in [28]: To select the lth minimum element of n k-bit number the area

$$A = \begin{cases} \Theta(\min(n, l(k - \log l))), & \text{for } k > \log l \\ \Theta(l), & \text{for } k = \log l \\ \Theta(2^k (\log l - k)), & \text{for } k < \log l \end{cases}$$

is needed. A special case of this theorem for $i = 1$ is presented in [95].

Applying Methods I and II, it is necessary to define the set Y_i of the variables which were not output until t_i. In this case, the following lemma is used similarly as in Consequence 1.

Lemma 1. If the variable y_j depends on at least one of the variables read in at time t_i, y_j belongs to Y_i.

Proof. It immediately follows from the definition of dependence and from Condition 4(b).

Note. The assumption in Lemma 1 is difficult to prove. That is why most often it is verified that y_j depends on every variable read in until the time t_i.

After [96] we introduce a very interesting application of Method II based on the use of Lemma 1. We say that $(y_1, y_2, ..., y_n) = f(x_i, x_2, ..., x_n, s_1, s_2, ..., s_p)$ is a transitive function of degree n, if after assigning values to variables s_i, $i = 1, 2, ..., p$, the output variable y_j is a permutation of variables x_i. Moreover, the set of all permutations forms the transitive group, i.e. each x_i can be mapped into each y_j. For example, cyclic shift in the transitive function of degree n defined as

$$y_i = x_{(i-k)(\mod n)}, \quad i = 1, 2, ..., n,$$

if $s_1 s_2 ... s_n$ is a representation of number k in binary code.

Now we introduce the notation $X_0 = \{x_1, x_2, ..., x_n\}$, $Y = \{y_1, y_2, ..., y_n\}$.

Theorem 5. Each VLSI circuit that computes a transitive function of degree n occupies an area $A = \Omega(n)$.

Proof. Sketch. Let t_i be a time instance in which the last variable was read in from X_0. From the definition of a transitive function it immediately follows that every output variable depends on every variable from X_0. Therefore $Y_i = Y$. Consider all the subfunctions that originated by assigning values to the variables from X_0. The variables that have been read in until t_i and that do not belong to X_0 are set to zero. All 2^n subfunctions are different, because if two subfunctions differ from each other in assigning a value to a variable x_j, for example, they also differ in the corresponding y_k into which x_j is mapped at a permutation given by value of $s_1, s_2, ..., s_n$. Thus, $A = \Omega(\log 2^n) = \Omega(n)$.

Problem	Degree of transitivity	Area
Cyclic shift of n-bit number	n	$\Omega(n)$
Multiplication of two n-bit numbers	n	$\Omega(n)$
Cyclic convolution of two n-component vectors with k-bit elements	nk	$\Omega(nk)$
Linear transformation of an n-component vector with elements in k-bit representation	nk	$\Omega(nk)$
Product of three matrices of order n with k-bit elements	$n^2 k$	$(n^2 k)$

According to Vuillemin [96], the following problems are described by transitive functions with corresponding lower bounds using Theorem 5.

With the exception of the cyclic shift, all the above results are related to the computations over the rings of residual numbers R_m with module $m = 2^k - 1$. Generalized results for arbitrary odd m, based on Consequence 1 are introduced in [94].

Obviously, these results are optimal, which can be demonstrated on the corresponding SALs in this chapter.

Lower bounds for AT^2

Now there follow three methods of proving lower bounds with respect to the measure AT^2. Later, we shall deal with the measure AT^α, for $1 \leqslant \alpha \leqslant 2$.

Method I

The first result in the theory of complexity of SAL was the lower bound for AT^2 for computation of the DFT [88]. The most important principle of this method is to estimate the amount of information that has to pass through the edges of the CG.

Let every output variable have assigned different output ports. Define $U(V)$ to be the set of input (output) variables. Let D be the diameter of the convex hull of the CG. We shall find a chord L perpendicular to D which divides the CG into two parts, where by this bisection the decomposition of the sets $U(V)$ is induced into U_1, U_2 (V_1, V_2) such that the input-output ports belonging to U_1, V_1 (U_2, V_2) lie to the left (right) of L, respectively. Furthermore,

$$|V_1| \leqslant |V_2| \leqslant |V_1| + 1.$$

Now assign fixed values to the variables in U_2 and define the number of all possible sets of their values of V_2 obtained for all possible assignments of values to the variables in U_1. Let Z_1 be the maximum number of such sets, if the maximum is taken over all assignments of values to the variables in U_2. Z_2 is defined by interchanging the indices. Let $Z = \max(Z_1, Z_2)$.

Definition. Under the information flow I we understand $I = \min_L \{\log Z\}$, where the minimum is taken over all the possible bisections of a CG by the chord L, which satisfy the above conditions. Hence, I defines how many bits of information have to pass through the edges intersected by L.

The Thompson method can be described by the following theorem [88].

Theorem 6. If A is the area of CG and T is the computation time, then

$$AT^2 = \Omega(I^2).$$

Proof. Let L be the chord of length $|L|$, at which the minimum flow is obtained. Let w edges intersect L. Through these w edges, during computations at least I bits of information must pass and thus, $T \geqslant I/w$. From the definition of area A is $A \geqslant |L|^2$ and $|L| \geqslant \lambda_w$, thus, $A = \Omega(w^2)$. From these inequalities the required lower bound is easy to obtain.

In [96], Vuillemin has derived an analogous theorem for the measure AP^2 and described a whole class of the so-called transitive functions, for which he has also found an information flow. A disadvantage of the Thompson method is that, that for $m = 1$ it yields only a trivial lower bound. Now we shall describe a stronger method, according to [37, 60, 91, 99], which yields a non-trivial lower bound for single-output functions.

Method II

Consider two processors, P_1 and P_2, that compute the above function f. Let the variables of the set $X_1 \subset X$, $|X_1| = n/2$ enter P_1 and P_2 calculate any set of output variables $Y_1 \subset Y$. Let the variables of $X - X_1$ enter the P_2 and P_2 compute the variables of $Y - Y_1$. π denotes the partition defined by the sets X_1 and Y_1.

Definition. $I(\pi)$ gives the maximum number of bits that have to be exchanged between P_1 and P_2 such that both P_1 and P_2 be able to compute their output variables. The maximum is taken over all the possible values assigned to input variables.

Definition. $I = \min I(\pi)$ is taken as information transfer for the function f, where the minimum is calculated over all possible partitions π.

Beginning with this definition, similarly to the preceding method, it is possible to derive the following theorem.

Theorem 7. $AT = \Omega(I^2)$.

In [37], the computation of I is reduced to a combinatorial problem of disjoint covering of zero-unit matrix with rectangles of equal elements. This makes it possible to derive lower bounds for the following problems.

Problem	AT^2
Computation of $2n$ bits of reciprocal value of an n-bit number	$\Omega(n^2)$
Computation of fixed root of an n-bit number	$\Omega(n^2)$
Product of two square ($n \times n$) matrices with k-bit elements	$\Omega(n^4 k^2)$
Solution of a system of n linear equations with n unknowns, with k-bit numbers	$\Omega(n^2 k^2)$

The results of the type $AT^2 = \Omega(n^2)$ for single-output functions have been proved in [60]. It can be shown [4] that Method II is stronger than Method I. For some problems, however, it only yields a trivial lower bound. For instance, it can be shown without any difficulty that the problem of addition of two n-bit numbers has information transfer $I = 1$. Since, if P_1 (P_2) knows the lower (upper) half of bits of the numbers and it has to compute the lower (upper) half of bits of the result, it suffices when P_1 sends to P_2 a single bit — a carry that originates on adding the lower halves of the numbers. In this bad case the following simple Method III works very well.

Method III

We have restricted ourselves to a constant model, but similar results hold also for other models. First we shall prove a simple but very useful theorem.

Theorem 8 [96]. $AT = \Omega(n)$.

Proof. If a CG has p input ports, $A = \Omega(p)$. On the other hand, to read in n input bits, a time $T = \Omega(n/p)$ is needed.

Without any additional assumptions on f, the above bound cannot be improved any more. As an example we use a serial adder of area $A = O(1)$ and time $T = O(n)$.

Theorem 9. Let at least one output variable depend on all input variables. Then it holds

$$AT^2 = \Omega(n \log n).$$

Proof. It follows immediately from Theorems 1 and 8.

The highest bit of a sum of two numbers depends on all input bits. Consequently, for this problem we have $AT^2 = \Omega(n \log n)$. As can be seen from results [15], the derived lower bound is optimal.

Methods for AT^α

Methods of searching the lower bound of the measure AT^α follow from the above methods. They can be summarized in Theorems 10 and 11.

Theorem 10. Let $A = \Omega(g(n))$ along with $AT^2 = \Omega(h(n))$. Then it holds $AT^\alpha = \Omega(g(n)^{1-\alpha/2} h(n)^{\alpha/2})$, $1 \leq \alpha \leq 2$.

Proof. It is obtained by simple algebraic operations and from assumptions.

Corollary. Let f be a single-output function with information transfer I, then it holds $AT^\alpha = \Omega(I^{1+\alpha/2})$, for $1 \leq \alpha \leq 2$.

Proof. The proof follows from the inequalities $A = \Omega(I)$, $AT^2 = \Omega(I^2)$ [60].

Theorem 11. If at least one output variable depends on all input variables, then $AT^\alpha = \Omega(n \log^{\alpha-1} n)$.

Proof. It is the same procedure as that used in Theorem 9.

Further modifications and stronger versions of the methods that have been described in this section are in [12, 21].

3.6 Conclusion

At present, the systolic algorithms go through a very fast development. The main trends of their development can be classified according to the following topics:

(1) The number of SALs for solving the case problems (especially in signal processing) grows. Along with synchronous algorithms also asynchronous systolic algorithms based on the principle of data-flow computation are proposed [51, 64]. Implementation of these algorithms on a single chip does not need any global synchronization of a network, which saves the area of circuits and accelerates computations.

Universal systolic systems that perform matrix operations are becoming still more important. Worth mentioning in this connection are the Warp-processor-linear systolic array for convolution, matrix multiplication and Fourier Transform [43], and the PSC (Programmable Systolic Chip) which represents the fundamental building block in constructing large systolic arrays [28]. Another example is the programmable systolic array for vector computations including convolution, Fourier Transform and vector product [5].

(2) Designs of algorithms are followed by works on technical implementation of systolic algorithms and systolic computers [29, 98]. This brings about the problem of a uniform description of algorithms, i.e. the SAL language. Such language should enable, to a certain extent, automatic transcription of the algorithm into logic, electric and geometric designs [46]. This problem is closely connected with the design of a silicon compiler of systolic arrays [30]. It turned out that the classical description of systolic algorithms, used also throughout this book is no more satisfactory. Numerous descriptions enabling simpler verification and simulation of SAL [62, 90] have been proposed. Transition from the design of algorithms by ad hoc methods to the systematic designing [24, 64] became inevitable. Worth mentioning is especially [59], in which SALs for recurrent relations are obtained by solving a system of vector equations. Solutions here are optimal and verified algorithms, such as those for matrix multiplication, filtration and deconvolution.

(3) Problems of SAL became also reflected in the theory of automata. Systolic automata for language recognition are defined and their computational power, limitation and relations to other computation models are studied in [23].

(4) Papers dealing with fault-tolerant systolic systems have a practical motivation. They express the aim to implement SALs not only on a chip but also on a wafer [58, 44].

(5) In the theory of complexity of algorithms efforts become manifest to develop a uniform universal computation model that would take into account the technological restrictions of the production of integrated circuits and would

be abstract enough. However, the problem of the crucial importance for the computation model of a VLSI is still not solved, irrespective of whether it is constant, logarithmic or linear.

It has been proved [93] that to achieve high transmission velocity in sublinear models it is unavoidably necessary to increase the area of conductors, too. The complexity of specified problems according to the known complexity measures is studied, new methods of finding lower bounds are proposed and new measures, such as electrical energy consumption by a circuit that has to compute a problem under consideration, are introduced in [18]. Still, there is a strict difference between the complexity of concrete problems (Boolean functions) and the complexity in average case. The hitherto known methods do not make it possible for us to obtain superlinear or superquadratic estimates of area A or AT^2. On the other hand, Leeuwen has shown that nearly all Boolean functions of n variables require the area $A = \Omega(2^n)$ [53].

Three-dimensional VLSI circuits and the complexity of algorithms, with respect to the measures V (volume) and V^2T^3 are studied in [57].

(6) Very important problems in the theory of complexity of SAL are the minimizations of the area of a VLSI circuit and the computation time. On abstracting these problems new questions arise: How to lay out a graph into a square grid such that

(a) it would occupy the minimum possible area,

(b) the length of the maximum edges would be as short as possible [54, 56, 70].

Analogical questions are also studied for the three-dimensional layouts of graphs in [57].

References

[1] A. Aggrawal, "Time with subpolynomial delay", *Proc. 17th Symp. on Theory of Computing* (Portland, 1985) pp. 59—68.

[2] H. M. Ahmed, J. M. Delosme and M. Morf, "Highly concurrent computing structures for matrix arithmetic and signal processing", *Computer* **1** (1982) 65—82.

[3] A. V. Aho, J. E. Hopcroft and J. D. Ullman, *The Design and Analysis of Computer Algorithms* (Addison-Wesley, Reading, Mass., 1976).

[4] A. V. Aho, J. D. Ullman and M. Xannakakis, "On notions of information transfer in VLSI circuits", *Proc. 25th Symp. on Foundations of Computer Science* (Boston, 1984) pp. 133—139.

[5] H. J. Alker, B. Solberg and O. Sorasen, "VLSI-implemented systolic array for vector processing", *Proc. on VLSI* (North-Holland, Amsterdam, 1983) pp. 307—316.

[6] G. Andrejková, "Systolic systems for the longest common subsequence problem", *Computers and Artif. Intelligence* **5** (1986) 199—212.

[7] M. Andrews and A. Eggerding, "A pipelined computer architecture for unified elementary function evaluation", *Comp. Electr. Engng.* **5** (1978) 189—202.
[8] J. P. Banatre, P. Frison and P. Quinton, "A systolic algorithm for connected word recognition", Techn. Rep. (IRISA, Rennes, 1982).
[9] G. M. Baudet, "On the area required by VLSI circuits", *Proc. CMU VLSI Conference* (Pittsburgh, 1981) pp. 100—107.
[10] G. M. Baudet, F. P. Preparata and J. Vuillemin, "Area-time optimal VLSI circuits for convolution", Techn. Rep. (INRIA, Le Chesny, 1980).
[11] J. L. Bentley and H. T. Kung, "A tree machine for searching problems", *Proc. Int. Conf. on Parallel Processing* (Bellaire, 1979) pp. 257—266.
[12] G. Bilardi, "The area-time complexity of sorting", Ph. D. Thesis (University of Illinois, Urbana, 1984).
[13] A. Bojanczyk, R. P. Brent and H. T. Kung, "Numerically stable solution of dense systems of linear equations using mesh-connected processors", Techn. Rep. (Comp. Sci. Dep., Carnegie-Mellon University, Pittsburgh, 1981).
[14] R. P. Brent and H. T. Kung, "Systolic VLSI array for polynomial GCD computation", *IEEE Trans. Comp.* **C-33** (1987) 731—737.
[15] R. P. Brent and H. T. Kung, "The chip complexity of binary arithmetic", *Proc. 12th Symp. on Theory of Computing* (Los Angeles, 1980) pp. 190—200.
[16] R. P. Brent and F. T. Luk, "A systolic array for the linear time solution of Toeplitz systems of equations", *J. VLSI and Comp. Syst.* **1** (1983) 1—23.
[17] R. P. Brent and F. T. Luk, "A systolic architecture for almost linear-time solution of symmetric eigenvalue problems", Techn. Rep. (Comp. Sci. Dep., Cornell University, Ithaca, 1982).
[18] B. Chazelle and L. Monier, "Optimality in VLSI", Techn. Rep. (Comp. Sci. Dep., Carnegie-Mellon University, Pittsburgh, 1981).
[19] B. Chazelle and L. Monier, "A model of computation for VLSI with related complexity results", Techn. Rep. (Comp. Sci. Dep., Carnegie-Mellon University, Pittsburgh, 1981).
[20] T. C. Chen, "Overlap and pipeline processing", In *Introduction to Computer Architecture*, Ed. H. S. Stone (Science Research Associates, Chicago, 1975) pp. 375-431.
[21] R. Cole and A. Siegel, "On information flow and sorting", *Proc. 17th Symp. on Theory of Computing* (Portland, 1985) pp. 208—221.
[22] L. Conway and C. Mead, *Introduction to VLSI Systems* (Addison-Wesley, Reading, Mass., 1980).
[23] K. Culik, J. Gruska and A. Salomaa, "Systolic automata for VLSI on balanced trees", *Acta Informatica* **18** (1983) 335—344.
[24] K. Culik and J. Pachl, "Folding and unrolling systolic arrays", *Proc. ACM SIGACT-SIGOPS Symp. on Principles of Distributed Computing* (Ottawa, 1982) pp. 254—261.
[25] Y. Dohi, A. L. Fischer, H. T. Kung, L. M. Monier and H. Walker, "Design of the PSC: A programmable systolic chip", *Proc. 3rd Conf. on VLSI* (Caltech, 1983) pp. 287—302.
[26] P. Ďuriš, O. Sýkora, C. D. Thompson and I. Vrťo, "Tight chip area lower bounds for DFT and DWHT", *Inform. Proc. Lett.* **215** (1985) 235—247.
[27] P. Ďuriš, O. Sýkora, C. D. Thompson and I. Vrťo, "Tight chip area bounds for sorting", *Computers and Artif. Intelligence* **4** (1985) 535—544.
[28] P. Ďuriš, O. Sýkora, C. D. Thompson and I. Vrťo, "Minimal area circuits for l selection", Techn. Rep. (Comp. Sci. Dep., University of California, Berkeley, 1985).
[29] M. J. Foster and H. T. Kung, "The design of special-purpose VLSI chips", *Computer* **13** (1980) 26—40.
[30] M. J. Foster, "Specialized silicon compilers for language recognition", Techn. Rep. (Comp. Sci. Dep., Carnegie-Mellon University, Pittsburgh, 1984).

[31] P. Frison and P. Quinton, "An integrated systolic machine for speach recognition", Techn. Rep. (IRISA, Rennes, 1983).
[32] Fu King-Sun (Ed.), *VLSI for Pattern Recognition and Image Processing*, Springer Series in Information Sciences (Springer-Verlag, Berlin, 1984).
[33] W. M. Gentleman and H. T. Kung, "Matrix triangularization by systolic arrays", *Proc. SPIE on Real-time Signal Processing IV* (Bellingham, 1981).
[34] L. J. Guibas, H. T. Kung and C. D. Thompson, "Direct VLSI implementation of combinatorial algorithms", *Proc. Conf. on VLSI: Architecture, Design, Fabrication* (California Institute of Technology, Pasadena, 1979) pp. 509—525.
[35] F. C. Hennie, *Iterative Arrays of Logical Circuits* (MIT Press — J. Wiley, New York, 1961).
[36] O. H. Ibarra and M. A. Palis, "Some results concerning linear iterative systolic arrays", *J. Parallel Distr. Comp.* **2** (1985) 182—218.
[37] J. Ja'Ja' and K. P. Kumar, "Information transfer in distributed computing with application to VLSI", *J. ACM* **31** (1984) 150—162.
[38] E. Katona, "Cellular algorithms for binary matrix operations", *Proc. COMPAR '81* (Nuernberg, 1981) pp. 203—216.
[39] Z. M. Kedem and A. Zorat, "On relation between input and communication/computation in VLSI", *Proc. 22nd Symp. on Foundations of Computer Science* (Nashville, 1981) pp. 37—44.
[40] R. Kolla, "Where oblivious is not sufficient", *Inform. Proc. Lett.* **17** (1983) 263—268.
[41] M. R. Kramer and L. van Leeuwen, "Systolische Rechnung und VLSI", *Informatik Spektrum* **7** (1984) 154—165.
[42] H. T. Kung, "Use of VLSI in algebraic computation: Some suggestions", *Proc. ACM Symp. on Symbolic and Algebraic Computation* (ACM SIMSAC, Snowbird, 1981) pp. 218—222.
[43] H. T. Kung, "Systolic algorithms for the CMU Warp processor", *Proc. 17th Int. Conf. on Pattern Recognition* (Int. Association for Pattern Recognition, 1984).
[44] H. T. Kung and M. S. Lam, "Fault-tolerance and two-level pipelining in VLSI systolic arrays", Techn. Rep. (Comp. Sci. Dep., Carnegie-Mellon University, Pittsburgh, 1983).
[45] H. T. Kung, "Why systolic architectures?", *Computer* **15** (1982) 37—46.
[46] H. T. Kung, "Let's design algorithms for VLSI systems", *Proc. Conf. on VLSI: Architecture, Design, Fabrication* (California Institute of Technology, Pasadena, 1979) pp. 65—90.
[47] H. T. Kung, "The structure of parallel algorithms", in *Advances in Computers*, Ed. M. C. Jovitz (Academic Press, New York, 1980) p. 19.
[48] H. T. Kung and P. L. Lehman, "Systolic VLSI arrays for relational database operations", *Proc. ACM SIGMOND Int. Conf. on Management of Data* (Los Angeles, 1980) pp. 105—116.
[49] H. T. Kung and S. W. Song, "A systolic 2-D convolution chip", Techn. Rep. (Comp. Sci. Dep., Carnegie-Mellon University, Pittsburgh, 1981).
[50] H. T. Kung and C. E. Leiserson, "Systolic arrays of VLSI", *Proc. Symp. on Sparse Matrix* (Knoxville, 1978) pp. 256—282.
[51] S. Y. Kung, K. S. Arun, R. J. Gal-Ezer and D. V. B. Rao, "Wavefront array processor", *IEEE Trans. Comp.* **C-31** (1982) 1054—1066.
[52] H. W. Lang, M. Schimler, H. Schmeck and H. Schröder, "Systolic sorting on a mesh-connected network", *IEEE Trans. Comp.* **C-34** (1985) 652—658.
[53] J. van Leeuwen, "VLSI complexity of Boolean functions", Techn. Rep. (Utrecht University, Utrecht, 1982).
[54] C. E. Leiserson, "Area-efficient graph layout for VLSI", *Proc. 21st Annual IEEE Symp. on Foundations of Computer Science* (Syracuse, 1980) pp. 270—281.
[55] C. E. Leiserson, "Systolic priority queues", Techn. Rep. (Comp. Sci. Dep., Carnegie-Mellon University, Pittsburgh, 1979).
[56] F. T. Leighton, "New lower bound techniques for VLSI", *Proc. 22nd Annual IEEE Symp. on Foundations of Computer Science* (Nashville, 1981) pp. 1—12.

[57] F. T. Leighton, "Three-dimensional VLSI layout", Techn. Rep. (Massachusetts Institute of Technology, Cambridge, 1983).
[58] F. T. Leighton and C. E. Leiserson, "Wafer-scale integration of systolic arrays", *Proc. 23rd Annual IEEE Symp. on Foundations of Computer Sciences* (San Francisco, 1982) pp. 279—311.
[59] G. J. Li and B. W. Wah, "The design of optimal systolic arrays", *IEEE Trans. Comp.* **C-34** (1985) 66—77.
[60] R. J. Lipton and R. Sedgwick, "Lower bounds for VLSI", *Proc. 13th Annual Symp. on Theory of Computing* (Milwaukee, 1981) pp. 300—307.
[61] C. A. Mead and M. Rem, "Cost and performance of VLSI computing structures", *IEEE J. Solid-State Circuits* **14** (1979) 455—462.
[62] Ch. Meinel, "A functional description of synchronous systems", *Proc. Conf. PARCELLA '84* (Berlin, 1984) (Akademie-Verlag, Berlin, 1985) pp. 192—201.
[63] J. Mikloško, "A fast algorithm for repeated computation of linear recurrence relations", *Bit* **17** (1987) 430—436.
[64] J. Mikloško, "Systolic systems for the systems of linear equations and matrix inversion", *Computers and Artif. Intelligence* **2** (1983) 361—372.
[65] D. I. Moldovan, "On the analysis and synthesis of VLSI algorithms", *IEEE Trans. Comp.* **C-31** (1982) 1121—1126.
[66] M. Morf and J. M. Delosme, "Matrix decomposition and inversions via elementary signature — orthogonal transformation", *Proc. ISMM on Control and Measurement* (San Francisco, 1981).
[67] D. Nath, S. N. Maheswari and P. C. P. Bhatt, "Efficient VLSI network for parallel processing based on orthogonal trees", Techn. Rep. (Electrical Engineering Dep., Indian Institute of Technology, New Delhi, 1981).
[68] J. von Neuman, *Theory of Self-reproducing Automata*, University of Illinois, Urbana, 1966).
[69] T. Ottmann, A. L. Rosenberg and L. J. Stockmeyer, "A dictionary machine for VLSI", Techn. Rep. (T. J. Watson Research Center, New York, 1981).
[70] M. S. Patterson, W. L. Ruzzo and L. Snyder, "Bounds on minimax edge length for complete binary tree", *Proc. 13th Symp. on Theory of Computing* (Milwaukee, 1981) pp. 293—299.
[71] F. P. Preparata and J. Vuillemin, "Area-time optimal VLSI networks for multiplying matrices", *Inform. Proc. Lett.* **11** (1980) 77—80.
[72] F. P. Preparata and J. Vuillemin, "Area-time optimal VLSI networks for computing integer multiplication and DFT", *Proc. ICALP Symp.* (Haifa, 1981) pp. 29—40.
[73] F. P. Preparata and J. Vuillemin, "Area-time optimal VLSI circuits for convolution", Techn. Rep. (INRIA, Le Chesney, 1980).
[74] F. P. Preparata and J. Vuillemin, "The cube-connected cycles, a versatile network for parallel computation", *Commun. ACM* **14** (1980) 300—309.
[75] A. Ralston, *A First Course in Numerical Analysis* (McGraw-Hill, New York, 1965).
[76] C. Savage, "A systolic data structure chip for connectivity problems", in *VLSI Systems and Computations*, Eds. H. T. Kung, R. F. Sproull and G. L. Steele (Carnegie-Mellon University, Pittsburgh, 1980) pp. 296—300.
[77] J. E. Savage, "Planar circuit complexity and the performance of VLSI algorithms", Techn. Rep. (Comp. Sci. Dep., Brown University, Providence, 1981).
[78] A. Siegel, "Tight area bounds and provably good AT^2 for sorting circuits", Techn. Rep. (Comp. Sci. Dep., New York University, New York, 1984).
[79] A. Siegel, "Minimal storage sorting circuits", *IEEE Trans. Comp.* **C-34** (1985) 355—361.
[80] L. Snyder, "Instruction to the configurable, highly parallel computer", *Computer* **1** (1982) 47—56.
[81] S. W. Song, "On a high-performance VLSI solution to database problems", Ph. D. Dissertation (Comp. Sci. Dep., Carnegie-Mellon University, Pittsburgh, 1981).

[82] H. S. Stone, "Parallel processing with the perfect shuffle", *IEEE Trans. Comp.* **C-20** (1971) 153—161.
[83] O. Sýkora, "Application of the orthogonal trees network for the parallel computing the visibility polygon", *Computers and Artif. Intelligence* **3** (1984) 341—346.
[84] O. Sýkora and J. Mikloško, "Special-purpose systolic arrays", *Computers and Artif. Intelligence* **2** (1983) 127—145.
[85] M. Šperka, "Design of integrated circuits", Master Thesis (Institute of Technical Cybernetics, Slovak Academy of Sciences, Bratislava, 1982).
[86] C. D. Thompson, "Area-time complexity for VLSI", *Proc. 11th Symp. on Theory of Computing* (Atlanta, 1979) pp. 81—88.
[87] C. D. Thompson, "The VLSI complexity of sorting", Techn. Rep. (University of California, Berkeley, 1982).
[88] C. D. Thompson, "Area-time complexity for VLSI", Ph. D. Thesis (Comp. Sci. Dep., Carnegie-Mellon University, Pittsburgh, 1980).
[89] C. D. Thompson, "Fourier transform in VLSI", Techn. Rep. (University of California, Berkeley, 1982).
[90] N. P. Turkedyev, "Description, functional analysis and simulation of parallel systolic architecture", *Proc. Conf. PARCELLA '84* (Berlin, 1984) (Akademie-Verlag, Berlin, 1985) pp. 225—231.
[91] J. D. Ullman, *Computational Aspects of VLSI* (Comp. Science Press, Rockville, 1984).
[92] V. Varshavsky, *Homogeneous Structures* (in Russian) Izd. Energiya, Moscow, 1973).
[93] P. M. B. Vitányi, "Area penalty for sublinear signal propagation delay on a chip", *Proc. 26th Annual IEEE Symp. on Foundations of Computer Science* (Syracuse, 1985) pp. 197—207.
[94] I. Vrťo, "Complexity of VLSI computation over integers modulo m", *Proc. Symp. SOFSEM '85* (Bratislava, 1985) pp. 245—247.
[95] I. Vrťo, "Optimal VLSI algorithms for selection the maximum element of a set", *Proc. PARCELLA '84* (Berlin, 1984) (Akademie-Verlag, Berlin, 1985) pp. 232—239.
[96] J. Vuillemin, "A combinatorial limit to the computing power of VLSI circuits", *IEEE Trans. Comp.* **C-32** (1983) 294—300.
[97] H. S. Wall, *Analytic Theory of Continued Fraction* (Van Nostrand Rheinhold, New York, 1948).
[98] H. Watanabe, "VLSI implementation of odd-even sorter using a uniform ladder", Techn. Rep. (Comp. Sci. Dep., University of Rochester, Rochester, 1981).
[99] A. Yao, "The entropic limitation on VLSI computation", *Proc. 13th Symp. on Theory of Computing* (Milwaukee, 1981) pp. 308—311.

Chapter 4

Algorithms for pipeline processors, matrix processors and multiprocessors

4.1 Introduction

Parallel algorithms for associative computers and systolic algorithms for specialized systolic arrays have been studied in the previous two chapters. Besides these types of parallel computers there also exist various other parallel architectures enabling the fast data processing. Some of them are presented and their algorithms described in this chapter.

From the point of view of organization of computation the basic types of parallel processors can be classified into pipeline processors, matrix processors and multiprocessors. The pipeline processors use the vectors on the principle of dividing the computational operation into many simultaneously operating functional subunits that perform their operations overlapping in time, similarly to a conveyer belt. The matrix processors also operate on vectors. Their instructions are performed sequentially, similarly to a classical computer, but in contrast to it, they operate in parallel on the data vectors. Multiprocessor computers are composed of at least a set of two processors that operate on the common memory. They are connected with control channels and information-sharing channels, their operation is controlled by an operating system.

All the three types of parallel computers are more or less specialized — their application is restricted only to some classes of algorithms.

In the second section of this chapter the pipeline vector computers and their algorithms will be studied. The general problems of realization of the algorithms on pipeline processors and questions of their implementation on the pipeline STAR-100 and CRAY-1 processors will be studied. Comparing the three algorithms for computation of tridiagonal systems of linear equations we shall explain their a priori timing. However, the main topic in this section is the description of the pipelined CRAY-1 processor, of its software and algorithms.

The third section is devoted to matrix processors and their algorithms. The reader can find here short descriptions of various interprocessor communication networks and of suitable data structures for realization of matrix algorithms. After a description of a ILLIAC-IV matrix processor there follows a description of the structure of the matrix processor DAP and of its software and algorithms, which actually is an essential problem in this section. Applicability of both the STARAN associative matrix processor and the MPP matrix processor specialized for image processing is given in the conclusion.

Multiprocessor computers, their algorithms, characteristic architecture features and basic principles of forming the algorithms are introduced in the last — fourth section. The EGPA hierarchical multiprocessor computer is discussed in more detail, and the method of implementation of the algorithm of matrix inversion by orthogonalization of its columns on this computer is given.

4.2 Pipeline vector computers and their algorithms

From the very beginning of the existence of computers overlapping of their individual operations occurred. However, this principle, a so-called pipelining of computation has fully developed only with pipeline computers, based on its parallel processing. On pipelining the computation parallelism is obtained such that the algorithm is realized on a pipeline unit composed of a linear chain of modules in which each module performs a certain subfunction of the implemented algorithm, but functionally depends on the preceding module. Thus, the computation proceeds as if on a conveyer belt of overlapping operations of a pipeline unit. This way of making computations parallel can be accomplished if the algorithm is split into a set of successive segments of nearly the same duration which are executed in the modules of a pipeline unit. To achieve high efficiency the input or output data of the algorithm must flow from memory of the pipeline unit or from the pipeline unit into memory. To secure a satisfactory speed of data input and output, the data flow width must be equal to at least three floating point numbers; most advantageous is to store these data as vectors of numbers. To avoid the conflicts in memory access, the vector can be defined as a set of successive memory positions. The transfers of vectors between the memory and the pipeline unit are performed with much higher efficiency when the vectors are not addressed individually, in opposite case the computation time is prolongated. The loss of addressability, however, means that computation cannot be accomplished between two vector elements but only between complete vectors, here all vector operands have to be defined prior to starting the vector operation. The computer implementing the pipeline processing of vectors is called a vector computer.

In this section we shall deal with general problems of implementation of algorithms on pipeline vector computers. The main attention will be devoted to the possibilities of STAR-100 and CRAY-1 vector computers.

Pipelining of computation can be used in the computer architecture at various levels, for example, at processing instructions, implementing arithmetic operations by specialized functional units or at pipelining processor that implement a more complex computational algorithms.

Implementation of every machine instruction can be divided into four segments [36] as follows

(1) read-in of instruction into memory,
(2) instruction decoding,
(3) choice of instruction operands from memory,
(4) instruction execution.

If these segments are realized in a linear chain of four modules of a pipeline unit, four of them can be executed in parallel in the continuous flow of instructions. While the first instruction is executing the fourth segment, the second instruction selects its operands in the third segment, the third instruction realizes the second segment and the fourth instruction reads from the memory. The implementation of all instructions is speeded up as much as four times in this case.

Pipelining of an arithmetic operation will be demonstrated on an example of floating point addition. This operation can be split into seven segments as follows

(1) reading of operands from memory,
(2) normalization of the operands and arrangement of their exponents,
(3) comparison of the exponents,
(4) shifting of the mantissa of an operand with a smaller exponent with respect to the larger exponent,
(5) summing of mantissas in the fixed point,
(6) normalization of the result,
(7) storing the result into the memory.

If each segment is realized in a single module of a pipeline unit, this unit can realize seven operations of addition simultaneously, each of them being in different stage of execution. This feature is especially advantageous in summing up two vectors

$$\boldsymbol{x} + \boldsymbol{y} = (x_i + y_i), \quad i = 1, 2, ..., n.$$

Let the execution time of the jth segment of operation of addition be t_j, $j = 1, 2, ..., 7$. Then, the time of serial summation of $\boldsymbol{x} + \boldsymbol{y}$ is $n \sum_{i=1}^{7} t_i$. Each of the seven segments in a pipeline functional unit is executed in another module; the execution time of each module is $t = \max t_j, j = 1, 2, ..., 7$. Each module performs its own segment on its own input operands and on realizing the next segment the obtained intermediate result is moved to the next module. The pipeline unit is successively entered in intervals of length t by operands x_1 and y_1, x_2 and y_2, etc. In its modules, the corresponding segments of each addition are executed one after another. Thus, the first result of addition of $x_1 + y_1$ is obtained at time $7t$, but each next result is obtained at time t, i.e. addition of two vectors is realized in time $(n + 6) t$.

Generally it holds that if a computation can be divided into k segments each of which has a realization time t, the time of vector operation over n elements will be $(n + k - 1) t$. Then, speeding up of this computation compared with its serial implementation is $nk/(n + k - 1)$, i.e., for $n \to \infty$, speeding up by k times is achieved.

We see that the average time per operation decreases with increasing length of vectors processed.

In a real pipeline vector computer — STAR-100, for example, the time to realize operation R with vectors of length n has two stages: the starting time of the vector operation, S, and the operation time for successive computation of all the results. S does not depend on the length of vectors and it lasts until the moment when the first result is started to be processed in the last module. It includes the time comprising the logics inevitable for correct orientation of the pipeline arithmetic unit to the required vector operation and of the time lasting until the computation of the last segment of the first pair of operands is started. The operation time depends on the length of vectors.

Time R depends on the number of linearly executed operations. In 40 ns units of the basic cycle of a STAR-100 computer it is expressed as $R = S + n/p$, where p is the number of results implemented in an arithmetic unit within a basic cycle. The values S, p, s (time of scalar operation) and $q = \lceil S/(s - p^{-1}) \rceil$ for floating-point arithmetic operations over 64-bit words are as follows: addition — 96, 2, 13, 8; multiplication — 156, 1, 17, 10; division — 156, 1/2, 47, 4.

From the above it follows that

— every algorithm implemented on a STAR-100 should have as minimum as possible number of vector operations with as maximum as possible length of vectors,

— on using short vectors, the efficiency of computation decreases due to many starting times,

— for $n > q$, it is more advantageous to use the vector operation than n scalar operations.

A small share of serial computation in algorithm has unfavourable effect on the overall efficiency of a vector computer. It has been found [43] that, if, for instance, 10% of program is realized 10 times slowlier than is the speed of a computer operating over vectors, then the whole realization speed of this program decreases by one half.

The STAR-100 computer was the first pipeline vector computer [9]. It was put under operation by the CDC Company in 1973. Its central processor has two pipeline floating-point arithmetic units that generate four 32-bit or 64-bit results per 40 ns. Thus, the computer achieves the speed as high as 100 million floating-point operations per second over 32-bit words. The STAR-100 has a set of 230 instructions, 65 of which are reserved for operations over vectors and 130 over scalars. It has 256 scalar registers and $512k$ of internal storage; it has no vector registers. Operation time of the cycles of internal storage is 1.2 µs.

The system only operates over vectors, i.e. over sets of words stored in n successive memory locations. Consequently, because of data transformation into vectors data manipulation has to be involved in the programming. Hence, a column of a matrix stored by rows does not represent a vector. Therefore, a summing up of two columns ($O(n)$ operations) must be preceded by extraction operation ($O(n^2)$ operations) which arranges the column elements into vector form.

The STAR-100 has several instructions, such as **compress** and **merge**, which do not have any analogy on classical computers. Both instructions use the control Boolean vector **z** that modifies some vector operations.

If **a**, **b** are the vectors and **z** is the control vector of dimension n, using **compress** the required elements **a** are, with respect to **z**, compressed onto vector **c** as follows:

$j:=1$; **for** $i = 1, 2, ..., n$ **do if** $z_i = 1$ **then** $(c_j:=a_i; j:=j+1;)$.

The instruction **merge** will generate vector **c** of vectors **a** and **b** with respect to **z** such that

$j:=1; k:=1;$
for $i = 1, 2, ..., n$ **do**
if $z_i = 1$ **then** $(c_i:=a_j; j:=j+1;)$ **else** $(c_i:=b_k; k:=k+1;)$.

Instructions **compress** and **merge** are applied especially when only some selected data of a large array are to be used. In TV signal processing, for example, it are the data that exceed a specified value. Similarly, on implementing the odd-even reduction in computation of a tridiagonal system of linear equation, **compress** will execute the operation of separating the vectors into even and odd components and **merge** will merge them into a single compact vector.

Once we know the implementation times of the individual instruction of the STAR-100, we may derive explicit relationships for the execution time of the given algorithm, such that different algorithms to solve the same problem are compared a priori. This can be demonstrated, for example, on a comparison of three algorithms for computation of a tridiagonal system of linear equations [31].

4.2 Pipeline vector computers and their algorithms

We have a tridiagonal system of linear equations

$$\begin{bmatrix} a_1 & b_1 & & & & \\ c_2 & a_2 & b_2 & & & \\ & \cdot & \cdot & \cdot & & \\ & & \cdot & \cdot & \cdot & \\ & & & \cdot & \cdot & \cdot \\ & & & & c_n & a_n \end{bmatrix} \begin{bmatrix} x_1 \\ x_2 \\ \cdot \\ \cdot \\ \cdot \\ x_n \end{bmatrix} = \begin{bmatrix} d_1 \\ d_2 \\ \cdot \\ \cdot \\ \cdot \\ d_n \end{bmatrix}. \tag{65}$$

The **LU**-decomposition of the system matrix and the following forward and reverse steps are given by algorithms that form the *GE*1 algorithm

$$f_1 = 1/a_1, \; g_i = c_i f_{i-1}, \quad f_i = 1/(a_i - g_i b_{i-1}), \quad i = 2, 3, \ldots, n,$$
$$y_1 = d_1, \quad\quad\quad\quad\quad\quad y_i = d_i - g_i y_{i-1}, \quad\quad\quad\quad\;\; i = 2, 3, \ldots, n,$$
$$x_n = y_n f_n, \quad\quad\quad\quad\quad x_i = (y_i - x_{i+1} b_i) f_i, \quad\quad\quad i = n-1, n-2, \ldots, 1.$$

In this case, the serial recurrent relationships are concerned, which cannot be implemented on a pipeline vector computer, since in vector operations all elements of input vectors must be known before. If, in the algorithm *GE*1, we substitute

$$t_i = b_{i-1} c_i, \quad i = 2, 3, \ldots, n,$$
$$f_1 = 1/a_1, \quad f_i = 1/(a_i - t_i f_{i-1}), \quad i = 2, 3, \ldots, n,$$
$$g_i = c_i f_{i-1}, \quad i = 2, 3, \ldots, n,$$

we get the algorithm *GE*2 containing two vector multiplications.

Timing of *GE*1 or *GE*2 for the STAR-100 is $273n$ or $312 + 247n$, respectively; hence for $n < 13$ the algorithm *GE*1 is faster, whereas for $n \geq 13$ it is *GE*2. In what follows, by *GE* we shall understand *GE*1 for $n < 13$ and *GE*2 for $n \geq 13$. The implementation time of *GE* on the STAR-100 will be denoted as T_1.

Parallel algorithm for computation (65) is the recursive doubling [28] described in Chapter 1. Timing of this algorithm for the STAR-100 is

$$T_2 = 15n \log n - n/2 + 2432 \log n - 230.$$

From the comparison of T_2 with the time of *GE* it follows that for $2^6 < n < 2^{17}$ we get $T_2 < T_1$, i.e. for the given n the recursive doubling on the STAR-100 represents an algorithm that is more efficient than *GE*, though for the term $n \log n$ it holds $\lim_{n \to \infty} T_2/T_1 = \infty$.

A much more efficient algorithm for the STAR-100 is that of cyclic odd-even reduction, described in the block form in Section 1.4.

If the given tridiagonal matrix is stored by the diagonals, the algorithm can be implemented on the STAR-100 in the vector form at time $T_3 = 339 \log n + 36n - 601$, which implies $\lim_{n \to \infty} T_3/T_1 \approx 0.14$, i.e. the cyclic odd-even reduction is asymptotically about 7 times faster than GE. This method is optimal for pipeline computers from the view-point of arithmetic operations shown in the comparison study in [41].

As we have seen in case of the STAR-100, even a small share of serial computations in a vector algorithm can substantially decrease its efficiency. Another disadvantage is that with respect to long starting times of vector operations these can be implemented with advantage only on long vectors, as well as that on simultaneous reading of operands from the storage and on storing the results, there appear memory conflicts, which also decreases computer's efficiency. CRAY-1 is a representative of computers which do not have this handicap. It is a highly efficient system based on the pipeline principle of vector and scalar information processing, reaching in certain applications the speed as high as 200 million floating-point operations [22]. This high speed is facilitated by suitable system architecture enabling parallel computation on several pipeline functional units as well as their pipelining into various chains where the results of one chain pass into the next one without being sent into memory. Vector instructions operate over vector registers and that is why no memory conflicts occur. On using non-reconfigurable functional units, the starting time of vector operations is short, hence also the vector operations of length 2 are applicable [24]. Another advantage of the computer are its small dimensions, hence the electrical signals in it travel only short distances.

Today the CRAY-1 computer is the only commercially available highperformance parallel computer in the world. According to [34], the CRAY Company has sold 29 pieces of this computer until 1981, in 1984 it were 24 pieces, the price of one computer being 7 million US $.

The central processor of the CRAY-1 consists of the computation, storage and input-output sections [38].

The computational section is divided into a control unit, operating registers and functional units. The control unit controls the execution of instructions, coordinates the operation of three types of data processing: vector, scalar and address ones. The operating registers and functional units are available to each type of processing.

A large set of operating registers that are readily accessible by program, are divided into registers V, S and A. Registers V and S operate over data, registers A over addresses and indices. In the system there are eight vector registers V

(each register has 64 elements and each element is represented by a 64-bit word), eight scalar registers S (each for one 64-bit word), and eight address registers A (each for a 24-bit word). Registers S are interconnected with operating memory through 64 buffer 64-bit registers T, and registers A through 64 buffer 24-bit registers B. Registers S and T speed up the scalar processing. The access time of the registers is 6 ns. Their total capacity is 4888 bytes.

Beside the above registers, the system also involves a register for vector length which determines the number of operations performed by a vector function, a 64-bit register for masking, whose bits correspond to the elements of vector registers and a 64-bit register of real-time clock.

Twelve specialized pipeline functional units of the system implement the vector and scalar arithmetic operations in both fixed and floating points, as well as shift and logic operations. Each functional unit can independently of other units operate in parallel. It works on a tree-address principle; the operands are obtained from registers and the results are stored again in the registers. In the computational section data flow from memory into registers, from the registers into functional units, and from there back again into the registers. Further, they travel either into the memory or, again, into the next functional unit.

The functional units perform address operations, scalar operations, floating-point operations and vector operations [24]. The address operations over registers A are executed by a functional unit for addition of integers (3), shift (3) and logic operations (1).

Furthermore, over registers S and V there is a functional unit for addition (6), multiplication (7) and reciprocal value (14). For vector operations over regis-

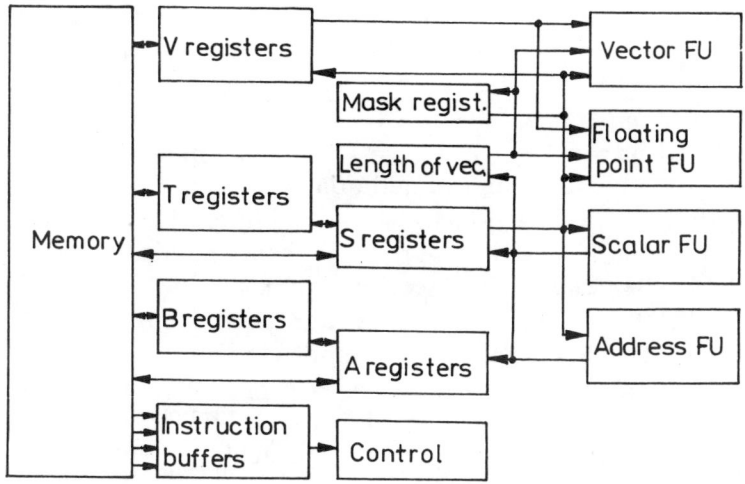

Fig. 57. Diagram showing the computation part of the CRAY-1 computer.

ters V there is a functional unit for addition of integers (3), shift (4) and logic operations (2).

Each functional unit operates in pipeline manner and executes its algorithm within a fixed time interval. Each of its segments executes its subfunction within the basic clock cycle of the computer, i.e. in 12.5 ns. Thus, each new result of the functional units is produced in each cycle of the basic clock cycle. The number of segments of functional units is given in parentheses. The computational block scheme of the CRAY-1 is shown in Fig. 57.

The system has 128 basic instructions of length 16 or 32 bits. For their fast processing they are implemented by four instruction buffers, with 64 16-bit registers each, which facilitates storing of sufficiently large program segments.

The capacity of operating memory is as much as 1 M 64-bit words, the cycle being 50 ns. The computer has 12 input and 12 output channels which can work in parallel. Each channel has the maximum transfer speed of 80 Mbit/s.

The CRAY-1 computer is able to implement four types of vector operations. In the first type, both operands are obtained from registers V, the result is also sent to register V. In the second type, one operand is obtained from register S and the second operand from V. The third type enables data transmission between memory and registers V, whereas the fourth type facilitates transmission from registers V into memory. The vector operations are performed in pipeline manner, i.e. two operands from registers V are sent into the functional unit within each basic clock cycle. Once the first result has been obtained, one result is always stored into register V in each basic clock cycle.

The required functional unit and operand registers per number of basic clock cycles depending on the length of vectors processed are reserved for vector operation. The next vector instruction demanding the same fuctional unit or registers has to wait until these are free. For example, instructions $V0:= = V1 + V2$; $V3:= V4 V5$; are independent over various registers, and thus they are executed in parallel. In contrast, instructions $V3:= V1 + V2$; $V6:= = V4 + V5$; or $V3:= V1 + V2$; $V6:= V1 V5$; are not like the above ones. In the first case, the functional unit of addition is reserved for the first addition, which postpones the execution of the second addition. In the second case, on addition the registers $V1$ and $V2$ are reserved, hence multiplication starts only, when $V1$ is free. In case of the sequence of instructions $V0:= V1 + V2$; $V3:= V1 + V5$; the second instruction is also postponed because of reservation of the unit of addition and reservation of $V1$ [24].

Only 64 elements can be stored into register V, such that the vectors of length exceeding 64 are automatically processed in a cycle by blocks of length 64. The most efficient use of the computer, however, is achieved with vectors that are multiples of 64.

A very important feature of vector processing on the CRAY-1 computer is

the possibility of pipeline treatment of a sequence of functional units. In this case the intermediate results flow from one functional unit into another without being stored into operating memory. If a certain register receives a result of some vector operation, this result can immediately become an operand of the following instruction, which is started to be executed as soon as at least one result that can be used as an operand is available. Pipelining of four successive instructions is demonstrated on the following example [36]
READ $(V0)$; (read-in of integer vectors)
$V2 := V0 + V1$; (addition of integer vectors)
$V3 := V2 < A3$; (shift of $V2$ to the left by $A3$ bits)
$V3 := V3 \wedge V4$; (logic multiplication of $V3$ by the masking vector)

Obviously, all the four instructions are overlapping in pipeline manner. Once the first result has been obtained in $V5$, each new result appears in $V5$ within one basic clock cycle.

The CRAY-1 computer has a CFT translator from FORTRAN IV into vector form of the program, it has a macroassembler CAL and an extensive library of standard programs. Its operating system COS executes processing of 63 tasks in multiprogramming mode [38].

The computer is designed especially for extensive tasks of vector signal processing. Testing a number of algorithms for signal processing yielded the following speeds (millions of floating-point operations per second — FLOPS [22] are given in parentheses): recurrent filtration (60), Fast Fourrier Transform (75), non-recurrent filtration (100), matrix multiplication (140).

In 1983 (1986) the CRAY Company produced CRAY XMP (CRAY-2) systems with 9.5 ns (5 ns) cycle, 2 (4) pipelines and maximum performance 400 (1000) million FLOPS. The 15 GFLOPS CRAY-3 with logic on the GaAs technology is planned for 1988.

4.3 Matrix processors and their algorithms

Various applications require a large number of operations on vectors and matrices. These operations are often independent and identical, so they can be implemented in parallel on a so-called matrix processor. They work on the following simple principle: If the problem solved can be split into N parallel branches, it is to be expected that the computation of this task on a network of N computers will be N times faster.

A matrix processor (MP) consists of an array of interconnected processors, each of which has a local memory. Using interprocessor communication network each processor can communicate (i.e. exchange data) with some of its neighbours.

The architecture of matrix processors is of the SIMD-type. The same operation is synchronously executed over various data in all processors. Thus, matrix processors operate over vectors. Instructions of a MP are executed serially but they operate in parallel over all data. The operation of a MP is controlled by its control unit that decodes instructions and transmits control signals to all processors of a matrix, controls the input-output operations and data transfers among the processors. The processors of an array cannot work independently. They just can execute, or, if masked, not execute an operation specified by the control unit.

If a processor needs data stored in another processor, it has to access it via an interprocessor communication network, that usually interconnects neighbouring processors. This network is a very important part of the MP, because it facilitates the speed of parallel computation.

Interprocessor connections are based on the most common functional relationships among the individual branches of algorithms suitable for matrix processors.

The most flexible interprocessor connection of an N-processor array in MP is a complete processor interconnection which each processor is directly connected with all the other processors. Such a network requires $N(N-1)/2$ two-way channels to connect the processors. Hence its complexity and price grow with N^2. Since the efficiency of the MP increases with N at a maximum linearly, in case of large N the complete interconnection is not convenient.

Another interconnection possibility presents connection by a cyclic shift. The processors are numbered as $0, 1, \ldots, N-1$, the ith processor is directly connected with the $(i-1)$st and the $(i+1)$st processor, addition is accomplished with mod N. For every i and j, the ith processor is indirectly connected with the jth processor via $(i-j-1) \bmod N$ processors, through which the data are successively moved from the ith into the jth processor. This scheme is based on iterative algorithms of $x_i = f(x_{i-1}, x_i, x_{i+1})$ type typical of one-dimensional partial differential equations. On using rectangular processor arrays, five-point iteration relationships for two-dimensional equations

$$x_{ij} = g(x_{i+1,j}, x_{i-1,j}, x_{i,j-1}, x_{i,j+1}, x_{ij})$$

lead to an "each-with-four-neighbours" interconnection.

A further interconnection scheme is the special permutation of a finite number of items, so-called perfect shuffle. Here, the set of subscripts of the vector x_i, $i = 0, 1, \ldots, N-1$, $N = 2^m$, is mapped into a new set by permuting according to the relationships

4.3 Matrix processors and their algorithms

$$P(i) = \begin{cases} 2i, & 0 \leq i \leq \frac{N}{2} - 1, \\ 2i + 1 - N, & \frac{N}{2} \leq i \leq N - 1. \end{cases}$$

If i is an subscript with binary representation

$$i = d_m 2^{m-1} + d_{m-1} 2^{m-2} + \ldots + d_2 2 + d_1 = (d_m d_{m-1} \ldots d_2 d_1),$$

$P(i)$ is the number which is obtained by cyclic rotation of these bits by 1 bit to the left, i.e.

$$P(i) = (d_{m-1} d_{m-2} \ldots d_1 d_m).$$

Interconnection of registers or processors by perfect shuffle is very important for efficient implementation of several parallel algorithms. For instance, the algorithm for bitonic sorting of N items [40] requires $O(N \log^2 N)$ operations on a serial computer. On an N-processor computer that is interconnected by perfect shuffle it can be performed in $O(\log^2 N)$ steps, provided, of course, the $N/2$ "compare–exchange" operations can be executed in parallel. The Fast Fourier Transform on N elements, serial implementation of which needs $O(N \log N)$ operations, takes $O(\log N)$ steps on an N processor computer; here one step involves a perfect shuffle, a multiplication–addition and a shift of results back to the inputs [40].

The third example of an algorithm effectively implemented by perfect shuffle, is the matrix transposition. Here from an N-dimensional matrix $\mathbf{A}$, the matrix $\mathbf{A}^T$ is obtained by perfect shuffle in $\log N$ steps.

Further interprocessor connections are defined by the following binary representations of indices [42]

$$i = (d_m d_{m-1} \ldots d_2 d_1), \quad P(i) = \begin{cases} (d_m d_{m-1} \ldots d_2 \bar{d}_1), \\ (d_1 d_m \ldots d_3 d_2), \\ (d_m d_{m-1} \ldots d_{j+1} \bar{d}_j d_{j-1} \ldots d_1), \\ j = 1, 2, \ldots, m, \end{cases}$$

where $\bar{x}$ is negation of x. The first interconnection facilitates exchange of neighbouring elements, while the second, so-called inverse perfect shuffle, is used with advantage in recurrent computations implementable by recursive doubling, the third being the interconnection "into a cube".

It has been shown in [13], that in some algorithms implemented on an MP with a regular two-dimensional interprocessor "each-with-four-neighbours" network the limiting factor need not be the number of arithmetic operations, but more likely the number of data transfers. It has been proved, for instance, that matrix inversion or multiplication of two matrices of dimension N requires $O(n)$

steps of data transfer, though the fastest algorithms to solve these problems have $O(\log^2 N)$ or $O(\log N)$ steps of arithmetic operations. Therefore, the complexity analysis of parallel computations must not ignore any details in the architecture of the computer applied.

The high efficiency of a MP requires suitable data and memory structures, since the distribution of data among the processors and the algorithm operators influences the frequency and the capacity of data transfers between the individual processors. It is most advantageous when n operands of a vector instruction are stored in n different memory modules — yet they can be read in simultaneously. Least advantageous is when all the operands are stored in the same memory module, hence they must be read in serially, one after another. For instance, if on multiplying two matrices of dimension N ($\mathbf{C} = \mathbf{AB}$) each scalar multiplication is executed by one processor, the ith row of $\mathbf{A}$ and the jth column of $\mathbf{B}$ must be stored into the memory of a processor to compute element c_{ij}, prior to computation. When $\mathbf{BA}$ is being computed, very fast access to the rows of $\mathbf{B}$ and columns of $\mathbf{A}$ is needed. However, the precondition that during computation the rows or columns of both matrices must be obtained at the same time is, under a fixed computer architecture, impossible to fulfil.

Take a matrix processor composed of $N+1$ processors p_i, $i = 0, 1, ..., N$, each having an index register r_i, through which an arbitrary element can be obtained from its memory. Let matrix $\mathbf{A} = (a_{ij})$, $i, j = 0, 1, ..., N$, be stored such that its ith column is in the p_ith processor. If i is stored in each r_i, the elements of the ith row are obtained in parallel. If the jth column is needed, N memory cycles are required; if this column is claimed by several processors, memory conflicts may occur. This disadvantage does not appear in the so-called skew storing of matrices [29]; here element a_{ij} is stored in p_k and it holds $i + j = = k \mod (N+1)$. Thus, by proper indexing one may get both the rows and columns of $\mathbf{A}$ at the same time. If we want to obtain the ith row, we send i to all r_i. If the jth column is needed, $i = 0, 1, ..., N$, $(i-j) \mod (N+1)$ is sent into r_i.

An algorithm suitable for an MP of the SIMD-type has to satisfy the following requirements

(a) it can be expressed by vector operations, whose operands can be read from the processor memories simultaneously;

(b) suitable data transfers can be readily implemented by a fixed interprocessor communication network.

Since these requirements are only satisfied by certain classes of computations (such as some algorithms of linear algebra, signal and image processing, numerical solving of partial differential equations), the MP is not a universal computer.

The ILLIAC-IV [4] computer is a matrix processor of SIMD-type very often quoted in literature. It was designed especially to solve extensive tasks of numerical computation of partial differential equations. The ILLIAC-IV was the first matrix processor, on which important experience of testing parallel computers were obtained. It had 64 processors, arranged in a two-dimensional array, with a memory of 2048 64-bit words each. The processors were controlled by a control unit. Instructions were executed synchronously over all processors unless blocked by a masking register. As regards data transfer, each processor i was directly connected with its four neighbours, i.e. with processors $i + 1$, $i - 1$, $i + 8$, $i - 8$ (mod 64). This interconnection coincides with the 5-point diagram of the finite difference method for two-dimensional elliptic equations. The data transfer to a non-neighbour was done as a series of single step transfers.

The ILLIAC-IV was a highly efficient computer for certain classes of computations. One of its main disadvantage was that it claimed highly efficient complex programs that would enable proper utilization of its facilities, as well as the inevitable time data exchanges between the pairs of its processors, which markedly prolongated the computations. These were the very reasons why for the ILLIAC-IV there were only few tasks available that mapped well onto its architecture.

The difficulties of the above matrix processor are not shared by the DAP matrix processor described in detail in the present section.

Today, the large-scale production of small and cheap microprocessors markedly influences also production of parallel matrix processors. That is why the latter are based especially on microprocessors.

From among all matrix processors of the SIMD-type, the most advanced is the DAP (Distributed Array Processor), which has been successfully developed by the ICL Company since 1972 [16].

Its original design, as with the ILLIAC-IV computer, was based on the idea that most programs for numerical calculation of partial differential equations are composed of multiple cycles, performing identical operations in small data arrays, where most interactions are only accomplished with the neighbouring elements of the arrays. This principle requires a large number of identical processors, connected in a regular array, which simultaneously perform the same instruction. The DAP matrix processor consists of a two-dimensional array of elementary microprocessors 32×32 (in 1976) and 64×64 (1980) in size.

All the processors are controlled by a simple control processor (CP). Each has its own local memory and operates on its own data and on the data recieved from its neighbours. The individual processors are not fast, but on arrays with 1024 or 4096 processors, the DAP can achieve (due to its architecture and modern technology of technical and programming tools) high speeds — by order 10 million instructions per second on 1000 processors [35].

Most matrix processors are connected to the host computer via fast channels.

The DAP is built in by its processors directly into the memory module of the ICL-2900 computer by connecting each of its processors to the memory chip in the module. There is no delay caused by data reading into the DAP, since the data enters the processor memory through the standard input devices of the ICL-2900 and it can be processed either by this computer or by the DAP.

As we have mentioned in the chapter dealing with associative computers, the physical separation of the memory from the computing unit is, due to slow transfers, the bottleneck of many computers. This problem does not arise in the DAP, since the processor matrix is stored directly in the memory of a standard serial computer. Thus, from the user's view-point, the DAP is an extension of the ICL-2900 computer. As a matter of fact, it is a kind of special-purpose active memory module.

Computation on the DAP proceeds as follows. Loaded into the host computer the program is executed serially. Suitable data are stored in a part of memory which is shared by the DAP. If the program requires a parallel operation, this is executed by the DAP. In the meantime, the host computer computes other tasks, whereas the part of memory shared by the DAP is blocked. After finishing the parallel operation, the host continues with the serial program.

A rough diagram of the architecture of the DAP computer with an array of 64 × 64 processors is shown in Fig. 58 [23].

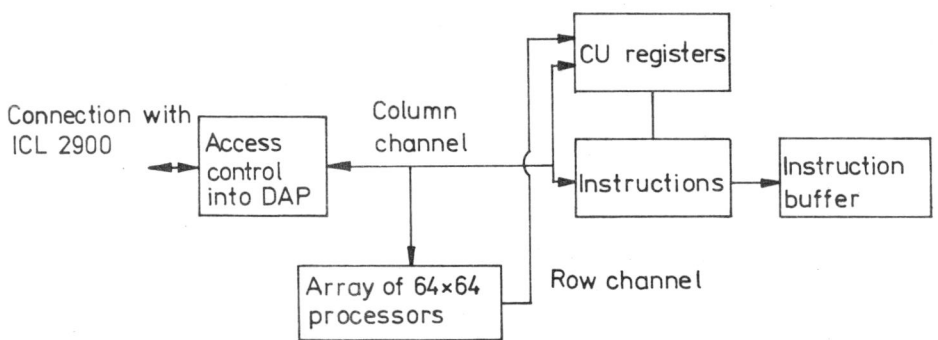

Fig. 58. Diagram of architecture of the DAP computer.

The DAP and the ICL-2900 are connected via an access controller and a column channel, which has one bit for each column of the array processors. One 64-bit word of the ICL-2900 corresponds to one row in the memory of DAP. The column channel serves as a path between the rows of an array and the registers of the control unit (CU) as well as a path that makes it possible for the CU to read instructions from memory. The row channel connects the processor array with the CU. It has one bit for each row of processors and it is only used to transfer the data into the CU registers and back.

The processors in the array are controlled by the CU which coordinates their operation and implements some functions. It selects instructions and sends them to the processor array where they are executed. Some of the special functions, such as scalar and global operations over processor memory (e.g. searching for maxima) are executed by the CU itself.

Each DAP instruction has 32 bits. Instructions are stored in memory rows of the processors, two instructions per row. To interpret the instructions for the processor array, instructions are called from the array memory during the reading phase and suitable control signals are sent into the processor array during the execution phase. Each phase is executed in one basic clock cycle of the computer, i.e. in 200 ns.

The CU has an instruction counter and eight length registers, the length being equal to one side of the processor array, i.e. 64 bits. The registers communicate with a processor array either through a row or a column channel.

The data in the DAP memory can be arranged in two formats. On using a vertical matrix format, each number is stored in the memory of one processor. However, when a horizontal vector format is used, which, compared with the vertical format, is less efficient, the number is divided within the row of processors in the same way as instructions are stored. Transformation between the two formats is performed automatically.

In a square processor array, each processor has six main connections. The processor is connected with its four neighbours. From their memory it can read in data. It also moves its own data to other processors by rows or columns. Interconnections with neighbours are important especially in computations in which the value of a node of a network depends on the values of surrounding nodes. Row or column interconnections are used as communications between the array and the CU.

A scheme of a DAP processor is in Fig. 59 [16].

It is a simple processor which has 4 kbits of memory and an arithmetic-logic unit (ALU) with three addressable 1-bit registers and a 1-bit adder. Register A has a control function, register Q serves as an accumulator, while the data transfer is facilitated by register C. Data channels are 1 bit wide. The upper multiplexor of the processor selects inputs into the ALU. The botton multiplexor selects the output from the processor. This can be either the output from the ALU, from memory or from the CU. Output from the processor may go either back to its memory or to an other processor. Both multiplexors allow communication with the CU via the row or column channels.

Each processor can, over its registers and memory, perform a set of simple instructions. Arithmetic operations are performed over registers Q, C and a memory bit. For instance, the instruction of addition will execute addition of these three bits, where the result and the carry are stored into registers Q and C. All computations in the processor are serial, they are executed bit by bit. The word length can be chosen according to the problem solved.

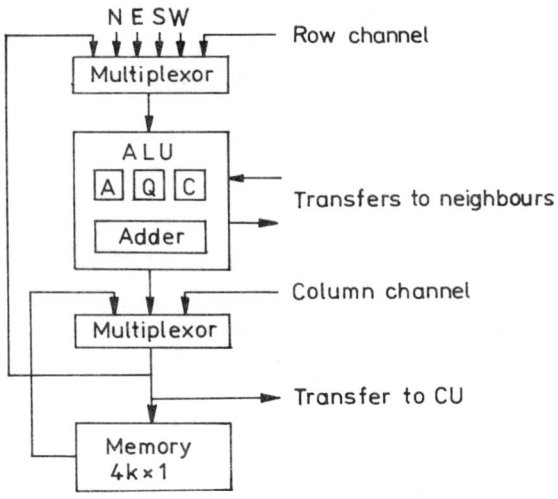

Fig. 59. Diagram of the DAP processor.

Computations are performed in the SIMD mode. When different algorithms are computed, a number of operations have to be performed only on a subset of array processors. These conditional operations are controlled by register A. This register operates as a switch preventing certain processors from executing an instruction that enters the array from the CU. Register A has a masking bit which does not allow modification of the memory in a processor — writing operation is performed only if the register A is set to 1. For instance, if a sign bit of a numeric array is put into the register A, the operation is only executed by the processors with positive elements.

Important properties of the DAP computer by which it differs from other parallel architectures are as follows.

(1) System processors are simple 1-bit processors, which implement bit-level arithmetic operations for a word length that is optimal for the system under consideration. Though a large number of processors are required, they are small and do not use much power.

(2) Processors are distributed directly into the memory of a serial computer, sharing the chip with the memory to which they belong, so that no requirements for transfer of large data volumes into them and out of them emerge.

A novel architecture of the DAP parallel matrix processor requires also new approach to its algorithmic and programming tools.

Simplicity of bit operations of the DAP processors needs such algorithms to be developed that would yield results iteratively — bit by bit and secure easy accuracy tests. For instance, to compute the elementary fuctions ($\sqrt{x}$, $\log x$,

$\sin x$, e^x, ...) the known algorithms based on orthogonal polynomials, continued fractions or Newton iterative method cannot be applied. Therefore, to compute these functions on the DAP, it was necessary to construct bit-by-bit methods. Such method for computation of $y = \sqrt{x}$ is described in [16].

For the given x, y has to be found such that with required accuracy it holds $y^2 = x$. We assume to have the first i bits of y satifying relationship $y_i^2 < x$, and we want to find the next approximation of y_{i+1}, which coincides in its first i bits with y_i and has the $(i + 1)$st bit b_{i+1} such that $(y_i + b_{i+1})^2 < x$ holds. If r_i is the error in the ith step, $r_i = x - y_i^2$ and $r_{i+1} = x - (y_i + b_{i+1})^2 = r_i - (2y_i + b_{i+1})b_{i+1}$. Consequently, we get $b_{i+1} = 1$, if $r_{i+1} > 0$, else $b_{i+1} = 0$.

The algorithm starts computing $y_0 = 0$ and then bit by bit it successively computes $\sqrt{x}$. If for some i, $r_i = 0$, then y_i is the exact square root of x.

For the computation, no arithmetic operations are needed. $2y_i$ is generated from y_i by shifting it one position to the left, where zero originates in the number on the right-hand side. Addition of b_{i+1} is a usual assigning of one to the zero and multiplication by b_{i+1} is a shift by $i + 1$ positions to the right.

Similarly, as we have stressed in the chapter dealing with algorithms for associative computers, the CORDIC technique which computes some elementary functions bit by bit is also suitable for the DAP computer.

Implementing parallel algorithms which have originated from serial algorithms on the DAP may completely differ from its serial counterparts. For instance, to solve a system of N linear equations of N unknowns, **Ax** = **b**, on serial computers the Gaussian or the Gauss–Jordan elimination is often used, where the matrix **A** is transformed to the upper triangular or unit matrix. In the first case, solution is obtained with the use of recursion by backward run. On a serial computer, the Gauss–Jordan elimination requires $N^3/2 + O(N^2)$ multiplications, i.e. the Gaussian elimination is faster. However, on a parallel DAP computer with $N^2 + N$ processors, the Gaussian elimination requires $O(2N)$ operations ($2N - 2$ multiplications and additions, and N divisions), while the Gauss–Jordan elimination needs only $O(N)$ operations (N multiplications, additions and divisions), i.e. the Gauss–Jordan elimination is one-time unit faster.

A similar situation occurs by pivotization, when searching for the maximum element to eliminate. On a serial computer partial pivoting (in columns) requires $O(N^2)$ comparisons, in complete pivoting (in the whole, still uneliminated matrix) it are $O(N^3)$ comparisons, which is very time-comsuming. On the DAP computer, however, the price of both partial and complete pivoting is the same, i.e. again, the characteristics of parallel algorithms substantially differ from their serial counterparts.

Let us note, that the special algorithm of matrix multiplication for DAP was described in Chapter 1.

Bit manipulations and logic operations on a DAP are easy to perform. Arithmetic operations are done in software, where the word size can be chosen arbitrarily. Operations on short words, such as arithmetic for fixed decimal points, image and signal processing, etc., are done quickly, whereas floating decimal-point arithmetic operations on long words are executed very slowly, though on several processors, a speed-up can be achieved. Implementation times (in μs) and computation speeds (in million operations per second) on a DAP computer with 64×64 processors for some programs of basic floating decimal-point operations with 32-bit words are given in Table 12 [12]. **X, Y, Z** are 64×64 matrices, S is a scalar and operations (except SUM and MAX) mean execution of the given function by components on all elements of argument matrices.

Table 12

Operation	Time (μs)	Speed (MOPS)
$Z = X + Y$	150	27
$Z = S * X$	40—130	32—102
$Z = X * Y$	250	16
$Z = X ** 2$	125	33
$Z = X\ Y$	330	12
$Z = \mathrm{SQRT}(X)$	170	24
$Z = \mathrm{LOG}(X)$	285	14
$S = \mathrm{SUM}(X)$	280	175
$S = \mathrm{MAX}(X)$	48	85

A number of important conclusions follow from Table 12. Obviously, the DAP makes use of the symmetry of computations — time for the square of the matrix equals just half the time of the matrix product by components. Multiplication of a matrix by a scalar depends on the scalar and on the fact whether the latter was known at compilation time. Square root and matrix logarithm operations are very fast compared to the time of multiplication. However, in spite of this, the time to sum all the matrix elements is not even twice as long as that for summation of two matrices. Nevertheless, from the viewpoint of the theoretically longest parallel algorithm of summation of 4096 elements by pairs it should by $\log 4096 = 12$ times faster. Although selection of the maximum in case of matrix processors represents a complex problem, the DAP is able to compute it very quickly. This is due to its bitwise computation.

To demonstrate the high speed of the DAP computer with 64×64 processors, we introduce the implementation times of various problems solved on this computer [10]:

one-dimensional FFT (4096 complex numbers) — 15 ms,
two-dimensional FFT (64 × 64 complex numbers) — 17 ms,
multiplication of square matrices of dimension 64—37 ms,
inversion of a 64 × 64 matrix by the Gauss–Jordan method by pivotization — 50 ms,
system of linear equations with 64 (500, 639) unknowns — 84 ms (8 s, 16.2 s),
computation of eigenvalues of a matrix of order 64 by Jacobi's method — 1.5 s,
sorting of 4096 (256 000) elements by the Batcher method — 125 ms (0.6 s).

The implementation time of the serial computer compared to that of the DAP depends on the size of the problem solved, as well as on the fact whether we succeed in adapting the structure of the algorithm selected to a parallel implementation. In [10] it is shown that suitable selection of a problem enables examples to be constructed in which the ratio of the times DAP/IBM 360/195 ranges between 0.1 and 1000. Real comparison studies from computational physics suggest that this ratio ranges for a large class of problems between 5 and 20. Advantage of the DAP is that this speed-up compared with other supercomputers is achieved at much lower hardware cost.

In the course of development of the DAP matrix processor, programming tools were developing. The DAP is equipped with a microassembler and DAP-FORTRAN. The DAP-FORTRAN is an extension to Standard FORTRAN and allows its users to usefully employ the parallel architecture of the DAP. Declaring the vector and matrix variables makes it possible to compute the whole arrays as simple items.

Solution of the Laplace equation on a square grid of $N \times N$ dimension by a point difference relationship, is written in DAP-FORTRAN as follows

$$\mathbf{X} = (\mathbf{Y}(+,) + \mathbf{Y}(-,) + \mathbf{Y}(,+) + \mathbf{Y}(,-))/4.0.$$

If we want the iterations of internal and boundary points differ from each other, we must write

$$\mathbf{X}(\text{INNER}) = \ldots \quad \mathbf{X}(\text{BOUNDARY}) = \ldots,$$

which allows complicated areas of solutions.

Basic arithmetic operations in DAP-FORTRAN are also extended to vector and matrix arguments. For example, to compute the roots of the equation $ax^2 + bx + c = 0$ for N^2 elements, a, b, c can be written in DAP-FORTRAN as

$$\mathbf{D} = \mathbf{B}**2 - 4.0*\mathbf{A}*\mathbf{C},$$
$$\mathbf{S} = \text{SQRT}(\mathbf{D}),$$

$$X1 = (-B + S)/(2.0*A),$$
$$X2 = (-B - S)/(2.0*A),$$

where **X**1, **X**2, **A**, **B**, **C** are matrices.

In FORTRAN a lot of time is spent indexing arrays. In vector and matrix operations, however, no indexing is needed, because the same operation is performed on all array elements simultaneously. In opposite case, however, a conditional command has to be added into the program. DAP-FORTRAN eliminates **IF** commands throughout program by the construction **X(MASK)** = = **EXPRESSION**, where **MASK** is a logic matrix and change of **X** occurs only in those elements for which **MASK** = 1. For example, in the above square equation, its discriminant must be tested prior to any computation of the square root. In this way, on the DAP all the array processors will compute, except those marked by register A, which is secured by the command

$$X(D.GE.0.0) = (-B + SQRT(D))/(2.0*A).$$

D.GE.0.0 is a Boolean expression that yields the matrix of values which equal 1 only for non-negative discriminants. This Boolean matrix is used as a mask to only change the values of **X**, for which the corresponding elements in the mask equal 1.

Computations in DAP-FORTRAN proceed as follows. The standard program is computed on the host computer. The program also involves some subroutines in DAP-FORTRAN, which are used by the DAP. The host computer activates the DAP on calling its procedure. Communication between FORTRAN and DAP-FORTRAN is performed via common blocks in the DAP memory. Since the data in this memory is accessible to both the host computer and the DAP, no time is spent by their transfer, which substantially speeds up all computations.

DAP-simulator is used to develop programs and replace technical hardware. Its speed is 10^3—10^4 times lower than that of the DAP. Except for program debugging it enables the programmer to estimate what is expected to be spent on a given problem on the DAP.

A special group of matrix processors is represented by so-called associative matrix processors, which originated by combining matrix data processing with associative memory. Associative matrix processors are frequently used for special purposes, such as data searching and processing in a quickly changing data base. Therefore, instead of passive cells, they have small specialized processors, which are able to simultaneously perform in all memory cells the operation of comparing their contents with a word they recieve via a channel connecting these processors with the rest of the computer.

In Chapter 2 of this book we have described several parallel algorithms for hypothetical parallel associative computers, without paying attention to any actual associative computer. The STARAN computer of the Goodyear Aerospace Corporation [39] may serve to illustrate actual associative matrix processors. It has a memory with multidimensional access, consisting of 256 words with 256 bits each. Further, it has 256 arithmetic processors and a permutation network. The STARAN computer system can involve as many as 32 associative matrix modules.

The STARAN differs from other parallel computers by parallel matrix arithmetic operations, a content-addressable memory, input and output by bit slices, and a permutation network.

An arithmetic unit is assigned to each memory word. Each of the 256 arithmetic units computes over the data in its memory word bitwise serially. Thus, the STARAN can execute arithmetic operations in parallel on hundred of thousands of pairs of operands. Therefore, irrespective of the number of operand pairs the implementation time of arithmetic operations only depends on the number of bits in the processed words.

The STARAN has an associative memory, i.e. a content-addressable memory. Each input word is compared with all data in the memory matrix within one cycle time; and all words which satisfy the given searching criterion are identified. Time of data retrieval according to a certain key is only proportional to the number of input items, and thus it is independent of the number of data in the memory. Advantage of the associative memory is that the data in it need not be stored in a fixed order.

Input and output operations can be performed by words, or, in case of associative operations, by bits. As many as 256 bits per word or one bit from each word of the memory matrix can be read or recorded in one memory cycle.

The STARAN has also an efficient permutation network that enables flexible data transfers and restructuralization facilitating the mutual intercommunication of processors as well as of processors with memory matrix.

Due to the above features the speed of the STARAN computer is several hundred of millions of operations per second, where the speed of data input and output increases up to several billions of bits per second.

The STARAN is suitable for applications which require high computation speed and have a large dynamic data base, or require implementation of the same operations over large data files. Typical applications of the STARAN include partial differential equations, weather forecast, matrix computations, pattern recognition, text processing, booking in transport, ballistic rockets security system, air traffic control, processing of signals from sensors and data processing.

According to the data from [33], satellites of the LANDSAT project produce cosmic photographs with more than 10^6 image elements-pixels per second, which results in a daily total of over 10^{13} information bits. For such an immense data volume, various tasks of image processing have to be solved rapidly; namely: transformation, correlation, filtration, enlarging, restoring, classification, etc., which provides a basis for extracting information from the image processed. Solving this complex task requires a specialized parallel computer, the speed of which would reach as many as 10^9—10^{10} operations per second. In 1979 the NASA signed a contract with the Goodyear Aerospace Corporation on a project of to date the largest matrix processor MPP (Massive Parallel Processor) specially designed for processing cosmic photographs [33].

The proposed architecture of the MPP is based on a synthetic study of architectures of both DAP and STARAN computers. Since image information is represented by integers, the MPP computer also processes the data in bit slices. The kernel of the MPP is a two-dimensional array of 16,384 processors arranged as a 128×128 array. The MPP processor is more complex than the DAP processor. It has six 1-bit registers and a programmable shifting register. Due to the optimum length of operands, arithmetic computations in the processor array are implemented serially in a bitwise manner. Each processor is connected with its four neighbours. The basic clock cycle of the processor matrix is 100 ns. The speed parameters of basic matrix operations by components on an MPP computer (in millions of operations per second) are listed in Table 13, where **A**, **B** are matrices of dimension 64×64, S is a scalar, 8-bit and 12-bit operations are operations on integers and 32-bit operation is a floating-point operation.

Table 13

Number of bits in the word	Operation		
	A + B	**AB**	**SA**
8	6553	1861	2824
12	4428	910	1489
32	470	291	373

From Table 13 it follows that the speed of floating-point addition (multiplication) of matrices is about 17 times (18 times) faster on the MPP than on the DAP.

The MPP is based on VLSI technology; 8 processors are on one VLSI chip. The memory of four processors is on one 4 kbit chip, such that the 8 processors and their memories occupy three chips (compared to the DAP, where one processor occupied five chips).

Because of its high speed and memory capacity the MPP is also useful for other applications, such as general tasks in image processing, weather forecast, aerodynamic simulation, processing of radar signals and matrix operations.

4.4 Multiprocessor computers and their algorithms

4.4.1 Introduction

Due to existence of some actual parallel computers (e.g. ILLIAC-IV, STARAN, ICL DAP), to date research in the field of parallel algorithms has been oriented towards the SIMD-type computers. Recently great attention is being paid to multiprocessor computers of the MIMD-type. These computers can solve a broader class of problems compared with the SIMD-type computers. On solving tasks by means of the MIMD computers, new problems are emerging, which did not exist with the SIMD computers (e.g. synchronization of computational processes, the assignment of individual processors to given tasks, etc.). In this section we shall point out the characteristic features of the architecture of these computers, introduce the most important principles underlying the process of designing their algorithms and we shall present a detailed description of the EGPA hierarchical multiprocessor computers.

The multiprocessor computer (MC) is defined as a computer with more than two processor units that share one memory and are controlled by a common unit [11]. The MC is controlled by a single operating system facilitating mutual interaction among the processors and the programs executed.

It is their interconnecting system that distinguishes computers of this type. It markedly influences efficiency (performance) of the computer as a whole in that it facilitates communication among its units. Time-shared bus, crossbar-switch and multiport memory are three basic types of interconnections [11].

The simplest alternative of interconnection is the time-shared bus. It is a common communication path to which all functional units of the system are connected. Transfer operations performed by the bus are controlled by the transmitting and receiving units. It is the possibility of adding or taking away separate functional units that makes a system with this type of interconnection flexible. Since all transfers proceed along a single transfer line, very often a situation occurs where the processors have to wait until the bus is released. This leads to a decrease in the performance of the whole computer. Transfer capacity of the whole system can be increased by adding one more one-way bus or by connecting several buses to enable a two-way transfer. Consequently, the interconnection system becomes more complex; to facilitate transfers with lowest possible rate of conflicts the switch points must be provided with additional switches, as well as with other types of control and logic functions. The Plessy

System 250 [45] can serve as an example of an MC with this type of interconnection, where one bus corresponds to each processor.

In a crossbar-switch, each memory module can use one independent transfer line. In multiprocessors with this type of interconnection, data can be transferred into all memory modules simultaneously, which enables the maximum possible transfer rate. Access to the individual memory modules is such that within one memory cycle time a single memory module is accessible to only one processor. This access strategy helps to prevent conflicts. The crossbar-switch is the most complex and largest interconnection system. Its typical example is the interconnection of 16 PDP-11 computers in a C.mmp multiprocessor [46].

In parallel computers with multiport memories, functions of the interconnection network are concentrated in each memory module. To prevent conflicts in accessing the memory, each of its ports is given a fixed number which specifies its priority. In this case, less circuits for switching and decision functions are needed than in the crossbar-switch. On the other hand, memory modules of the computers with this type of interconnection are most complex and expensive.

4.4.2 Algorithms for multiprocessor computers

An algorithm is implemented on the MC as a set of parallel processes which can intercommunicate. A process is executed by a processor to which it has been allocated by the operating system. Special parts of the program are so-called critical sections; only one processor can be in the critical section at a fixed time interval. On a given processor, the execution of the allocated process is passivated in the critical section and it is activated only when in the critical section there is no other process.

Parallel algorithms for these computers are classified according to the kind of communication among the individual processes. To date, algorithms for multiprocessors have usually been designed on the selection of such parts of serial algorithm that could be executed in parallel. After independent partial problems (subtasks) had been identified, a graph showing the dependence of their execution was constructed. This approach leads to designs of synchronous algorithms in which the starting time of each process depended on the termination of all preceding processes. Such algorithms, however, require large-scale communication and many synchronization steps. An example of a synchronous algorithm is Jacobi's method for iterative computation of the solution of linear systems with N unknowns. Since it is the multiplication of a vector by a matrix of size $N \times N$, the simplest alternative is to split the whole work among N processors such, that each of them computes one element of the new iteration vector. The implementation of computation of each iteration involves a computational section (CS), waiting sections (WS) and a critical section (CrS), which form a string (CS—WS—WS—CrS). Having computed the next iteration values, the first waiting section is needed to synchronize all processes. The second waiting is caused by the critical section, in which the processors stay during reading in and restoring the values of successive iterations. Since the computation of the iteration vector is divided among all the processors by equal measure, it could be expected that the execution time of a given subtask would be the same for all the processors. However, practical experiments have shown that this time is a random variable and the time spent by a processor in the CS section (expressed in relative units) is about $1/\ln N$ of the total run-time of the iteration [6]. Thus, for large N, despite the high degree of parallelism, the processors are mostly in idle state, because they have to wait for each other.

The above example suggests that the computation efficiency is substantially decreased by synchronization in algorithms. From this it follows that in designing an algorithm to solve a task, a subdivision into large independent subtasks has to be chosen such that the number of synchronization phases in the algorithm be as small as possible. For this reason, so-called asynchronous algorithms [30] are most suitable for the MC. In these algorithms, the processes communicate with each other by means of global variables, whose values are used in another process immediately after the afore process has terminated. There are several examples of numerical and non-numerical asynchronous algorithms in references [5, 7, 8].

In the next section we shall study the possible asynchronous implementation of iterative methods to solve the system of linear equations, resulting from discretization of the Poisson equation in N^2 grid points of a unit square. These problems are discussed in detail in Chapter 1, where a number of fast parallel algorithms to solve this task are introduced. In iterative methods the time of asynchronous implementation of one iteration involves three sections that form a string (CS—WS—CrS). Since the processes need not be synchronized after the computation of the new iteration value, waiting is exclusively caused by the presence of the critical section. Using the asynchronous Jacobi method (AJ), the computation is performed in k processes where iteration values are calculated in N^2/k grid points and the computation of the values of the individual processes does not have to wait for the others. In the critical section those values are restored and duplicated, which are necessary for the computation of the next iteration. In asynchronous Gauss—Seidel method (AGS), values newly computed in every process are used as soon as they are available. Values of a new iteration are restored after the computation at all the points corresponding to the given process has been finished.

In the AJ and AGS methods, the asynchronous principle is applied at the process level. The iterative computation can be implemented more efficiently if the asynchronous principle is introduced to the inside of the individual processes. In this completely asynchronous method (PA), the iteration value at the grid point is computed from the latest accessible neighbouring values. Once computed this value is immediately passed to be used by other processes. In contrast to the above-mentioned methods, this method has no critical section, since after computation of the iteration there is no need of reading in and restoring the vectors of iteration values in the process.

Results of solving the boundary value problem for the Poisson equation by the use of these methods on a multiprocessor C.mmp in a six-processor configuration [46] are introduced in [6]. Computations were performed for a 504-point grid using different numbers of processes. The obtained values of computation speed-up for individual methods are summarized in Fig. 60. The effect of synchronization as manifested in the computational efficiency follows from the comparison of the results obtained by Jacobi's and PA methods.

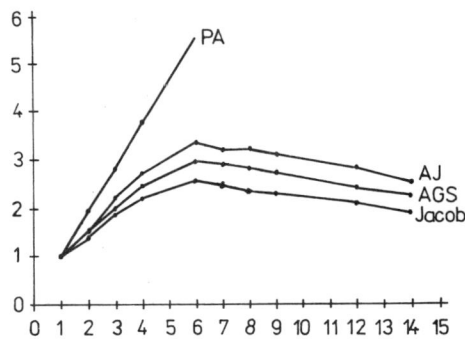

Fig. 60. Speed-up of iterative methods on the C.mmp computer.

The PA method also served as a testing example for the Cm* multiprocessor with 50 processors, where in case of some operating systems the linear factor of speeding up the computations was also achieved [25].

Another interesting example of synchronized implementation was introduced in Chapter 1. In this case, a strictly serial task divided into independent subtasks can be solved on the basis of duration variation of individual processes, provided none of the subtasks can be parallelized at the given level.

4.4.3 Hierarchical EGPA multiprocessor

A hierarchical multiprocessor computer EGPA (Erlangen General Purpose Array) is a multiprocessor computer developed at the University in Erlangen

[19]. Its designers followed the aim to employ in it a number of well-known principles of organizing parallel computations without the necessity of developing new hardware.

Its interconnecting subsystem should secure large-scale interprocessor communication without using any crossbar-switch. The above requirements resulted in a design of a computer with dynamically extensible hierarchical structure [21]. Its basic unit consists of five "processor—memory" pairs arranged in a pyramidal structure shown in Fig. 61 [18].

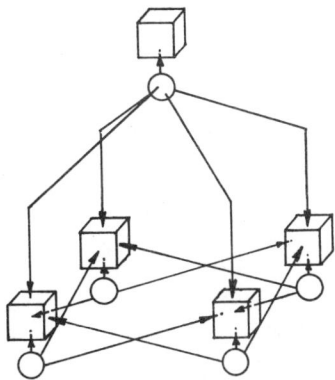

Fig. 61. Diagram of the EGPA pyramidal multiprocessor.

Each of four processors at the base of the pyramid can be replaced by another elementary pyramid, which enables to dynamically generate multilevel structures of the same form. Dimension of a pyramid can be chosen to match the implemented algorithm as much as possible. The processor array at the base of the pyramid executes computation of the given task. Higher-level processors fulfil the functions of the operating system, they also may be involved in computations. Multiport memory modules ensure interconnection. Interconnection chart of processors at the same level is shown in Fig. 62 [3]. Each processor outside its level is connected with its master processor and with four processors at lower level. In this way the processor can communicate, except for its memory, with memories of its eight neighbours. Its memory is also accessible (except itself) to its neighbours at the same level.

Compactness of such interconnection mechanism secures that the system can also operate in case of breakdown of one or more processors. Operating processors perform computations separately, as a group of parallelly operating processors that solve the same or different tasks or as pipeline processors. Execution of the data flow operating mode is also possible. Another possibility (based on vertical data processing) is a pseudoassociative organization of com-

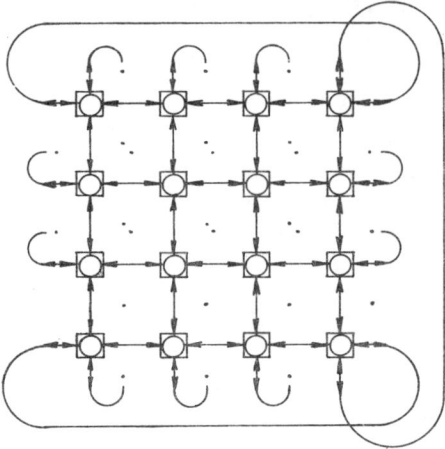

Fig. 62. Diagram of an interconnecting network of a hierarchical multiprocessor.

putation; here all processors perform comparison operations serially in a bit-wise manner, and arithmetic-logical operations are executed using the access to the memory of their neighbours.

The functioning configuration of the EGPA computer is formed by a five-processor elementary pyramid. The interconnection of the processors at the base of the pyramid (further, the A processors) is implemented in both directions along its perimeter without interconnection among the processors lying on diagonal lines. The processor at the top of the pyramid (further, the B processor) controls the operation of the multiprocessor, since it can access the memories of all A processors. Parameters of this interconnection depending on the implemented parallel principles of computation are given in [20, 21]. The optimal distribution of tasks to the individual processors of a hierarchical multiprocessor and the corresponding evaluations for the EGPA computer are in [26]. The data flow principle and its application to an algorithm from image processing are described in [27]. Various parallel implementations of program systems (software packages) on hierarchical multiprocessors are analysed in [37]. A number of papers are devoted [1, 2, 17] to the problems of vertical data processing. It was found that application of the above principle resulted in a substantial speeding up of the retrieval, comparison and arithmetic operations; in some cases, the computations were as much as 80 times faster compared with serial computations. Implementation of the FFT algorithm on the EGPA computer is analysed in [3]. Fast parallel algorithms for the elementary elliptic differential equations and results of their implementation are presented in [44]. Parallelization of the multigrid method of computation of the Navier–Stokes equation is proposed in [14].

4.4.4 Algorithms for the EGPA multiprocessor

Implementation of a matrix inversion on the EGPA computer will be demonstrated and the times of implementation of several algorithms presented in this section. The operating processors will be labelled as AJ, $J = 1, 2, 3, 4$, and the notation of the left (AJL), or right (AJR) neighbour of each of them follows according to Table 14.

Table 14

AJ	$A1$	$A2$	$A3$	$A4$
AJL	$A4$	$A1$	$A2$	$A3$
AJR	$A2$	$A3$	$A4$	$A1$

In constructing algorithms for this computer we shall consider two types of variables. A local variable x is labelled by x. If x will be a global variable shared by several processors, its value on a special processor AJ will be labelled as $x(J)$. For simplicity, we shall suppose that the dimensions of applied arrays are multiples of 4. Then, these arrays can be divided into four horizontal or vertical blocks, each of the same order. The vertical slices of an array $\boldsymbol{X}$ are denoted by $\boldsymbol{X}_J$, $J = 1, 2, 3, 4$, where the leftmost slice is $\boldsymbol{X}_1$. Analogically, the horizontal slices are $\boldsymbol{X}_{\bar{J}}$, $\bar{J} = 1, 2, 3, 4$, with the uppermost array $\boldsymbol{X}_{\bar{1}}$. The function **Wait**(Q) is used for synchronization. If the condition Q is satisfied, the processor can execute the successive step of an algorithm. **Trans**$x(J)$ serves to describe the transport of $x(J)$ which is stored in the memory of the right neighbouring processor AJR of a processor AJ, to its left neighbour AJL. In other words, by **Trans**$x(J)$ the processor AJ executes the transport between diagonally positioned processors AJR and AJL.

In numerical computations there often arises a situation when all intermediate results, evaluated on individual processors, need to be available to each of them. Since the neighbouring processors are interconnected directly, the mutual data exchange has to be performed among the pairs of processors ($A1$, $A3$) and ($A2$, $A4$). The transfer of values $x(J)$, $J = 1, 2, 3, 4$, can be implemented simultaneously on all processors by the procedure **Transportalle** whose formulation for the initial values **false** of global variables *ber* (denoting the termination of computation) and *trans* (denoting the termination of transfer) is as follows

Wait $(ber(JR)) \rightarrow$ **true** ;
Trans (x_{JR});
$trans(JL) \rightarrow$ **true** ;

Wait $(ber\,(JL)) \rightarrow$ **true**;
Wait $(trans\,(J)) \rightarrow$ **true**.

To compute the inversion of a regular matrix **M** of dimension N, the method of orthogonalization of its columns m_i, $i = 1, 2, ..., N$, will be chosen. From the initial basis $v_j^{(0)} = m_j^T$, $j = 1, 2, ..., N$ (T being the sign of transposition), for $i = 1, 2, ..., N$, the vectors

$$v_i^{(i)} = (v_i^{(i-1)} m_i)^{-1} v_i^{(i-1)},$$

$$v_k^{(i)} = v_k^{(i-1)} - (v_k^{(i-1)} m_i) v_i^{(i)},$$

$$k = 1, 2, ..., i-1, i+1, ..., N$$

are calculated.

If the matrix resulting from computation of the ith step of orthogonalization is denoted as $\mathbf{V}^{(i)}$, $i = 1, 2, ..., N$, $\mathbf{V}^{(N)}$ is the calculated inverse matrix $\mathbf{M}^{-1}$. Since we suppose that N is a multiple of 4, this method is implementable on four processors. Each processor AJ, $J = 1, 2, 3, 4$, will compute for $L = N/4$ the row vectors v_k, $k = (J-1)L + 1, ..., JL$, which form the block $\mathbf{V}_J^{(i)}$ of matrix $\mathbf{V}^{(i)}$. In order to perform this computation for given i in parallel, vector $v_i^{(i)}$ must be available to each processor. This vector is solely computed on a single processor AP in every step. In the course of computation, the number P is successively changing from the value 1 to $P = 2, 3, 4$ for $i = L, 2L, 3L$, respectively. In this way, the vector $v_i^{(i)}$ becomes directly accessible to the processor AP and its neighbours APL and APR. However, it must be transported to the processor on a diagonal. For this reason, it is necessary for every i to synchronize the process just once. In this case, the processor APL waits until AP computes $v_i^{(i)}$, and then it performs the necessary transfer. Now, the parallel computation of all the four horizontal blocks of the matrix $\mathbf{V}^{(i)}$ can be executed. The computation can be written for each AJ, $J = 1, 2, 3, 4$, using the following algorithm (algorithm $O1$):

```
         i ← 1;
         P ← 1;
         m ← 0;
LAB:     i ← i + 1;
         m ← m + 1;
         if m = L
            then m ← 1;
                 P ← P + 1;
         fi;
         if J = P
            then ber(P) ← false;
```

$$y \leftarrow \mathbf{v}_m^{(i-1)} \mathbf{m}_i;$$
$$x \leftarrow \frac{1}{y} \mathbf{v}_m^{(i-1)};$$
$$\mathbf{v}_m^{(i)} \leftarrow \mathbf{x} + \frac{1}{y} \mathbf{x};$$
$ber(P) \leftarrow \mathbf{true};$
 else if $J = PL$
  then $trans(PL) \leftarrow \mathbf{false};$
   Wait$(ber(P) \leftarrow \mathbf{true});$
   Trans$(X);$
   $trans(PL) \leftarrow \mathbf{true};$
 else if $J = PR$
  then Wait$(ber(P) \leftarrow \mathbf{true});$
  else Wait$(trans(PL) \leftarrow \mathbf{true});$
 fi
fi
fi;
for $k = (J-1)L + 1, \ldots, JL$ **do**
 $\mathbf{v}_k^{(i)} = \mathbf{v}_k^{(i-1)} - (\mathbf{v}_k^{(i-1)} \mathbf{m}_i) \mathbf{x};$
od;
if $i < N$
 then go to LAB
fi.

After its execution, each processor has in its memory L corresponding rows of the inverse matrix. It is worth noting that in this algorithm the whole matrix **M** must be stored in each processor.

If the dimension of matrix **M** is sufficiently large, and the memory of individual processors does not suffice the computation, another algorithm has to be constructed such that each processor AJ would store in its memory only the horizontal block $\mathbf{M}_J$ of the matrix. According to this method, four vertical blocks $\mathbf{V}_J^{(i)}$ will be computed for each i. To this aim, all components of vector $\mathbf{v} = \mathbf{V}^{(i-1)} \mathbf{m}_i$ must be available for each processor. Vector $\mathbf{v} = (v_1, \ldots, v_N)$ is computed as a sum

$$\mathbf{v} = \sum_{J=1}^{4} \mathbf{t}_J = \sum_{J=1}^{4} \mathbf{V}_J^{(i-1)} [\mathbf{m}_i]_J,$$

where $[\mathbf{m}_i]_J$ is the Jth section of the column $\mathbf{m}_i$. Now, **Transportalle** executes cyclic transport of vectors $\mathbf{t}_J$. A vector transported into the memory will be labelled as $\mathbf{t}_{\text{diag}}$. Finally, the vertical blocks $\mathbf{V}_J^{(N)}$ of the inverse matrix are computed on four processors AJ, $J = 1, 2, 3, 4$, from the input values $\mathbf{V}_J^{(0)} = [\mathbf{M}_J]^T$ as follows (algorithm $O2$)

for $i = 1, 2, \ldots, N$ **do**
    $ber(J) \leftarrow$ **false**;
    $trans(J) \leftarrow$ **false**;
    $t_J \leftarrow v_J^{(i-1)}[m_i]_J$;
    $ber(J) \leftarrow$ **true**;
    Transportalle (t_{JR});
    $t \leftarrow t_J + t_{JR} + t_{JL} + t_{\text{diag}}$;
    $[v_i^{(i)}]_J \leftarrow \dfrac{1}{v_i} [v_i^{(i-1)}]_J$;
    for $k = 1, \ldots, i-1, i+1, \ldots, N$ **do**
        $[v_k^{(i)}]_J \leftarrow [v_k^{(i-1)}]_J - v_k [v_i^{(i)}]_J$;
    od
od.

Both parallel algorithms were implemented and tested on the EGPA computer. The parallel run-times t_1 (in seconds) and speed-up values z (defined as a ratio t_0/t_1, where t_0 is the time of sequential realization) are listed in Table 15.

Table 15

	Algorithm			
	O1		O2	
N	t_1	z	t_1	z
10		< 1		< 1
15	0.701	< 1	0.674	1.02
20	1.135	1.43	0.973	1.67
30	2.176	2.53	2.155	2.56
40	4.206	3.09	4.487	2.89
50	7.769	3.36	8.101	3.22
60	12.610	3.48	12.408	3.54
70	20.350	3.52	20.355	3.52
80	29.595	3.55	28.703	3.66
90	42.567	3.53	41.337	3.63
100	57.175	3.64	54.984	3.79
110	77.142	3.6	74.145	3.74
120	98.289	3.68	94.248	3.83
130	126.010	3.72	121.757	3.85
140	155.226	3.72	149.134	3.87
150	193.206	3.75	185.593	3.90
160	230.711	3.75	221.821	3.90

With the first algorithm a speed-up of 3.75 was achieved. The second parallel version yielded a speed-up of 3.90 because it needed less transport of data than the first one.

One of the most frequently used methods to invert a matrix is the Gauss–Jordan elimination. Two versions of this method for the EGPA are presented in [15].

In the first version (algorithm $E1$), pivoting is included and new values in all elements of the matrix are evaluated for each elimination stage. It is a parallel modification of the original algorithm, where a global synchronization of the computation process through the processor at the top of the pyramid is demonstrated. Its main idea is based on the fact, that to compute new values of an arbitrary submatrix of **M** it suffices to know the submatrix, the pivot, and the corresponding sections of the pivot row and of the pivot column. The structure of the pilot pyramid enables each processor to get access to the desired data.

In the second version (algorithm $E2$), the elimination phase serves to calculate N^2 elements of N factorization matrices

$$\mathbf{F}^{(i)} = \begin{bmatrix} 1 & & & f_{1i} & & 0 \\ & \ddots & & \vdots & & \\ & & 1 & f_{ii} & & \\ & & & 1 & & \\ & & & \vdots & \ddots & \\ 0 & & & f_{Ni} & & 1 \end{bmatrix}, \quad i = 1, 2, ..., N.$$

In this way, it is easy to complete the inverse matrix as a product

$$\mathbf{M}^{-1} = \mathbf{F}^{(N)} \mathbf{F}^{(N-1)} ... \mathbf{F}^{(1)}.$$

The computation times and speed-up values of both algorithms run on matrices up to 200×200 in size are given in Table 16. As seen, the speed-up ratio of the second algorithm approaches the optimum value of 4.

The inversion of matrix **M** of order N can also be efficiently computed by dividing the matrix into four square blocks of order $N/2$

$$\mathbf{M} = \begin{bmatrix} C & D \\ E & F \end{bmatrix}$$

from which the corresponding blocks of the inverse matrix

$$\mathbf{M}^{-1} = \begin{bmatrix} P & R \\ S & T \end{bmatrix}$$

Table 16

	Algorithm			
	E1		E2	
N	t_1	z	t_1	z
10	0.525	< 1	0.664	< 1
15	0.671	< 1	0.559	< 1
20	0.874	1.41	0.660	1.26
30	1.678	2.5	1.322	1.93
40	3.225	3.15	2.094	2.87
50	5.697	3.38	3.736	3.46
60	9.517	3.5	5.646	3.54
70	14.534	3.67	8.799	3.64
80	21.300	3.73	12.490	3.79
90	29.912	3.79	18.278	3.66
100	40.761	3.81	24.066	3.83
120	70.419	3.83	41.353	3.91
140	111.924	3.83	64.645	3.93
160	165.505	3.89	95.828	3.98
180	233.269	3.95	135.862	3.97
200	323.500	3.95	186.017	3.97

can be obtained by

$$P = (C - DF^{-1}E)^{-1}, \quad R = PDF^{-1}, \quad T = F^{-1} - F^{-1}ER, \quad S = -F^{-1}EP.$$

Having the procedure for matrix inversion available, two matrices of order $N/2$ can be inverted in place of inversion of the original matrix of order N. The efficiency of the method increases if one of the diagonal blocks of **M** is easy to invert. To implement this method on the EGPA computer, a programming module for each processor AJ, $J = 1, 2, 3, 4$, can be written in the following form

    berfertig $(J) \leftarrow$ **false**
    transfertig $(J) \leftarrow$ **false**
Compute F_J^{-1}
$F_J \leftarrow F_J^{-1}$
$D_{J+} \leftarrow DF_J = DF_J^{-1}$
    berfertig $(J) \leftarrow$ **true**
Transportalle (F_{JR})
    berfertig $(J) \leftarrow$ **false**
    transfertig $(J) \leftarrow$ **false**
$E_J \leftarrow FE_J = F^{-1}E_J$

$berfertig\ (J) \leftarrow$ **true**
Transportalle $(\mathbf{E}_{JR})$
 $berfertig\ (J) \leftarrow$ **false**
 $transfertig\ (J) \leftarrow$ **false**
$\mathbf{C}_J \leftarrow \mathbf{C}_J - \mathbf{D}_J\mathbf{E} = \mathbf{C}_J - \mathbf{D}_J\mathbf{F}^{-1}\mathbf{E}$
 Compute $(\mathbf{C} - \mathbf{DF}^{-1}\mathbf{E})_J^{-1} = \mathbf{P}_J$
 $berfertig\ (J) \leftarrow$ **true**
Transportalle $(\mathbf{P}_{JR})$
 $berfertig\ (J) \leftarrow$ **false**
 $transfertig\ (J) \leftarrow$ **false**
$\mathbf{C}_J \leftarrow \mathbf{P}_J$
$\mathbf{D}_J \leftarrow \mathbf{CD}_{J+} = \mathbf{P}(\mathbf{DF}_J^{-1}) = \mathbf{R}_J$
$\mathbf{F}_J \leftarrow \mathbf{F}_J - \mathbf{ED}_J = \mathbf{F}_J^{-1} - \mathbf{F}^{-1}\mathbf{ER}_J = \mathbf{T}_J$
$\mathbf{E}_J \leftarrow -\mathbf{EC}_J = -\mathbf{F}^{-1}\mathbf{EP}_J = \mathbf{S}_J$.

The "next upper" horizontal slice to $\mathbf{D}_J$ is denoted by $\mathbf{D}_{J+}$, i.e. $J^+ = J + 1$ for $J = 1, 2, 3,$ and $J^+ = 1$ if $J = 4$. It is introduced to store $\mathbf{DF}_J^{-1}$ which cannot be stored in $\mathbf{D}_J$, because this slice of $\mathbf{D}$ is needed for evaluation of $\mathbf{D}_J$ from which the inverse $\mathbf{P}_J$ is computed. In the parallel implementation of the partitioning method [15], both inverses in the algorithm were computed by the parallel Gauss–Jordan elimination. Because of the nearest neighbour connection, each of the six matrix multiplication steps in the algorithm was realized in a macrosystolic manner.

Another problem solved on the EGPA computer was the Dirichlet problem for the Poisson equation on the unit square. In this case, the parallel algorithm of matrix decomposition, described in Chapter 1, was implemented. The algorithm was realized by one synchronization and a cyclic transfer of the matrix blocks using the procedure **Transportalle**. The results achieved for the function $u(x, y) = x^2 + y^2$ with various discretization parameters are listed in Table 17 [44].

The computation time of a serial algorithm on one processor is labelled as t_1.

Table 17

N	t_1 [s]	t_p [s]	z	e [%]
32	6.959	4.837	1.44	36.0 (28.8)
40	12.988	6.494	2.00	50.0 (40.0)
64	49.834	16.449	3.03	75.8 (60.6)
80	94.852	28.610	3.32	82.9 (66.3)
128	374.624	103.237	3.63	90.7 (72.6)

The values t_p give the times of its parallel realization on the EGPA computer. The speed-up z is defined as t_1/t_p ratio. The efficiency of computation e depends on z and on the number of processors involved in the computation such that $e = (z/n) 100\%$. The efficiency values given in Table 12 hold for $n = 4$. Because the EGPA is a five-processor computer, in parentheses there are also values for $n = 5$. It is clear, that the larger N the more efficient is the computation. In this case, the time necessary for arithmetic computations prevails over the time necessary for synchronization and transfers.

It is worth mentioning in the conclusion to this chapter, that the knowledge of the architecture, algorithms and performance of the EGPA computer has recently been employed in the development of the modular reconfigurable, fault-tolerant parallel multiprocessor system DIRMU [32].

References

[1] B. Albert, A. Bode and W. Händler, "A case study in vertical migration: The implementation of a dedicated associative instruction set", *Microprocessing and Microprogramming* **8** (1981) 257—262.

[2] B. Albert, A. Bode, R. Jacob, R. Kilgenstein and M. Ratke, "Vertikalverarbeitung: Beschleunigung von Anwendeprogrammen durch mikroprogrammierte Assoziativbefehle", in *Hardware für Software*. Tagung der German Chapter of the ACM (Konstanz, 1980) (B. G. Teubner, Stuttgart, 1980) pp. 114—123.

[3] F. Arnold, L. Benker and M. Grutz, "Die Fast Fourier-Transformation und Möglichkeiten ihrer Implementierung auf EGPA", Arbeitsbericht IMMD (Universität Erlangen-Nürnberg, 1977).

[4] G. Barnes et al., "The ILLIAC-IV Computer", *IEEE Trans. Comp.* **C-17** (1968) 746—757.

[5] G. M. Baudet, "Asynchronous iterative methods for multiprocessors", *J. ACM* **25** (1978) 226—244.

[6] G. M. Baudet, "Parallel Algorithms: Design, analysis and experiments", Proc. CREST Course on Design of Numerical Algorithms (Bergamo, 1981).

[7] G. M. Baudet, R. P. Brent and H. T. Kung, "Parallel execution of a sequence of tasks on an asynchronous multiprocessor", *Austr. Comp. J.* **12** (1980) 105—112.

[8] G. M. Baudet and D. Stevenson, "Optimal sorting algorithms for parallel computers", *IEEE Trans. Comp.* **C-27** (1978) 84—87.

[9] Control Data Corporation, STAR-100 Computer Hardware, Reference Manual (1974).

[10] "DAP support unit", Techn. Rep. (Comp. Centre, Queen Mary College, London, 1982).

[11] P. H. Enslow, Jr., "Multiprocessor organization — a survey", *Comp. Surv.* **9** (1977) 103—112.

[12] P. M. Flanders, D. J. Hunt, S. F. Reddaway and D. Parkinson, "Efficient high speed computing with the distributed array processor", in *High Speed Computers and Algorithm Organization* (Academic Press, London, 1977) pp. 113—128.

[13] W. M. Gentleman, "Some complexity results for matrix computations on parallel processors", *J. ACM* **25** (1978) 112—115.

[14] L. Geus, "Parallelisierung eines Mehrgitterverfahrens für die Navier – Stokes-Gleichungen auf EGPA-Systemen", Arbeitsbericht IMMD (Universität Erlangen-Nürnberg, 1985).
[15] L. Geus, W. Hennig, M. Vajteršic and J. Volkert, "Matrix inversion algorithms for the parallel computer EGPA" *Computers and Artif. Intelligence* (in press).
[16] R. W. Gostick, "Software and algorithms for the distributed array processors", DAP Unit Mark. Div., *Inform. Comp. Lett.* **20** (1981).
[17] W. Händler, "Unconventional computation by conventional equipment", Arbeitsbericht IMMD (Universität Erlangen-Nürnberg, 1974).
[18] W. Händler, "Technology in computing and architectural considerations", *Proc. SEAS Anniversary Meeting '81* (Nice, 1981) pp. 17—38.
[19] W. Händler, F. Hofmann and H. J. Schneider, "A general purpose array with a broad spectrum of applications", *Proc. of the Workshop on Computer Architecture* (Springer-Verlag, Berlin, 1975) pp. 311—335.
[20] V. Herzog, W. Hofmann and W. Kleinöder, "Performance modelling and evaluation for hierarchically organized multiprocessor computer systems", *Proc. Int. Conf. on Parallel Processing* (Bellaire, 1977) pp. 103—114.
[21] U. Hercksen, R. Klar and W. Kleinöder, "Hardware measurements of storage access conflicts in the processor array EGPA", *Proc. 7th Annual Symp. on Computer Architecture* (La Baûle, 1980) pp. 317—324.
[22] L. Higbie, "Applications of vector processing", *Comp. Design* **2** (1978) 1—7.
[23] R. W. Hockney and C. R. Jesshope, *Parallel Computers — Architecture, Programming and Algorithms* (Adam Hilger, Bristol, 1981).
[24] P. M. Johnson, "An introduction to vector processing", *Comp. Design* **2** (1978) 89—97.
[25] A. K. Jones and E. F. Gehringer, "The Cm* multiprocessor project: A research review", Techn. Rep. 131 (Comp. Sci. Dep., Carnegie-Mellon University, Pittsburgh, 1980).
[26] W. Kleinöder, "Stochastische Bewertung von Aufgabenstrukturen für heirarchische Mehrrechnersysteme", Arbeitsbericht IMMD (Universität Erlangen-Nürnberg, 1982).
[27] F. Kneissl, "Realisierung von Makro-Datenflussmechanismen auf hierarchischen Mehrrechnersystemen", Arbeitsbericht IMMD (Universität Erlangen-Nürnberg, 1982).
[28] P. Kogge and H. S. Stone, "A parallel algorithm for the efficient solution of a general class of recurrence equation", *IEEE Trans. Comp.* **C-22** (1973) 786—790.
[29] D. Kuck, "ILLIAC-IV software and application programming", *IEEE Trans. Comp.* **C-17** (1968) 758—770.
[30] H. T. Kung, "Synchronized and asynchronous parallel algorithms for multiprocessors", in *Algorithms and Complexity*, Ed. J. F. Traub (Academic Press, New York, 1976) pp. 153—200.
[31] J. J. Lambiotte and R. G. Voigt, "The solution of tridiagonal systems of equations on the CDC STAR-100 computer", *ACM Trans. Math. Soft.* **4** (1975) 308—329.
[32] E. Maehle, "Fehlertolerantes Verhalten in Multiprozessoren-Untersuchungen zur Diagnose und Rekonfiguration", Arbeitsbericht IMMD (Universität Erlangen-Nürnberg, 1982).
[33] *MPP — Massively Parallel Processor* (Goodyear Aerospace Corp., NASA Goddard Space Flight Center, Ohio, 1981).
[34] Neue Rechnerarchitekturen, Vorwort, *Proc. 3rd Coll. with CRAY*, Paper 22 (Regionales Rechenzentrum, Universität Hannover, 1982).
[35] D. Parkinson, "Computers by the thousand", *New Scientist* **5** (1976) 626—627.
[36] C. V. Ramamoorthy and H. F. Li, "Pipeline architecture", *Comp. Surv.* **9** (1977) 61—102.
[37] M. Rathke, "Parallelisieren ordnungshaltender Programmsysteme für hierarchische Multiprozessorsysteme", Arbeitsbericht IMMD (Universität Erlangen-Nürnberg, 1985).
[38] R. M. Russell, "The CRAY-1 computer system", *Commun. ACM* **21** (1978) 63—72.

[39] *STARAN: System Description, A New Class Computer* (Goodyear Aerospace Corp., Akron, 1974).
[40] H. S. Stone, "Parallel processing with perfect shuffle", *IEEE Trans. Comp.* **C-20** (1971) 153—161.
[41] H. S. Stone, "Parallel tridiagonal equation solver", *ACM Trans. Math. Soft.* **1** (1975) 289—307.
[42] C. D. Thompson, "Generalized connection networks for parallel processor intercommunication", Techn. Rep. (Comp. Sci. Dep., Carnegie-Mellon University, Pittsburgh, 1977).
[43] P. G. Tuttle, "Implementation of selected eigenvalue algorithms on a vector computer", Techn. Rep. (NPGD-TM-330, Babcock and Wilcox Comp., 1975).
[44] M. Vajteršic, "Parallel Poisson and biharmonic solvers implemented on the EGPA multiprocessor", *Proc. Int. Conf. on Parallel Processing* (Bellaire, 1982) pp. 72—81.
[45] R. K. Williams, "System 250-basic concepts", *Proc. Conf. on Computers — Systems and Technology* (IERE, London, 1972).
[46] W. A. Wulf and C. G. Bell, "C.mmp a multi-miniprocessor", *Proc. AFIPS Conf.* (New York, 1972) pp. 765—777.

Chapter 5

Fast algorithm for solution of a system of linear algebraic equations on specialized VLSI computers

5.1 Introduction

New VLSI technology has opened new ways of constructing specialized computer structures. The goal of this chapter is to suggest some specialized VLSI computers that could be used to solve dense systems of linear algebraic equations and concurrently calculate the determinant of the matrix involved. Having analysed several types of elimination algorithms, we have chosen the Gauss–Jordan–Rutishauser elimination with partial pivoting (GJR), which is described in [1] as so-called rotation (Umwälzung) algorithm, for our example in this chapter. The algorithm is parallel and sufficiently homogeneous, which is the main condition for implementation in VLSI technology. With a detailed knowledge of this algorithm, we suggest and analyse four specialized VLSI computers for modified GJR algorithms: single chip computer, P-processors computer with on-chip cache memory and off-chip active memory, orthogonal pipeline vector processor (row and column variants), and systolic array. The scheme of each computer is given, their specialized (restricted) instruction sets are described, the programs executing the GJR algorithm on these computers are formulated and their complexity is evaluated.

The most frequent numerical task in scientific-technical calculations is the solution of a dense system of linear algebraic equations [2]. The question of a fast, precise and inexpensive solution of this problem is, therefore, significant.

Given a system of linear algebraic equations expressed in matrix notation,

$$\mathbf{AX} = \mathbf{B}, \qquad (66)$$

$\mathbf{A} = (a_{ij})$ is a regular matrix of order n, and $\mathbf{X} = x_i^{(j)}$ and $\mathbf{B} = (a_{i, n+j})$, $i = 1, 2, ..., n$; $j = 1, 2, ..., m$, are n by m matrices.

First let's look at the simpler Gauss–Jordan elimination with partial (column) pivoting for solving (66) [1, 2]. We begin by constructing the augmented matrix $\mathbf{C} = (\mathbf{A} | \mathbf{B}) = (a_{ij})$, $i = 1, 2, ..., n$; $j = 1, 2, ..., n + m$. With appropriate exchanges of rows, the matrix $\mathbf{A}$ is eliminated by a column at a time, replacing the matrix **A** with a unit matrix **I**. The same operations are done on **B** simultaneously, so that **C** becomes (**I**|**X**). Thus the solution **X** is obtained after the nth elimination step in the place where we originally put **B**.

C, in the sth elimination step, is

$$\mathbf{C}_s = \begin{bmatrix} 1 & 0 & \cdots & 0 & a_{1s}^{(s-1)} & \cdots & a_{1,n+m}^{(s-1)} \\ 0 & 1 & \cdots & 0 & a_{2s}^{(s-1)} & \cdots & a_{2,n+m}^{(s-1)} \\ \vdots & \vdots & \ddots & \vdots & \vdots & & \vdots \\ 0 & 0 & & 1 & a_{s-1,s}^{(s-1)} & \cdots & a_{s-1,n+m}^{(s-1)} \\ 0 & 0 & \cdots & 0 & a_{ss}^{(s-1)} & \cdots & a_{s,n+m}^{(s-1)} \\ \vdots & \vdots & & \vdots & \vdots & & \vdots \\ 0 & 0 & & 0 & a_{ns}^{(s-1)} & \cdots & a_{n,n+m}^{(s-1)} \end{bmatrix}.$$

Then Gauss–Jordan elimination can be described by these steps [1]:
Let $a_{ij} = a_{ij}^{(0)}$.
For $s = 1, 2, \ldots, n$ do:
 (1) find i such that $a_{is} = \max_{j \geq s} |a_{js}^{(s-1)}|$, (find the best pivot)
 (2) exchange sth and ith rows of $\mathbf{C}_s$, (pivot)
 (3) calculate $c_s = 1/a_{ss}^{(s-1)}$, (reduce)
 (4) multiply the sth row of matrix $\mathbf{C}_s$ with c_s,
 (5) for $i = 1, 2, \ldots, n$ do: (for each row)
   for $j = s, s+1, \ldots, n+m$ do: (for all remaining columns)

$$a_{ij}^{(s)} := a_{ij}^{(s-1)} - a_{is}^{(s-1)}(a_{sj}^{(s-1)}/a_{ss}^{(s-1)}),$$

where the expression in brackets was calculated in step (4). After n steps we get

$$\mathbf{C}_n = \begin{bmatrix} & & \vdots & a_{1,n+1}^{(n-1)} & a_{1,n+2}^{(n-1)} & \cdots & a_{1,n+m}^{(n-1)} \\ & \mathbf{I} & \vdots & a_{2,n+1}^{(n-1)} & a_{2,n+2}^{(n-1)} & \cdots & a_{2,n+m}^{(n-1)} \\ & & \vdots & \vdots & \vdots & & \vdots \\ & & \vdots & a_{n,n+1}^{(n-1)} & a_{n,n+2}^{(n-1)} & \cdots & a_{n,n+m}^{(n-1)} \end{bmatrix},$$

where $a_{i,n+j}^{(n-1)} = x_i^{(j)}$. The determinant of **A** can be calculated, too:

$$d = (-1)^J \prod_{i=1}^n a_{ii}^{(i-1)}, \tag{67}$$

where J is the total number of exchanges of rows, i.e. after each exchange in step (2) of the Gauss–Jordan algorithm, the sign of the intermediate product must be changed.

The Gauss–Jordan–Rutishauser algorithm is also used in the calculation of the matrix inversion [1]. After each elimination step we make a cyclic shift of columns to the left and rows upwards, so that we always get the pivot in position a_{11}. The advantages of this approach are only seen in parallel implementations of this algorithm.

Systolic arrays for the GJR algorithm without pivoting for the matrix solution of problem (66) and for calculating $\mathbf{A}^{-1}$ are described in [3]. In this chapter we give four specialized VLSI computers that will calculate (66) and (67) using a modified GJR algorithm.

In Section 5.2 we describe the single VLSI chip computer SLEC1 (System of Linear Equation Computer 1). In Section 5.3 we describe a VLSI chip with P-processors and cache memory and off-chip active memory: SLEC2. Section 5.4 combines two different VLSI orthogonal pipeline vector processors, SLEC3r, that does row-by-row elimination, with SLEC3c, that performs column-by-column elimination. In Section 5.5 the VLSI systolic array SLEC4 is described. The chapter ends with some remarks and a brief conclusion in Section 5.6.

The SLEC1 chip implements the Gauss—Jordan (GJ) elimination with partial pivoting algorithm. SLEC2 and SLEC3r execute GJR, where **C** is shifted to the left after each elimination step (GJR1). SLEC3r and SLEC4 calculate GJR, where **C** is shifted to the left and cyclically upwards after each elimination step (GJR2). We note that in this algorithm, a cyclic shift to the left is not necessary, since the column just eliminated is not needed for the next calculation.

In Sections 5.2 through 5.5 we describe the schemes of the required chips (computers), their specialized instruction sets and we present programs for an n by $n + m$ matrix **C**. We also briefly evaluate the complexity of these programs under these assumptions:

— we give only the terms with the highest power of n and m,
— for pivoting we always calculate the maximal distance row exchange,
— I/O instructions are not considered,
— some simple restoring of index registers and register instructions are neglected,
— we evaluate only the longest instruction, in each row of the program.

If we had upper-bound time estimates for our instructions — which we do not have — then some comparison of the time performances of the different programs would be possible. Without such knowledge it is difficult to compare the various programs for various architectures, so we did not make such comparisons, except for those in Table 26. Our tables are therefore of theoretical, not practical use.

The input data for the programs that will evaluate equations (66) and (67) are the integers n, m, b, a Boolean p and the real matrix **C**. The programs produce the determinant d and matrix **X** as output.

Integer b determines how many bits per register and memory word will be used to store one floating-point number and, consequently, to configure floating-point arithmetic operations $-$, $\times$ and $/$. Thus b allows variable precision arithmetic.

In the floating-point (FP) number fp will be normalized [4], $fp = \pm$ man $\times 2^{\exp}$, where man is the mantissa ($2^{-1} \leqslant |\text{man}| < 1$) and exp is its integer exponent, then b determines the number of bits needed to store fp, i.e. its signs, man and exp. We assume that the hardware in our computers is automatically configured to this b-bit arithmetic, when b is input. This yields sufficient but not excessive precision arithmetic. Further, we assume that $b \leqslant b_{\max}$, where $b_{\max}$ is the maximum possible number of bits in the needed registers and for the FP operations.

The Boolean p flags partial pivoting on or off. If $p = 1$, then partial pivoting is performed, if $p = 0$, then the algorithm will be executed without pivoting (e.g. set $p = 0$, if **A** is a positive definite or a diagonally dominant matrix).

On our SLEC1 $-$ 3 chips, the matrix **C** will be stored row by row in memory. We denote the rows and columns of **C** by $r(i)$, $i = 1, 2, ..., n$, and $c(j), j = 1, 2, ..., n + m$, respectively. We assume that this memory always has NM bits. When **C** is an n by $n + m$ matrix, then, for b-bit FP arithmetic it must hold that $nb \leqslant N$ and $(n + m)b \leqslant M$. Here we solve system (66) with an n by $n + m$ matrix, $n \leqslant N/b$ and $n + m \leqslant M/b$.

The FP multiplication and division in our computers will be executed by the bit-by-bit Cordic algorithm [5]. Its advantage is that only addition and shift operations are required for each iteration and each iteration calculates one precise bit of result. The Cordic algorithm is useful for variable-precision FP arithmetic. A general Cordic algorithm implemented in a VLSI chip is described in [6].

Some vector operations in SLEC2, SLEC3r and SLEC3c will be calculated through the Boolean mask register (Mr). This means that if the operation O_1 (O_2) with the vector v_1 (vectors v_1 and v_2) is executed through the Mr mask register, then this operation is only performed on the components v_1 (v_1 and v_2), where the corresponding Mr bit component is 1 (v_1, v_2 and Mr have the same dimensions).

We note that in SLEC2, SLEC3r and SLEC3c the time required to execute a vector instruction No. 19 and No. 5 will depend on b, and not on n, since it will be executed in an associative memory.

5.2 Single VLSI chip computer: SLEC1

5.2.1 Introduction

In a conventionally organized computer the processor is separated from the memory. Many of the instructions must access this remote memory. In such a system a major bottleneck is the traffic between the processor and the off-chip memory. It becomes necessary to reduce the movements of data in the system in order to avoid this bottleneck and thus increase performance.

According to [7], the off-chip—on-chip transmission times differ by a factor of 10. With improving chip integration paving the way to more complex chips, further increases in this speed gap can be expected. According to [8], there is a trend to improve the overall performance of the computer by incorporating a greater portion of memory directly onto the chips. Memory may actually dominate the silicon area in the future. Another tendency is to build a universal single chip computer with a small set of frequent instructions. An example of this is the RISC I [9], a 32-bit single chip microprocessor. It has 31 simple instructions, most of them at the register-to-register level, which operate entirely on chip.

In this section we combined these ideas to propose a special architecture tailored to efficiently solve equations (66) and (67). These chips have a small processor and a large RAM on chip.

5.2.2 Structure of SLEC1

On our SLEC1 computer, because we have both the memory and the processor unit (PU) on the same chip, there are no off-chip memory accesses. For the

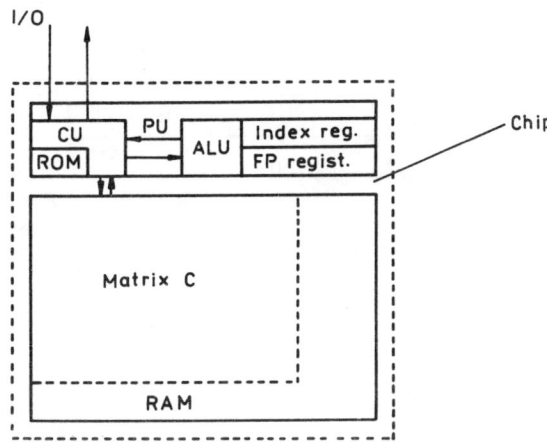

Fig. 63. Structure of a SLEC1 computer.

PU we have chosen 10 specialized instructions. Out program resides in a ROM control unit (CU), and matrix **C** is in RAM. A parallel arithmetic-logic unit (ALU) rounds out the chip design.

The structure of SLEC1 is shown in Fig. 63.

The ALU has 7 index registers (rn, rm, rb, rp, rs, ri, rj) and 4 FP registers (Ra, Rx, Ry, Rd).

5.2.3 Instructions and program P1 for SLEC1

The SLEC1 instruction set contains instructions for input/output (2), memory access (2), index register usage (1), floating-point arithmetic (4) and for conditional jumps (1).

A description of the SLEC1 instruction set is given in Table 18, where $c(i, j)$ means the contents of the ith row and the jth column cell of RAM.

Table 18

SLEC1 Instruction Set

No.	Instruction	Description
1	**INPUT**$(n, m, b, p, C(1:n, 1:(n+m)))$;	Input of data. Values $n, n+m, b, p$ are stored into index registers rn, rm, rb, rp. Hardware is set for b-bit arithmetic. C is stored row by row into RAM. Set $Rd := 1$ and $rs := 0$
2	**OUTPUT**$(Rd, C(1:rn, (rn+1):rm))$;	Output of data. Output of d and X from the $(n+1)$-, $(n+2)$-, ..., $(n+m)$th column of C in RAM
3	$FPr \Leftarrow c(i, j)$;	Load contents of $c(i, j)$ from RAM into FPr (Ra, Rx or Ry)
4	$FPr \Rightarrow c(i, j)$;	Store FPr (Ra or Ry) into $c(i, j)$ in RAM
5	$ir1 := ir2 + k$;	Integer add. $ir1$ and $ir2$ are index registers, k is $-1, 0, 1$
5a	$ri := 0$;	Reset ri
6	$FPr1 := \pm Rd$;	Restoring of $FPr1$ (Rx or Rd) with contents of $\pm Rd$ ($+$ is not written)
7	$Ra := Ra - Ry$;	FP subtraction
8	$FPr := Rx \times Ry$;	FP multiplication, where FPr can be Ra, Ry or Rd
9	$Ry := 1/Ry$;	FP reciprocal value
10	**if** CON **then** L;	If CON is true, then jump to an integer label L

5.2 Single VLSI chip computer: SLEC1

The program, P1, for the SLEC1 chip is the following (instructions on the same row are calculated in parallel):

INPUT$(n, m, b, p, C(1:n, 1:(n+m)))$;	Input of data
$1: rs := rs + 1$;	Elimination of the rsth column
if $rp = 0 \lor rs = rn$ then 4;	Not necessary to search for a pivot
$ri := rj := rs$;	
$Ra \Leftarrow c(rs, rs)$;	Choice of maximum in the rsth column
$2: ri := ri + 1$;	and rith row ($ri \leq rs$)
$Ry \Leftarrow c(ri, rs)$;	Maximum is in Ra; the number of
if $abs(Ry) \leq abs(Ra)$ then 7;	row is in rj
$Ra := Ry; rj := ri$;	
$7:$ if $ri < rn$ then 2;	
if $rj = rs$ then 4;	Not necessary to exchange rows
$Rd := -Rd; ri := rj$;	Change of the determinant sign
$rj := rs - 1$;	Exchange of the rsth and the rith row
$3: rj := rj + 1$;	
$Ra \Leftarrow c(rs, rj); Ry \Leftarrow c(ri, rj)$;	
$Ry \Rightarrow c(rs, rj); Ra \Rightarrow c(ri, rj)$;	
if $rj < rm$ then 3;	
$4: Ry \Leftarrow c(rs, rs); Rx := Rd$;	
$Rd := Rx \times Ry$;	Calculation of the determinant
$Ry := 1/Ry; rj := rs$;	Reciprocal value of a pivot
$8: rj := rj + 1$;	Multiplication of the rsth row
$Rx \Leftarrow c(rs, rj)$;	
$Ra := Rx \times Ry$;	
$Ra \Rightarrow c(rs, rj)$;	
if $rj < rm$ then 8;	
$ri := 0$;	
$5: ri := ri + 1$;	Elimination of the $rs+1, rs+2, \ldots,$
if $ri = rs$ then 6;	rmth columns of matrix **C**
$Rx \Leftarrow c(ri, rs); rj := rs$;	
$9: rj := rj + 1$;	
$Ra \Leftarrow c(ri, rj); Ry \Leftarrow c(rs, rj)$;	
$Ry := Rx \times Ry$;	
$Ra := Ra - Ry$;	
$Ra \Rightarrow c(ri, rj)$;	
if $rj < rm$ then 9;	
$6:$ if $ri < rn$ then 5;	
if $rs < rn$ then 1;	
OUTPUT$(Rd, C(1:rn, (rn+1):rm))$;	Output of results

5.2.4 Complexity of program P1

The number of times each instruction is executed in P1 is given in Table 19 (instructions No. 1, 2, 5a, 6 are not considered; $q_1 = 2n + 3m$).

Table 19

Instr. No.	3	4	5	7	8	9	10
Count	$n^2 q_1$	$n^2\left(q_1 - \dfrac{n}{2}\right)$	$n^2 q_1$	$n^2\left(\dfrac{n}{2} + m\right)$	$n^2(n + 2m)$	n	$n^2\left(q_1 + \dfrac{n}{2}\right)$

We see that the complexity of the sequential program P1 is $O(n^3) + O(n^2 m)$ but there are no time penalties for off-chip communication in the SLEC1.

5.3 VLSI chip with *P*-processors and cache memory: SLEC2

5.3.1 Introduction

In the previous section we described a specialized, single-processor computer with its entire main memory on chip. For a large memory this is currently impossible. But integration of a cache memory onto a processor chip is currently feasible [7]. Here, the major portion of the memory traffic moves only a short distance, and the slower off-chip traffic, occurs much less frequently [10].

In this section we describe the VLSI chip computer SLEC2, specialized for equations (66) and (67) to be solved by the GJR1 algorithm. It has a single *P*-processor ($P \leq m$) on-chip cache memory and off-chip active memory (AM) which has some calculation capacity.

Our active memory will be an orthogonal memory (dual-access memory [11]) with horizontal bit-parallel word-parallel loading and storing of rows and vertical bit-sliced selection of the maximum value in the first column of the array. We note that some associative array processors have a similar kind of orthogonal multidimensional access memory (e.g. the associative array processor STARAN [12]). Its memory allows bit-sliced access for parallel operations and word-sliced access for I/O operations.

5.3.2 Structure of SLEC2

The architecture of SLEC2 is shown in Fig. 64.

The SLEC2 consists of one VLSI chip and an off-chip AM. On chip there is a control unit (CU), P-processors $\{p_i\}$, and on-chip cache memory. All calculations in the SLEC2 are controlled by the CU. The CU executes program P2, does some arithmetic operations on scalars, and transfers single constant values to all of the processors. The cache memory is divided into two parts, Cache 1 and Cache 2. Each has on M bit (i.e. a maximum of m b-bit FP numbers denoted by $c1(j)$ and $c2(j), j = 1, 2, ..., m$). Since $P \leqslant m$ there exists some mapping which allows us to read (store) from (into) Cache 1 or Cache 2 some continuous segment from AM consisting of P b-bit words scattered into (from) the registers of all P-processors.

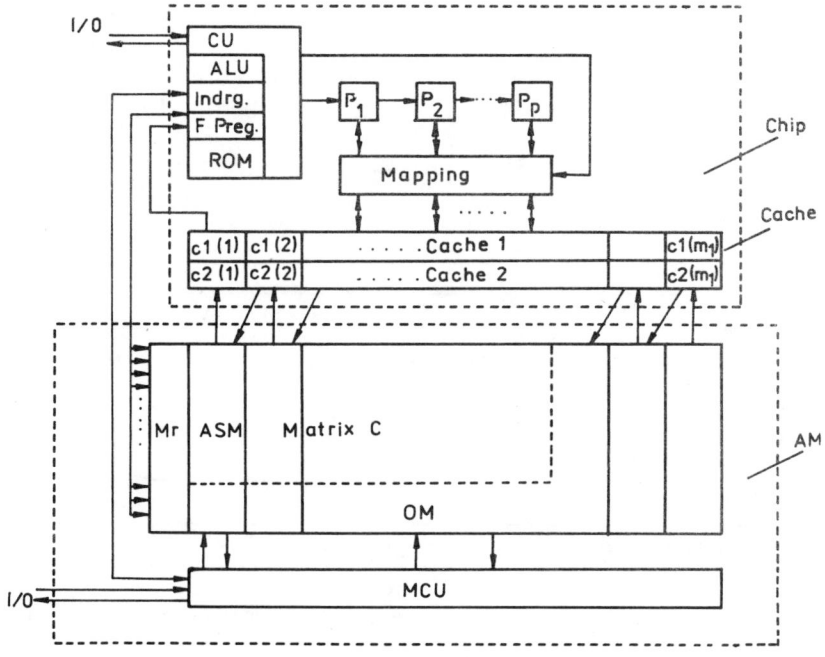

Fig. 64. Structure of a SLEC2 computer.

The off-chip AM is specialized for pivoting. It consists of a memory control unit (MCU) and the previously described orthogonal memory (OM). The MCU can independently search for a pivot. The first column of the OM creates an associative memory (ASM) that is b_{max}-bit wide. The **MAX** instruction executes through the mask register (Mr) a bit-serial word-parallel search for a maximum pivot, which is an operation done naturally on an ASM. The OM is configured into M-bit rows, $r(j), j = 1, 2, ..., N$, which contain the rows of the matrix **C**. The exchange instruction, **EXCH**, exchanges 2 rows in the OM. The OM is bidirectionally bit-parallel word-parallel connected with cache. In the direction from OM into cache, one row from OM can be transferred into Cache 1 or Cache 2. In the opposite direction, from Cache 1 or Cache 2 into some row of OM, the storing is shifted one word to the left, so that the word in ASM is cancelled.

The CU has 11 index registers ($rn, rm, rb, rp, rmx, rs, rj, rd, rk, rq, P$) and 2 FP registers ($Sr, Rd$). In the P register the number of processors on chip is given. Each processor, p_i, has 3 FP registers ($Ra(i), Rx(i), Ry(i)$). The MCU has a mask register, Mr, and 6 index registers (rn, rm, rb, rs, rj, rmx) which are shared with the CU.

5.3.3 Instructions and program P2 for SLEC2

On the SLEC2 computer there are separate instruction sets for the CU, the set of P-processors, and the MCU. They are described in Tables 20a – c.

Table 20a

No.	Instruction	Description
		Instructions of CU
1	**ZERO**;	Reset OM, cache and all registers
2	**input** (n, m, b, p);	Input $n, n + m, b, p$ into rn, rm, rb, rp. Hardware of all necessary instructions is configured for b-bits words. Set $rd := 1$ and $Rd := 1$
3	**output** (Rd);	Output d from Rd
4	$Sr \Leftarrow$ **read** $cj(1)$;	Load $cj(1), j = 1$ or 2, into Sr register
5	$Sr \Rightarrow Rx(\forall i)$;	Transfer Sr to all $Rx(i), \forall i$
6	$ir := $ AE (indregs);	Assign result of arithmetic expression AE on the set of index registers (indregs) into some index register ir, $+, -, \times,$ and $//$ in AE mean integer addition, subtraction, multiplication and division (ir first integer $\geq$ than results of AE)
7	$Rd := rd \times Rd$;	Multiplication by ± 1
8	$Rd := Rd \times Sr$;	FP multiplication
9	$SR := -1/Sr$;	FP negative reciprocal value
10	**if** CON **then** L;	Analogical to instruction 10 in SLEC1

Table 20b

Instruction of p_i, $\forall i$

No.	Instruction	Description
11	$\forall i: Ra(i) \Leftarrow$ **pread** $cj(rf + 1)$;	$\forall i$, parallel load of contents of $cj(rf + i)$ from Cache j, $j = 1$ or 2, into $Ra(i)$ or $Ry(i)$
12	$\forall i: Ra(i) \Rightarrow$ **pstore** $cj(rf + i)$;	$\forall i$, parallel store of $Ra(i)$, into $cj(rf + i)$ in Cache j, $j = 1$ or 2
13	$\forall i: Ra(i) := Ra(i) - Rx(i) Ry(i)$;	$\forall i$, parallel FP execution of elimination step
13a	$\forall i: Ra(i) := 0$;	$\forall i$, parallel reset of $Ra(i)$

Table 20c

Instructions of MCU

No.	Instruction	Description
14	∗ **INPUT** $(C(1:n, 1:(n+m)))$;	Input C into OM row by row
15	∗ **OUTPUT** $(C(1:rn, 1)(rm - rn)))$;	Output X from the 1, 2, ..., mth columns of OM
16	∗ Cache $j \Leftarrow r(ir)$;	Parallel load of $r(ir)$ row from OM into Cache j, $j = 1$, or 2 (ir can be rs or rj)
17	∗ Cache $j/ \Rightarrow r(ir)$;	Parallel skew store of Cache j, $j = 1$ or 2, into $r(ir)$, ir can be rs or rj. Storing is shifted one word to the left ($cj(1)$ is not stored)
18	∗ $Mr := ((rs - 1)\|0, (rn - rs + 1)\|1, 0)$;	Assign a bit-pattern into Mr. Set first $rs - 1$ bits to 0, set further $rn - rs + 1$ bits to 1 and others to 0
19	∗ $rmx := $ **MAX**;	Search for maximum absolute value in ASM through Mr. Index of this row will be in rmx
20	∗ **EXCH** (rs, rmx);	Exchange $r(rs)$ row with $r(rmx)$

The program P2 for SLEC2 is the following (instructions of p_i (MCU) begin with $\forall i: (*)$, again, instructions in one row can be done in parallel):

ZERO;
input (n, m, b, p); ∗**INPUT** $(C(1:n, 1:(n+m)))$;
1: $rs := rs + 1$;   Elimination of the rsth column
  if $rp = 0 \vee rs = rn$ **then** 2;   Without pivoting?

$*Mr := ((rs - 1)\|0, (rn - rs + 1)\|1, 0);$	Set mask register
$*rmx := \mathbf{MAX};$	Pivoting
if $rs = rmx$ **then** 2;	
$rd := -rd;$	
$*\mathbf{EXCH}(rs, rmx);$	Exchange rows
2: $rq := (rm - rs + 1)//P;$	Load one row of OM into P-processors
$*$Cache $1 \Leftarrow r(rs);$	Load row with a pivot
$Sr \Leftarrow \mathbf{read}\, c1(1);$	Load the pivot
$Rd := rd \times Rd;$	Change the determinant sign
$Rd := Rd \times Sr;$	Calculation of the determinant
$Sr := -1/Sr;$	Negative reciprocal value of the pivot
$Sr \Rightarrow Rx(\forall i);$	
$rk := 0;$	
3: $rk := rk + 1;$	rq times: mapping of a row into process
$rf := (rk - 1) \times P;$	
$\forall i: (Ra(i) := 0;\ Ry(i) \Leftarrow \mathbf{pread}\, c1(rf + i);\ );$	
$\forall i: Ra(i) := Ra(i) - Rx(i) \times Ry(i);$	Multiplication of the rsth row
$\forall i: Ra(i) \Rightarrow \mathbf{pstore}\, c1(rf + i);$	
if $rk < rq$ **then** 3;	
$*$Cache $1/ \Rightarrow r(rs);$	Skew store of Cache 1 into OM
$rj := 0;$	
4: $rj := rj + 1;$	
if $rj = rs$ **then** 6;	
$*$Cache $2 \Leftarrow r(rj);$	Sequential loading of all rows
$Sr \Leftarrow \mathbf{read}\, c2(1);$	
$Sr \Rightarrow Rx(\forall i);$	
$rk := 0;$	
5: $rk := rk + 1;$	rq times: elimination step on one row
$rf := (rk - 1) \times P;$	
$\forall i: (Ra(i) \Leftarrow \mathbf{pread}\, c2(rf + i);\ Ry(i) \Leftarrow \mathbf{pread}\, c1(rf + i);\ );$	
$\forall i: Ra(i) := Ra(i) - Rx(i) \times Ry(i);$	
$\forall i: Ra(i) \Rightarrow \mathbf{pstore}\, c2(rf + i);$	
if $rk < rq$ **then** 5;	
$*$Cache $2/ \Rightarrow r(rj);$	Skew store of Cache 2 into OM
6: **if** $rj < rn$ **then** 4;	
if $rs < rn$ **then** 1;	

output (Rd); *OUTPUT $(C(1:rn, 1:(rm-rn)))$. Output of results

5.3.4 Complexity of program P2

The number of instructions calculated in P2 is given in Table 21 (instructions No. 1, 2, 3, 7, 13a, 14, 15 are not considered).

Table 21

Instr. No.	4, 5	6			8, 9	10, 11, 12	13	16, 17	18, 19, 20
		±	×	//					
Count	n^2	$2rn$	rn	n	n	rn	rn	n^2	n

Since it holds $r = \sum_{s=1}^{n} r_s$, whereby $r_s = (n + m - s + 1)//P$, then for r we have the estimation

$$r \leqslant O\left(\frac{n^2}{2P}\right) + O\left(\frac{nm}{P}\right).$$

As we would expect, the total number of steps in P2 depends on the number of processors in SLEC2.

5.4 VLSI orthogonal pipeline vector processors: SLEC3r and SLEC3c

5.4.1 Introduction

In this section we use both an orthogonal memory [11] and a pipeline vector processor [13]. We suggest two variants of VLSI orthogonal pipeline vector processors SLEC3r and SLEC3c. SLEC3r or SLEC3c are specialized processors designed to implement equations (66) and (67) using algorithms GJR1 and GJR2, respectively. Our orthogonal memory has horizontal bit-parallel word-parallel reading (writing) of rows from (into) horizontal vector registers (HVr) and vertical bit-serial word-parallel loading (storing) of column into (from) vertical vector register (VVr).

In the SLEC3r computer, the matrix **C** is eliminated row by row in the horizontal vector registers XVr and YVr. The only column operations — searching for a pivot — is done through the AMr mask register using the associative vector register AVr. After each step of elimination, the matrix **C** is shifted one word to the left, thus the just eliminated column is removed, and the next column to be reduced is moved into its place.

In the SLEC3c, the matrix **C** is eliminated column by column using the vertical vector registers Xr and $AVr1$. The search for a pivot is the same as in the SLEC3r. The only row operation in the SLEC3c processor is the pipelined vector multiplication of the first row of memory, which is moved into vector register RVr, and is multiplied by the reciprocal value of a pivot which is in the Sr register. After each elimination step, the matrix **C** is shifted one word to the left and cyclically upwards, so that the diagonal element of the next column to be reduced is always in the first row and the first column of memory.

In both computers the only arithmetic pipelined vector operations needed are vector multiplication by a scalar, and vector multiplication by a scalar followed by vector substraction; both operations are executed through the AMr mask in the pipeline arithmetic-logic unit (PALU).

5.4.2 Structures of SLEC3r and SLEC3c

The structure of the SLEC3r is in Fig. 65.
It consists of the control unit (CU), an orthogonal memory (OM), with

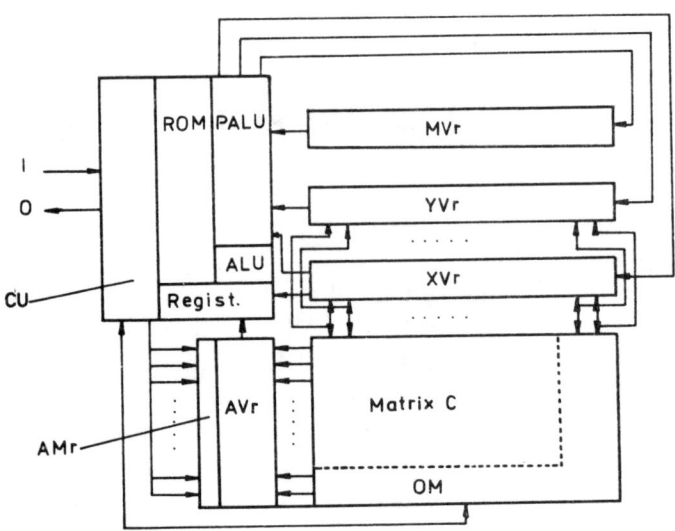

Fig. 65. Structure of a SLEC3r computer.

horizontal vector registers XVr, YVr and mask register MVr, a vertical associative vector register AVr, and a vertical mask register AMr.

The structure of SLEC3c is in Fig. 66.

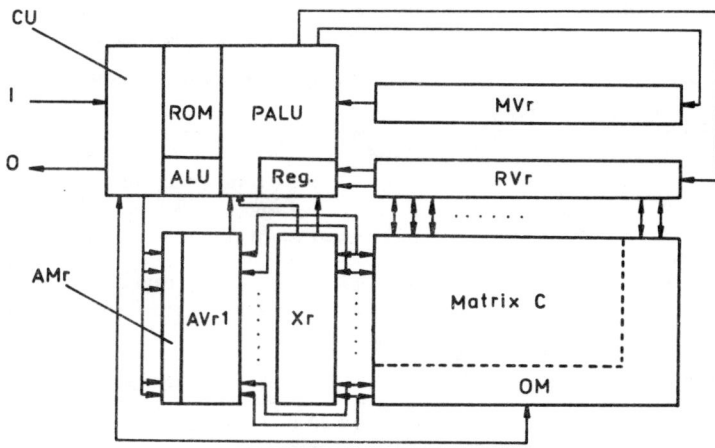

Fig. 66. Structure of a SLEC3c computer.

It consists of the CU, an OM with vertical vector register Xr, a vertical associative vector register $AVr1$, a vertical mask register AMr, a horizontal vector register RVr, and a horizontal mask register MVr.

In both computers the CU has a PALU, a scalar ALU, 6 index registers (rn, rm, rb, rp, rs, ri) and 2 FP registers (Sr and Dr). The OM is addressable through its rows $r(1)$, $r(2)$, ..., $r(N)$ or its columns $c(1)$, $c(2)$, ..., $c(m + N)$.

5.4.3 Instructions and programs P3r and P3c for SLEC3r and SLEC3c

SLEC3r and SLEC3c have basically the same instruction set. It is described in Table 22 (horizontal directions between VVr and OM are $\Leftarrow$ (load into register) and $\Rightarrow$ (store into OM), vertical directions between HVr and OM are ↘ (read into register) and ↘ (write into OM); transfers in the directions $\Leftarrow$ and $\Rightarrow$ are bit-serial word-parallel, transfers in the direction ↘ and ↘ are bit-parallel word-parallel).

The program P3r for SLEC3r is the following

Table 22

No.	Instruction	Description
1	**ZERO**;	Reset OM and all registers. Set $Dr := 1$
2	**INPUT** $(n, m, b, p, C(1:n, 1:(n+m)))$;	Input n, $n+m$, b, p into rn, rm, rb, rp. Hardware of necessary instructions is configured for FP b-bit words. C is stored row by row into OM
3	**OUTPUT** $(Dr, c(1:(rm-rn)))$;	Output d and X from the columns $c(i)$, $i = 1, 2, \ldots, m$, of OM
4	$Mr := (AE1\|0, AE2\|1, 0)$;	Assign a bit-pattern into mask Mr (MVr or AMr). Set first $AE1$ bits (from the left or the top) to 0, set further $AE2$ bits to 1 and others to 0. $AE1$ and $AE2$ are arithmetic expressions on index registers
5	$ri := $ **MAX**;	Search for AVr ($AVr1$) through AMr for the address of the element with maximum absolute value and set it into ri index register
6	$ir := ir + 1$;	Add 1 to ir index register (ir can be rs or ri)
6a	$ir := k$;	Assign k (0 or 1) to ir
7	if CON then L;	Analog to instruction 10 in SLEC1
8	$Dr := -Dr$;	Exchange of sign in Dr
9	$Dr := Dr \times Sr$;	FP scalar multiplication
10	$Sr := 1/Sr$;	FP scalar reciprocal value
11	**EXCH** (ir, ri);	Exchange $r(ir)$ row with $r(ri)$ in OM (ir can be rs or 1)
12	$HVr \searrow $ **read** $r(ir)$;	Parallel reading of $r(ir)$ row from OM into HVr. In the SLEC3r (SLEC3c) HVr can be XVr, YVr, (RVr), ir can be ri, rs (1)
13	$HVr \searrow $ **write** $r(ir)$;	Parallel writing of HVr into $r(ir)$ row. In the SLEC3r (SLEC3c) HVr can be XVr, YVr, (RVr), ir can be ri, rs (1, rn)
14	$VVr \Leftarrow $ **load** $c(ir)$;	Bit-serial word-parallel loading of the irth $c(ir)$ column of OM into VVR. In the SLEC3r (SLEC3c) VVR and ir can be AVr and 1 (AVr, Xr and 1, ri)
15	$Sr \Leftarrow VVr(ir)$;	Assign the irth term from VVr into Sr. In the SLEC3r (SLEC3c) VVr can be AVr, XVr (RVr, Xr), ir can be rs, ri (1, ri)
16	$Xr \Rightarrow $ **store** $c(ri)$;	Store in parallel Xr into $c(ri)$ column of OM (use only in SLEC3c)
17	**SHIFT** L;	Shift the whole OM and MVr register b-bits to the left; $c(1)$ is cancelled

Table 22 (Continued)

No.	Instruction	Description
18	**SHIFT** U;	Shift the whole OM 1 bit upwards; $r(1)$ is cancelled (used only in SLEC3c)
19	$HVr := \mathbf{MULT}(Sr, HVr)$;	Do the FP pipeline vector multiplication of HVr by scalar in Sr and assign the result to HVr. In the SLEC3r (SLEC3c) HVr can be YVr (RVr)
20	$Vr := SUBf(Vr, MULTf(Sr, Vr1))$;	Do the FP pipeline term-by-term vector operation $Vr := Vr - Sr \times Vr1$, where Vr and $Vr1$ are vector registers. In SLEC3r it is a row operation ($f = r$), Vr is XVr and $Vr1$ is YVr. In the SLEC3c it is a column operation ($f = c$), Vr is Xr and $VR1$ is $AVr1$

ZERO;
INPUT $(n, m, b, p, C(1:n, 1:(n + m)))$;
$MVr := (rm \times rb | 1, 0)$;
1: $rs := rs + 1$;
   $AMr := ((rs - 1)|0, (rn - rs + 1)|1, 0)$;
   $AVr \Leftarrow \mathbf{load}\ c(1)$;
   $Sr \Leftarrow AVr(rs)$;
   if $rp = 0 \lor rs = rn$ **then** 2;
   $ri := \mathbf{MAX}$;
   if $rs = ri$ **then** 2;
   $Dr := - Dr$;
   EXCH (rs, ri);
2: $Dr := Dr \times Sr$;
   $Sr := 1/Sr$;
   $YVr \searrow \mathbf{read}\ r(rs)$;
   $YVr := \mathbf{MULT}(Sr, YVr)$;
   $YVr \searrow \mathbf{write}\ r(rs)$;
   $ri := 0$;
3: $ri := ri + 1$;
   if $ri = rs$ **then** 4;
   $XVr \searrow \mathbf{read}\ r(ri)$;
   $Sr \Leftarrow XVr(ri)$;
   $XVr := SUBr(XVr, MULTr(Sr, YVr))$;
   $XVr \searrow \mathbf{write}\ r(ri)$;
4: **if** $ri < rn$ **then** 3;
   SHIFT L;
   if $rs < rn$ **then** 1;
OUTPUT $(Dr, c(1:(rm - rn)))$.

The program P3c for SLEC3c is the following:

ZERO;
INPUT $(n, m, b, p, C(1:n, 1:(n+m)))$;
$MVr := (rm \times rb | 1, 0)$;
$1: rs := rs + 1$;
  $AMr := ((rn - rs + 1)|1, 0)$;
  $AVr1 \Leftarrow$ **load** $c(1)$;
  if $rp = 0 \vee rs = rn$ **then** 2;
  $ri := $ **MAX**;
  if $rs = ri$ **then** 2;
  $Dr := -Dr$;
  EXCH $(1, ri)$;
$2: RVr \searrow$ **read** $r(1)$;
  $Sr \Leftarrow RVr(1)$;
  $Dr := Dr \times Sr$;
  $Sr := 1/Sr$;
  $RVr := $ **MULT** (Sr, RVr);
  $RVr \searrow$ **write** $r(1)$;
  $AVr1 \Leftarrow$ **load** $c(1)$;
  $ri := 1$;
$3: ri := ri + 1$;
  $Xr \Leftarrow$ **load** $c(ri)$;
  $Sr \Leftarrow Xr(ri)$;
  $Xr := SUBc(Xr, MULTc(Sr, AVr1))$;
  $Xr \Rightarrow$ **store** $c(ri)$;
  if $ri < rm - rs + 1$ **then** 3;
  SHIFT L;
  SHIFT U;
  $RVr \searrow$ **write** $r(rn)$;
  if $rs < rn$ **then** 1;
OUTPUT $(Dr, c(1:(rm - rn)))$.

5.4.4 Complexity of P3r and P3c programs

The number of instructions executed in P3r and P3c are given in Table 25 (instructions No. 1, 2, 3, 6a, 8 are not considered; $q_2 = n^2/2 + nm$).

We see that P3c is better for $m = 1$, and that P3r is better for $m \times n$. Thus for given n and m we can always choose the lowest complexity computer for our calculation.

Table 23

Instr. No.	4, 5	6	7	9, 10, 11	12	13	14	15	16	17	18	19	20
P3r count	n	n^2	$2n^2$	n	n^2	n^2	n	n^2	—	n	—	n	n^2
P3c count	n	q_2	q_2	n	n	$2n$	q_2	q_2	q_2	n	n	n	q_2

We note that vector instructions No. 19 and 20 are pipelined through the PALU, i.e. times of their executions are proportional to $(L + k - 1)t$, where L is the length of the vectors. Arithmetic operations in the PALU are divided into successive steps, where t is the duration of the longest step [13]. Instructions No. 19 and 20 in the SLEC3r and No. 19 in SLEC3c are executed on rows of the matrix with $L = n + m - s + 1$, $s = 1, 2, ..., n$. Instruction No. 20 in SLEC3c is realized on columns with $L = n$.

Please note that it is also possible to construct a SLEC3 computer which can work like the SLEC3r or the SLEC3c, depending on the ratio between n and m.

5.5 VLSI systolic array: SLEC4

5.5.1 Introduction

The first systolic system designed to solve equation (66) was described by Kung and Leiserson in [14]. The system implements an **LU**-decomposition of the matrix **A** on a hexagonal array using inner product step processors with one special processor to calculate the reciprocal value. The design of the systolic array with a local communication network for the calculation of equation (66) by Givens' method is also described in [14]. The advantage of the above algorithm lies in its not being necessary to pivot **A**. The disadvantage is that, in contrast to elimination methods which require solely arithmetic operations, Givens' method requires a sequence of planar rotations which involve the trigonometric functions $\sin x$, $\cos x$, $\sqrt{x}$ and $\arctan x$. Specialized systolic array for (66) and for matrix inversion with **GJR** without pivoting are given in [3]. A universal and almost homogeneous systolic array which uses an array of processors and implements the GJR2 algorithm without pivoting to solve equations (66) and (67) and to invert the matrix **A** is given in [15].

In this section we describe the VLSI systolic array SLEC4, which uses algorithm GJR2 to solve equations (66) and (67).

5.5.2 Structure of SLEC4

SLEC4 will be composed of an array of n_1 by $(n_1 + m_1)$ processors p_{ij} ($i = 1, 2, ..., n_1, j = 1, 2, ..., n_1 + m_1$) which will be connected by a square communication network. Our systolic array SLEC4 has, except for p_{11}, a homogeneous structure given in Fig. 67.

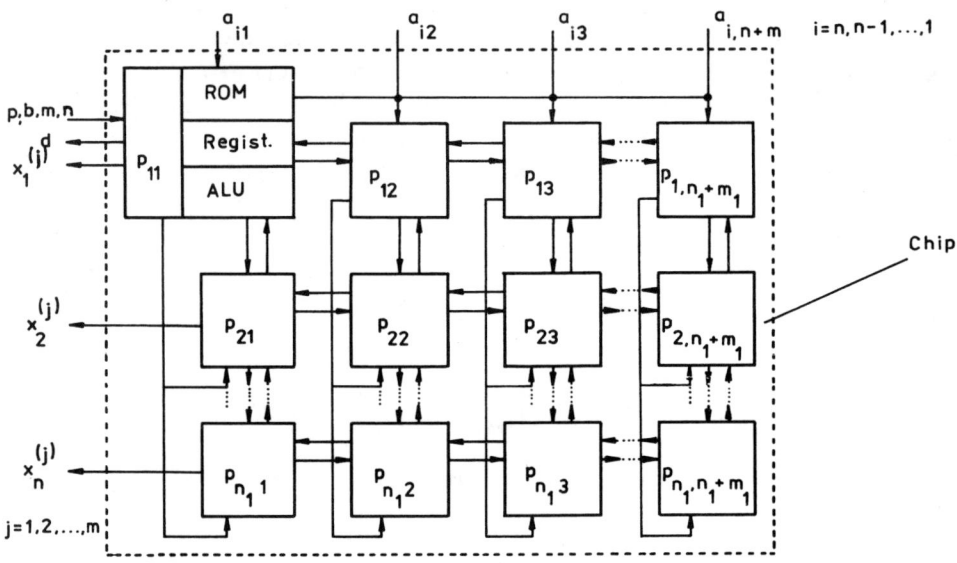

Fig. 67. Structure of a systolic array SLEC4.

The processor p_{11} will act as the CU, search for a pivot, calculate its negative reciprocal value, and calculate the determinant d. It has 8 index registers (rn_{11}, rm_{11}, rb_{11}, rp_{11}, rs_{11}, ri_{11}, rj_{11}, rc_{11}) and 4 FP registers (Ra_{11}, Rx_{11}, Ry_{11}, Rd_{11}) which are used to calculate the FP multiplication and negative reciprocal value. All other processors p_{ij}, $i \neq 1$ or $j \neq 1$, are the same. They have 3 FP registers (Ra_{ij}, Rx_{ij}, Ry_{ij}) which execute the FP operations $Ra_{ij} := Ra_{ij} - Rx_{ij} \times Ry_{ij}$.

The communication network is rectangular, connecting the processors in "each-with-four-neighbours" manner. In addition, the first row of processors is directly connected with all other rows in the array.

5.5.3 Instructions and program P4 for SLEC4

The following symbols have been chosen to describe our systolic program:

$\forall i$ means $i = 1, 2, ..., n$,
$\forall j$ $j = 1, 2, ..., n + m$,
$\forall i(k)$ $i = 1, 2, ..., k - 1, k + 1, ..., n$,
$\forall i(i \leqslant n - s + 1)$ $i = 1, 2, ..., n - s + 1$,
$\forall j(j \leqslant m)$ $j = 1, 2, ..., m$,

where the values of the indices i, j, n, $n + m$, s are stored in index registers ri_{11}, rj_{11}, rn_{11}, rm_{11}, rs_{11}, respectively. The communication path markers $\Downarrow$, $\Uparrow$, $\Leftarrow$, $\Rightarrow$ mean the direction of data flow in the given operation. The prefix **par-** (p- in the description) means that they are executed in parallel. The symbol $f \wedge g$ means that both f and g are done in parallel, and the program is blocked until both f and g are finished.

The instructions executed by p_{11} are in Table 24a.

Table 24a

No.	Instruction	Description
1	**parinput** $\Rightarrow$ $\Rightarrow (n \wedge m \wedge b \wedge p)$;	p-Input of n, $n + m$, b, p into rn_{11}, rm_{11}, rb_{11}, rp_{11}. Hardware configured for b-bit FP words
2	**output** $\Leftarrow Rd_{11}$;	Output of d to the left
3	$ira_{11} := irb_{11} + k$;	Same as instruction 5 in the SLEC1
4	**if** CON **then** L;	Same as instruction 10 in the SLEC1
5	$Rx_{11} := Ra_{11}$;	Restoring of Rx_{11} by Ra_{11}
6	$Rd_{11} := Rd_{11} \times Ra_{11}$;	Same as instruction 8 in the SLEC2
7	$Ry_{11} := -1/Ry_{11}$;	Same as instruction 9 in the SLEC2

Table 24b

No.	Instruction	Description
8	**ZERO**;	Reset all registers and index registers in SLEC4. Set $Rd_{11} := 1$
9	$\forall i \forall j$ **parinput** $a_{ij} \Downarrow Ra_{ij}$;	p-Input of a_{ij} from the top to the bottom into register Ra_{ij} ($\forall i \forall j$: take $Ra_{i-1,j}$, store it into Ra_{ij} and send it into $Ra_{i+1,j}$ till a_{nj} is not in Ra_{nj}; Ra_{0j} means input from outside)

Table 24b (Continued)

No.	Instruction	Description
10	$\forall i$ **partransfer** $Ra_{i1} \Rightarrow Rx_{ij} \; \forall j(1);$	p-Transfer of Ra_{i1} to the right into $Rx_{ij} \; \forall j(1)$ ($\forall i$: take $Ra_{i,1}$, store it into Rx_{i2}; $\forall i \forall j \; (j \neq 1 \wedge j \leqslant n + m)$: take Rx_{ij} and send it into $Rx_{i,j+1}$, until these waves have passed through to $Rx_{j,n+m})$
10a	**partransfer** $Ry_{11} \Rightarrow Ry_{1j} \; \forall j(1);$	Same as the previous instruction, but only in the first row of processors
11	$\forall i \forall j$ **parshift** $Ra_{i,j-1} \Leftarrow Ra_{ij};$	p-Shift of Ra registers to the left, where $Ra_{i1} \; \forall i$ are cancelled ($\forall i \forall j(1)$: take Ra_{ij} and store it into $Ra_{i,j-1}$)
12	$\forall i \forall j$ **parcyclshift** $(a, b) \; Ra_{ij} \Uparrow Ra_{i-1,j};$	In the first b rows of processors do a times a p-cyclic shift of the Ra registers upwards ($\forall i \; (i \leqslant b) \; \forall j \; a$ times do: take Ra_{ij} and store it into $Ra_{i-1,j}$, where $Ra_{0j} \equiv Ra_{bj}$)
12a	$\forall i \; (i \leqslant n - s + 1)$ **parcyclshift** $(1, rc_{11}) \; Ra_{i1} \Uparrow Ra_{i-1,1};$	Same as the previous instruction, but only in the first rc_{11} processors of the first column of the array
13	$\forall i \forall j \; (j \leqslant m)$ **paroutput** $\Leftarrow Ra_{ij};$	p-Output of X, i.e., $Ra_{ij}, \forall i, \; \forall j \; (j \leqslant m)$ ($\forall i \; m$ times do: p-output Ra_{i1} to the left, $\forall j(j \leqslant m)$: take Ra_{ij} and store it into $Ra_{i,j-1}$)

Table 24c

No.	Instruction	Description
14	$\forall i(1) \forall j(1)$ **pardo** $Ra_{ij} := Ra_{ij} - Rx_{ij} \times Ry_{ij};$	p-Performance of elimination step on the appropriate registers and storage of results into Ra_{ij}
14a	$\forall j(1)$ **pardo** $Ra_{1j} := Ra_{1j} - Rx_{1j} \times Ry_{1j};$	Same as the previous instruction, but only in the first row of processors
14b	$\forall j(1)$ **pardo** $Ra_{1j} := 0;$	Reset $Ra_{1j}, \forall j(1)$

The instructions calculated by all processors p_{ij} (except p_{11}) are given in Table 24b (Table 24c). When necessary, a brief description of the activity involved for the processor is given in parentheses.

The program P4, written for SLEC4, is the following (if the step is only executed by p_{11} then the second column is blanc) (1st column — step number, 2nd column — number of processors used, third column — action of the processors).

0	$n(n+m)$	**ZERO**;
1		**parinput** $\Rightarrow (n \wedge m \wedge b \wedge p) \wedge$
	$n(n+m)$	**for** $\forall i \forall j$ **parinput** $a_{ij} \Downarrow Ra_{ij};$

5.5 VLSI systolic array: SLEC4

2		$rs_{11} := rs_{11} + 1 \wedge$ **if** $rp_{11} = 0$ **then** 11;
3		$Rx_{11} := Ra_{11} \wedge ri_{11} := 0 \wedge rj_{11} := 0 \wedge rc_{11} :=$
		$= rn_{11} - rs_{11} + 1;$
4		**if** $rs_{11} = rn_{11}$ **then** 11;
5		$rj_{11} := rj_{11} + 1 \wedge$
	$n - s + 1$	**for** $\forall i (i \leq n - s + 1)$ **parcyclshift** $(1, rc_{11})$
		$Ra_{i1} \Uparrow Ra_{i-1,1};$
6		**if** $\text{abs}(Ra_{11}) \leq \text{abs}(Rx_{11})$ **then** 8;
7		$Rx_{11} := Ra_{11} \wedge ri_{11} := rj_{11};$
8		**if** $rj_{11} < rc_{11}$ **then** 5;
9		**if** $ri_{11} = 0$ **then** 11;
10	$(n - s + 1)(n + m)$	**for** $\forall i (i \leq n - s + 1) \forall j$ **parcyclshift** (ri_{11}, rc_{11})
		$Ra_{ij} \Uparrow Ra_{i-1};$
11	$n(n + m)$	**for** $\forall i$ **partransfer** $Ra_{i1} \Rightarrow Rx_{ij} \forall j(1);$
12		$Ry_{11} := -1/Ra_{11} \wedge Rd_{11} := Rd_{11} \times Ra_{11};$
13	$n + m$	**partransfer** $Ry_{11} \Rightarrow Ry_{1j} \forall j(1) \wedge$
	$n + m - 1$	**for** $\forall j(1)$ **pardo** $Ra_{1j} := 0;$
14	$n + m - 1$	**for** $\forall j(1)$ **pardo** $Ra_{1j} := Ra_{1j} - Rx_{1j}Ry_{1j};$
15	$n(n + m - 1)$	**for** $\forall j(1)$ **partransfer** $Ra_{1j} \Downarrow Ry_{ij} \forall i(1);$
16	$n(n + m) - 2n - m + 1$	**for** $\forall i(1) \forall j(1)$ **pardo** $Ra_{ij} := Ra_{ij} - Rx_{ij}Ry_{ij};$
17	$n(n + m - 1)$	**for** $\forall i \forall j$ **parshift** $Ra_{i,j-1} \Uparrow Ra_{ij};$
18	$n(n + m)$	**for** $\forall i \forall j$ **parcyclshift** $(1, rn_{11}) Ra_{ij} \Uparrow Ra_{i-1,j};$
19		**if** $rs_{11} < rn_{11}$ **then** 2;
20		**output** $\Leftarrow Rd_{11} \wedge$
	n	**for** $\forall i \forall j (j \leq m)$ **paroutput** $\Leftarrow Ra_{ij}.$

Program P4 is distributed through the array of processors, so that each processor needs only the current step number and the microcode necessary to implement the desired instruction. p_{11} synchronizes the calculation of SLEC4 by setting the current step number and broadcasting this information to all processors in the array. Each processor receives this information and, if it is to do anything during this time step, it executes the corresponding instruction and, after finishing, sends an unsigned finished signal back to p_{11}. When p_{11} gets responses from all active processors (it counts the number of signals it is expecting — see the second column of program P4), the next step of the program can be executed.

5.5.4 Complexity of program P4

The number of instructions executed in P4 is given in Table 25 (instructions No. 1, 2, 5, 8, 9, 13 are not considered, No. 6 and 14b are not counted because

Table 25

Instr. No.	3	4	7	10 + 10a	11	12 + 12a	14 + 14a
Count	$2n$	$n^2 + 5n$	n	$2n^2 - n$	n	$n^2 + n$	$2n$
Pivoting only	—	$n^2 + n$	—	—	—	n^2	—

they are calculated in parallel with other instructions). We assume that instruction No. 4 (No. 7) takes more time than No. 3 (No. 6).

In P4, arithmetic requires only $O(n)$ steps, but both transferring data and pivoting require $O(n^2)$ steps. We have assumed that pivoting always occurs between rows separated by the maximum distance.

5.6 Conclusion

In this chapter we have shown that, by tailoring architectures to the exact requirements of an algorithm, it is possible to achieve an effective implementation. The algorithm used was the Gauss—Jordan—Rutishauser elimination with partial pivoting [1] and some modifications. We suggested the following specialized computers: single chip computer, P-processors computer with on-chip cache memory and off-chip active memory, orthogonal pipeline vector processors (row and column variants), and systolic array. For each computer we described its structure, gave a specialized set of instructions, coded variations of the GJR algorithm, and calculated the complexity. Table 26 shows the comparison of complexity for all of the programs (remember, lower order terms are omitted).

We propose that these computers can be realized in hardware resulting in specialized high-performance machines, which can quickly calculate accurate results for large-scale dense systems of linear algebraic equations. The real cost and performance of these specialized computers must, of course, be proved by simulating or building them. This was not our intention.

Notes

(1) In our computers, we do not calculate the residual of equation (66) **AX** − **B**. If we want our programs to produce the residual vector, these programs must be slightly modified, since **A** and **B** are eliminated in place during the calculation of equation (66).

(2) Our computers can also be modified so that they calculate $\mathbf{A}^{-1}$ along with equations (66) and (67). Some specialized systolic arrays for solving equations (66) and (67) and $\mathbf{A}^{-1}$, by the GJR algorithm without pivoting are described in [15].

Table 26

Program	FP arithmetic	Memory access	Index reg.	Condit. jump	Other	Total complexity	Note
P1	$3n^2\left(\frac{n}{2}+m\right)$	$n^2\left(2q_1-\frac{n}{2}\right)$	$n^2 q_1$	$n^2\left(q_1+\frac{n}{2}\right)$	—	$O(n^3)+O(n_2 m)$	$q_1=2n+3m$
P2	rn	$2rn$	$3rn$	rn	$3n$	$\leq O\left(\frac{n^3}{2P}\right)+O\left(\frac{n^2 m}{P}\right)$	$r\leq O\left(\frac{n^2}{2P}\right)+O\left(\frac{nm}{P}\right)$
P3r	$n^2 v + nw + 2n$	$3n^2$	n^2	$2n^2$	$4n$	$O(n^2 v)$	$v(w)$: pipeline vector $\times$ ($-$ and $\times$)
P3c	$q_2 v + nw + 2n$	$3q_2$	q_2	q_2	$5n$	$O(q_2 v)$	$q_2=\frac{n^2}{2}+nm$
P4	$3n$	—	$2n$	n^2	$3n^2$	$O(n^2)$	only $O(n)$ arithmetic

References

[1] F. L. Bauer, J. Heinhold, K. Samelson and R. Sauer, *Moderne Rechenanlagen* (B. G. Teubner, Stuttgart, 1965).

[2] H. Rutishauser, *Vorlesungen über numerische Mathematik*, Bd. 1 (Birkhäuser Verlag, Basel, Stuttgart, 1976).

[3] J. Mikloško, "Systolic system for the linear equation system and matrix inversion", *Computers and Artif. Intelligence* **2** (1983) 361—372.

[4] F. L. Bauer and G. Goos, *Informatik*, Bd. 1 (Springer-Verlag, Berlin, Heidelberg, New York, 1982).

[5] V. D. Baikov and V. B. Smolov, *Hardware Implementation of Elementary Functions in Computers* (in Russian) (Izd. Leningradskogo universiteta, Leningrad, 1975).

[6] H. M. Ahmed, J. M. Delosme and M. Morf, "Highly concurrent computing structure for matrix arithmetic and signal processing", *Computer*, **1** (1982) 65—82.

[7] E. Hörbst, "Interdependence of architecture, circuit design and technology", *Proc. VLSI Architecture*, Eds. B. Randell and P. C. Treleaven (Prentice-Hall, Englewood Cliffs, 1983) pp. 255—275.

[8] D. J. Kinniment, "Memory system design", *Proc. VLSI Architecture*, Eds. B. Randell and P. C. Treleaven (Prentice-Hall, Englewood Cliffs, 1983) pp. 44—53.

[9] C. H. Sequin and D. A. Patterson, "Design and implementation of RISC I", *Proc. VLSI Architecture*, Eds. B. Randell and P. C. Treleaven (Prentice-Hall, Englewood Cliffs, 1983) pp. 276—298.

[10] D. J. Kinniment, "VLSI and machine architecture", *Proc. VLSI Architecture*, Eds. B. Randell and P. C. Treleaven (Prentice-Hall, Englewood Cliffs, 1983) pp. 24—33.

[11] R. W. Hockney and C. R. Jesshope, *Parallel Computers* (Adam Hilger Ltd., Bristol, 1981).

[12] C. C. Foster, *Content Addressable Parallel Processors* (Van Nostrand Rheinhold, New York, 1976).

[13] C. V. Ramamoorthy and H. F. Li, "Pipeline architecture", *Comp. Surv.*, **9** (1977) pp. 61—80.

[14] H. T. Kung and C. E. Leiserson, "Systolic arrays for VLSI", Introduction to VLSI Systems, Eds. C. Mead and L. Conway (Addison-Wesley, Reading, 1980) pp. 260—292.

[15] J. Mikloško and B. Zaťko, "Universal systolic array processors for fast matrix operations", *Proc. Artificial Intelligence and Information-Control Systems of Robots*, Ed. I. Plander (Elsevier/ /North-Holland, Amsterdam, 1984) pp. 259—263.

Chapter 6

Lower time bounds for SIMD-type algorithms

6.1 Introduction

In the previous chapter, concrete algorithms for specialized computers were given that demonstrated the increased power over the von-Neumann architecture. But, of course, these specialized computers have restrictions that may be characterized by lower time bounds. To demonstrate this general idea of comparing computer architectures and computational problems, a general method called the data transfer for obtaining lower time bounds is described in this chapter [1, 3, 4, 10]. This method will be illustrated applying a variety of different parallel processing architectures. The unifying feature of these parallel processes will be that they are SIMD models that employ an interconnection network and use no shared memory. Our parallel processing systems will be abstract models of computation where the level of abstraction may be compared with that of a random access machine, cf. [2]. For computational problems such as those mentioned in the present chapter refer to [5, 9]. Proofs omitted in this chapter may be found in [4].

6.2 The general SIMD model

The general SIMD model used in this chapter is characterized by a finite or infinite set of processing elements (PEs), an interconnection network and a central processing unit (CPU). For a rough scheme of an SIMD system that the reader may keep in mind throughout this chapter, see Fig. 68.

CPU. The CPU has a central random access memory which consists of a finite or infinite sequence of registers $r_0, r_1, r_2, \ldots$ with a distinguished accumulator r_0. Let D_{CPU} be the depth of this random access memory, i.e. the number of CPU registers, where $1 \leqslant D_{\text{CPU}} \leqslant \infty$. Furthermore, let W_{CPU} be the word length of these registers (number of bit positions), where it is assumed to be constant for all CPU registers and $1 \leqslant W_{\text{CPU}} \leqslant \infty$. The CPU spreads a single instruction stream to the synchronized working PEs. The programs of the system are stored

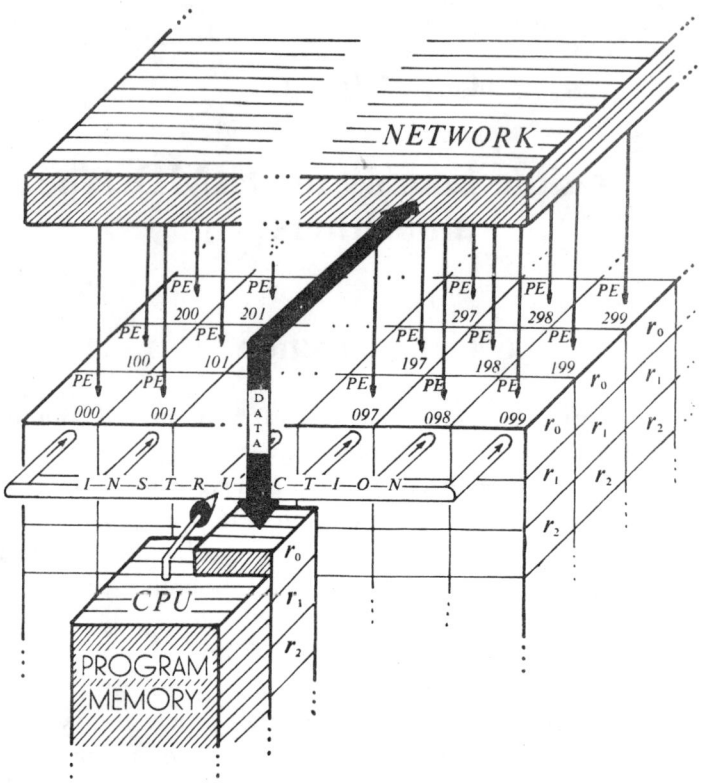

Fig. 68. Scheme of an SIMD system.

in a potentially size-unlimited, special program memory of the CPU. Part of any instruction addressed to the PEs is an enable/disable mask to select a subset of the PEs that are to perform the instruction; the remaining PEs will be idle. The CPU may read the accumulator content of each PE of a specified subset of all PEs, and is able to transfer this content to any of the PE accumulators. All data transfers between the CPU and PEs are restricted to serial mode.

PEs. Each PE has a (local) random access memory which consists of a finite or infinite sequence of registers $r_1, r_2, \ldots$ and a distinguished register r_0, called the accumulator. Let D_{PE}, $1 \leq D_{PE} \leq \infty$, be the depth of these random access memories, i.e., this depth is assumed to be constant for all PEs of a given system. Furthermore, let W_{PE}, $1 \leq W_{PE} \leq \infty$, be the unique word length of PE registers. Each PE can perform in its accumulator some elementary operations. Direct data access is restricted to its registers, to the accumulators of the directly connected PEs in the sense of the given interconnection network, and, possibly, also to the accumulator of the CPU. The PEs are indexed by integers or tuples of integers. Each PE knows its index. Let N_{PE}, $0 \leq N_{PE} \leq \infty$, be the number of PEs of a given system, and ind $= \{j_1, j_2, ..., j_{N_{PE}}\}$ be the set of all PE indices of a given SIMD system.

Interconnection network. Each PE is located in a node of an undirected graph that represents a two-way interconnection scheme. Each PE identifies only the different edges connected to its node by using a given coding scheme. Let N_{IN}, $0 \leq N_{IN} \leq \infty$, be the branching degree of the network, i.e. the maximum degree of the nodes of the given graph.

The system features that are to be taken into account in a specialized SIMD model are specified as follows:
— off-line or on-line communication with the outside world,
— special values for N_{PE}, N_{IN}, D_{PE}, W_{CPU}, or W_{PE},
— the set ind,
— the interconnection network structure and the edge coding scheme,
— the CPU instruction set and the available set of enable/disable masks, as well as the method of the data exchange between CPU and PEs,
— the restrictions on the system in communication with the outside world, i.e. input and output control.

Note that with regards to the technical realization of an SIMD computing facility, one implementation may offer, on principle, different ways to run such a system, i.e. the working principles of several SIMD models may be unified in one implementation. Essentially, this is the problem of constructing reconfigurable, flexible interconnection network, and/or to run a system that uses different modes, for example. Such flexible approaches are considered in a cellular processor project [7].

6.3 OFF-NETs and ON-NETs

A common one-accumulator computer, e.g. random access machine (RAM), according to [2], may be used as the simplest model for an abstract SIMD system — $N_{PE} = 0$ and $D_{CPU} = W_{CPU} = \infty$. We shall use it as underlying model for serial data processing. In contrast to [2], infinite precision and real number arithmetic are assumed, which is convenient for our considerations, since computational problems avoid discussions of round-off errors. In this sense, our standardized system features start with the declaration of abstract registers.

Abstract registers. For an SIMD system with abstract registers we assume that any register may store without any special encoding tricks one real number at fixed time. For the theoretical considerations in this paper, it is not important to specify how the reals are stored in the abstract registers by special bit representations.

Standard register enumeration. Here we use a special enumeration of all registers as follows. For registers r_m of the PE with index j or (j, k), called PE(j) or PE(j, k), we use the integer tuples (j, m) or (j, k, m), respectively, and for register r_m of the CPU the integer m.

Uniform network structure. Either $N_{IN} = 0$, or $N_{IN} = p \geq 1$; the network structure is characterized by p different functions $f_0, f_1, ..., f_{p-1}$ on the set ind of all PE indices in the following way. For $j, k \in$ ind, PE(j) and PE(k) are directly connected iff there exists an $i, 0 \leq i \leq p - 1$, such that $f_i(j) = k$. Because of our assumption that all connections are two-way connections, it follows

$$(\wedge j, k \in \text{ind})[(\vee i \in \{0, 1, ..., p-1\}) f_i(j) = k$$
$$\equiv k(\vee h \in \{0, 1, ..., p-1\}) f_h(k) = j]. \tag{68}$$

In [10], the functions $f_0, f_1, ..., f_{p-1}$ were called interconnection functions. Except for a fixed set of PEs at the network border, all other PEs must be directly connected to exactly p-different PEs. If $f_i(j) = k$, PE(k) is called the ith neighbour of PE(j). In this way, the edge coding scheme for uniform networks is defined. The neighbourhood of each PE involves all (i.e. at most p) neighbouring PEs. Models of infinite as well as finite networks that satisfy our requirements for uniformity are given in Table 27. In the sequel, we shall use these networks as defined in it.

Some remarks are necessary regarding Table 27. Both the left-right 2^i (LR2I) and the left-right-up-down 2^i (LRUD2I) networks were used for vector machines in [6, 8] without the restriction by integer m. Note that we have restricted ourselves to interconnection networks with a finite branching degree. Special form of the set ind in the Quadtree network is determined by our standard PE address masking scheme that is defined later. The finite uniform networks presented in Table 27, namely the perfect shuffle (PS), the ILLIAC, the Cube, the plus-minus 2^i (PM2I), and the wrap-around plus-minus 2^i (WPM2I) network, modified such that the PS network was an undirected graph to match out uniform network convention, i.e. the inverse shuffle function was added to the PS network, were studied in [10]. For $j \in$ ind $= \{0, 1, ..., 2^m - 1\} a_{m-1} ... a_1 a_0$ denotes the binary representation of j and $\bar{a}_i$ denotes the complement of a_i. Then

$$\text{exch}(a_{m-1} ... a_1 a_0) = a_{m-1} ... a_1 \bar{a}_0,$$
$$\text{shuf}(a_{m-1} ... a_1 a_0) = a_{m-2} ... a_1 a_0 a_{m-1},$$
$$\text{shuf}^{-1}(a_{m-1} ... a_1 a_0) = a_0 a_{m-1} ... a_2 a_1,$$
$$\text{cube}_i(a_{m-1} ... a_{i+1} a_i a_{i-1} ... a_0) = a_{m-1} ... a_{i+1} \bar{a}_i a_{i-1} ... a_0,$$
$$\text{WPM}_{+i}(a_{m-1} ... a_i ... a_0) = b_{m-1} ... b_i ... b_0,$$

Table 27

Network	ind	N_{IN}	Case	Edge coding scheme							
				0	1	2	3	4	5	6	7
LINEAR	integers	2	all	$j-1$	$j+1$	—	—	—	—	—	—
LR2I^m	integers	$2m$	all	$f_{2i}(j) = j+2^i$ and $f_{2i+1}(j) = j-2^i$ for $0 \leq i < m$ and $m \geq 2$							
BINTREE	positive integers	3	$j \geq 2$ all	$\lfloor j/2 \rfloor$ —	$2j$ —	$2j+1$ —	— —	— —	— —	— —	— —
TRIANGLE	positive integers	5	$j \geq 2$ all $j \neq 2^i$ $j \neq 2^i - 1$	$\lfloor j/2 \rfloor$ — — —	$2j$ — — —	$2j+1$ — — —	— — $j-1$ —	— — — $j+1$	— — — —	— — — —	— — — —
QUADTREE	$\bigcup_{i=0}^{\infty} \{4^i, ..., 2 \times 4^i - 1\}$	5	$j \geq 4$ all	$\lfloor j/4 \rfloor$ —	— $4j$	— $4j+1$	— $4j+2$	— $4j+3$	— —	— —	— —
HEXAGONAL	tuples of integers	3	all $j+k$ even $j+k$ odd	$(j, k-1)$ — —	$(j, k+1)$ — —	— $(j-1, k)$ —	— — —	— — —	— — —	— — —	— — —
SQUARE	tuples of integers	4	all	$(j, k-1)$	$(j, k+1)$	$(j-1, k)$	$(j+1, k)$	—	—	—	—
TRIAGONAL	tuples of integers	6	all	$(j, k-1)$	$(j, k+1)$	$(j-1, k)$	$(j+1, k)$	$(j-1, k-1)$	$(j+1, k+1)$	—	—
DIAGONAL	tuples of integers	8	all	$(j, k-1)$	$(j, k+1)$	$(j-1, k)$	$(j+1, k)$	$(j-1, k-1)$	$(j+1, k+1)$	$(j-1, k+1)$	$(j+1, k-1)$
LRUD2I^m	tuples of integers	$4m$	all	$f_{4i}(j, k) = (j+2^i, k), f_{4i+1}(j, k) = (j-2^i, k), f_{4i+2}(j, k) = (j, k+2^i),$ $f_{4i+3}(j, k) = (j, k-2^i)$, for $0 \leq i < m$ and $m \geq 2$							
PS^m	$\{0, 1, ..., 2^m - 1\}$	3	all	exch	shuf	shuf^{-1}	—	—	—	—	—
ILLIAC^m	$\{0, 1, ..., 2^m - 1\}$	4	all	$+1 \bmod 2^m$	$-1 \bmod 2^m$	$+\frac{m}{2} \bmod 2^m$	$-\frac{m}{2} \bmod 2^m$	—	—	—	—
CUBE^m	$\{0, 1, ..., 2^m - 1\}$	m	all	$f_i(j) = \text{cube}_i(j)$, for $0 \leq i < m$							
PM2I^m	$\{0, 1, ..., 2^m - 1\}$	$2m$	all	$f_{2i}(j) = j + 2^i \bmod 2^m, f_{2i+1}(j) = j - 2^i \bmod 2^m$, for $0 \leq i < m$							
WPM2I^m	$\{0, 1, ..., 2^m - 1\}$	$2m$	all	$f_{2i}(j) = \text{WPM}_{+i}(j), f_{2i+1}(j) = \text{WPM}_{-i}(j)$, for $0 \leq i < m$							

where $b_{i-1} \ldots b_0 b_{m-1} \ldots b_{i+1} b_i = (a_{i-1} \ldots a_0 a_{m-1} \ldots a_{i+1} a_i) - 1 \mod 2^m$,

$$\text{WPM}_{-i}(a_{m-1} \ldots a_i \ldots a_0) = b_{m-1} \ldots b_i \ldots b_0,$$

where $b_{i-1} \ldots b_0 b_{m-1} \ldots b_{i+1} b_i = (a_{i-1} \ldots a_0 a_{m-1} \ldots a_{i+1} a_i) - 1 \mod 2^m$, for $0 \leqslant i < m$ and $m \geqslant 1$.

Standard PE masking scheme. As standard masks we shall use the simple bit patterns for PE indices used, also in [10]. In the case of integer indices, standard PE address mask is given by an arbitrary, non-empty word on the alphabet $\{0, 1, x\}$, where x represents the "don't care" situation. The only PEs that will be active are those whose address (i.e. index) matches the mask from right to left. The indices are given in binary representation; 0 matches 0, 1 matches 1, and either 0 or 1 matches x. By mask [x], for example, all PEs are activated. To represent concrete standard masks within programs, we take liberty such as [all PEs] instead of [x] or [odd PEs] instead of [$1x$], if the rightmost bit position is assumed to be the sign position. In the case of integer tuple indices, the standard PE address masks are arbitrary tuples of non-empty words on $\{0, 1, x\}$. Note that in the infinite networks given in Table 27, any given PE address mask can activate an infinite manifold of PEs. For example, the mask [$0xx$] applied to the bintree network will activate the processing elements PE(2) and PE(3) on layer 1 of the bintree, it will disable layer 2, and enable the first four PEs of layer 3, etc. Here, the common binary representation of non-negative integers is assumed for the PE indices of the bintree network.

Abstract CPU instruction set. Assume that in any of our theoretical SIMD systems the CPU instruction set may be obtained by special interpretation and selection of instructions of an abstract CPU instruction reservoir defined as follows. There are two different types of instructions, parallel instructions to activate some PEs, and serial instructions where the CPU itself is addressed to a certain activity. Each parallel instruction consists of a PE address mask, an operation code (**READ, WRITE, LOAD, STORE, OP** or **OP**$_{2+l}$, $l \leqslant 1$) and of an operation address a, where we shall use the standard register enumeration to explain the meaning of these operation addresses. In serial instructions, we assume branching instructions **JUMP** b, **JGTZ** b, **JZERO** b, **JLTZ** b (where b symbolizes an instruction number in a CPU program and the content of the CPU accumulator is tested), the **HALT** instruction, and instructions consisting of an operation code (**READ, WRITE, LOAD, STORE, OP**$_1$ or **OP**$_2$). For a complete abstract CPU instruction set without jump and stop instructions, see Table 28. In parallel instructions, **OP**$_1$ denotes a unary operation that determines the new accumulator contents of all activated PEs by a certain transformation of the contents of the register addressed by a as well as the old accumulator contents of the activated PEs; **OP**$_{l+1}$ denotes an $(l + 1)$-ary opera-

6.3 OFF-NETs and ON-NETs

Table 28

Instruction	Possible operation address a			
[mask] **READ** a	m;	$*m$		
[mask] **WRITE** a	m;	$*m$		
[mask] **LOAD** a	m;	$*m$;	$: i$	
[mask] **STORE** a	m;	$*m$;	$: i_1, i_2, ..., i_l$	
[mask] **OP$_1$** a	m;	$*m$;	$: i$	
[mask] **OP$_2$** a	m;	$*m$;	$: i$	
[mask] **OP$_{l+1}$**	$: i_1, i_2, ..., i_l$			
READ a	m;	$*m$		
WRITE a	$= x$;	m;	$*m$	
LOAD a	$= x$;	m;	$*m$;	(j)
STORE a	m;	$*m$;	(j)	
OP$_1$ a	$= x$;	m;	$*m$;	(j)
OP$_2$ a	$= x$;	m;	$*m$;	(j)

tion in the same sense. In activated PE(j), the operation address m indicates the contents of register (j, m), $*m$ indicates the contents of register (j, n) if the non-negative integer n is in the register (j, m) at that moment (i.e. indirect operand addressing in case of incorrect programming; e.g. when (j, m) does not contain a non-negative integer at that moment, an interrupt of the programmed system is assumed) and the operand: $i_1, i_2, ..., i_l$, $l \leq 1$, indicates the contents of accumulators of those neighbours of activated PEs that are encoded $i_1, i_2, ..., i_l$, according to the edge coding scheme of the interconnection network. **LOAD** and **STORE** mean that the accumulator contents of the activated PEs are replaced by the addressed value, or copied into the addressed registers, respectively. **READ** and **WRITE** denote the necessary operations of communication with the outside world, where the source and destination of data in the "outside world" remain unspecified places in a computing environment that not belong to the SIMD system as such. In a serial instruction, the unary operation, **OP$_1$**, and the binary operation, **OP$_2$**, produce new CPU accumulator contents by a certain transformation of the addressed values, where in the case of **OP$_2$** the old CPU accumulator contents is used as operand in first position. **READ**, **WRITE**, **LOAD**, and **STORE** have their obvious fixed meanings. Operands $= x$, m, $*m$, and (j) indicate the data unit x, the contents of the CPU register m, the contents of the CPU register n if register m contains non-negative integer n at that moment, and the contents of register ($j, 0$), respectively. Note that with this abstract CPU instruction set, data transfer between the CPU and the PEs via the accumulators is only possible when performed serially. Furthermore, in a specialized SIMD model, it is useful to harmonize the basic computational power of the PEs and CPU with that of the RAM, see the RAM instruction set

[2, Fig. 1.5]. Using equation (69) in Example 1 we shall explain how the PEs are able to perform local logical decisions in SIMD mode.

Off-line I/O convention. For the off-line communication of an SIMD system with the outside world we assume that there is a special set of input registers of the system fixed such that all other registers of the system contain zero at the beginning of each computation (moment $t = 0$), i.e. analogously to input registers that need not store input data. Each of the input registers may contain at most one item of data. Thus, to solve a concrete problem, it is necessary to specify

— the structure of the given input data,
— the manner of storing this data in a fixed input register set.

It is also necessary to fix the set of output registers of the system. Hence, to solve a concrete problem we must know.

— the desired data structure of the output data, and the manner of storing or computing this data in the predetermined output register set.

In an off-line I/O convention we declare that for a certain L, $1 \leqslant L \leqslant D_{\text{CPU}}$, the CPU registers $0, 1, ..., L - 1$ are input and output registers, and for any PE(j), if there exists a certain $m \geqslant 0$ such that register (j, m) is an input register (output register), register ($j, 0$) is an input register (output register) as well. The same holds also for the accumulator.

On-line I/O convention. In the on-line communication of an SIMD system with the outside world some registers are predetermined to act as input and/or output registers. In the on-line I/O convention we adopt the same rules as in the off-line convention. But, at the beginning of each on-line computation (moment $t = 0$), all registers of the system are assumed to hold the value zero. Input or output data may enter or leave the system at a moment specified by the **READ** or **WRITE** instructions of the CPU program. In each correct program, these input (output) instructions have to be addressed to a proper subset of all registers specified as input (output) registers. It is assumed that for the input (output) data there exists a memory facility in the outside world from where (to where) the input (output) data are obtained (supplied) by the system. Thus, to solve a concrete problem it is necessary to specify

— the structures of the input and output data,
— how these data are to be partitioned into waves of information such that one wave may enter (leave) the system per input (output) operation performed to the CPU program.

The size of these waves of information, i.e. the number of data units to form these waves, may change during a computation process. Only one data unit, for example, by **LOAD** $= x$, will be considered to be the simplest section of a wave of information.

Uniform cost criterion. In measuring the time complexity of computations we assume that one unit of time is needed to perform a basic instruction on the SIMD system.

Definition 1. A model of computation SYS is called a standard off-line network system (SYS ∈ OFF-NET) iff SYS is defined by

— a CPU and a fixed set of indexed PEs, with concrete values for D_{CPU} and D_{PE},

— abstract registers, if not otherwise specified, and a standard register enumeration,

— a uniform interconnection network with $0 \leqslant N_{\text{IN}} < \infty$,

— a standard PE masking scheme,

— a special interpretation and selection of instructions of the abstract CPU instruction set, where

(OFF.1) no **READ** and **WRITE** instructions are contained in the instruction set of SYS;

(OFF.2) for the CPU, all RAM instructions [2, Fig. 1.5] except for **READ** and **WRITE** are available;

(OFF.3) for $N_{\text{IN}} = p \geqslant 1$, at least one instruction of the type [all PEs] $\mathbf{OP}_{p+1}$: $0, 1, \ldots, p-1$ is available; and

(OFF.4) for any output register $(j, 0)$, i.e. accumulator of PE(j), at least one instruction of the type $\mathbf{OP}_2(j)$ is available, i.e. the CPU may control any outputting PE;

— the off-line I/O convention,

— the uniform cost criterion.

For a fixed class OFF-NET, we may define subclasses, for example, OFF-NET$_p$ will be the set of all SYS ∈ OFF-NET having the branching degree $p = N_{\text{IN}}$, OFF-SQUARE will be the set of all SYS ∈ OFF-NET having a square network (see Table 27), OFF-BINTREE (see also Table 27), OFF-PS = $\bigcup_{m=1}^{\infty}$ OFF-PS^m, or just OFF-RAM.

Example 1. Let us consider the following special SIMD system EXAMP1 ∈ ∈ OFF-SQUARE. Let $D_{\text{CPU}} = D_{\text{PE}} = \infty$. Additionally, all accumulators $(j, k, 0)$, $0 \leqslant j < M$ and $0 \leqslant k < N$, for some $M, N \geqslant 1$, are fixed to each CPU registers $0, 1, \ldots, L-1, L \geqslant 1$ as input and output registers of EXAMP1. The system has the following instruction set

[mask] **ADD** a, a for m, *m, :i_1, ..., i_l for $i_1, \ldots, i_l \in \{0, 1, 2, 3\}$,
[mask] **OP**$_l$ a, a for m, *m, :i for $i \in \{0, 1, 2, 3\}$, $l = 1, 2$,
[mask] **LOAD** a, a for m, *m, :i for $i \in \{0, 1, 2, 3\}$,
[mask] **STORE** a, a for m, *m, :i_1, ..., i_l for $i_1, \ldots, i_l \in \{0, 1, 2, 3\}$,
        LOAD a, a for $= x$, m, *m, (j, k),
        STORE a, a for m, *m, (j, k),
        OP$_2$ a, a for $= x$, m, *m, (j, k),

JUMP b, **JGTZ** b, **JZERO** b, **JLTZ** b, and **HALT**. Here, [mask] represents an arbitrary PE address mask, **OP**$_1$ is **ABS** (absolute value) or **SIGN** (signum function), **OP**$_2$ is **ADD**, **SUB**, **MULT**, or **DIV** for tuples (j, k) with $0 \leq j < M$ and $0 \leq k < N$.

To illustrate in few words the computing power of EXAMP1, consider the computation of the parallel Roberts gradient (cf. [9] for its importance to digital image processing), where the input image $A = (a_{jk})$ of size $M \times N$ is assumed to be stored in the PE input registers (a_{jk} in register $(j, k, 0)$) at the beginning of the computation. At the end of the computation, value $\max\{|a_{jk} - a_{j+1, k+1}|, |a_{j+1, k} - a_{j, k+1}|\}$ must be stored in register $(j, k, 0)$.

Performing the following sequence of parallel instructions

(1) [all PEs] **STORE** 1
(2) [all PEs] **LOAD** :2
(3) [all PEs] **STORE** 2
(4) [all PEs] **LOAD** :1
(5) [all PEs] **SUB** 1
(6) [all PEs] **ABS** 0
(7) [all PEs] **STORE** 3
(8) [all PEs] **LOAD** 1
(9) [all PEs] **LOAD** :1
(10) [all PEs] **SUB** 2
(11) [all PEs] **ABS** 0
(12) [all PEs] **STORE** 4

all registers $(j, k, 3)$ contain value $|a_{jk} - a_{j+1, k+1}|$, and all registers $(j, k, 4)$ the value $|a_{j+1, k} - a_{j, k+1}|$, for $0 \leq j < M$ and $0 \leq k < N$. These values may be considered as two $M \times N$ matrices, **B** and **C**. For $\max(\mathbf{B}, \mathbf{C}) = (\max\{b_{jk}, c_{jk}\})$ we have

$$\max(\mathbf{B}, \mathbf{C}) = b \times \mathrm{sign}(\mathbf{B} - \mathbf{C}) + \mathbf{C} \times \mathrm{sign}(\mathbf{C} - \mathbf{B}) + \mathbf{B} - \mathbf{B} \times \mathrm{sign}|\mathbf{B} - \mathbf{C}|, \tag{69}$$

where $\times$ means the parallel **MULT** operation (cross product of two matrices) and sign — the parallel **SIGN** operation. On using this formula, the reader may check easily that the parallel Roberts gradient may be computed on the defined special OFF-SQUARE system within time 29 or less, independently of the values of M and N. Note that formula (69) describes the way the PEs are able to perform local logical decisions in SIMD mode.

Example 2. The system EXAMP1 may dramatically change using some simple modifications. Replace the square network by LRUD2I^m, for $m < \max\{\log_2 M, \log_2 N\}$, let $W_{\mathrm{PE}} = 1$, and replace the parallel operations **ADD**, **OP**$_1$ and **OP**$_2$ by logical operations **AND**, **NOT** and **OR**, respectively. What results is a special OFF-LRUD2I^m system EXAMP2.

Definition 2. A model of computation SYS is called a standard on-line network system (SYS $\in$ ON-NET) iff SYS is defined by

— a CPU and a fixed set of indexed PEs, with concrete values for D_{CPU} and D_{PE},

— abstract registers, if not otherwise specified, and the standard register enumeration,
— a uniform interconnection network with $0 \leqslant N_{IN} < \infty$,
— a standard PE masking scheme,
— a special interpretation and selection of instructions of the abstract CPU instruction set, where, for $N_{IN} \geqslant 2$, an integer tuple (p, q) may denote the characteristic of SYS in the following sense:

(ON.1) $P = N_{IN}$ and $1 \leqslant q < p$;

(ON.2) a proper subset $\{i_1, i_2, ..., i_q\}$ of all directions $\{0, 1, ..., p - 1\}$ is specified;

(ON.3) at least one instruction of the type [all PEs] $\mathbf{OP}_{q+1}: i_1, i_2, ..., i_q$ is available;

(ON.4) for any of the instructions [mask] $\mathbf{LOAD}: j$ or [mask] $\mathbf{OP}_{k(+1)}: j_1, j_2, ..., j_k$, $k \geqslant 1$, it follows that $j, j_1, j_2, ..., j_k \in \{i_1, i_2, ..., i_q\}$;

(ON.5) for any of the instructions [mask] $\mathbf{STORE}: j_1, j_2, ..., j_k$, $k \geqslant 1$, it follows that $j_1, j_2, ..., j_k \in \{0, 1, ..., p - 1\} - \{i_1, i_2, ..., i_q\}$, i.e. the results of consecutive parallel operations may be shifted through the system only in directions $\{0, 1, ..., p - 1\} - \{i_1, i_2, ..., i_q\}$;

(ON.6) for the CPU, all RAM instructions (including **READ** and **WRITE**) are available;

(ON.7) for any output register $(j, 0)$, at least one instruction of the type $\mathbf{OP}_2(j)$ is available;

— the on-line I/O convention, and
— the uniform cost criterion.

For the defined class ON-NET, we may define subclasses, for example, ON-NET$_{p,q}$ will be the set of all ON-NET systems with characteristic (p, q), ON-LR2I^m will be the set of all SYS $\in$ ON-NET having a left-right 2^i network (see Table 27), ON-ILLIAC^m (see also Table 27), ON-PM2I $= \bigcup_{m=1}^{\infty}$ ON-PM2I^m, or just ON-RAM.

Any infinite OFF-LINEAR or ON-DIAGONAL network class may be considered an abstraction of a finite network system or a union of classes of finite network systems in the following way.

Definition 3. Let OFF-IN be the set of all OFF-NET systems which are defined by a special infinite network IN, e.g. IN = LINEAR or IN = LRUD2I^m. A model of SYS computation is called a finite OFF-IN system (SYS $\in$ FIN-OFF-IN) iff there exists a system SYS$_0 \in$ OFF-IN such that SYS may be obtained as a restriction of SYS$_0$ in the following sense.

Let ind$_0$ and D_{PE}^0 be the PE index set and the PE memory depth for SYS$_0$, respectively. A finite cut-off of the PE register set of SYS$_0$ is defined by a finite subset ind of ind$_0$ and a (possibly infinite) memory depth $D_{PE} \leqslant D_{PE}^0$. The work of SYS may be described as follows. All registers in a finite cut-off of SYS$_0$ are available in SYS but all registers outside this finite cut-off will be considered dummy, i.e. they are supposed to store zero if addressed as an operand, and to "forget" each value handed over to them; this is the only difference between SYS_0 and SYS.

The FIN-ON-IN set may be defined analogously.

Example 3. An example of a FIN-ON-BINTREE system may be specified as follows. Let $D_{CPU} = \infty$ and $D_{PE} = m \geq 2$. The finite cut-off of the bintree network is given by ind $= \{1, 2, ..., 2^m - 1\}$. Additionally, registers $(2^{m-1}, 0)$, $(2^{m-1} + 1, 0), ..., (2^m - 1, 0)$, i.e. accumulators of the 2^{m-1} leaf node PEs, are fixed as input registers, and register $(1, 0)$, i.e. the accumulator of the top node PE as output register to the CPU accumulator which then acts as an input and output register ($L = 1$). Instruction set of the system is as follows

[mask] **ADD** a, a for m, *m, : 1, : 2, : 1, 2,
[mask] **OP**$_l$ a, a for m, *m, : 1, : 2 and $l = 1, 2$,
[mask] **LOAD** a, a for m, *m, : 1, : 2,
[mask] **STORE** a, a for m, *m, : 0,
[subset leaf nodes] **READ** 0,
[top node] **WRITE** 0,
    LOAD a, a for $= x$, m, *m, (1),
    STORE a, a for m, *m, (1),
    OP$_l$ a, a for $= x$, m, *m, (1), and $l = 1, 2$,
    READ 0,
    WRITE a, a for $= x$, 0,
    JUMP b, **JGTZ** b, **JZERO** b, **JLTZ** b, **HALT**.

Here, [mask] represents an arbitrary PE address, **OP**$_1$ either **ABS** or **SIGN**, **OP**$_2$ one of the operation codes **ADD**, **SUB**, **MULT**, or **DIV**. Altogether, a FIN-ON-BINTREE system EXAMP3 is defined which may be obtained by a restriction of an infinite ON-BINTREE model, where infinite sets of input and output PE registers are available in the infinite origin.

To illustrate in few words the computational power of the EXAMP3 system we consider the computation of the arithmetic average $\frac{1}{N} \sum_{i=0}^{N-1} a_i$, $N = 2^{n-1}$, n odd, for M consecutive waves of information $(a_0, a_1, ..., a_{N-1})$, where a_i is fed to the accumulator of the $PE(2^{n-1} + i)$, $i = 0, 1, ..., N - 1$. In order of the M consecutive waves of information the arithmetic average has to leave the system via register $(1, 0)$.

To activate the system, first instruction **LOAD** $= N$, **STORE** (1), [top node] **STORE** 1 is to be performed in the following order. For $M \geq (n-1)/2$, the following sequence of instructions are executed $(n - 1)/2$ times:

[leaf nodes]   **READ** 0,
[all PEs]   **ADD** : 1, 2,
[leaf nodes]   **LOAD** 1,
[all PEs]   **ADD** : 1, 2,

then follow instructions which are executed $M - [(n - 1)/2]$ times:

[top node]   **DIV** 1,
[top node]   **WRITE** 0,
[leaf nodes]   **READ** 0,
[all PEs]   **ADD** : 1, 2,
[leaf nodes]   **LOAD** 1,
[all PEs]   **ADD** : 1, 2.

Finally, the following sequence of instructions is executed $(n - 3)/2$ times:

[top node]   **DIV** 1,
[top node]   **WRITE** 0,
[all PEs]   **ADD** : 1, 2,
[all PEs]   **ADD** : 1, 2,

followed by the last two instructions [top node] **DIV** 1 and top node **WRITE** 0. Thus, the arithmetic averages of $M \geqslant (n - 1)/2$ consecutive waves of information $(a_0, a_1, \ldots, a_{N-1})$ may be computed altogether within $6M + n$ basic operations of EXAMP3, instead of $O(NM)$ basic operations in the serial case using RAM as model for computation.

To conclude we point out that now SIMD represents not a general concept but a well-defined class of models for computation, i.e. it unifies system classes given in Definitions 1, 2 and 3.

6.4 Local, global and total data transfer measures

Let $SYS \in SIMD$; a special parallel processing system, i.e. a standard system for considerations of data transfer restrictions in computing systems, will be used throughout this chapter. Each computational process performed on a model SYS may be uniquely specified by a CPU program π and a concrete input situation I characterized by storing input values into the set of input registers if off-line mode is used, or, by the partitioning input data into consecutive waves of information fed to some input registers of the system from the outside world if on-line mode is used.

Applications to visual perception suggest that the set of input registers of the SYS model is some kind of retina of the system, and that each new wave of information to this set of input registers represents a snapshot of the outside world. In this sense, after t steps of a computation process characterized by program π and input situation I, any register r of the system can be ascribed a certain receptive field $\mathrm{rec}_\pi^I(r, t)$ containing all the names of those input registers which have had any influence on the contents of register r up to the moment t and where new waves of information to the retina of the system produce new names of the input registers, formally represented by $r^{(0)}$, $r^{(1)}$, $r^{(2)}$, ..., $r^{(i)}$, ... for register r.

Standard register names. At time $t = 0$, each register r, in a computation process has in our standard enumeration the name $r^{(0)}$. Also at $t = 0$, let the wave number $WN = 0$. Assume that a serial or parallel **READ** instruction, or instruction **LOAD** $= x$, **OP**$_1 = x$, or **OP**$_2 = x$ has to be performed at time $t + 1$. Consequently, we get $WN \leftarrow WN + 1$ and the new names $r^{(WN)}$ for all registers which were addressed by these instructions. For example, the number $(j, c(j, m))^{(WN)}$ in case of instruction [mask] **READ** $*m$ for all activated processing elements PE(j), where $c(j, m)$ denotes the actual contents of register (j, m), or the name $O^{(WN)}$ in case of instruction **OP**$_2 = x$.

Definition 4. Let SYS $\in$ SIMD. Standard register names are assumed. For program π of SYS, input situation I of SYS, register r of SYS, and arbitrary moment $t \geqslant 0$, the receptive field $\mathrm{rec}_\pi^I(r, t)$ is recursively defined as follows moment $t = 0$:

$$\mathrm{rec}_\pi^I(r, 0) = r^{(0)} \quad \begin{array}{l} \text{if input register } r \text{ stores an} \\ \text{input value according to } I, \\ \text{for off-line mode,} \\ \text{empty set, otherwise} \end{array}$$

moment $t + 1$, $t \geqslant 0$:
At moment $t + 1$, a given instruction has to be applied according to π and I, or the **HALT** instruction is assumed for this moment.

(i) Depending on the instruction: if it is one of those listed in Table 29, changes of receptive fields given in the table are defined, indices π and I are omitted for simplification of the expressions. In the case of parallel instructions, the mentioned changes are valid for all activated PEs PE(j), where j matches [mask].

(ii) For the parallel or serial **LOAD** instructions the changes of receptive fields are analogous to those of the corresponding **OP**$_1$ instructions.

(iii) In the case of **WRITE**, **JUMP** or **HALT** instructions no changes of receptive fields appear.

(iv) In the case of **JGTZ**, **JZERO** or **JLTZ** instructions no changes of receptive fields appear in step $t + 1$, but the set $\mathrm{rec}\,(0, t)$ will be added at moment

6.4 Local, global and total data transfer measures

Table 29

Instructions	Changes of receptive fields
[mask] $\mathbf{OP}_1\ m$	$\mathrm{rec}((j, 0), t + 1) = \mathrm{rec}((j, m), t)$
[mask] $\mathbf{OP}_1\ *m$	$\mathrm{rec}((j, 0), t + 1) = \mathrm{rec}((j, m), t) \cup \mathrm{rec}((j, c(j, m)), t)$
[mask] $\mathbf{OP}_1 : i$	$\mathrm{rec}((j, 0), t + 1) = \mathrm{rec}((f_i(j), 0), t)$
[mask] $\mathbf{OP}_2\ m$	$\mathrm{rec}((j, 0), t + 1) = \mathrm{rec}((j, 0), t) \cup \mathrm{rec}((j, m), t)$
[mask] $\mathbf{OP}_2\ *m$	$\mathrm{rec}((j, 0), t + 1) = \mathrm{rec}((j, 0), t) \cup$ $\cup \mathrm{rec}((j, m), t) \cup \mathrm{rec}((j, c(j, m)), t)$
[mask] $\mathbf{OP}_{l+1} : i_1, i_2, \ldots, i_l$	$\mathrm{rec}((j, 0), t + 1) = \mathrm{rec}((j, 0), t) \cup \mathrm{rec}((f_{i_1}(j), 0), t) \cup$ $\cup \mathrm{rec}((f_{i_2}(j), 0), t) \cup \ldots \cup \mathrm{rec}((f_{i_l}(j), 0), t)$
[mask] $\mathbf{STORE}\ m$	$\mathrm{rec}((j, m), t + 1) = \mathrm{rec}((j, 0), t)$
[mask] $\mathbf{STORE}\ *m$	$\mathrm{rec}((j, c(j, m), t + 1) = \mathrm{rec}((j, 0), t) \cup \mathrm{rec}((j, m), t)$
[mask] $\mathbf{STORE} : i_1, i_2, \ldots, i_l$	$\mathrm{rec}((f_{i_1}(j), 0), t + 1) = \mathrm{rec}((j, 0), t), \mathrm{rec}((f_{i_2}(j), 0), t + 1) =$ $= \mathrm{rec}((j, 0), t), \ldots, \mathrm{rec}((f_{i_l}(j), 0), t + 1) = \mathrm{rec}((j, 0), t)$
[mask] $\mathbf{READ}\ m$	$\mathrm{rec}(j, m), t + 1) = \{(j, m)^{(WN)}\}$
[mask] $\mathbf{READ}\ *m$	$\mathrm{rec}((j, c(j, m), t + 1) = \mathrm{rec}((j, m), t) \cup \{(j, c(j, m))^{(WN)}\}$
$\mathbf{OP}_1 = x$	$\mathrm{rec}(0, t + 1) = \{0^{(WN)}\}$
$\mathbf{OP}_1\ m$	$\mathrm{rec}(0, t + 1) = \mathrm{rec}(m, t)$
$\mathbf{OP}_1\ *m$	$\mathrm{rec}(0, t + 1) = \mathrm{rec}(m, t) \cup \mathrm{rec}(c(m), t)$
$\mathbf{OP}_1\ (j)$	$\mathrm{rec}(0, t + 1) = \mathrm{rec}((j, 0), t)$
$\mathbf{OP}_2 = x$	$\mathrm{rec}(0, t + 1) = \mathrm{rec}(0, t) \cup \{0^{(WN)}\}$
$\mathbf{OP}_2\ m$	$\mathrm{rec}(0, t + 1) = \mathrm{rec}(0, t) \cup \mathrm{rec}(m, t)$
$\mathbf{OP}_2\ *m$	$\mathrm{rec}(0, t + 1) = \mathrm{rec}(0, t) \cup \mathrm{rec}(m, t) \cup \mathrm{rec}(c(m), t)$
$\mathbf{OP}_2\ (j)$	$\mathrm{rec}(0, t + 1) = \mathrm{rec}(0, t) \cup \mathrm{rec}((j, 0), t)$
$\mathbf{STORE}\ m$	$\mathrm{rec}(m, t + 1) = \mathrm{rec}(0, t)$
$\mathbf{STORE}\ *m$	$\mathrm{rec}(c(m), t + 1) = \mathrm{rec}(0, t) \cup \mathrm{rec}(m, t)$
$\mathbf{STORE}\ (j)$	$\mathrm{rec}((j, 0), t + 1) = \mathrm{rec}(0, t))$
$\mathbf{READ}\ m$	$\mathrm{rec}(m, t + 1) = \{m^{(WN)}\}$
$\mathbf{READ}\ *m$	$\mathrm{rec}(c(m), t + 1) = \mathrm{rec}(m, t) \cup \{c(m)^{(WN)}\}$

$t' \geqslant t + 2$ to each receptive field that changes at moment t' according to (i) or (ii), if at moment t' an instruction has to be performed covered by cases (i) and (ii). For example, the instruction mask $\mathbf{OP}_2\ m$, at moment $t' \geqslant t + 2$, will produce changes $\mathrm{rec}((j, 0), t') = \mathrm{rec}((j, 0), t' - 1) \cup \mathrm{rec}((j, m), t' - 1) \cup \mathrm{rec}(0, t)$ for all activated PEs.

To illustrate this definition, consider the special OFF-SQUARE system defined in Example 1. Let I be the input situation in computing the parallel Roberts gradient and let π be the sequence of 12 parallel instructions. At moment $t = 0$, we have $\mathrm{rec}((j, k, 0), 0) = \{(j, k, 0)^{(0)}\}$ for $0 \leqslant j < M$ and $0 \leqslant k < N$, and for any other register r of the system EXAMP1, $\mathrm{rec}(r, 0)$ is an empty set. Having performed the 12 instructions of π, the reception fields of maximum cardinality 2 belong to the registers $(j, k, 0)$, $(j, k, 3)$ and $(j, k, 4)$, $0 \leqslant j \leqslant M - 2$, $0 \leqslant k \leqslant N - 2$, where, e.g. $\mathrm{rec}((j, k, 0), 12) = \{(j + 1, k, 0)^{(0)},$

$(j, k + 1, 0)^{(0)}\}$. Consider the program and the input situation for the system defined in Example 3. Then after performing the $6M + n$ instructions, the receptive field of maximal cardinality $NM + 1$ belongs to the register $(1, 0)$, i.e. to the accumulator of the top node PE.

Definition 5. Let $SYS \in SIMD$. For a set R of registers of SYS and a moment $t \geq 0$ define
the local data transfer function λ_{SYS} by

$$\lambda_{SYS}(R, t) = \max_{\pi} \max_{I} \max_{r \in R} \operatorname{card}(\operatorname{rec}^{I}(r, t)),$$

the global data transfer function γ_{SYS} by

$$\lambda_{SYS}(R, t) = \max_{\pi} \max_{I} \operatorname{card}\left(\bigcup_{r \in R} \operatorname{rec}_{\pi}^{I}(r, t)\right),$$

and the total data transfer function τ_{SYS} by

$$\lambda_{SYS}(R, t) = \max_{\pi} \max_{I} \bigcup_{r \in R} \operatorname{card}(\operatorname{rec}_{\pi}^{I}(r, t)).$$

With this definition, it follows immediately that the functions λ_{SYS}, γ_{SYS} and τ_{SYS} are monotonically increasing for any set R of SYS registers and increasing values of t. Furthermore,

$$\lambda_{SYS}(R, t) \leq \gamma_{SYS}(R, t) \leq \tau_{SYS}(R, t) \tag{70}$$

for all models SYS of SIMD, register sets R and moments $t \geq 0$. If within t steps of an arbitrary program π for any model SYS that starts with an arbitrary input situation I where at most $\omega_{SYS}(t)$ input data may be fed to the system, then

$$\gamma_{SYS}(R, t) \leq \omega_{SYS}(t), \quad \text{and} \tag{71}$$

$$\tau_{SYS}(R, t) \leq \lambda_{SYS}(R, t) \operatorname{card}(R) \tag{72}$$

for any set R of SYS registers and $t \geq 0$.

Example 4. In Section 6.6 we shall explain how to use the data transfer functions in order to get lower time bounds for concrete computational problems. In serial data processing, the system RAM_L, cf. [2, Fig. 1.5] will be used for computation model, where $R_L = \{0, 1, 2, ..., L - 1\}$, $L \geq 1$, is assumed to be the set of all input/output registers of such a machine ($D_{CPU} = \infty$, $N_{PE} = 0$, $W_{CPU} = \infty$). For $t \geq 0$, we have $\omega_{OFF\text{-}RAM_L}(t) = L + t$ and $\omega_{ON\text{-}RAM_L}(t) = t$. For

OFF-RAM = $\bigcup_{L=1}^{\infty}$ OFF-RAM$_L$, note that $\omega_{\text{OFF-RAM}}(t) = \max_L \omega_{\text{OFF-RAM}_L}(t)$ is not defined.

If the RAM$_L$ in off-line mode is used, we get

$$\lambda_{\text{OFF-RAM}_L}(R_L, t) = \begin{cases} 2t + 1 & \text{for } 0 \leqslant t \leqslant \lfloor (L-1)/2 \rfloor \\ \lfloor (L+1)/2 \rfloor + t, & \text{otherwise,} \end{cases} \quad (73)$$

$$\gamma_{\text{OFF-RAM}_L}(R_L, t) = L + t, \quad (74)$$

$$\tau_{\text{OFF-RAM}_L}(R_L, t) = L(t - \lfloor L/2 \rfloor + 1) \quad \text{for } t \geqslant \lfloor L/2 \rfloor,$$

if it is used in on-line model, we get

$$\lambda_{\text{ON-RAM}_L}(R_L, t) = \gamma_{\text{ON-RAM}_L}(R_L, t) = t, \quad (75)$$

$$\tau_{\text{ON-RAM}_L}(R_L, t) = \begin{cases} t(t+l)/2 & \text{for } t \leqslant L \\ L(t - (L/2) + 1/2) & \text{for } t \geqslant L. \end{cases} \quad (76)$$

The maximum data flow to obtain equation (73) is possible by indirect addressing **OP**$_2$ *m, followed by **OP**$_2 = x$ operations. For (75), the same sequence of operations is extended by $L - 1$ instructions **STORE** m. For (76), t operations of the type **OP**$_2 = x$ may be considered. For small t, the exact derivation of the function $\tau_{\text{OFF-RAM}_L}$ represents a sophisticated problem on this quite simple model of serial computation.

Example 5. To further illustrate the concrete derivation of these data transfer functions, consider the above-defined systems EXAMP1 and EXAMP3.

For the system EXAMP1, we first see that $\omega_{\text{EXAMP1}(t)} = MN + L + t$ for $t \geqslant 0$. Let $R_{M,N}$ be the set $\{(j, k, 0): 0 \leqslant j < M \text{ and } 0 \leqslant k < N\}$ of all PE input/output registers of the system. Using t operations of the type

[all PEs] **ADD**: 0, 1, 2, 3

we get the maximum local and total data transfer within the field of PE accumulators, where

$$\lambda_{\text{EXAMP1}}(R_{M,N}, t) = 2t^2 + 2t + 1,$$

$$(2t^2 + 2t + 1)MN - \left(\frac{t+1}{3} - (t+1)^2 + \frac{2(t+1)^3}{3}\right)(M+N) \leqslant$$

$$\leqslant \tau_{\text{EXAMP1}}(R_{M,N}, t) \leqslant (2t^2 + 2t + 1)MN,$$

for $2t + 1 \leq \min\{M, N\}$, by elementary combinatorial consideration, and for $t \geq t_0 = \lfloor M/2 \rfloor \lfloor N/2 \rfloor$, we get

$$MN + (t - t_0) \leq \lambda_{\text{EXAMP1}}(R_{M, N}, t) \leq MN + L + t.$$

For $t \geq t_0 = M + N - 2$ we can easily see that

$$M^2 N^2 + (t - t_0) \leq \tau_{\text{EXAMP1}}(R_{M, N}, t) \leq MN(MN + L + t).$$

Finally, for a global data transfer we obtain

$$\gamma_{\text{EXAMP1}}(R_{M, N}, t) = \begin{cases} MN & \text{for } t = 0, \\ MN + 2t + 1 & \text{for } 2t + 1 \leq L \text{ and } t > 0, \\ MN + \lfloor (L - 1)/2 \rfloor + t & \text{for } 2t + 1 > L, \end{cases}$$

where, the maximum global data transfer for $2t + 1 \leq L$, is possible by t operations of the type **ADD** $*m_t$ and one operation **STORE** (j, k), for example.

For the system EXAMP3, we first have $\omega_{\text{EXAMP3}}(t) = tN$, for $N = 2^{n-1}$ and $t \geq 0$ by using t operations of the type

[leaf nodes]   **READ** 0.

Let $R_0 = \{0, (1, 0)\}$ be the set of the two distinguished output registers of the system EXAMP3. By using the instruction pair

[leaf nodes]   **READ** 0,
[all PEs]   **ADD**: 1, 2

repeated $(m - 1)$ times, $m \geq 1$; the single instruction

[leaf nodes]   **READ** 0

again; and finally $(n - 1)$ instructions

[all PEs]   **ADD**: 1, 2,

we get the maximum local data transfer for register $(1, 0)$ in any case $t \geq m$. We have

6.4 Local, global and total data transfer measures

$$\lambda_{\text{EXAMP3}}(R_0, t) = \begin{cases} 0 & \text{for } t = 0, \\ 2^{t-1} & \text{for } 1 \leqslant t \leqslant n-1, \\ mN & \text{for } t = n + 2m - l, m \geqslant 1 \\ & \text{and } l = 1 \text{ or } l = 2, \end{cases}$$

for all $t \geqslant 0$. Analogously, for the same set R_0 and $t \geqslant 0$

$$\gamma_{\text{EXAMP3}}(R_0, t) = \begin{cases} 0 & \text{for } t = 0, \\ 2^{t-1} & \text{for } 1 \leqslant t \leqslant n-1, \\ mN & \text{for } t = n + 2m - 2, m \geqslant 1, \\ mN + 1 & \text{for } t = n + 2m - 1, m \geqslant 1, \end{cases}$$

$$\tau_{\text{EXAMP3}}(R_0, t) = \begin{cases} 0 & \text{for } t = 0, \\ 2^{t-1} & \text{for } 1 \leqslant t \leqslant n+1, \\ 2mN & \text{for } t = n + 2m - 1, m \leqslant 1, \\ 2mN + 1 & \text{for } t = n + 2m, m \geqslant 1. \end{cases}$$

Of course, the values of λ_{EXAMP3}, γ_{EXAMP3} and τ_{EXAMP3} depend on the choice of set R_0 and may be quite different for some other sets of registers.

Definition 6. Let CLASS $\subseteq$ SIMD. For such a set of models of computation the general data transfer functions for $t, n \geqslant 0$, are defined as follows

$\Lambda_{\text{CLASS}}(t)$ denotes the maximum value of all
  $\lambda_{\text{SYS}}(R, t)$,
$\Gamma_{\text{CLASS}}(n, t)$ denotes the maximum value of all
  $\gamma_{\text{SYS}}(R, t)$ with card$(R) = n$, and
$T_{\text{CLASS}}(n, t)$ denotes the maximum value of all
  $\tau_{\text{SYS}}(R, t)$ with card$(R) = n$, where SYS is an arbitrary element of CLASS, and R denotes a set of registers of SYS.

Interesting examples of CLASS are sets like OFF-NET$_p$, ON-NET$_{p,q}$, OFF-SQUARE, OFF-BINTREE, or ON-HEXAGONAL, where the general data transfer functions are fully defined.

Theorem 1. For standard off-line network systems and $2 \leqslant p < \infty$ we get

$$\Lambda_{\text{OFF-NET}_p}(t) = \begin{cases} 2t + 1 & \text{for } p = 2, \\ p\left(\dfrac{(p-1)^t - 1}{p - 2}\right) + 1 & \text{for } p \geqslant 3, \end{cases}$$

and
$$\Gamma_{\text{OFF-NET}_p}(n, t) = T_{\text{OFF-NET}_p}(n, t) = n\Lambda_{\text{OFF-NET}_p}(t) \quad \text{for } n, t \geq 0.$$

Example 6. From Theorem 1 it follows that $\Lambda_{\text{OFF-RAM}}(t) = \lambda_{\text{OFF-NET}_2}(t) = 2t + 1$, for $t \geq 0$. Of course, this coincidence is not true in the total and global cases. According to Theorem 1, we have $\Gamma_{\text{OFF-NET}_2}(n, t) = T_{\text{OFF-NET}_2}(n, t) = n(2t + 1)$, for $n, t \geq 0$, but according to elementary considerations $\Gamma_{\text{OFF-RAM}}(n, t) = 2t + n$, for $n \geq 1$, and $T_{\text{OFF-RAM}}(n, t) = 2n(t - n + 2) - 2$, for $t \geq n \geq 2$.

The general local data transfer functions for some classes of off-line systems (defined in Section 6.3) are given in Table 30. For these classes, the functions $\Lambda_{\text{OFF-NET}_p}$, given in Theorem 1, serve as upper bounds, where the proper value of p has to be specified. The classes OFF-LINEAR, OFF-PS, OFF-BINTREE, and OFF-QUADTREE are examples of maximum transfer situations characterized by Theorem 1, for $p = 2, 3, 5$, respectively.

Table 30

CLASS	p	$\Lambda_{\text{OFF-CLASS}}(t)$	$t = 4$	$t = 8$
LINEAR	2	$2t + 1$	9	17
HEXAGONAL	3	$\frac{3}{2}t^2 + \frac{3}{2}t + 1$	31	109
SQUARE or ILLIAC	4	$2t^2 + 3t + 1$	41	145
TRIAGONAL	6	$3t^2 + 3t + 1$	61	215
DIAGONAL	8	$4t^2 + 4t + 1$	81	289
PS	3	$3 \times 2^t - 2$	46	766
BINTREE top node	3	$3 \times 2^t - 2$ $2^{t+1} - 1$	46 31	766 511
TRIANGLE top node	5	$3 \times 2^{t+1} + t^2 - 2$ $2^{t+1} - 1$	99 31	1,579 511
QUADTREE top node	5	$(5 \cdot 4^t - 2)/3$ $(4^{t+1} - 1)/3$	426 341	109,226 87,381

Here are some remarks to Table 30 and some other networks:

(1) Note that for the bintree, triangle and quadtree networks the maximum receptive fields may only be obtained for central nodes and not the top node of these three structures. The maximum possible cardinalities of receptive fields of top node accumulators are given to illustrate this fact.

(2) $\Gamma_{\text{OFF-CLASS}}(n, t) = T_{\text{OFF-CLASS}}(n, t) = n\Lambda_{\text{OFF-CLASS}}(t)$, for $n, t \geq 0$, holds for all CLASS examples given in Table 30.

(3) The hexagonal, square, triagonal, and diagonal networks are special examples of infinite graphs of constant degree p, where the general local data transfer function is equal to $(p/2)t^2 + (p/2)t + 1$. Such networks naturally correspond to the usual digital metrics for the orthogonal grid, e.g. the metrics d_4 or d_8 used in digital image processing, cf. [9], correspond to the square or diagonal network, respectively.

(4) Derivation of the three general data transfer functions for the networks CUBE^m, PM2I^m, WPM2I^m, LR2I^m or LFUD2I^m represents a very sophisticated problem. Of course, the values of these functions depend on the value of m, and the consideration of classes like

$$\text{CUBE} = \bigcup_{m \geq 2} \text{CUBE}^m$$

would lead to undefined general data transfer functions. For the system CUBE^m, the exact derivation of the local transfer function should be a solvable task. We have

$$\Lambda_{\text{OFF-CUBE}^m}(t) \begin{cases} = \sum_{i=0}^{t} \binom{m}{i} & \text{for } t < m, \\ \geq 2^m & \text{for } t = m, \\ \geq 2^{m+1}(t-m) & \text{for } t > m. \end{cases}$$

For example, $\Lambda_{\text{OFF-CUBE}} 256(4) = 177{,}589{,}057$ and $\Lambda_{\text{OFF-CUBE}} 256(8)$ is about 4×10^{14}. For the systems PM2I^m, WPMZI^m, LRZI^m, and LRUD2I^m values of the data transfer functions may be found in [4].

Theorem 2. For standard on-line network systems and $2 \leq p < \infty$, $1 \leq q \leq p - 1$,

$$\Lambda_{\text{ON-NET}_{p,q}}(t) = \begin{cases} 0 & \text{for } t = 0, \\ 2t - 1 & \text{for } t \geq 1 \text{ and } q = 1, \\ (q^t - 1)/(q - 1) & \text{for } t \geq 1 \text{ and } q \geq 2, \end{cases}$$

and

$$\Gamma_{\text{ON-NET}_{p,q}}(n, t) = T_{\text{ON-NET}_{p,q}}(n, t) = n\Lambda_{\text{ON-NET}_{p,q}}(t) \quad \text{for } n, t \geq 0.$$

Example 7. From (76) it follows that $\Lambda_{\text{ON-RAM}}(t) = \Gamma_{\text{ON-RAM}}(n, t) = t$, for $t \geq 0$ and $n \geq 1$, and thus $\Lambda_{\text{ON-RAM}}(t) < \Lambda_{\text{ON-NET}_{p,1}}(t)$ as well as $\Gamma_{\text{ON-RAM}}(n, t) < \Gamma_{\text{ON-NET}_{p,1}}(n, t)$, for $t \geq 2$ and $n \geq 1$. Furthermore, $T_{\text{ON-RAM}}(n, t) =$

Table 31

CLASS	p	$\{i_1, i_2, ..., i_q\}$	$\Lambda_{\text{ON-CLASS}}(t)$	$t=4$	$t=8$
LINEAR	2	$\{0\}$	$2t-1$	7	15
HEXAGONAL	3	$\{0, 1\}$	$t(t+1)/2$	10	36
		$\{0\}$	$2t-1$	7	15
SQUARE or ILLIAC	4	$\{0, 1, 2\}$	t^2	16	64
		$\{0, 2\}$	$t(t+1)/2$	10	36
		$\{0, 1\}, \{0\}$	$2t-1$	7	15
TRIAGONAL	6	$\{0, 1, 2, 3, 4\}$	$\frac{5}{2}t^2 - \frac{5}{2}t + 1$	31	121
		$\{0, 2, 3, 4\}$	$\frac{3}{2}t^2 - \frac{1}{2}t$	22	92
		$\{0, 2, 4\}$	t^2	16	64
DIAGONAL	8	$\{0, 1, 2, 3, 4, 6, 7\}$	$\frac{7}{2}t^2 - \frac{7}{2}t + 1$	43	197
BINTREE	3	$\{1, 2\}$	$2^t - 1$	15	255
		$\{0, 1\}$	$t(t+1)/2$	10	36
TRIANGLE	5	$\{1, 2, 3, 4\}$	$2^t - 1$	15	255
QUADTREE	5	$\{1, 2, 3, 4\}$	$(4^t - 1)/3$	85	21,845
PS	3	$\{0, 1\}$	$([(1+\sqrt{5})^{t+3} - (1-\sqrt{5})^{t+3}]/\sqrt{5} \times 2^{t+3}) - 2$	11	87

$= n(t - (n/2 + 1/2))$, for $t \geq n \geq 1$, and thus $T_{\text{ON-RAM}}(n, t) < T_{\text{ON-NET}_{p,1}}(n, t)$, for $t \geq n \geq 2$.

Some results of the analysis of general local data transfer functions for classes of on-line systems mentioned in Section 6.3 are given in Table 31. For these classes, the functions given in Theorem 2 serve as upper bounds, where the proper values of p and q have to be correlated. By ON-IN$_{\{i_1, i_2, ..., i_q\}}$ we denote a special ON-IN system with fixed set $\{i_1, i_2, ..., i_q\}$ according to (ON.2). The classes ON-LINEAR$_{\{0\}}$, ON-BINTREE$_{\{1, 2\}}$ and ON-QUADTREE$_{\{1, 2, 3, 4\}}$ are examples of maximum transfer situations characterized by Theorem 2.

Here are some remarks to Table 31 and some other networks given in Table 27.

(1) $\Gamma_{\text{ON-CLASS}}(n, t) = T_{\text{ON-CLASS}}(n, t) = n\Lambda_{\text{ON-CLASS}}(t)$, for $n, t \geq 0$ holds of all CLASS examples given in Table 31.

(2) The class ON-PS$_{\{0, 1\}}$ denotes special SIMD systems using the PS network in its original meaning [10]. Let $f_0 = 1, f_1 = 1, f_2 = 2, ..., f_{n+2} = f_n + f_{n+1}, ...,$

where

$$f_n = [(1 + \sqrt{5})^{n+1} - (1 - \sqrt{5})^{n+1}]/\sqrt{5}\, 2^{n+1}$$

denotes the nth Fibonacci number, $n \geq 0$. We get

$$\Lambda_{\text{ON-PS}_{(0,1)}}(t) = \sum_{t=1}^{t} f_n = f_{n+2} - 2 \quad \text{for } t \geq 0;$$

cf. [3] for a similar result.

(3) Note that for the bintree, triangle and quadtree networks the maximum receptive fields may be obtained for the top node accumulator, for $\{i_1, i_2, ..., i_q\}$ equal to $\{1, 2\}$, $\{1, 2, 3, 4\}$, $\{1, 2, 3, 4\}$, respectively.

6.5 Local, global and total data dependence measures

For parallel processing systems, the optimum time for the solution of a computation problem depends on the data transfer abilities of the given system as well as on the possibilities of parallelization of a solution process. The first may be characterized by the data transfer fuctions Λ_{SYS}, Γ_{SYS}, T_{SYS} using a general system analysis considered in Section 6.4. The second property, however, requires individual consideration of the given computation problem.

For example, consider the multiplication of two $N \times N$ real matrices $\mathbf{AB} = \mathbf{C}$. For a given system SYS, assume that all N^2 elements of matrix $\mathbf{C}$ have to be computed in N^2 different output registers represented by set R_{OUT}. Let $r \in R_{\text{OUT}}$, $R_0 \subseteq R_{\text{OUT}}$ and R_1 be the set of N distinctive registers for outputting the N diagonal elements of $\mathbf{C}$. If the product $\mathbf{AB}$ is to be computed on SYS in time t^*, then it follows that $\lambda_{\text{SYS}}(r, t^*) \geq 2N$, $\gamma_{\text{SYS}}(R_1, t^*) \geq 2N^2$ and $\tau_{\text{SYS}}(R_0, t^*) \geq \geq 2N \operatorname{card}(R_0)$. Thus, if the functions Λ_{SYS}, Γ_{SYS} or T_{SYS} are known, lower time bounds for the immediate solution time t^* are derivable from these inequalities where the maximum lower time bound from the three possible values is taken as the result. For example, according to out considerations in Section 6.4 for the system EXAMP1, on the assumption that $M = 2N$ we get $t^* \geq N - 1$. However, note that a better lower time bound for this system and the matrix multiplication problem may be obtained by more specialized considerations demonstrated in [3, Theorem 1]. Each data unit transfer from a register r_1 to a register r_2 of the system EXAMP1 may be performed in the same time in the reverse direction from r_2 to r_1. The proof of Theorem 1 in [3] matches the situation given by the system EXAMP1, i.e. for $r \in R_{\text{OUT}}$ we get

$$\lambda_{\text{EXAMP1}}(r, 2t^*) \geq N^2, \quad \text{and thus} \quad t^* \geq \tfrac{1}{4}(2N^2 - 1)^{1/2} - \tfrac{1}{4}.$$

In a general approach to the derivation of lower time bounds for parallel processing systems, we shall use for computation problems which may be identified with special functions that will be described later the quantitative description of data dependences of the desired output data in relation to the input data specification.

Definition 7. Let $n, m \geq 1$. Let f be an n-ary function defined on a certain set domain (f) of n-tuples of real numbers, into the set of m-tuples of real numbers. For an n-tuple $(x_1, x_2, \ldots, x_n) \in \text{domain}(f)$, define

$$\text{sub}_i(x_1, x_2, \ldots, x_n) =$$
$$= \{j: 1 \leq j \leq n \,\&\, (\vee x' \neq x_j)(x_1, x_2, \ldots, x_{j-1}, x', x_{j+1}, \ldots, x_n) \in \text{domain}(f) \,\&$$
$$\&\, \text{proj}_i(f(x_1, x_2, \ldots, x_n)) \neq \text{proj}_i(f(x_1, x_2, \ldots, x_{j-1}, x', x_{j+1}, \ldots, x_n))\}$$

as a set of all positions j such that changes in the jth component of $(x_1, x_2, \ldots, x_n)$ have an effect on the projection $\text{proj}_i f$, for $1 \leq i \leq m$. Then, define

$$\lambda_f = \max_{(x_1, x_2, \ldots, x_n)} \max_{1 \leq i \leq m} \text{card}(\text{sub}_i(x_1, x_2, \ldots, x_n)),$$

$$\gamma_f = \max_{(x_1, x_2, \ldots, x_n)} \text{card}\left(\bigcup_{i=1}^{m} \text{sub}_i(x_1, x_2, \ldots, x_n)\right),$$

and

$$\tau_f = \max_{(x_1, x_2, \ldots, x_n)} \sum_{i=1}^{m} \text{card}(\text{sub}_i(x_1, x_2, \ldots, x_n)).$$

The function f is called locally d-dependent iff $d \leq \lambda_f$, globally d-dependent iff $d \leq \gamma_f$ and totally d-dependent iff $d \leq \tau_f$, for an integer $d \geq 0$.

From this definition, for arbitrary functions f defined on n-tuples of real numbers into the set of m-tuples of real numbers, it immediately follows that $\lambda_f = \gamma_f = \tau_f$ if $m = 1$, and for $m \geq 1$

$$\lambda_f \leq \gamma_f \leq \tau_f, \tag{77}$$

$$\gamma_f \leq n,$$

and

$$\tau_f \leq m\lambda_f. \tag{78}$$

For example, in the case of the following function f,

$$f(x_1, x_2, x_3, x_4, x_5) = \begin{cases} x_1 + x_2 & \text{if } x_5 = 0, \\ x_3 + x_4 & \text{if } x_5 \neq 0, \end{cases}$$

6.5 Local, global and total data dependence measures   249

we have $\text{sub}_1(x_1, x_2, x_3, x_4, 0) = \{1, 2, 5\}$ if $x_1 + x_2 \neq x_3 + x_4$; and $\text{sub}_1(x_1, x_2, x_3, x_4, 0) = \{1, 2\}$ if $x_1 + x_2 = x_3 + x_4$. Because $\lambda_f = \gamma_f = \tau_f = 3$, this function is local, global or total 1-, 2- and 3-dependent, but not 4- or 5-dependent.

Now, the data dependence measures given by Definition 7 will be analysed for certain computational problems in a sequence of examples. The results are summarized in Table 32. The following examples may be used as explanations to this table.

Table 32

Computational problem f	n	m	λ_f	γ_f	τ_f
MATRIX MULTIPLICATION	$2N^2$	N^2	$2N$	$2N^2$	$2N^3$
MATRIX INVERSION IP	N^2	N^2	N^2	N^2	N^4
DETERMINANT	N^2	1		N^2	
LINEAR EQUATIONS	$N^2 + N$	N	$N^2 + N$	$N^2 + N$	$N^3 + N^2$
TRANSPOSITION IP	N^2	N^2	1	N^2	N^2
MATRIX π IP	N^2	N^2	2 for $\pi \neq id$	N^2	$2N^2 - \#\{(i,j): \pi(i,j) = (i,j)\}$
2D-DFT	$2N^2$	$2N^2$	$\geq 2N^2 - 4$ $\leq 2N^2 - 1$	$2N^2$	$\geq 2N^4$ $\leq 4N^4 - 2N^2$
2D-WT	N^2	N^2	N^2	N^2	N^4
ROBERTS GRADIENT	MN	NM	4	MN	$4MN - 2M - 2N - 2$
CH SIPOL	$2N$	$2N$	$2N$	$2N$	$\geq 2N^2 - 8N + 12$ $\leq 4N^2$
VORONOI DIAGRAM	$2N$	$18N - 33$	$2N$	$2N$	$\geq 12N - 30$ $\leq 36N^2 - 66N$
PATTERN MATCHING	$N + M$	$N - M + 1$	$2N$	$M + N$	$2M(N - M + 1)$
PATTERN SIGNALIZATION	$N + M$	1	$\geq \max\{2M, M + \lfloor N/M \rfloor\}$,		$\geq M + N$
SORTING	N	N	N	N	N^2

Example 8. The multiplication of two $N \times N$ real matrices may be considered as a $2N^2$-ary function into the set of N^2-tuples of real numbers. For this computation problem, it holds that

$$\lambda_{\text{MATRIX-MULTIPLICATION}} = 2N,$$

$$\gamma_{\text{MATRIX-MULTIPLICATION}} = 2N^2, \quad \text{and} \quad \tau_{\text{MATRIX-MULTIPLICATION}} = 2N^3,$$

where the maximum values of data dependence are true for each input vector of length $2N^2$ that contains non-zero values in all positions. From this example it follows that the upper bounds (77) and (78) cannot be reduced in general. The inversion of an $N \times N$ real matrix in place may be considered as an N^2-ary function defined into the set of N^2-tuples of real numbers. We have

$$\lambda_{\text{MATRIX-INVERSION-IP}} = \gamma_{\text{MATRIX-INVERSION-IP}} = N^2,$$

and

$$\tau_{\text{MATRIX-INVERSION-IP}} = N^4,$$

where the maximum data dependence appears for each matrix that contains non-zero values in all N^2 positions. The data dependence quantities may be considered a direct consequence of the data dependence quantities for the determinant of an $N \times N$ real matrix,

$$\lambda_{\text{DETERMINANT}} = \gamma_{\text{DETERMINANT}} = \tau_{\text{DETERMINANT}} = N^2.$$

The solution of a system of N linear equation with N unknowns may be considered as an $(N^2 + N)$-ary function into the set of N-tuples of real numbers. We obtain

$$\lambda_{\text{LINEAR-EQUATIONS}} = \gamma_{\text{LINEAR-EQUATIONS}} = N^2 + N$$

and

$$\tau_{\text{LINEAR-EQUATIONS}} = N^3 + N^2.$$

Transposing an $N \times N$ real matrix in place may be considered as an N^2-ary function defined into the set of N^2-tuples of real numbers,

$$\lambda_{\text{TRANSPOSITION-IP}} = 1 \quad \text{and} \quad \gamma_{\text{TRANSPOSITION-IP}} = \tau_{\text{TRANSPOSITION-IP}} = N^2.$$

For binary operations on permuted $N \times N$ real matrices in place,

$$(a_{ij}) \; i, j = 0, 1, \ldots, N-1 \Rightarrow (\mathbf{op}_2(a_{ij}, a_{(i, j)})), \quad i, j = 0, 1, \ldots, N-1,$$

can be considered as N^2-ary functions into the set of N^2-tuples of real numbers

$$\lambda_{\text{MATRIX-}\pi\text{-IP}} = 2 \quad \text{for } \pi \neq \text{id},$$

$$\gamma_{\text{MATRIX-}\pi\text{-IP}} = N^2$$

and
$$\tau_{\text{MATRIX-}\pi\text{-IP}} = 2N^2 - \text{card}\{(i,j): 0 \leq i,j \leq N-1 \ \& \ \pi(i,j) = (i,j)\}.$$

The transposition may be considered as a special permutation π^*, $\tau_{\text{MATRIX-}\pi^*\text{-IP}} = 2N^2 - N$, and $\mathbf{op}_2$ as exchange operation, in this case $\mathbf{op}_2(a_{ij}, a_{\pi^*(i,j)}) = (a^*_{\pi^*(i,j)}, a_{ij})$, where the second component of these resulting tuples will be considered as a dummy result.

Example 9. Here, three two-dimensional transforms of $N \times N$ pictures will be treated. First, the Fourier Transform of an $N \times N$ complex matrix may be considered as a $2N^2$-ary function into the set of $2N^2$-tuples of real numbers. In this case, we get

$$2N^2 - 4 \leq \lambda_{\text{2D-DFT}} \leq 2N^2 - 1,$$

$$\gamma_{\text{2D-DFT}} = 2N^2 \quad \text{and} \quad 2N^4 \leq \tau_{\text{2D-DFT}} \leq 4N^4 - 2N^2,$$

where the maximum values of data dependence hold for each input vector of length $2N^2$ that contains non-zero values in all positions. In order to exactly determine $\lambda_{\text{2D-DFT}}$ and $\tau_{\text{2D-DFT}}$, it is necessary to study the influence of different values of N. The Walsh transform of an $N \times N$ real matrix (2D-WT, two-dimensional Walsh transform, cf. [9]) may be considered as an N^2-ary function into the set of N^2-tuples of real numbers,

$$\lambda_{\text{2D-WT}} = \gamma_{\text{2D-WT}} = N^2 \quad \text{and} \quad \tau_{\text{2D-WT}} = N^4,$$

where the maximum values of data dependence hold for any input vector of length N^2. The computation of the parallel Roberts gradient (see Example 1) on images of size $M \times N$ may be considered as an MN-ary function into the set of MN-tuples of real numbers. For this function,

$$\lambda_{\text{ROBERTS-GRADIENT}} = 4,$$

$$\gamma_{\text{ROBERTS-GRADIENT}} = MN \quad \text{and} \quad \gamma_{\text{ROBERTS-GRADIENT}} = 4MN - 2M - 2N - 2,$$

which follows by considering the case of non-zero values in all MN positions and by paying attention to border effects.

Example 10. The computation of the convex hull of a simple polygon, cf. [5], where the N extreme points of the polygon are given by coordinate tuples of real numbers starting with the uppermost-leftmost point, may be considered as a $2N$-ary function into the set of $2N$-tuples of real numbers. All coordinate tuples or extreme points of the conves hull of the polygon appear in the resulting vector of length $2N$ starting with the uppermost-leftmost point and in the same run direction as the polygon. Positions that are not needed in this resulting $2N$-tuple contain zero. In this case, it follows that

$$\lambda_{\text{CH-SIPOL}} = \gamma_{\text{CH-SIPOL}} = 2N$$

and

$$2N^2 - 8N + 12 \leqslant \tau_{\text{CH-SIPOL}} \leqslant 4N^2$$

by analysing the input situation of special convex polygons with N extreme points illustrated in Fig. 69, for $N \geqslant 4$. Analogously to the simple polygon

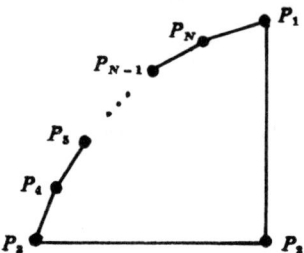

Fig. 69. Convex polygon for analysing the maximum possible data dependence situation, for $N \geqslant 4$.

situation the computation of the convex hull of N planar points, cf. [5], given by coordinate tuples of real numbers, may be considered as a $2N$-ary function into the set of $2N$-tuples of real numbers. For this problem,

$$\lambda_{\text{CH-POINT}} = \gamma_{\text{CH-POINT}} = 2N,$$

and

$$\tau_{\text{CH-POINT}} = 4N^2,$$

where the maximum values hold for every input situation. The computation of the Voronoi diagram of N planar points, cf. [5], given by coordinate tuples of real numbers, may be considered as a $2N$-ary function into the set of $(18N - 33)$-tuples of real numbers in the following sense. The Voronoi diagram may have at most $2N - 5$ vertices and, as a special planar graph, at most $3N - 6$ edges for $N \geqslant 3$. See Fig. 70 which illustrates the construction of such a "maximum Voronoi diagram", where the number of $v(N)$ vertices and the number of $e(N)$ edges satisfy the recursive equations

$$v(3) = 1, \quad e(3) = 3,$$

$$v(N + 1) = v(N) + 2 \quad \text{and} \quad e(N + 1) = e(N) + 3,$$

for $N \geqslant 3$. We consider that $18N - 33 = 3(2N - 5) + 4(3N - 6)$ positions of the resulting vector of a Voronoi diagram computation as a unique characterization of the Voronoi diagram by a linearization of the adjacency lists for this special graph structure with the positions for each vertex. Two positions are reserved for the coordinate values and one for a common pointer, two times two positions are reserved for each edge, i.e. for the index of the vertex at the other end of the edge, of or for the slope of the edge and for a common pointer. For

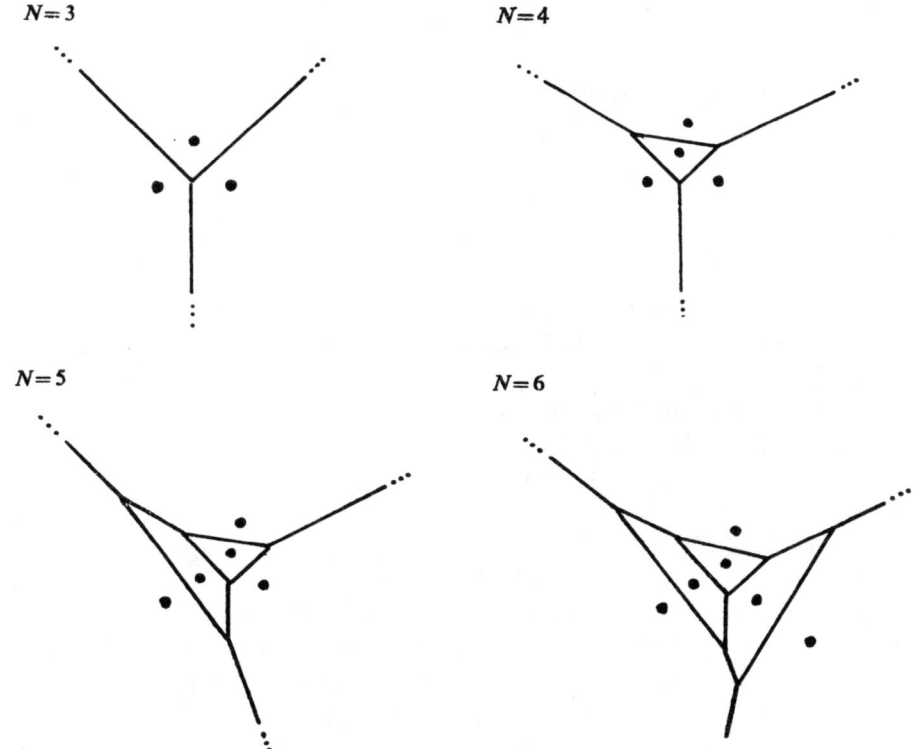

Fig. 70. Voronoi diagrams for $N = 3, 4, 5, 6$ with $2N - 5 = 1, 3, 5, 7$ vertices and $3N - 6 = 3, 6, 9, 12$ edges, respectively.

concrete inputs of N points, positions actually not needed in the resulting $(18N - 33)$-tuple contain value zero. Then, we get

$$\lambda_{\text{VORONOI-DIAGRAM}} = \gamma_{\text{VORONOI-DIAGRAM}} = 2N,$$

and

$$12N - 3 \leq \tau_{\text{VORONOI-DIAGRAM}} \leq 2N(18N - 33),$$

for $N \geq 3$, where the local and global cases may be analysed using a regular N-gon. For the total case, a Voronoi diagram with $2N - 5$ points, according to

Fig. 70 where each point of the diagram essentially depends on there input points, i.e. on six coordinate values, was used.

Example 11. Matching of a pattern of length M against a string of length N ($M \leq N$ and the elements of the pattern and string are assumed to be reals) may be considered as an $(N + M)$-ary function into the set of $(N - M + 1)$-tuples on $\{0, 1\}$ where, for

$$f_{\text{PATTERN-MATCHING}}(p_1, p_2, \ldots, p_m; s_1, s_2, \ldots, s_m) = (e_1, e_2, \ldots, e_{N-M+1})$$

we get $e_i = 1$ iff $s_{i+j} = p_{j+1}$, for all $j = 0, 1, \ldots, M - 1$, and $e_i = 0$ otherwise, for $i = 1, 2, \ldots, N - M + 1$. We have

$$\lambda_{\text{PATTERN-MATCHING}} = 2M,$$

$$\gamma_{\text{PATTERN-MATCHING}} = M + N \quad \text{and} \quad \tau_{\text{PATTERN-MATCHING}} = 2M(N - M + 1).$$

In all three cases, the maximum dependence may be analysed for the trivial input situation $p_i = s_j = \text{const}$, $i = 1, 2, \ldots, M$ and $j = 1, 2, \ldots, N$. Detection of the pattern of length M within the string of length N, $M \leq N$, may be considered as an $(N + M)$-ary function into the set $\{0, 1\}$, where the output is equal to $\max\{e_i: i = 1, 2, \ldots, N - M + 1 f_{\text{PATTERN-MATCHING}}(p_1, p_2, \ldots, p_M; s_1, s_2, \ldots, s_N) = (e_1, e_2, \ldots, e_{N-M+1})\}$ for input $(p_1, p_2, \ldots, p_M; s_1, s_2, \ldots, s_N)$. Then

$$\max\{2M, M + \lfloor N/M \rfloor\} \leq \lambda_{\text{PATTERN-SIGNALIZATION}} \leq M + N.$$

Note that this is the first example of a computation problem where the equality $\gamma_f = n$ for an n-ary function f with $n = N + M$ in the case of pattern detection remains an open problem. The last example, i.e. sorting of N real numbers may be considered as an N-ary function into the set of N-tuples of real numbers. For this very important problem, we have

$$\lambda_{\text{SORTING}} = \gamma_{\text{SORTING}} = N \quad \text{and} \quad \tau_{\text{SORTING}} = N^2,$$

where the maximum values are true for N pairwise different input values.

6.6 Data transfer lemma and applications

There is a direct relationship between the quantitative description of data transfer for SIMD systems (Section 6.4) and the description of data dependence for computational problems (Section 6.5).

6.6 Data transfer lemma and applications

Lemma 1. (Data Transfer Lemma). Let SYS ∈ SIMD. Let π be an arbitrary program for SYS to compute a function f which is n-ary and has m-tuple values. Let R denote the set of output registers of SYS, where the m-tuples appear at the end of the computation (card $(R) = m$, off-line mode), or output registers of SYS through which the computed values of the m-tuples leave SYS in certain waves of information (card $(R) \leq m$, on-line mode). Then, the computation of $f(x_1, x_2, \ldots, x_n)$ on SYS by π requires at least t_0 steps of computation for a given input $(x_1, x_2, \ldots, x_0) \in \mathrm{domain}(f)$, where $\Lambda_{\mathrm{SYS}}(t_0) \leq \lambda_f$, $\Gamma_{\mathrm{SYS}}(\mathrm{card}(R), t_0) \geq \gamma_f$, and $T_{\mathrm{SYS}}(\mathrm{card}(R), t_0) \geq \tau_f$.

Corollary 1. Let CLASS ⊆ SIMD. For any system SYS ∈ CLASS, the computation of a function f which is into the set of m-tuples of real numbers, requires at least t_0 steps of computation in the worst case, where $\Lambda_{\mathrm{CLASS}}(t_0) \geq$ $\geq \lambda_f$, $\Gamma_{\mathrm{CLASS}}(m, t_0) \geq \gamma_f$ and $T_{\mathrm{CLASS}}(m, t_0) \geq \tau_f$.

Example 12. Let CLASS = {EXAMP1} and consider the computation of the parallel Roberts gradient described in Example 1. In this case we get only the trivial lower time bound 1; the upper bound is 29. Now, let CLASS = = {EXAMP3} and consider the computation of the arithmetic averages of M consecutive waves of information of length $N = 2^{n-1}$ described in Example 3. Here, by Corollary 1 we obtain the lower time bound $n + 2M - 2 = \max\{n - 1, n + 2M - 2, n + M - 1\}$, cf. equations (79), (80), for values $\lambda_f = N$, $\gamma_f = NM$ and $\tau_f = NM$. The upper bound is $6M + n$.

Using common asymptotic notations in both examples, the optimum times $\Theta(1)$ and $\Theta(M + n)$ are known.

Theorem 3. For any system SIS ∈ OFF-NET$_p$, $p \geq 2$, the computation of a function f which is into the set of m-tuples of real numbers requires at least t_0 steps of computation in the worst case, where for $p = 2$

$$t_0 \geq \max\{(d_1 - 1)/2, (d_2 - m)/2m, (d_3 - m)/2m\}, \qquad (79)$$

and for $p \geq 3$

$$\begin{aligned} t_0 \geq \max\{&\log_{p-1}(d_1(p-2) + 2) - 1.586, \\ &\log_{p-1}(d_2(p-2) + 2) - \log_{p-1} m - 1.586, \\ &\log_{p-1}(d_3(p-2) + 2) - \log_{p-1} m - 1.586\}, \end{aligned} \qquad (80)$$

if f is locally d_1-dependent, globally d_2-dependent and totally d_3-dependent.

The lower time bounds (for the classes of off-line systems defined in Section 6.3) that may be obtained by using Corollary 1 are given in Table 33. Because the classes OFF-LINEAR, OFF-PS, OFF-BINTREE, and OFF-QUADTREE are examples of maximum transfer situations (characterized by Theorem 1), their lower time bounds will be given by Theorem 3. If a function f into the set of m-tuples is globally or totally d'-dependent, then the value d has to be replaced

Table 33

CLASS	p	lower time bound	$d = 128$	$d = 128^2$
LINEAR	2	$(d-1)/2$	64	8,192
HEXAGONAL	3	$\left(\left(\frac{8}{3}d - \frac{5}{3}\right)^{1/2} - 1\right)/2$	9	105
SQUARE or ILLIAC	4	$((2d-1)^{1/2} - 1)/2$	8	91
TRIAGONAL	6	$\left(\left(\frac{4}{3}d - \frac{1}{3}\right)^{1/2} - 1\right)/2$	7	74
DIAGONAL	8	$(d^{1/2} - 1)/2$	6	64
PS	3	$\log_2(d+2) - 1.586$	6	13
BINTREE	3	$\log_2(d+2) - 1.586$	6	13
top node		$\log_2(d+1) - 1$	7	14
TRIANGLE	5	$t_0 \geq \log_2(d - t_0^2 + 2t_0 + 5) - 2.586$	5	12
top node		$\log_2(d+1) - 1$	7	14
QUADTREE	5	$\log_4(3d+2) - 1.161$	4	7
top node		$\log_4(3d+1) - 1$	5	7

by d'/m from the lower time bounds given in Table 33 to obtain the corresponding values for the global or total situation.

Theorem 4. For any system $\text{SYS} \in \text{ON-NET}_{p,q}$, $2 \leq p < \infty$, $1 \leq q < p$, the computation of a function f which is into the set of m-tuples of real numbers requires at least t_0 steps of computation in the worst case, where for $q = 1$

$$t_0 \geq \max\{(d_1 + 1)/2, (d_2 + m)/2m, (d_3 + m)/2m\}$$

and for $q \geq 2$

$$t_0 \geq \max\{\log_q(d_1(q-1) + 1), \log_q(d_2(q-1)/m + 1), \log_q(d_3(q-1)/m + 1)\},$$

if f is locally d_1-dependent, globally d_2-dependent, and totally d_3-dependent.

The lower time bounds (for the classes of on-line systems defined in Section 6.3) that may be obtained by using Corollary 1 are presented in Table 34. Because the classes ON-LINEAR$_{\{0\}}$, ON-BINTREE$_{\{1,2\}}$, and ON-QUADTREE$_{\{1,2,3,4\}}$ are examples of maximum transfer situations (characterized by Theorem 2) their lower time bounds will be given by Theorem 4. Analogously to Table 33, if a function f into the set of m-tuples is globally or totally d'-dependent, the value d has to be replaced by d'/m from the lower time bounds

Table 34

CLASS	p	$\{i_1, ..., i_q\}$	Lower time bound	$d = 128$	$d = 128^2$
LINEAR	2	$\{0\}$	$(d+1)/2$	65	8,193
HEXAGONAL	3	$\{0, 1\}$	$((8d+1)^{1/2} - 1)/2$	16	181
SQUARE or ILLIAC	4	$\{0, 1, 2\}$	$d^{1/2}$	12	128
TRIAGONAL	6	$\{0, 1, 2, 3, 4\}$	$\left(\left(\frac{8}{5}d - \frac{3}{5}\right)^{1/2} - 1\right)/2$	7	81
DIAGONAL	8	$\{0, 1, 2, 3, 4, 6, 7\}$	$\left(\left(\frac{8}{7}d - \frac{3}{7}\right)^{1/2} - 1\right)/2$	6	64
BINTREE	3	$\{1, 2\}$	$\log_2(d+1)$	8	15
TRIANGLE	5	$\{1, 2, 3, 4\}$	$\log_2(d+1)$	8	15
QUADTREE	5	$\{1, 2, 3, 4\}$	$\log_4(3d+1)$	5	8
PS	3	$\{0, 1\}$	$f_{t_0+2} \geq d + 2$ for the Fibonacci numbers $f_0, f_1, f_2, ...$	11	21

given in Table 34 to obtain the corresponding values for the global or total situation. Note that the value m may be replaced by a value $m_0 \leq m$ for special ON-NET systems.

Using Tables 32 to 34 the interested reader may obtain lower time bounds for different combinations of SIMD systems and computation problems, e.g. the lower time bound $\log_2(N^2 + 1)$ for the two-dimensional Walsh transform on ON-TRIANGLE systems. Of course, asymptotic notations should generally suffice to describe the lower time bounds as, for example, $\Omega(\log N)$ for on-line quadtree-net systems and the computation of Voronoi diagrams for N planar points, $\Omega(N)$ for off-line diagonal-net systems and the two-dimensional Discrete Fourier Transform, and $\Omega(\sqrt{N})$ for off- or on-line ILLIAC-net systems and sorting of N items.

In this chapter we have given a general idea of how to describe parallel (SIMD-type) processing systems and explained how the data transfer may be used in analysing the lower time bounds in general. Note that this approach may be applied to supercomputers as well as to on-chip realizations. Problems concerning technical features of architecture elements were by-passed by a selected level of abstract system description. Thus, discussing parallel algorithms for a given model SYS ∈ SIMD we may have in mind quite different technical implementations, though we may discuss parallel algorithms for all of them at once using the abstract model SYS ∈ SIMD. For example, an important problem is given by the necessary decision between different structures of parallel processing systems to ensure efficient algorithmic solutions for classes of computational problems mentioned in Example 8 (matrix-type computations), Example 9 (two-dimensional transforms), Example 10 (geometric problems), or in Example 11 (combinatorial problems). In the previous chapters we have shown that the selection of parallel algorithms crucially depends on the respective parallel processing system, and comparisons between different SIMD systems on the basis of knowledge about optimal algorithms represent a difficult task. Also, there are nearly as many different models for parallel processing as papers on this topic, making comparative studies of different parallel structures quite impossible. In this chapter an attempt was made to propose a classification of special parallel processing systems which have been of widespread interest in the past.

References

[1] H. Abelson, "Lower bounds on information transfer in distributed computations", *J. ACM* **27** (1980) 384—392.
[2] A. V. Aho, J. E. Hopcroft and J. D. Ullman, *The Design and Analysis of Computer Algorithms* (Addison-Wesley, Reading, 1974).
[3] W. M. Gentleman, "Some complexity results for matrix computation on parallel processors", *J. ACM* **25** (1978) 112—115.
[4] R. Klette, "Analysis of data flow for SIMD systems", *Acta Cybernetica* **6** (1984) 389—423.
[5] R. Klette, "Geometrische Probleme der digitalen Bildverarbeitung", *Bild und Ton* **35** (1982) 101—110.
[6] R. Klette and R. Lindner, "Zweidimensionale Vektormaschinen und ihr Leistungsvermögen bei der Lösung von Entscheidungsproblemen der Aussagenlogik", *EIK* **15** (1979) 37—46.
[7] T. Legendi, "A cellular processor project", *Int. Workshop on Parallel Processing by Cellular Automata* (Berlin, 1982).
[8] V. R. Pratt and L. J. Stockmeyer, "A characterization of the power of vector machines", *J. Comp. System Sci.* **12** (1976) 118—121.
[9] A. Rosenfeld and A. C. Kak, *Digital Picture Processing*, 2nd Ed. (Academic Press, New York, 1982).
[10] H. J. Stegel, "A model of SIMD machines and a comparison of various interconnection networks", *IEEE Trans. Comp.* **C-28** (1979) 907—917.

Subject index

Adder, serial 153
Algorithm
— asynchronous, systolic 17, 154
— CORDIC 21, 122, 177
— synchronous, systolic 11, 154
Area 146
Arithmetic expression 3, 208
— -geometric mean 10
Aspect ratio 146
Associative
— computer system 56
— memory 57
AT 147
AT^2 147

Band matrix 113
Binary tree 140, 230
Bit reversal code 74, 137
Bit slice 21, 59, 82
Boolean function 145
Border network 228
Broadcasting of data 124

Cache memory 199, 206
Carry look ahead 147
Cellular automaton 112
Chaotic iteration 24
Communication graph 145
— network 115, 170, 183, 227
Combinational circuits 145
Comparison 138
Computer
— associative 60, 69, 77
— Cm* 186
— C.mmp 184
— CRAY-1 160, 166
— CRAY XMP 47, 169
— CYBER-205 43

— DAP 161, 173, 183
— EGPA 183
— ILLIAC IV 160, 172, 183
— MIMD-type 41, 45, 183
— SIMD-type 21, 44, 169
— SOLOMON II 47
— STARAN 75, 161, 181
— Single VLSI chip 203
Complexity
— measure 146
— of systolic algorithm 144
Connected components 116, 142
Continued fraction 128
Convention
— off-line I/O 232
— on-line I/O 232
Convex
— domain 146
— hull 146
Crossbar switch 183
Cyclic shift 78, 150

Data
— flow 115, 241
— transfer functions 241, 247
Database operation 116
Decomposition
— matrix 37
— orthogonal 37
Dependence 247
Diagram, Voronoi 249, 252
Difference, relationship 95
Discrete Fourier transform 72, 148
Divide et impera 8
Dynamic programming 116

Elementary function 116, 128
Elimination

— Gaussian 6, 84, 122, 177
— Gauss—Jordan 84, 122, 177, 199
Enumeration, standard 233

Fast
— algorithm 1, 199
— Fourier Transform 23, 57, 136, 188
— parallel algorithms 1, 56
Fault-tolerant systolic algorithm 154
Fourier Transform 72, 117, 134, 251
Function
— Boolean 145
— interconnection network 115, 228

Geometry, computational 116
Global synchronization 154
Graph, communication 145
Greatest common divisor 116

Hexagonal array 35, 113, 116
Histogram 77
Horner's method 67
Hull convex 146

Image processing 77, 178
Input-output operation 145
Instruction set 230
Integrated circuit 111
Interprocessor communication 115, 183
Iteration
— chaotic 24
— stationary method 92
— synchronous 24
Iterative array 112

Laplace equation 95
Layout 155
Leaf processor 140
Linear
— array 116
— equation 8, 17, 23, 126, 165, 199, 249
— model 147
— recurrence relation 116, 126
Lower bound 144, 247
Logarithmic model 147
LU-decomposition 116, 119, 165

Machine, random access 225
Mask 226, 230, 236
Masking scheme 230

Matrix
— inversion 57, 116, 124, 190, 217, 249
— multiplication 28, 113, 247
— orthogonal 41
— processor 31, 160
— symmetric 100
— transposition 117, 250
— triangulation 116
— tridiagonal 32, 38, 44
Maximum element 61, 116, 141
Merging 117
Method
— ADI 49
— column orthogonalization 190
— cyclic reduction 38
— Fast Fourier Transform 116, 134
— Gauss—Seidel 17, 48
— Given's 121
— matrix decomposition 37, 42
— multigrid 45
— successive over-relaxation 49
Minimum spanning tree 116
Model
— of VLSI circuit 145
— PE 225
Multiprocessor 160, 183

Navier—Stokes equation 188
Network
— border 228
— interconnected function 228, 233
— system standard 228
— — — off-line 232, 243
— — — on-line 232, 245

Orthogonal
— array 116
— pipeline vector processors 119, 211, 222
Orthogonalization column method 190

Partial differential equation 36, 92
Pattern
— matching 61, 137, 249
— recognition 133, 249
Perfect shuffle 67, 116, 170, 228
Period 146
Permutation 150
Pipeline vector processors 161
Pivoting 122, 177, 200
Polynomial, multiplication 116, 130

Processor
— CHIP 121
— root 141

Random access machine 225
Recurrence relation 43, 126
Register 79, 86, 225
Ring of residual numbers 151
Robert's gradient operator 234, 249, 255

Scheme
— masking 228
— PERMOPRY 103, 107
— PERORD 103, 108
— PERSAM 102, 107
— PERSEQ 101, 108
Searching 116
Sequential circuit 145
Serial adder 153
Signal processing 133, 178
SIMD
— model 225, 231
— type computer 21, 41, 169
Sorting
— Batcher's 67, 179
— rank 140
Spanning tree, minimum 116
Speech recognition 116
Standard
— enumeration 228
— names 238
— off-line network system 227, 232
— on-line network system 227, 232
State variable 146
Systolic
— architecture 111
— array 9, 35, 111, 199, 217
— automaton 154
— system 121

Time
— determinate 146
— tradeoff area 146
Transitive
— closure 116, 143
— function 156
— group 150
Tree
— binary 140
— of processors 140
Triangular system of linear equation 116, 120
Tridiagonal, matrix 38
— system of linear equations 6, 44
Two-dimensional convolution 116, 133

Upper bound 144

Variable
— input 146
— state 146
Vector
— computer 161, 228
— iteration 6, 92
— processor 199
VLSI circuit 145
— model 145
— technology 23, 111

Wafer 154
Word recognition 116

FAST ALGORITHMS AND THEIR IMPLEMENTATION ON SPECIALIZED PARALLEL COMPUTERS

RNDr. Jozef MIKLOŠKO, DrSc. (vedúci autorského kolektívu),
Dr. Reinhard KLETTE, RNDr. Marián VAJTERŠIC, CSc.,
RNDr. Imrich VRŤO, CSc.

Prepracovaný a rozšírený originál Rýchle algoritmy a ich realizácia na špecializovaných počítačoch, ktorý vyšiel vo vydavateľstve Veda v Bratislave roku 1985, preložila Jana Hajnovičová.

Zodpovedné redaktorky publikácie Zuzana Malíková a Eva Zikmundová
Výtvarná redaktorka Viera Miková
Technická redaktorka Marcela Janálová

Rukopis zadaný do tlačiarne 27. 12. 1987.

Prvé vydanie. Vydala Veda, vydavateľstvo Slovenskej akadémie vied, a vydavateľstvo North-Holland, Holandsko, v Bratislave roku 1988 ako svoju 2799. publikáciu. Počet strán 264. AH 19,32 (text 17,71, ilustr. 1,61), VH 20,04. Formát B5, väzba V2. Náklad 1300 výtlačkov.
Vytlačili Západoslovenské tlačiarne, z. p., závod Svornosť, Bratislava.
SÚKK 1728/I-87

071–005–88 FAA
03   Kčs 35,—